Sexuality in Modern German History

THE BLOOMSBURY HISTORY OF MODERN GERMANY SERIES

Series Editors: Daniel Siemens (Newcastle University, UK),
Jennifer V. Evans (Carleton University, Canada) and
Matthew P. Fitzpatrick (Flinders University, Australia)

The Bloomsbury History of Modern Germany Series is an open-ended series of thematic books on various aspects of modern German history. This ambitious and unique series offers readers the latest views on aspects of the modern history of what has been and remains one of the most powerful and important countries in the world. In a series of books aimed at students, leading academics and experts from across the world portray, in a thematic manner, a broad variety of aspects of the German experience, over extended periods of time, from roughly the turn of the nineteenth century to the modern day. Themes covered include class, religion, war, race, empire, sexuality and gender. Each volume contains an appendix of documents, illustrations and other material to enhance understanding.

Published:
Technology in Modern German History, Karsten Uhl (2022)
Sexuality in Modern German History, Katie Sutton (2023)

Forthcoming:
Dictatorships and Authoritarianism in Modern German History,
André Keil
Imperialism in Modern German History, Eva Bischoff
Philosophy in Modern German History, Cat Moir
Revolutions in Modern German History, Andrew Bonnell
War in Modern German History, Rüdiger Bergien

Sexuality in Modern German History

1800 to the Present

Katie Sutton

BLOOMSBURY ACADEMIC
LONDON • NEW YORK • OXFORD • NEW DELHI • SYDNEY

BLOOMSBURY ACADEMIC
Bloomsbury Publishing Plc
50 Bedford Square, London, WC1B 3DP, UK
1385 Broadway, New York, NY 10018, USA
29 Earlsfort Terrace, Dublin 2, Ireland

BLOOMSBURY, BLOOMSBURY ACADEMIC and the Diana logo are
trademarks of Bloomsbury Publishing Plc

First published in Great Britain 2023

Series design by Jade Barnett
Cover image: Street in Hamburg known as *Die Gasse*, 1955–56.
(© Imagno/Getty Images)

A catalogue record for this book is available from the British Library.

A catalog record for this book is available from the Library of Congress.

ISBN: PB: 978-1-3500-1006-2
        HB: 978-1-3500-1007-9
        ePDF: 978-1-3500-1008-6
        eBook: 978-1-3500-1009-3

Typeset by Integra Software Services Pvt. Ltd.

To find out more about our authors and books visit www.bloomsbury.com
and sign up for our newsletters.

For KB

CONTENTS

FIGURES

ACKNOWLEDGEMENTS

A book always takes a village, and I'm tremendously grateful to the people and institutions who have supported this one. After spending a while in the planning stages – don't they always? – this project ended up being my constant companion through these topsy-turvy past years of pandemic. I've welcomed the chance to momentarily escape lockdowns and news cycles by delving into the rich scholarship in this field, and to read across periods and topics that were often quite new to me – from early modern witchcraft to GDR divorce stories. I've learnt so much along the way, and have the greatest respect for the wonderful scholars around the world who make this field such an exciting one to be part of. I'm only sorry that I couldn't include even more of that work here – a survey like this requires, I've realized, making lots of difficult choices in order to crystallize a larger narrative. I hope the result offers a fresh eye and useful tool on this immensely exciting area of modern German and European history.

Warm thanks to the ANU College of Arts and Social Sciences for funding that enabled research assistance support during the early stages of this project, and to Stephanie Borst for her meticulous bibliographical work. Thanks to my always supportive supervisors, Kate Mitchell and Catherine Travis, and others who have had my back in the delicate juggle of research and administrative roles – in particular Julieanne Lamond as a wonderful Deputy Head. A warm shout out, too, to the School of History book writing group led by Carolyn Strange, whose feedback instrumentally shaped not only a chapter, but also some of the larger threads of the book.

I am grateful to the editors of this exciting series, Jennifer Evans, Daniel Siemens and Matt Fitzpatrick, for entrusting me with this project – I'm delighted to be part of such a great line-up. I thank the peer reviewers for Bloomsbury for their thoughtful and productive engagement with the manuscript, steering me in welcome directions, as well as the fabulous editorial team, including the ever-patient Laura Reeves and Rhodri Mogford, and Emma Tranter and her team in Production, including Sudhagaran Thandapani and Viswasirasini Govindarajan.

This book contains quite a few images, and I'm thankful to those who helped out as I was scrabbling around for high-resolution files and copyright permissions to a tight timeframe: Marion Schneider at the German Hygiene Museum, Dresden; Ralf Dose at the Magnus-Hirschfeld-Gesellschaft in Berlin; Karin Buch at Ullstein; Liam Sims and Johanna Ward at Cambridge

University Library; Hannah Hien at the Staatsarchiv Würzburg; Karl Sand at the Landesarchiv Berlin; Wolfgang Baaske of Baaske Cartoons; Glen Menzies at the Copyright Agency, Sydney; Jennifer Carding at akg; Andreas Schlüter at the Klassik Stiftung Weimar; Andrea Terzer-Grahn at ddrbildarchiv.de; Eva Rothkirch in special collections at the Staatsbibliothek Berlin; Sylvia Schönwald at the Deutsche Nationalbibliothek; Karin Buch at Axel Springer – and many others who pointed me in the right direction.

As I received the proofs for this book, I was deeply saddened to learn that one of the shining lights of German queer history and literary studies, Robert Deam Tobin, had died at his home in Massachusetts. We had been in touch in the weeks before his death, and I am so honoured that in those final months, Bob made time to read and blurb this manuscript. He was someone who always modelled warm collegiality, encouraging mentorship, and queer kinship, and I am so glad to have known him. He made huge contributions to this field, and many people whose work is cited in this book will miss him.

Finally, this project was only possible thanks to family and friends who have offered ongoing support and at times welcome distraction from the peaks and troughs of book research and writing – especially Birgit Lang, a most trusty longstanding collaborator and friend. And last but most, I dedicate this project to Katharina, who together with the gorgeous Austin the dog made all the difference. This one, again and again, is for you.

Introduction
Sexuality in modern German history

In 1955, in the redlight district of Germany's northern industrial city of Hamburg, one of the largest ports in Europe and for centuries a space in which sailors, dockworkers, emigrants and people of all classes, racial backgrounds, genders, abilities and sexual identities would regularly brush shoulders – and sometimes a little more – four white women of various ages gather behind an open shop window, brightly lit and elevated, on clear display to passers-by. Framed by the darkness of the evening and the decorative iron bars of the window itself, three of the women, probably in their twenties or early thirties, are in pale, elegant eveningwear and jewellery – outfits more suggestive of an elegant ballroom in an upmarket Hamburg merchant villa than the neat but pragmatic furnishings and lampshades of the room in which they sit on display. One of the women leans over the front window-ledge, leisurely smoking a cigarette as she gazes over her shoulder, one eye on her colleagues and the other on the street below. The second sits back, arms crossed, with a distanced, somewhat sceptical gaze, while the third is slightly out of focus, coyly gazing downwards towards a blurred figure just outside. The fourth presents a point of contrast: decked out in a no-nonsense housecoat, 1950s cat eye glasses and a short, sensible haircut, she bustles about in the background, seemingly shuffling the others into position, perhaps readying them for the evening shift. This is an image that, even as it invites the viewer to share the eroticizing gaze of the invisible observer on the street, conceals as much as it reveals. The women on display emanate a sense of agency and purpose, of being in control of their image, and well aware of the photographer's prying lens. Yet we can only speculate about the specific familial, socio-economic and gendered structures that may have led to their involvement in the city's commercial sex industry on this particular evening, in a street known simply as 'Die Gasse' (the alley).

FIGURE 0.1 *Street in Hamburg known as 'Die Gasse,' Hamburg. 1955–6.*
Source: Imagno/Getty Images

Ten years after the most horrific war and genocide that the world has ever seen, Germany in 1955 was still reeling from the destruction, turmoil and guilt of twelve years of National Socialist dictatorship. It had also, by this stage, become not one but two Germanies, split in 1949 into the Federal Republic in the West, already enjoying the first fruits of the 'economic miracle' of 1950s consumerism and industry, and the German Democratic Republic in the East, strongly aligned with the Soviet Union, with leaders working to establish state socialism as a 'really existing' rather than purely ideological entity. Against this backdrop of postwar splits and upheavals, this photograph presents a conflicted message. On the one hand, the women on display reference norms of 1950s gender and sexuality, and in particular, a brand of femininity associated with attractiveness, consumption, display and objectification. Such ideals complemented the dominant conservative celebration of postwar domesticity: strong male providers, nuclear families and women supposedly embracing a return to the celebrated trio of 'children, church, and kitchen' (*Kinder, Kirche, Küche*). Yet the image also complicates those ideals. The women's very presence in the shopfront might suggest at least some men's failure to provide – or even to return from the war in the first place; equally, it points to these women's determination to self-consciously harness their feminine and erotic charms into economies of sexual exchange.

The ambiguities of this image point to several questions central to this book. While *Sexuality in Modern German History* takes a broadly chronological format, with chapters aligning with conventional periodizations of nineteenth- and twentieth-century German history (pre-unification, Empire, Weimar Republic, Third Reich and postwar division), its narrative is shaped by the overarching question: How does a focus on shifting ideas of the 'normal' change our understanding of the history of sexuality in modern Germany? This leads to further questions and concerns: How and why do ideas about certain sexual behaviours, desires and identities come to be seen as 'normal' in certain times and places? How are these ideas tied up with questions of gender – of femininity, masculinity or behaviours and expressions not so clearly categorizable? When and how do ideas of what is 'normal' become 'norms' that can be enforced – sometimes subtly, by shaping expectations about 'acceptable' behaviours or 'attractive' appearances, but often in more confronting, even violent ways? What happens to those who find themselves situated outside of the 'norm'? Why has the challenging of sexual norms so often attracted such fierce reactions – and how might understanding these processes help us to better understand debates in our own time, such as the pitting of supposedly 'gender-critical' perspectives against trans lives? As feminist scholar Sara Ahmed remarks, '[a] norm is a restriction that can feel like freedom to those it enables. To challenge a norm is thus almost always treated as restricting other people's freedoms.'[1] By foregrounding and interrogating ideas of norms and the normal, this book offers an alternative window onto several centuries of German society, politics and culture, from the late Enlightenment to the present day. It aims not only to synthesize rich bodies of existing scholarship, but also to generate new insights into the turbulent history of one of Europe's and the world's most powerful and influential nations in the modern era.

Sexuality in Modern German History homes in on an aspect of human experience unique in its significance for people's understanding of their place in the world. 'Sexuality' is itself a concept that only crystallized as a distinct phenomenon in the modern era, from around the late nineteenth century. Examining the period of early modern civil society in the German-speaking world, historian Isabel Hull suggests that it would be 'anachronistic and methodologically misleading to use it for the period before 1815'; instead, Hull suggests the 'inelegant, but more accurate, phrases "sexual behavior" or "sexual matters"' in writing about earlier periods.[2] The concept of sexuality, scholars broadly agree, constitutes a distinctly modern way of thinking about the self. This view has been particularly prominent since French philosopher Michel Foucault published the first volume of his influential three-part *History of Sexuality* in 1976 and aligns with broader philosophical and sociological ways of thinking about the development of the individual, subject and citizen in the modern era.[3] It is also not without its critics, as I explore below.

The story of sex in the modern era has frequently been told as one of progress: a story of reform, emancipation and ongoing liberalization despite repeated setbacks. Such approaches tend to situate sex as a site of struggle between progressive and socially conservative movements, often framed by ideas about morality and religion. As we shall see, however, the complex ways in which people negotiate ideas about sex, gender and relationships have rarely followed such straightforward lines, and nor have they adhered to neat periodizations. We must take seriously, observes historian Jennifer Evans, 'the category of sexuality as both a marker and agent of modernity, one which reflects the twin goals of emancipation and domination'.[4] The modern era is understood in this book to cover the period from around 1800 to the present. There can be no doubt that ideas of the 'modern' and 'modernity' are crucial in shaping the way people have thought about sexuality across these two centuries of German history. Yet what counts as 'modern' is as contested as what counts as 'normal', and requires our critical attention. At a political, social and economic level, modernity is closely associated with the rise of capitalism, which saw mass population shifts away from traditional, rural and agricultural forms of work into urban, industrialized factory and office settings. It is linked to the rising economic and cultural influence of the middle classes, even where they did not (yet) hold the political reins, and roughly aligns with the emergence of modern political and state structures such as democracy and the nation state. Yet modernity is not just about parliaments and paychecks – it also describes a period of new forms of cultural and aesthetic expression often dubbed 'modernist', from avant-garde experiments in dance, theatre and art to the new mass media of illustrated newspapers, film, radio and photography.

People's experience of living in 'modern' times was equally shaped by new ways of speaking and thinking about these phenomena. What it meant to be modern was closely tied to certain kinds of space – such as the hustle and bustle of the metropolis and larger towns – but also to a shifting experience of time, especially thanks to new technologies that seemed to accelerate and compress the pace of life, such as trains, telegraphs and motion pictures.[5] Historian Geoff Eley observes that '"the modern" emerged as a set of discursive claims about the social world seeking aggressively to reorder that world in terms of itself'.[6] This book seeks to highlight competing visions of the 'modern' shaping German society and attitudes to sex across two centuries, and to hold concepts of sexuality and modernity in critical tension. It recognizes that while ideas of modernity sometimes aligned with socially progressive reforms such as improved access to contraception or the introduction of gender equality laws, at other times modern technologies and forms of knowledge were used to support much more sinister goals, including the 'racial hygiene' principles of the Nazi state.

This is no minor point. For decades, scholars have debated how to view the rise of National Socialism from 1933 to 1945 in the broader context of German and European modernity. Was Adolf Hitler's so-called Third Reich rooted in distinctly German historical traditions, and essentially 'backwards' and antimodern, or was it in fact a peculiarly modern phenomenon in its embrace of industrialism, technology, science and rationalized population governance – the ultimate tale of modernity gone wrong?[7] This latter position has gained traction over time, as historians remind us that there was never just one version of modernity. Instead, it is more productive to view these two centuries through a lens of competing moderni*ties*: complex entanglements of political, social and cultural forces that reached across social classes, genders, ethnicities, political affiliations and national boundaries, and that shaped conflicting visions of the present and the future.[8] We do not do justice to this complexity when we insist on thinking about sex and its history only in terms of 'progress' towards an ever more tolerant future, as an older form of history-writing tended to do. 'We have to tell a different story', emphasizes Evans, than one that revolves around

> moral regulation and social control. To be effective and lasting, the generation of new knowledge about sex relied on mechanisms of enticement as well as coercion, power and pleasure, surveillance and seduction, in an uneven process of fits and starts. This haphazard evolution of new sexual norms created possibilities for subversion alongside ongoing social regulation.[9]

We must, in short, remain attentive to what historian Dagmar Herzog describes as 'the inextricability of repression and liberalization' shaping attitudes to and experiences of human sexuality and intimacy – not only under fascist rule, but in the modern era more broadly.[10]

Nationhood, identity and norms

During the two centuries covered by this book, the German-speaking world has played a crucial role in shaping modern understandings of sexuality not only within, but also beyond national borders. At the same time, those borders have been highly contested. It is barely possible to speak of 'Germany' in any straightforward geographical, political, religious or social sense for the period conventionally summarized as modernity, let alone the centuries that preceded it. 'Germany? Where is it? I do not know where to find such a country,' wrote the famous poet Friedrich Schiller in 1796.[11] Nonetheless, 'Germany' and 'German' are useful shorthand for describing the shared cultural assumptions, traditions and language variations that connected the various German-speaking towns and regions of Europe even well before the modern era, before a distinct sense of 'greater Germany' began to crystallize in the nineteenth century, spurred by the mid-century revolutionary fervour of 1848. Until unification in 1871, 'Germany' was a loose alliance of states rather than a coherent political entity. Following the Congress of Vienna in

1815, these states formed part of the German Confederation, with Austria also a member. Austria and its northern neighbour, Prussia, struggled for supremacy over the Germany territories, until, following the Austro-Prussian war of 1866, the southern German states joined Prussia and others in the north to form the new German empire.[12]

Germany thus only established a modern sense of nationhood in 1871, with other major German-speaking entities at this period including the vast Austro-Hungarian Empire and the much smaller Switzerland to the south. During the decades that followed, ideas of what it meant to be 'German' remained hotly contested. As David Blackbourn provocatively asks, 'what did it mean around 1900 to be a German who was also a Pfälzer and a (reluctant) Bavarian, the more so when you lived on the French border, probably had family members who had settled in the Banat two centuries earlier, and had an uncle in Milwaukee?'[13] Following the defeat of the Empire and fall of the monarchy in the First World War, Germany established its first democracy: the much-celebrated and almost as frequently maligned Weimar Republic, before the seizure of power by Hitler's National Socialist party turned the country into a brutal dictatorship from 1933 to 1945. Following the Second World War, Allied victors and occupiers oversaw the separation of what remained of the former German Reich into two separate, neighbouring states that remained in place for a good four decades. Separated by the at once symbolic and very real Iron Curtain, the division of GDR and FRG was most loudly proclaimed by the heavily guarded cement wall erected in 1961 right through the middle of Berlin. Following the peaceful revolution and 'fall' of the Wall in 1989, the two states were again merged into a joint entity in 1990 – with the Eastern states now viewed politically as 'new' (if in other ways decidedly 'old') states of a reunited Federal Republic. Sometimes dubbed the 'Berlin Republic', the capital of the former West Germany returned from Bonn to the metropolis on the Spree.

Examining this *longue durée* of ruptures, wars, divisions and (re) unifications, *Sexuality in Modern German History* adopts a critical approach that highlights competing and at times unpredictable ideas of the normal and the modern. The modern era brought with it new ways of thinking about sex and bringing it into political debate: from new ideas about individual identity and the body to broader movements for legal and social reform. Yet understanding what was distinct about this era requires us to take a step back, to consider what 'modern' thinkers were reacting against. This book thus begins by examining the longer history of key institutions and events in the history of sexuality, from the sexual transgressions and policing of 'witches' in the medieval period to debates about marriage and divorce during the Protestant Reformation of the sixteenth century. It traces the at-times bumpy evolution of these ideas through to nineteenth-century ideals of love-centred marriage and the bourgeois nuclear family overseen by a patriarchal father figure, and into the era of so-called 'sexual revolution' in the later decades of the twentieth century – all the while also attending to the stories of people whose sexual behaviours and desires fell outside of emerging norms.

Recent scholarly efforts to historicize the 'normal' emphasize that this term has encompassed multiple meanings since it first gained widespread currency in the mid-nineteenth century. At first, it was generally used to refer to that which was typical in a statistical sense – the 'norm' reflecting the highest point on a probability bell curve. During the twentieth century, the 'normal' increasingly came to be understood as the 'average' and 'healthy'. Yet even as medicalized definitions came to dominate, they remained in tension with older religious or moral frameworks.[14] The late nineteenth century represents a moment of particular importance in tracking this evolution of the normal and the deviant, at a time when the country's politicians were becoming increasingly concerned with modern 'biopolitical' concerns (another term coined by Foucault[15]) such as tracking and promoting the birth rate and health of the population. German-speaking Europe during these decades was the birthplace of a modern science of sexuality, with doctors and scientists coining new names for so-called perversions such as homosexuality, masochism and transvestism, and investigating male and female sexual 'dysfunctions' in ever more detailed ways. The rise of scientific modernity combined with the German Empire's distinctive legal framework – and especially its punitive approach to male same-sex acts – to spur activists and doctors alike to develop new medical categories and diagnoses such as 'invert' and 'urning', and to precipitate the world's first organized gay rights movement from the 1890s. Towards the end of the century, the emergence of Freudian psychoanalysis forced a further rethinking of 'normal' sexual development, drawing attention to the role of the subconscious in shaping sexual pleasures and identities. These medical and scientific developments not only intersected with modern legal and political movements centred on notions of human 'rights', but also came into play in socially conservative and often religious-inspired campaigns advocating censorship and moral purity. During these decades, too, Germany's imperialist ambitions shaped a decidedly racialized, Eurocentric sense of superiority. This had a pervasive impact on discussions of sexuality, from anthropological studies of the sexual lives of 'primitive' others to new legislation around 'mixed' marriages in the colonies.

The twentieth century saw further radical, but also more subtle changes to norms of sexual activity and gendered behaviour – for it is difficult to imagine sexual relations, desires or identities completely removed from ideas of gender, and these two categories intersect strongly throughout the chapters of this book. At times these shifting norms broadly coincided with major political and historical events: the two World Wars created significant social as well as sexual mobility, for example, while the forty-year East-West division provided a framework for quite distinct legal frameworks governing things like abortion, contraception, homosexuality and divorce. But we also find evidence of perhaps surprising continuities in sexual attitudes and practices across what are commonly assumed to be pervasive historical breaks. A long-view look at German history like this can shed light on lines of connection, for example, between the flourishing of queer and trans communities during Germany's Weimar Republic and again in the post-1968 era of sexual 'liberation'. It can also help us to bring a historicizing lens to how that term was understood against the very different political and economic structures of the capitalist, democratic West and socialist East. At other times, those continuities were of a more repressive, even violent kind – such as between debates about eugenics among left-wing reformers during the Weimar Republic and the forced sterilizations and abortions overseen by doctors during the 'Third Reich', or between imperialist bans on 'miscegenation' and the stigmatization of German women who had flings with occupying US forces in the 1950s – especially if those GIs were African Americans. Throughout these two centuries of German history, sex has variously functioned, as it continues to today, as a vehicle of violence and pleasure, power and knowledge – sometimes all at once.

The following chapters trace this history to argue for the central place of sexuality in understanding modern German history. They aim, firstly, to offer a 'big picture' survey of the burgeoning literature in the field, and thus a springboard for future research. The focus leans towards English-language scholarship, but the German history of sexuality is completely unthinkable without the work of scholars working and publishing in German. The many references in this book are aimed towards pointing readers in productive directions, even as the field is – thankfully – growing too quickly to offer an exhaustive review. Just as importantly, this book seeks to make its own intervention into the historical scholarship on modern Germany by taking up a critical lens on ideas of norms and the normal. It contributes to wider scholarly attempts to disrupt still widely held assumptions that attitudes towards sexuality have followed a more or less straightforward path towards liberation. Instead, it highlights the diversity of ideas around sexual propriety, subjectivity, eroticism and fulfilment that have always existed, even under conditions of extreme state surveillance and persecution. It shows the power of sexuality not only to trouble dominant political and social relations, but also to act as a readily comprehensible symbol of social change. Taking sex seriously as a category of historical analysis means examining the diverse and often contradictory ways in which activists, doctors, politicians, artists, social movements, cultural commentators, and everyday women, men and gender-diverse people have defined 'normal' or 'natural' sexuality over the past two centuries. It means examining how these definitions have been used to shape and direct bodies and behaviours, often to align with ideals of heterosexual, marital, reproductive sex – but also how people have challenged such normative policing of individuals and practices deemed 'abnormal', 'deviant' or 'perverse'.

Far more than a niche subfield, histories of gender and sexuality, with their focus on bodies, desires and how these are overlaid with broader political, cultural and social meanings, have repeatedly challenged conventional patterns of historical explanation. We must avoid, scholars emphasize, the temptation to view larger transformations of state and political structure as an 'explanatory black box' for shifts in areas such as manners or social comportment – for this merely underscores political factors as the key principle underlying historical change.[16] Even as it follows conventional periodizations, *Sexuality in Modern German History* seeks to highlight moments at which historical breaks – the transition from Weimar democracy to Nazi dictatorship, or the split into East and West – offer inadequate frameworks for thinking about changes and continuities in sexual attitudes and behaviours.

Doing the history of sexuality

The history of sexuality has grown rapidly since its emergence as a discrete academic field during the final decades of the twentieth century. Its beginnings are frequently linked to Foucault's aforementioned *History of Sexuality*, which argued that the concept of sexuality itself has a history – or, to follow Foucault's language, a 'genealogy' – and that it was only in the modern era, from around 1800, that people started to conceive of themselves as 'having' a sexuality, and to see this as a fundamental pillar of their own sense of self or identity.[17] The very word 'sexuality' (*Sexualität* in German), broadly defined as 'the constitution or life of the individual as related to sex' only entered into English and most other Western languages in this modern era. As early modern historian Merry Wiesner-Hanks emphasizes, its emergence aligned with 'new ideas about the body, changes in marriage patterns, new concepts of gender differences, and new methods of controlling peoples' lives'.[18]

Yet there are also risks in assuming that premodern people had a fundamentally different sense of self to those living in more recent centuries. Notions of 'identity' or the modern 'subject' may well reflect decidedly nineteenth-century ways of thinking about the relationship of individual citizens to the state, the rising influence of the middle-classes, or the emergence of cultural formations such as the novel, but as early modernist Lyndal Roper observes, we also have much to gain from being prepared 'to view individuals in the past as having individual subjectivities and conflicts not entirely unfamiliar to our own'.[19] People living before the modern era likely *did* have some sense of themselves as individual subjects, and this was likely shaped, at least in part, around distinctly sexual behaviours and desires – even if people did not yet see themselves as 'having' or 'being' a sexuality. In this vein, *Sexuality in Modern German History* at times adopts the more capacious language of sexual 'subjectivity' to think about the role of sex in shaping individual lives.[20] The term 'sexuality' also connects ideas about the intimate self to larger ideas of community and belonging, nation and citizenship. Historians of sexuality working on the German-speaking world have made major contributions to expanding upon and complicating Foucault's still highly influential account.[21] More broadly, sex has become ever more central to historians' accounts of the modern era, and few countries have been as influential in shaping the history of modern sexuality as Germany.

The emergence of the history of sexuality as a discrete area of study occurred against a backdrop of broader cultural and political shifts that enabled works such as Foucault's *History* not only to be written, but also to find a ready audience in the post-Second World War era. These included the rise of left-wing student, feminist and gay and lesbian movements from the late 1960s, in which many historians of gender and sexuality were involved as activists. Until that point, 'history' had been largely understood as that written by and about white, straight, cisgendered (i.e. identifying with the sex assigned to them at birth), financially well-to-do men whose racial, class and gender privilege enabled them significant influence on their social and political surroundings. Marxist and other left-wing historians made important inroads into telling history 'from below', foregrounding social and working-class histories using different kinds of sources, while feminist scholars forged the subfield of women's history, arguing for the significance of research on the family, marriage, abortion, contraception, prostitution and witchcraft alongside more traditional areas of inquiry.[22]

Marriage soon became a particular concern of histories of women, the family and social history, for the way it opened up examinations of women's changing status in relation to men. Somewhat paradoxically, marriage has at times been sidelined by more recent historians of sexuality, who have tended to pay more attention to socially marginalized or 'deviant' sexual practices, such as male same-sex relations. This book seeks to bridge such divides, not least by emphasizing the social institution of marriage as a fundamental site for expressing sexual attitudes across very different political and cultural contexts. Through marriage, ideas about family, inheritance, gender, race, religion and pleasure have been and continue to be contested and affirmed.[23] Situated on the cusp between domestic intimacy and the world at large, between public recognition and private consent, marriage has always involved conforming to collective norms and regulations. Yet as historians remind us, norms and laws are not the same as lived reality, rather, 'they represent the way people conceptualized their world, hoped things would be, or tried to make them'.[24] That the shape of norms surrounding marriage has changed considerably during the modern era has been especially evident since the late twentieth century, with the legal recognition and social normalization of same-sex marriages in many parts of the globe.[25]

While feminist historians pioneered the neglected field of women's history, they also made important conceptual innovations to the field, pushing for historians across the board to take gender seriously as a category of historical analysis. There was an urgent need, argued scholars such as Joan W. Scott, to re-evaluate inherited histories of economics, war, work and political change through a gendered lens.[26] This work has entailed thinking creatively about how to bring into view the stories of individuals not belonging to the social and cultural elites, and looking to alternative sources as legitimate forms of evidence. Early modern historians began turning their attention to little-studied documents and material fragments such as plays, woodcuts, marriage and funeral sermons, and popular stories to offer insights into women's lives. For the modern era, historians of same-sex intimacies and gender-diverse identities have often turned to literary or autobiographical texts to explore more subjective and embodied accounts of intimate experience than those offered by court cases or police records.[27]

The rapid evolution of women's and gender history provided a crucial foundation for the turn towards sexuality as a subject of historical inquiry in the final decades of the twentieth century. Scholarly journals such as the *Journal of Women's History* and *Gender and History* reflect moves to complement the 'history of women' with a critical focus on gender relations and identities, and increasingly also to show how the history of gender and sexuality are intricately intertwined. Wiesner-Hanks even suggests that 'scholars may need to be reminded of distinctions between gender and sexuality rather than convinced of the importance of gender as a category of analysis when exploring sexuality'.[28] One area in which this is particularly the case is the history of prostitution. Female prostitution remains far more studied than sex work involving men or gender-diverse people, although this is starting to change; meanwhile, the labels used to describe this work are hotly debated. Those working in the industry today overwhelmingly prefer 'sex work', a term coined by activist artist Carol Leigh, which avoids older connotations of criminality. Yet others argue that 'prostitution' better encompasses the potential for exploitation and vulnerability that have often been associated with paying and being paid for sexual services, and that sex work is either never, or only sometimes, truly consensual. Historians have tended to favour the latter term in examining the legal, criminal and social aspects of sex work and trafficking.[29] In this book I follow this usage, even as I seek to highlight how prostitution has functioned as a practice that can both support and challenge social norms of sexuality and gender.

Another trigger for the emergence of the history of sexuality as a discrete subfield was the political activism associated with the era of 'gay liberation' and 'sexual revolution'. Although often linked to the famous riots in New York City around the Stonewall Inn in 1969, *Sexuality in Modern German History* draws on a rich body of historical scholarship to remind readers that modern queer and trans rights movements go back much further than this, with origins traceable in Germany back to at least the late 1860s.[30] From the 1970s onwards, social attitudes around nonnormative sexual practices were widely debated in the public sphere, and older medical and psychiatric models that framed them in terms of illness were vocally challenged. That it was becoming easier to publish research on topics such as homosexuality or sex work was heralded in 1990 by the establishment of *The Journal of the History of Sexuality*.[31] 'Claiming a history for sexuality is no longer controversial', many scholars now agree, with historians of queer and trans lives 'no longer feel[ing] much pressure to defend the enterprise'.[32] Even so, many historians working on these topics have had to contend with marginalization and precarity within the academy, or found themselves needing to work outside of the university system altogether. This has been particularly the case in Germany, where until very recently the history of sexuality, and LGBTIQ lives in particular, has been spearheaded by researchers and archivists working with little institutional support. In a field acutely attuned to historical processes of inclusion and exclusion, it is crucial to acknowledge this excellent yet often sidelined research.[33]

Because of its capacity to challenge traditional ways of thinking about the past, some scholars describe sex as itself a 'queer' subject – an adjective that encompasses not only challenges to sex-gender norms, but to ideas of the 'normal' more broadly.[34] Sex is always both a 'discursive construct and a deeply experienced reality', its archival traces at once fragmentary and pervasive, as one recent special issue emphasizes:

> Its imprint on the past can be found in a wide range of sources associated with social and cultural history, the history of science, medicine and technology, material history, and the history of ideas. It intersects with histories of gender, race and racism, class, and disability and is concerned with the production and experiential realities of sexual lives, ideas, and bodies, and their affective reach.[35]

Yet even as it presents important challenges to dominant modes of history writing, the historiography of sexuality has not been without its own blindspots, or immune to privileging some voices over others. Some of the most prominent early historians, including Foucault, focused overwhelmingly on (cis)male experience, even as they opened up discussions of same-sex desire. Less attention has been paid to lesbianism, bisexuality, trans or intersex identities, and much work also remains to be done on more 'heteronormative' topics, from sex education to pornography.[36] As prominent queer theorist Eve Kosovsky Sedgwick once observed, 'making heterosexuality historically visible' is so difficult 'because, under its institutional pseudonyms such as Inheritance, Marriage, Dynasty, Domesticity, and Population, heterosexuality has been permitted to masquerade so fully as History itself'.[37]

Seeking to offer a more comprehensive history of sexuality in modern Germany, this book deliberately brings together histories of 'normal' and 'deviant' sexual behaviours and identities. In doing so, it draws on a rich literature, in both English and German, dealing with much more specific themes and periods – from the emergence of sexual science and modern ideas of homosexuality through to organized LGBTIQ rights movements, from Wilhelmine and Weimar-era debates around 'sex reform', including birth control, abortion and prostitution, to the confronting sexual history of the 'Third Reich'. Historians of National Socialism have been particularly influential in unpacking the interplay between pronatalist and antinatalist policies, and in complicating notions of 'persecution' and 'victimhood', including in relation to queer and trans experience – for gays, lesbians and trans people experienced violence and persecution in very different ways under Nazism, and race always played a role. The history of sexuality during the postwar decades is another rigorous field of inquiry, as scholars work to complicate assumptions about the conservative 1950s, challenge one-sided views of life under state socialism, and present a diverse picture of 1960s and 1970s countercultures on both sides of the Iron Curtain. Scholars have pointed to the benefits of dwelling in the 'entangled' histories of sexuality during these postwar decades, 'the myriad ways in which people found their path through the abnormal, unnatural, and strange world of occupied and divided Germany'.[38]

The following chapters each introduce themes of particular relevance to the history of sexuality – marriage, divorce, birth control, abortion, prostitution, homosexual persecution and emancipation and gender-diverse experiences – and connect these to broader questions of gender, race, class and nation. This simultaneously chronological and thematic structure invites readers to draw larger connections, tracing shifts and continuities in norms of desire, intimacy and morality across two centuries of German history.

Gender, sexuality and a note on terminology

The history of sexuality in modern Germany has shaped sexual identities and language well beyond the German-speaking world. A swathe of recent studies highlights the German 'invention' of categories such as the 'homosexual' or 'transvestite' – labels still in circulation today, although their meanings have changed – with one book even proclaiming the 'German discovery of sex'.[39] Yet such narratives of 'invention' and 'discovery' also raise a pervasive question for historians of sexuality, namely: what is gained, and what is lost, by applying modern identity categories (such as 'gay', 'heterosexual', 'queer' or 'trans') to individuals who likely viewed their behaviours and desires in very different ways to ourselves? Medieval and early modern historians have been especially vocal in warning against the dangers of over-simplifying how individuals in the past viewed their own practices and subjectivities. Instead, they advocate 'a more localized reading of past sexualities – an analysis that allows for a vast array of meanings, contestations, and diverse appropriations by historical actors'.[40] 'That we can find persistent patterns in the construction of sexuality from the ancient Greeks to twentieth-century New York,' observes Ruth Mazo Karras, 'does not mean that the modes of sexual categorization were the same .... It does mean, however, that we cannot identify a sharp break that comes with modernity.'[41] Interrogating and historicizing categories of identity, gender and sexuality will be a pervasive theme of the following chapters, for language not only reflects, but also actively shapes how people have understood, and continue to understand, their most intimate selves and their relations with others. This becomes particularly important when it comes to considering the intertwined histories of same-sex desires and gender-diverse embodiments and behaviours.

There are different ways of approaching these issues. On the one hand, there are powerful political arguments for seeking to 'uncover' sexual lives and experiences in the archives that seem to resemble our own – particularly when it comes to marginalized experiences. Sometimes described as the 'ancestral genealogy' model of queer history, over several decades this mode of history writing has proven to be an emotionally compelling resource for LGBTIQ rights movements. Contemporary rhetoric of gay and trans (and more recently, bisexual, intersex and non-binary) 'rights' and 'pride' are underscored with reference to long and proud histories of queer ancestors.[42] Notably, this strategy is not as new as it might seem, but was also familiar to an earlier generation of German gay rights activists. Turn-of-the-century sexologist Magnus Hirschfeld and late nineteenth-century writer Karl-Maria Kertbeny each included lists of famous 'homosexuals' or 'sexual intermediaries' from history in their medical and legal writings, often featuring the likes of Michelangelo, Shakespeare and Frederick the Great. Their goal was clear: to advocate for greater scientific and legal recognition for same-sex desiring individuals.[43] This strategy even featured in the early silent film *Different from the Others* (*Anders als die Andern* 1919, dir. Oswald), one of the first films to tackle the question of homosexuality head-on. Its opening scenes featured a re-enacted stream of famous gay men from history parading through the visions of depressed gay violinist Paul Körner, prodding Weimar-era audiences to reflect on the life and death stakes of overturning the notorious Paragraph 175 that criminalized male homosexuality.[44]

Such strategies of recovery can, however, obscure the different ways in which individuals in the past may have conceived of themselves, their sexual behaviours and relationships. Many historians of sexuality thus urge us to embrace the 'topsy-turvydom' of historical representations of gender and sexual intimacy.[45] It is important, they emphasize, to remain open to forms of embodiment and desire that do not align neatly with our own twenty-first century or western-centric perspectives, and that might even at times disrupt our own understandings of sex and gender identity.[46] 'The act of mapping a category onto subjects who may not have recognized the practices, lifestyles, notions of body and self, and so forth that it references', argues María Elena Martínez, can cause us to 'miss[] an opportunity to discover in the past human possibilities and imaginings that were suppressed or left unfulfilled but that can provide guidance in the present for creating better worlds in the future'.[47]

To take such a critical stance towards terminology, and by extension, to ideas of identity, is not to do away with them altogether. On the contrary, using terms like 'heterosexual', 'queer' and 'trans' is crucial to writing histories that are accessible and meaningful to readers in the present. In this book I thus persist in using these and other terms to describe individuals across several centuries of German history, even where it may be anachronistic do so. I use 'queer' to encompass a wide range of sexual subjects and practices seen as challenging social norms of heterosexuality, and that sometimes, but not always, aligned with gender-nonconforming presentations and identities. Such practices and identities have been described over time under very different labels, such as 'sodomy', 'urning', 'homosexual', or 'sexual intermediary'.[48] Similarly, I use 'trans' to describe gendered expressions and identities that differed from or challenged binary norms and expectations of masculinity and femininity, particularly where an individual's experience of their gender did not align with the 'sex' assigned to them at birth. I at times deploy the prefix 'cis' to describe non-trans individuals whose birth-assigned sex did align with social norms and expectations of gender, and 'heteronormative' to refer to still-dominant social expectations that sexual relationships should centre on a man and a woman, preferably in a long-term, married, monogamous relationship oriented towards reproduction and family. Finally, I use the terms 'subcultures' and 'scenes' to describe some of the historical communities and networks created by socially marginalized groups such as queer and trans people, who worked in the shadow of mainstream laws and norms to create alternative spaces of sociality, political activism and sexual fulfilment.[49]

An enduring concern of this book is how and why certain labels to describe gender and sexuality come into circulation at certain points in time. Often, this has occurred when political, legal, medical or cultural forces pushed people towards new ways of thinking about their bodies and intimate relationships – sometimes in conjunction with reassessing their relation to family, community or state. I highlight how such labels took twists and turns as they moved in and between official, institutional and more informal and subcultural contexts – for rarely, if ever, have groups with acknowledged social privilege, such as politicians, doctors, lawyers or even concentration camp guards, been able to straightforwardly force their views about sex-gender categories onto voiceless patients and subjects. Rather, looking closely at the historical sources shows that this almost always involved complex processes of negotiation and exchange. In such ways, the history and historiography of sexuality opens up important new ways of thinking about power, resistance and agency, and about the place of the individual in modern society. Across two centuries of German history, the following chapters show how sex was shaped by, and actively shaped, understandings of gender, race, class, ability and religion. Understanding the history of sex is integral to understanding the complex social positionings of life in the modern era.

1

Enlightening intimacy: From Reformation to unification

On a now unknown date sometime in the 1670s, a baby was born to a wayman in Dörverden in Germany's north, declared by those attending the birth to be a girl, and given the name Anna Ilsabe Buncke. This is in itself the most everyday of occurrences, hardly warranting our closer attention. Yet the life of this individual, to whom later sources assigned the decidedly gender-nonconforming appellation 'Maiden Heinrich', developed in intriguing ways. As an adult, in around 1698, Buncke travelled to Bremen, assumed the male name Heinrich Lohmann, and 'had men's clothing made for herself'.[1] Sometime later, moving via Rotterdam to Amsterdam, Heinrich organized for a dildo – 'an instrument shaped like a male member', or *membrum virile* – to be attached to their body by prostitutes working in an Amsterdam brothel.[2] According to evidence given at trial some years later, in 1701, 'she then noticed a small scrotum hanging on her [body], and she did not know from whence it came. Once the said *membrum virile* was firmly set on her, she ate a cold soup with the whores'.[3] At this time it was not unusual to attribute to prostitutes the supernatural powers of witchcraft, capable of variously enlarging or destroying a man's penis, among other things, and folkloric beliefs in magical 'sex change' (*Geschlechtswechsel*) were widespread. In the years that followed, Heinrich used this appendage with various wives, reporting pleasure in its use in ways that went beyond what one may expect:

> the virile member did not always remain in the same size [and shape] as did her other limbs, rather when she wished to cohabit, she got regular erections and in the act of fornication felt the common lusts [of a man], spilled her seed [like a man], and when the member had done its work well, it went limp.[4]

Heinrich's wives, too – presumably with some pleasure – told of how it moved and ejaculated. On 23 January 1702, Heinrich and two other suspects were sentenced to the medieval execution method of death on the wheel on homicide charges, a year after officials fished out 'a woman's torso, naked, and missing its head' from the public privy in the beast market in the centre of Hamburg. Wild speculation surrounded this most public of legal trials and executions, including stories of transvestism, 'female sodomy' and magical harm.[5]

Reading closely with and through the sources – sources evidently produced in circumstances of forced testimony under torture, and almost certainly incorporating elements of fabrication – can allow us, argues historian Mary Lindemann in a careful unpacking of this case, to grasp some sense of this subject's agency. It becomes possible to seek out Heinrich's own voice rather than just those of their prosecutors, 'to fathom how she composed her storyline(s), how she selected and plaited together the many different strands of her life into a tale she felt was convincing or useful or that allowed her to make sense of her own existence'.[6] We do those who lived in earlier centuries a disservice, as the introduction to this book has pointed out, by assuming that it was only in the modern era, broadly speaking, that people developed a sense of themselves as social actors and subjects. And while it is anachronistic to assign to Heinrich, as I do here, the twenty-first-century singular pronoun 'they', I do so to highlight their clear claiming of a gender-diverse, rather than straightforwardly female, identity. Heinrich pushed against early modern norms of sex and gender. Their experiences weaved in and around dominant social, legal and religious structures governing acceptable sexual expression, including multiple marriages, as well as in and around ideas of nonnormative sexual embodiment and behaviour, as they were variously labelled a 'hermaphrodite', 'tribade' and 'sodomite'.

Heinrich's story represents a fitting beginning for this chapter, which seeks to lay out a broader historical context for the study of sexuality in modern Germany. I argue that what constitutes 'norms' of sexual behaviour and expression, as well as what was considered outside of those norms, has changed enormously over time. The historiography of sexuality in the German-speaking world has tended to focus on the period beginning in the second half of the nineteenth century. These decades, as observed in the introduction, saw some of the first explicit calls for homosexual rights and law reform anywhere in the world, as well as the emergence of a new field of 'sexual science' largely pioneered by German-speaking doctors, scientists and intellectuals. 'Seldom', notes one scholar, 'do historians dip further back'.[7] Yet it is crucial to situate these distinctly 'modern' developments against earlier political, cultural and social events and patterns. This book thus begins by looking back to the medieval and early modern periods as the crucible of modern ideas about love, marriage, and 'normal' and 'abnormal' sexualities, drawing on a rapidly growing body of scholarship foregrounding gender and sexuality during these centuries.[8]

In the Middle Ages the ideas of Church leaders became increasingly central to norms of marriage and divorce, while the later medieval period saw the increasing persecution of those deemed outside of social and legal norms of sexual propriety – people given labels such as 'witches', 'sodomites' and 'tribades'. The early modern era, lasting from approximately 1500 to 1800, then witnessed a series of major religious and political upheavals. The Protestant Reformation in the sixteenth century was particularly significant in shaping German attitudes around sexual behaviours, especially as the Reformers granted marriage a much greater status than in medieval times as the focus of sexual and social organization. This period also saw crackdowns on urban prostitution, sharper policing of same-sex behaviours and highly sexualized attacks on so-called witches within and beyond Germany – mostly women, but sometimes also men and children.

The early modern German-speaking world was 'a highly complex society', historians remind us, 'politically polycentric, made up of territorial courts, imposing Imperial cities, strong village communities, small archbishoprics, supra-regional alliances, and Imperial political and legal institutions'.[9] Following the 1555 Peace of Augsburg, 'Germany became a truly extraordinary patchwork' of Catholic, Protestant and bi-confessional cities, with Protestants further split into Lutheran and Calvinist traditions. The seventeenth century saw political and religious tensions reach a climax in the Thirty Years' War (1618–48), and increased attempts to consolidate state control through social regulation.[10] Moving towards the eighteenth century, meanwhile, Germany underwent a transition towards a form of modern civil society. During this period, widely associated with the optimism and rationalizing intellectual currents of the 'Enlightenment', we witness a series of changes in models of sex, love and friendship. In the decades that followed, men's and women's public and private roles were reimagined, cultural models of close friendship and brotherhood developed in ways often regarded as distinctly German, and the middle classes vastly increased their social and cultural dominance.

This first chapter takes us through to 1871, the year of Germany's unification and emergence as a modern nation state. Histories of nineteenth-century Germany highlight the revolution of 1848 and federal unification several decades later as the most significant political milestones of this era. These events are generally narrated as part of a larger story of industrialization, capitalist development and the expanding 'colonial fantasies' of European imperialism.[11] While the following pages examine the history of sexuality in light of these and other developments, they also show that focusing on the sexual as our main category of analysis can cause us to reflect critically on such conventional periodizations. Historian Isabel Hull points out, for example, that by as early as 1815 – some decades before these 'key' events – 'the distinction between the modern state and modern civil society had already been drawn and the main lines of the modern sexual system largely laid down'.[12] Furthermore, we can already see the emergence of new ways of thinking about same-sex relations in works by German-speaking lawyers, doctors and intellectuals in the years prior to unification. Chapter 2 interrogates these writings in more detail, exploring late nineteenth-century Germany's reputation as the 'birthplace' of modern ideas of sexuality.

This chapter is organized thematically rather than chronologically, guided by the critical focus on norms outlined in the introduction. The first stop is marriage. Across several centuries, this institution transformed into the dominant framework for socially acceptable sexuality, becoming a cornerstone of the early modern German family, household, and community and civic life. It was also a site of scandals, pleasures and challenges to social norms and expectations. By the turn of the nineteenth century, most marriages in Germany consisted of heterosexual unions between two people of similar socio-economic background, with love idealized as a central value underpinning the union's validity. This had not always been the case: 'if there is any constant in the history of marriage, it is *variety* – the sheer number and diversity of sexual pair-bonds that Western societies have recognized, formally or informally.'[13] Examining where marriage was celebrated, and where it was seen to transgress social norms, offers rich insights into how people have experienced themselves as sexual beings at different moments in time, and how this intersected with ideas about religion, work, race, family, class and gender. The chapter then turns its attention to forms of sexual behaviour and ways of categorizing people who, like 'Maiden Heinrich', challenged dominant norms proscribed by the law, medicine or religion – for the treatment of 'witches', 'prostitutes' or 'sodomites' can tell us much about shifting sexual norms over the centuries. Brothels and prostitution were crucial to medieval urban structures, for example, but were sharply condemned and regulated during the Reformation and Counter-Reformations of the sixteenth and early seventeenth centuries. Tracing the persecution of witches and people who desired others of their own sex, meanwhile, points to the ways in which gender and sexuality intersected to shape ideas about who was considered outside of mainstream society, and how new structures of political and social organization did not always equate to more progressive sexual politics.

Marriage, family and norms in the medieval and early modern eras

Since at least the early modern era, marriage has served as a cornerstone of a desirable life path. Marital unions have been critical to reproducing social structures, linking individuals and couples to families, inheritance and society at large. Yet this has not always been the case, and the focus on love as the basis of legal union is also a relatively recent phenomenon. The early Christian Church was far less interested in marriage than in later centuries.

Early medieval marriages were largely a secular matter, with the consent of spouses all that was required to validate a union, although religious sacraments and blessings did exist. The Church – which in medieval western Europe meant the Roman Catholic church – celebrated celibacy over family life. Single-sex communities of nuns and monks dedicated to serving God represented a demographically significant alternative to marriage, a safe and honourable place for women and men who chose not to marry or remarry. Only with the Fourth Lateran Council in 1215 did the western Church declare marriage a sacrament, enabling it to become a significant focus of canon, or church, law. By this stage, most European societies had come to see themselves as broadly 'Christian', and this perception increasingly coloured social rituals around marriage, 'even if in fact they were largely or entirely pagan in origin'.[14]

In the German-speaking lands, these rituals included the tradition of the *Morgengabe*, the payment of a sum in addition to the bride price or dowry the morning after the wedding. Originally a practice of literally paying for the woman's virginity, this was later folded into regular prenuptial property settlements, while the size of the dowry depended on social class. The early medieval period also saw the tradition of the *Friedelehe* – 'quasi' or 'abduction' marriage – where a woman contracted a marriage without the standard property payments; sometimes, it involved a husband secretly taking the bride-to-be from her family. Although frowned upon by the church, such marriages – sometimes romanticized as love matches, though they benefited the husband more than the wife – were generally permitted to continue provided the families could reach a property agreement. This was important, as the woman was presumably no longer a virgin, lessening her future value as a bride.[15] At the same time, remarriage was not just possible, but in rural areas even common, particularly following the death of a spouse. Perhaps most surprising from a twenty-first-century perspective is that during much of the medieval period, only priests were required to be married in church – the ban on clerical marriage and insistence on celibacy were only introduced with the reform movement of the eleventh century.[16]

The medieval Christian Church developed numerous laws around when, where and how to have sex in marriage. Historians who have done the sums have established that less than half the days of the year were available for intercourse – the Penitentials or books of church rules banned sex between wives and husbands on feast and fasting days, during menstruation, pregnancy and lactation, or at times that coincided with confession or receiving the Eucharist. Sundays, Wednesdays, Fridays, Advent and Lent were also off the menu. Further prohibitions on both marital and extramarital sex also applied, and while some of these are less shocking to us today – intercourse with other people or animals was seen to conflict with the vows of marriage – others were decidedly more restrictive, with bans on oral and anal sex, mandates for strict hygiene practices and limitations on sexual positions. Broadly speaking, the male superior or 'missionary' position was the normative expectation of marital intercourse, and reproduction the goal.[17] Needless to say, having sex in a church – a safe, dry place for illicit encounters, as historian Ruth Mazo Karras points out – attracted scandal, with rumours circulating widely about one couple who allegedly became stuck together 'like dogs', only to be discovered by a bewildered congregation the following day.[18] Monks and nuns were explicitly prohibited from engaging in same-sex practices including 'sodomy' or 'a woman fornicating with a woman' (more on these below). There were also strict bans on abortion, contraception, bestiality, infanticide and the use of sexual objects – even as the very existence of such bans suggests that such practices were far from unheard of.[19]

For married couples, fertility and reproduction were surrounded by further restrictions and recommendations. Women who had given birth had to wait forty days before they could re-enter a church following a cleansing ritual. 'For a culture that made reproduction the basis of marriage,' Karras observes, 'it seems strange that it would have been seen as at the same time polluting, but the very conflicted relation between the medieval church and the flesh made this contradiction possible.'[20] It is hard to know how seriously everyday people treated these regulations: many likely viewed them 'as guidelines rather than absolute commands'.[21] And despite wide-ranging restrictions on reproductive sexuality, much effort went into promoting marital fertility, from medical handbooks to advice books. Perhaps surprisingly, these also included more or less coded advice on how to practice contraception. One influential medieval compilation of women's medicine, the 'Trotula', recommended the following, slightly peculiar method:

> Take a male weasel and let its testicles be removed and let it be released alive. Let the women carry these testicles with her in her bosom and tie them in goose skin or in another skin, and she will not conceive.[22]

Other books recommended cures for infertility, often thought to be due to a lack of balance in the 'humours' of one or other partner – too hot, cold, moist or dry. This could be remedied with a range of 'baths, diets, lotions, and fumigations … as well as sexual techniques (what might today be called foreplay) that would promote the release of the female seed'.[23] Overindulgence in sex was thought to risk fertility, particularly in men, with doctors recommending moderation (as opposed to chastity). Sexually transmitted diseases with names such as 'burning sickness' were also a problem once multiple sexual partners were involved, and it was widely believed that sexual intercourse could lead to leprosy – a name applied to a range of conditions during the medieval period.[24]

Marriage and marital sex were also important elements of family, religious and community life in Jewish communities in medieval Germany – and in Muslim communities, too, although these were far less prominent than elsewhere in Europe during this period, such as Iberia or Sicily.[25] Rabbinical laws and traditions oversaw Jewish marriages, including blessing a marriage with words from the Talmud. Such practices may also have influenced Christian rituals at a time when non-Jewish marriages were becoming less secular.[26] Jewish marriage partners tended to be younger than their Christian counterparts, and parents often played a greater role in the choice of spouse. There was a greater emphasis on marital companionship, and a greater capacity for divorce – sometimes justified on the spiritual grounds that the spouses were not 'predestined' for each other.[27] Finally, some traditions were in stark contrast to Christian practices: where Christians were forbidden from sexual intercourse on Sundays, Karras points to 'the Jewish *mitzvah* or commandment of sexual relations on the Sabbath except if the wife is menstruating'.[28] This urging to intercourse suggests very different, yet historically synchronous, understandings of when it was 'moral' or 'normal' to have sex within marriage.

The idea that marriage should be based on romantic love, such a dominant norm of marriage in our own time, only became widespread during the later Middle Ages. Before the twelfth century, Christians' relationships to their spouses were expected to be closer to sibling affection or parental devotion than centred on erotic or romantic attraction. Love was a desirable consequence rather than necessary precursor to marriage, and medieval literature highlighted this 'ambivalent role'.[29] And the meaning of love itself also changed significantly across these centuries. German literature from the late Middle Ages shows a growing turn to themes of love, sex and marriage, and sometimes even 'a drastic and uninhibited interest in the topic of sex'.[30] In one of numerous erotic stories in the Karlsruhe Codex 408, copied around 1430, an innocent monk travelling with a fatherly abbot finds himself at close quarters with an innkeeper's daughter, who cooks up plans to seduce the monk that night. 'I will try to find out at night whether his body is able to discover how to use women in bed,' she plots, before inducting him into the secrets of 'bed games' later that evening.[31] Yet 'love' in the later medieval era was not just about intimate or romantic relationships between individuals. Above all, it centred on the love of God as a force legitimizing worldly power and overseeing social relations, unified in the notion of charity or *caritas*.[32]

The Protestant Reformation, the beginning of which is often linked to the moment when a monk named Martin Luther (Figure 1.1) hammered a piece of paper containing his *Ninety-Five Theses* to the door of the Castle Church in Wittenberg in 1517, ushered in decades of radical debates about religion between Catholics and Protestants.[33] These debates decisively shifted the boundaries of marriage and altered the ways in which individuals organized their intimate lives, even as they also instigated much broader changes to social structures and political organization. The Catholic Church, as we have seen, had long tended to view human sexuality as impure and requiring strict regulation, with the convent and monastic life of nuns

FIGURE 1.1 *Martin Luther as an Augustinian Monk. Print from engraving by Lucas Cranach the Elder, 1520. Metropolitan Museum of Art.*

Source: CC0, via Wikimedia Commons.

and monks the holiest option. Protestant Reformers, under the guidance of leaders such as Luther, took a more positive view. For them, marriage was 'the estate expected of all but the rarest Christian, lay and clergy alike', and carried a great moral burden.[34] They thus elevated the status of monogamous heterosexual marriage, granting a newly spiritual significance to the emotional bond between husband and wife. Clerical celibacy, by now dogma within the Catholic Church, was also sharply criticized by Luther and others, who declared life without sex too great a challenge for the weak human constitution. He especially attacked the hypocrisy of priests commonly living, often quite publicly, in so-called 'unmarriages' or *Unehen* with concubine 'wives' and children.[35]

Of course, people did not necessarily do what theologians recommended, and the Reformers' emphasis on spiritualized marriage and moral order existed alongside a diversity of views and lived realities. Dowries continued to play a role in many marriages, and monetary exchanges could also be used to settle human obligations that did not result in marriage. Thus when Barbara Sontheimer in the rural Swabian district of Ottobeuren fell pregnant to her employer's stepson, Jacob Magg, but could not afford the necessary dowry to marry the much wealthier man, the notaries settled on a cash payment of 155 *gulden* as the price of premarital 'defloration and impregnation' – a sum she could then take into her subsequent marriage to Caspar Herz.[36]

Divorce is another example of the diversity and contradictions surrounding marital norms during this period, and formed a key point of difference between Protestants and Catholics. Religious leaders and lawmakers had long debated the legitimate foundation of marriage, and in particular, whether a union rested on freely given consent, or on consummation – the act of sexual intercourse to 'seal' the marriage vows. Catholic theologians in the twelfth century had settled on the former – largely due to the problem otherwise posed by the virginal marriage between Mary and Joseph.[37] They strongly condemned divorce, even though for centuries it had been possible, at least for wealthy or well-connected individuals, to arrange an official 'annulment' declaring that a marriage had never been legitimate in the first place. Other reasons accepted by the Catholics included forced marriage, non-consummation (failure to have intercourse) or the subsequent discovery of a prohibited level of kinship (incest). Separating from one's partner while remaining married was also possible in some cases, especially where adultery or violence played a role.[38]

Despite some reluctance, Luther and his followers substantially challenged these positions on divorce. They allowed the official dissolution of marital unions on the grounds of adultery, desertion or impotence, representing a significant expansion of legal and religious norms around marriage, at least for their Protestant adherents. There is a definite pragmatism to Luther's argument in his 1522 work *The Estate of Marriage* that 'certain strange, stubborn, and obstinate people, who have no capacity for toleration and are not suited for married life at all, should be permitted to get a divorce .... Frequently something must be tolerated ... to prevent something worse from happening.'[39] Luther offered advice on this issue to such notable figures as Henry VIII of England and Philipp, Landgrave of Hesse – a key protagonist of German Protestantism – and even secretly endorsed the latter's bigamous marriage to Margarete von der Saale in 1540. Catholics, meanwhile, viewed all Protestants who divorced and remarried as engaging in non-permissible bigamy.[40]

Even with this greater flexibility to dissolve unhappy marriages, Protestant attitudes to marriage also imposed new restrictive norms. This was especially the case for women, expected to one-sidedly uphold sexual morality: 'The reformed religion was patriarchal and Reformation Europe is characterized as the heyday of the patriarchal nuclear family.'[41] And even though this picture is complicated by evidence that many Reformation-era men were loving and sympathetic husbands and fathers, wives nonetheless occupied a lower place on the family hierarchy than husbands.[42] Similarly, children were expected to be submissive to their parents, and servants to their masters in an economy dominated by the guild ideal of the household workshop. This prominent medieval and early modern model of social organization combined family and work, with the master craftsmen often also the heads of large households.[43]

Examining changing ideas around 'transgressive' marriages sheds further light on the norms and limits of acceptable social and sexual organization. At times, marital unions were tolerated in the medieval and early modern eras that appear quite progressive even from the perspective of much of the twentieth century. Although never in the majority, these included interfaith, interracial and incestuous alliances. At times they involved marriages involving more than two people (such as the aforementioned Landgrave of Hesse), and the evidence suggests that sometimes even same-sex unions were able to be formalized – these were never widespread, but at least well-known enough to become a literary trope in places such as early modern England.[44] Some scholars – most notably, John Boswell in his 1994 book *Same-Sex Unions in Premodern Europe* – have argued that same-sex unions were quite common in the medieval Christian era.[45] More recently, though, historians have questioned whether such claims rely on inappropriate comparisons between contemporary 'gay' marriage and medieval rituals such as the 'creation of the brothers' or other male friendship ceremonies. Those ceremonies, however erotic or passionate the friendship between men may have been, did not prevent men from also carrying out their marital duties. Viewing them as precursors to today's gay marriage, moreover, risks misunderstanding the highly transactional purpose of medieval marriage, which was to secure legal inheritance:

> Marriage in the Middle Ages was not an affirmation and official recognition of love between two people as much as it was the establishment of a legal unit that legitimized children and facilitated the transfer of property from one family to another and one generation to another. Same-sex unions were clearly not this.[46]

In considering such ceremonies from a twenty-first-century perspective, we must acknowledge the possibility that there existed socially and even religiously condoned relationships between members of the 'same' sex that do not align with our own legal and social institutions. At the same time, accusations of 'sodomy', discussed below, were often pursued with the full force of the law.

The splits in German society caused by the Reformation meant that most marriages took place within confessional groupings, the largest being the Catholics, Lutherans and Reformed Protestants. Marriages across these Christian confessional lines were not illegal, but tended to be avoided for social reasons. Where they did occur, it seems partners often arrived at reasonably equitable compromises concerning freedom of conscience and how offspring were to be raised. Case studies of peasants in Osnabrück reveal that confessionally mixed couples tended to raise sons in the religion of the father and daughters in that of the mother. Elsewhere, children were raised in the faith adopted by the rulers of the territory.[47] Alliances between Christians and Jews, on the other hand, were rare and subject to sharp taboos. In some places, state laws forbade Christians to even socialize with Jews, whether for eating, bathing, letting houses or having sex. Yet once again, the presence of such laws suggests that mixing between these groups did indeed take place.[48]

Studies of incestuous marriage are particularly illuminating for understanding shifting religious and social boundaries around sexual relations. In 1525 Luther, himself a former Augustinian monk, married former nun Katharina von Bora. Although not related by blood, their marriage was considered incestuous by many at the time because both had vowed to live in chastity and were regarded as married to God; in this sense they were related by spiritual kinship (*cognation spiritualis*). Based on similar reasoning, godparents had for centuries been prohibited from marrying their godchildren, or even the relatives of those children, pointing to a quite different understanding of 'incest' to our own.[49] The historical German term for incest is *Blutschande*, literally 'disgrace of the blood'. It carries implications of racial as well as familial transgression, although it has been understood and applied very differently over the centuries. Fourteenth-century canon law prohibited marriage up to the fourth degree, including unions between second cousins. In contrast, sixteenth-century Reformers restricted prohibitions to a much tighter kinship circle. But they still considered incest an abominable sin, and transgressions were susceptible to the severest consequences. According to the 1532 Imperial Criminal Code (the 'Carolina'), incestuous unions were even punishable by death. This penalty was not always applied, though, and by the eighteenth century was decidedly rare.[50]

By the time of the Enlightenment in the eighteenth century, prominent intellectuals tended to agree that while incestuous marriage transgressed social norms, it did not necessarily conflict with natural or divine law. Johann Zedler's 'bellwether' Enlightenment publication, the *Universal-Lexikon* (universal encyclopaedia), concluded that 'incest ... does not contradict nature', but cautioned that prohibiting it might be necessary for practical reasons, to uphold social order. As Mary Lindemann points out, '[i]t is hardly clear that incest in the European past was so defined [as we understand it today,] or that the practice was clearly abhorrent.'[51] Equally, she notes that it is important to avoid reading incestuous relationships – whether involving marriage or not – too narrowly through the modern lenses of domestic violence or child abuse, even if intrafamilial abuse was sometimes a factor. It is almost impossible to know how common incest was in the eighteenth century, with many instances unreported. We do know, though, that during the eighteenth century many prohibitions on marriages between kin, including between cousins or brother- and sisters- in law, began to be rolled back or no longer enforced, and that by the nineteenth century, marriage between cousins had become fairly widespread.[52] This formed part of a larger move towards more endogamous unions – people of all socio-economic backgrounds now tended to marry within their same class and kinship groups – which in turn served inheritance goals: it made it easier to retain money and resources, keeping these in the family.[53] In such ways, the definition of incest changed, with intrafamilial marriages becoming both easier and more 'normal' over time – although always within limits defined by Church and state.

Love, marriage and gendered citizenship in the age of Enlightenment

The Reformation is commonly understood to have 'changed marriage profoundly, giving rise to an ideal that the modern protagonists of traditional [marriage] take for eternal'.[54] Yet this institution, and the understandings of love and gender that underpinned it, underwent further significant changes during the eighteenth century. Germany is widely regarded as a centre of the European Enlightenment (in German *Aufklärung*), and the eighteenth century as a period of cultural and intellectual blossoming, from the proto-Romantic passions of the *Sturm und Drang* ('Storm and Stress') movement in literature and music in the 1760s to 1780s, to the humanist era of Weimar Classicism (1780s to early 1800s). Philosophers Johann Gottlieb Fichte and Immanuel Kant and authors Johann Wolfgang von Goethe, Sophie von La Roche and Friedrich Schiller were among those beginning to reassess not only women's and men's public roles, but also the more intimate spheres of marriage and sexual relationships during this period, sometimes toying with more egalitarian forms of heterosexual intimacy.

There are two main understandings of the shifts associated with the era of Enlightenment in the European context. Many philosophers and public intellectuals, even today, view it as a coming together of secularizing, liberalizing and modernizing tendencies in religion, politics, philosophy and science. Enlightenment ideals of light, knowledge, rationality and progress came to be 'identified with the "modern," and, increasingly, with "modernity" itself'.[55] Historians, on the other hand, are more cautious about such broad causal narratives – which at times conflate political and intellectual developments that may have been unrelated. Viewing the past from the perspective of sexuality can offer alternative views on such wider explanatory structures, and in particular, challenge narratives of 'progress' that imagine gender roles and sexual relations as moving inexorably towards liberation.[56]

Following the Reformation the German territorial states greatly increased their powers, including in areas once overseen by the church. Ever more sophisticated state bureaucracies decentred the authority of medieval structures such as the *Gemeinde* (community), the craft guilds and the family when it came to regulating sexuality. This era of 'absolutism' forged a new relationship between state and subjects. As Isabel Hull explains, individuals faced greater state regulation, sometimes referred to as 'social disciplining', as the 'common man' of the medieval era became the 'citizen' of seventeenth-century civil society.[57] This citizen was defined by gender as well as class, with Germany's numerous absolutist states of this era taking a firm hand against women and those without property via so-called 'discipline ordinances'. The gap between the bourgeoisie and working classes grew, as did the regulation of female sexuality, non-marital sex and illegitimacy. At the same time, the German absolutist states were often more in tune with their 'subjects' than the social-disciplinary model suggests. State regulation frequently enforced the kinds of sexual norms that were already widespread among the population, reserving discipline and punishment for the most egregious acts considered likely to harm the local economy or social stability.[58]

The eighteenth century saw a push away from state absolutism and towards ideas of bourgeois civil society, or *bürgerliche Gesellschaft*, with greater emphasis on the responsibility of individuals. Christian principles merged into a secularized concept of the public good, and those seeking to reimagine society and its relationship to the state frequently turned to sexual arguments: the bourgeoisie argued that its sexual morality was superior to that of both the nobility and the poorer classes, portrayed as victims of their own sexual incontinence.[59] Shifts in the basic assumptions underlining civil society also affected gender relations and lasted well into the nineteenth century. Middle-class men were starting to enjoy greater freedoms as self-determining, active citizens. For middle-class women this situation was reversed – or was, at least, far less emancipatory than Enlightenment ideals of progress might suggest. Women's shifting status also complicated ideas of public and private, with lasting effects: 'not independent, emancipated, or a citizen, [woman] could not be sexually self-determining. ... The resulting schematic dichotomy of male-active/female-passive is familiar to any observer of the nineteenth century.'[60] This shift was also palpable in rural areas, where new forums of public debates between men on agricultural matters ranging from fodder beets to new farming technologies aligned with a decline in the older authority of the moral household, in which women had played an important role.[61] Whether in the towns or in the countryside, men enjoyed a growing sense of participation in the public sphere, complemented by a sense of private individuality independent of society. Women, on the other hand, had little access to such public agency, even as they remained subject to society's judgment. Such increasingly polarized understandings of men and women's roles and status survived the revolution of 1848 and unification of 1871 'largely untouched and unquestioned', permeating institutions and ideologies across the political spectrum.[62]

Whether despite or because of such gender polarization, the mid-century saw fledgling feminist developments that challenged dominant ideas about gender and sex roles. Nineteenth-century German feminism had its roots in the religious dissenting movement of the 1840s, when an alliance of German Catholics and Protestants objecting to conservatism and monarchical authority had advocated for more democratic congregations and a separation of church and state. Women constituted as many as 30–40 per cent of these groups, and their contribution led one women's activist, Louise Otto, to observe in 1847 that 'it is above all the religious movement to which we are indebted for the rapid advance of female participation in the issues of the times'.[63]

The literary history of the Enlightenment and subsequent cultural epoch of Romanticism offer further perspectives on the position of women and men in German society, and marriage, during this era. The late eighteenth-century plays of Gotthold Ephraim Lessing illustrate the strict constraints on women and female passion in bourgeois culture, although not necessarily in a negative light: 'Religion suits feminine modesty very much, it gives to beauty a certain noble, earnest, and yearning appearance,' declares one character in the play *Der Freigeist* (The Freethinker) of 1749.[64] Others were less convinced. Marriage, declared feminist Jewish writer and literary salon host Rahel Levin (later Varnhagen) in the early 1800s, constituted no less than a 'bourgeois anvil' for women.[65] In response, novels by women authors such as Sophie von La Roche and Friederike Helene Unger drew on the emancipatory language of the French Revolution and women's rights developed by actors such as Olympes de Gouges to develop more liberating representations of femininity. Karoline von Günderrode went so far as to develop a radical critique of the contradictions of bourgeois female existence, proclaiming to her friend Gunda Brentano in a letter penned in around 1800 the 'unfeminine desire to throw myself into the wild thick of battle, to die – why was I not a man! I have no sense for female virtues, for female happiness. Only the wild, great, resplendent pleases me.'[66] Such railing against gendered constraints came up against resistance from male colleagues, however: famous writers Goethe and Schiller were not alone in condescendingly proclaiming the 'dilettantism of broads' and 'little gentlewomen' who dared pick up a pen.[67]

Despite such feminist protests, late eighteenth-century marriage was more focused on love, or at least affection, between the partners than in earlier eras. Equally, forced marriages were frowned upon, particularly among the educated middle classes, or *Bildungsbürgertum*, suggesting a shift towards more equitable norms of partnership.[68] In 1774 German jurist and social theorist Justus Möser likely expressed the wish of many men of his class when he outlined his catalogue of desirable qualities in a future wife:

> I wish for a virtuous, Christian woman with a good heart, healthy sense of reason, comfortable domestic interactions and a lively yet restrained nature, a hard-working and industrious housekeeper, a clean and prudent cook and an attentive gardener.[69]

Such separation between the masculine world of work and the feminine world of the home was held up by many as the middle-class ideal at the dawning of the modern era.

By the early nineteenth century, Germany was starting to transform into a modern, industrial and capitalist society. German marriages of this era were increasingly shaped by the forces of nationalism, imperialism and industrialization and dominant models of sexual reproduction, family and respectability came to reflect the values of the ever more influential bourgeoisie. The family, with marriage at its centre, became 'one of the key institutions that provided a model through which the German bourgeoisie was able to generalize its outlook and values within the larger society'.[70] The family was the symbolic, intimate heart of the emerging private realm, forming a counterpart to the competitive public realm of business and industry. The 'triumph of the nuclear family', historian George Mosse has argued, 'coincided with the rise of nationalism and respectability'.[71] While men were to be strong, active protectors of the family, women were to be passive upholders of morality with a strong sense of beauty and decorum. It was not unusual for there to be a considerable age difference between spouses, underlining the patriarchal positioning of the husband as the older partner; generally, he also had the last word in matters ranging from the family finances to the hiring and firing of servants.[72] Between 1700 and 1914 the average age for men at (first) marriage remained reasonably stable, between thirty-one and thirty-three, while for women it rose from twenty-two in the eighteenth century to twenty-seven by 1900–14 – an increase that historians attribute largely to women's increased educational and professional opportunities.[73]

As the nineteenth century progressed, economists and politicians began to argue for a 'family wage' for married male workers that would allow wives to focus on domestic tasks and childrearing. Bourgeois marriage also relied on structural, socio-economic factors such as servants and a non-working mother. These were beyond the reach of many lower-class families, though, including peasants and unskilled workers, among whom 'there was little imitation of bourgeois family norms, certainly before the First World War'.[74]

On the contrary: the economic conditions of the industrial era meant that in many working-class families, child labour was necessary to survive. Demand for contraception increased, and this in turn prompted religious leaders to make statements condemning the practice. In 1869 Pope Pius IX declared that the foetus acquires a soul at conception, several months earlier than had traditionally been assumed. This effectively recategorized all post-conception methods of contraception as 'abortion', and had severe consequences for working-class Catholics who struggled to cater to more mouths to feed. In such ways, new moral strictures were imposed on reproductive sexuality, even if statements by the Pope did not necessarily reflect people's actual behaviours and choices.[75] By the final decades of the nineteenth century, a growing women's movement had begun to vocally criticize such constraints and norms surrounding women's sexuality and respectability, while also articulating other demands: the right to work, to vote, to study and to access more liberating forms of dress.[76]

Germany's emerging status as an imperial power in an era of European colonial expansion also influenced social norms around acceptable marriage partners. Where religious and class differences had long functioned as barriers to marriage, increasingly differences of skin colour and ethnicity played a role. At the same time, colonialism and overseas merchant trade brought with them more geographic mobility and interethnic unions.[77] Assumptions about racial difference and European 'superiority' over colonized or 'primitive' peoples frequently produced hypocritical reasoning about appropriate gender roles. 'Europeans and Americans often criticized the societies they were colonizing for requiring women to be secluded in the home, but at the same time they created a stronger ideal of domesticity for women at home,' as Merry Wiesner-Hanks observes.[78] These nineteenth-century developments, and the growing significance of race as an organizing category, are explored further in Chapter 2.

Marriage remained the primary socially acceptable outlet for sexuality and a central focus of social and economic organization throughout the medieval, early modern and Enlightenment periods, even as the terms of this legal and social contract differed significantly over time. What, though, of the many individuals whose behaviours and desires defied its limits altogether – people that one historian of nineteenth-century Britain dubbed the 'other Victorians', such as prostitutes, pornographers, 'hysterics' and 'sodomites'?[79] It is to such individuals that the remainder of this chapter turns.

Unruly sexualities

As religious and political leaders held up marriage as both an ideal and a norm for all, many women, men and gender-diverse individuals found themselves outside of its safe harbour, and variously feared, marginalized, a focus of sexual fantasies, or an object of political critique and persecution.

Figures commonly associated with such nonconforming sexual behaviours in the late medieval and early modern eras were often coded female, such as prostitutes and witches. On the other hand, 'sodomites' were generally conceived of as male. Other individuals, as we saw with Maiden Heinrich, experienced their gender and sexuality in ways that we might today variously describe as queer, non-binary, trans or non-heteronormative. The increasing regulation of prostitution and the persecution of witches during the early modern era point to ways in which societal attitudes especially towards unmarried women were changing. And it was not only individuals engaged in the sex trade or accused of sorcery and superstition who challenged social norms of gender and sexuality. Educated women, as well as women and men who chose to devote themselves to religious life in same-sex communities, were increasingly suspected of embodying their sexuality in socially nonconforming and even dangerous ways.

Lascivious nuns, monks and scholars

Trapped between the pursuit of Renaissance humanist ideals and the restrictive bourgeois female roles idealized during the Enlightenment, most early modern German women who chose a life of scholarship were compelled to live in chaste solitude and give up on family life. Certainly, they were unable to aspire to the combination of political and public service and family life that was the ideal for many early modern men.[80] Nuns were viewed with particular suspicion for the way their status as 'brides of Christ', living in single-sex monastic communities, blurred lines of wifehood, sisterhood and daughterhood. Anti-convent writings by sixteenth-century Reformers often portrayed lusty heterosexual nuns as at once virginal and intensely sexual, while others decried the 'unnatural acts' allegedly rife among women in religious orders. For some devout women choosing to live in single-sex communities, such sexualized attacks meant that they experienced the Reformation as a period of sexual vulnerability and repression. Particularly as convents began to close in Protestant areas from the sixteenth century, many former nuns were forced either to marry or move back in with their biological families, with marriage held up as their only natural vocation.[81]

Such policing of sexuality and gender by Protestant Reformers, who now deemed certain women's life choices to be unruly that had once been considered morally upstanding, also played out on a more symbolic level in the battles over religion. One telling 1523 woodcut pamphlet depicted the pope as a feminized and sexualized ass, a monstrous figure intended to link the papacy with femininity, self-centredness and embodied pleasure (Figure 1.2). Such popular images connected ideas of purity, pollution and antisocial or dangerous passions with ideas about gender non-conformity. As Ulinka Rublack points out, they worked to critique the existing social order in powerful ways: 'The equation of the papacy with a hybrid male-female,

FIGURE 1.2 *The Pope-Ass, 1523.*

Source: Cambridge University Library, Classmark: F152.d.1.10.[82]

effeminate-animal monster touched the audience's fear of mixed categories, and also a desire for clear codes of reliable and civilized "male" and "female" behaviour.'[83] In similar ways, in the early phases of the Reformation monks, like nuns, were depicted as highly sensual beings, their vows of celibacy now viewed with suspicion and negatively contrasted with the sober male artisans of the guilds. Reformers denounced Catholic priests as whores of the Devil, and such sexualized, feminized attacks helped to spread the Reformation's popular appeal, especially in the towns, where men of good social standing were expected to conform to honour codes based in ideas of fearlessness, combativeness and restraint.[84] Meanwhile, the fears of monstrous hybridity this woodcut highlights can help to explain the many medieval and early modern laws prohibiting bestiality, or sexual contact with animals.[85]

Bodily symbols, especially sexual ones, often take on considerable significance in times of crisis or socio-political reorganization.[86] It is, of course, important to distinguish between politicized 'scripts' of appropriate feminine and masculine behaviour and the actual feelings and experiences of people in the past – who, after all, always had some degree of agency over their sexual behaviours and gendered expressions. Yet sources like this woodcut remind us not only of the need to examine the history of sexuality and gender together, but to think about how both categories were used to come to terms with major social and political shifts like the wars of religion. One way of understanding how they did so is to draw on approaches from psychoanalysis, a school of thought that first emerged with the writings of psychiatrist and neurologist Sigmund Freud in Vienna from the final decade of the nineteenth century, and which emphasizes the role of unconscious desires and fantasies as well as early childhood relations with one's parents in shaping human identity and behaviour. Lyndal Roper presents a strong case for drawing on such 'modern' theoretical approaches as a means to understand earlier periods, as she suggests that images like this woodcut might even have constituted a 'psychic necessity' for a new generation of Protestant clergy as they found themselves called to abandon old vows of celibacy and instead marry and join the ranks of other male heads of household and citizens.[87] Viewed through this theoretical lens – and we will encounter further examples of using psychoanalysis to dig deeper into the history of sexuality below – we see that cultural representations can constitute an important vehicle through which to negotiate social transformations, whether dealing with an individual priest's changing sense of masculine identity and belonging, or a wider German society coming to terms with the tumult of the Reformation era.

Prostitutes, witches and children

Prostitution, sometimes dubbed the 'oldest' profession, has over the centuries had a hugely varied relationship with structures such as the law, religion, urban geography and marriage. Studying the history of prostitution can tell us much about changes and continuities in society more broadly, from expectations placed on husbands and wives to what was required to be recognized as a citizen of a particular town, region or nation. In the Middle Ages, public brothels were widespread and widely tolerated. Although some people saw them as a necessary evil, others viewed them in more positive terms, as a valuable outlet for the disruptive influence of young male lust, or even as a civic space to show off to visiting dignitaries. The brothel, declared one medieval ordinance from the southern German city of Ulm, improved the 'good piety, and honour of the whole community'.[88] Both prostitutes and the places in which they worked continued to be viewed as a significant civic resource into the early modern period, when nearly every major city and many smaller ones had an official *Frauenhaus* (literally, 'house of women').[89]

There were, though, important differences between urban and rural areas when it came to attitudes to prostitution and men's access to women outside of marriage. In a close study of several centuries' worth of records from the rural Benedictine monastery of Ottobeuren, Govind Sreenivasan cites several cases in which sexual violence seems to have played a far greater role in extramarital relations than monetary exchange. In one, farmer's son Paul Heffelin was charged with impregnating his own maid in 1569 before committing adultery with at least two other maids during the next decade. In another, nine men in the village of Sontheim were prosecuted for having sex with the maid of the local miller, including the miller himself, two of his sons, a baker, the aforementioned Heffelin and a widowed farmer, leaving the woman pregnant. As Sreenivasan observes, such cases were 'worlds apart from the urban brothel, where prostitutes enjoyed a measure of institutional protection and qualified public acceptance' – for 'the debauched rural maid was a ruined woman', unable to remain in the village and work in her usual occupation, and reliant on the local monastery to force some child support from the men charged.[90]

During the sixteenth century, many town brothels were closed down as part of a new wave of Reformation-era regulations, with prostitutes moved from the margins of society to beyond its boundaries, in a very literal sense. The powerful guilds in the cities were increasingly vocal in policing moral conduct, often forbidding their members contact with prostitutes, and even preventing them from dancing or standing next to them in public.[91] If the Reformers attacked brothels as symbols of a corrupt society, though, the Enlighteners of the eighteenth century were notable for avoiding much explicit discussion of this or other sexually confronting topics, such as homosexuality and venereal disease. Rather than focus on deviance, Enlightenment-era thinkers were more concerned 'with laying down the principles of "normality"'.[92] This meant that for a time, women involved in commercialized sex (for women were the overwhelming focus of these discussions, even if sex work also involved men and gender-diverse individuals) were not seen to pose the same degree of symbolic threat as they had during the Reformation. Sex work would become more politicized again during the later nineteenth century, however, when discourses around prostitution collided with concerns about urban degeneracy and decline in the wake of rapid industrialization.[93]

Even more transgressive than the prostitute in the early modern period was the sexuality of individuals accused of witchcraft. This crime was understood in overtly sexualized terms, with witches accused of sleeping with the devil in 'diabolic union'. Witchcraft trials in Germany began in the fifteenth century, but took off with a vengeance during the sixteenth, in both Catholic and Protestant regions. Some men and children were also persecuted under witchcraft laws, but women were considered particularly impressionable and carnal, and were by far the most numerous victims of these laws.[94] Contemporaries argued that they were more likely to succumb to Satanic temptations, including Upper German Dominican Inquisitors Heinrich Kramer and Jacob Sprenger in the work *Malleus Maleficarum* (the Hammer of the [Female] Witches) in 1486, a work which went through no fewer than fourteen editions by 1520. Because only dishonourable individuals were considered capable of entering into abhorrent Satanic unions, witch trials placed great emphasis on establishing the prior honour and reputation of the accused. This often worked against those not living within male-dominated households: older, single women became the primary victims of this widespread and often horrific practice of social and legal persecution.[95] Today, plaques around Germany commemorate these victims, who faced ghastly deaths and punishments, while moves to formally rehabilitate the persecuted through official pardons have continued into our own century.

The figure of the witch has been held up as 'the classic early modern European example' of stereotypical gender imagery, linking femininity to narrow self-interest and weaker control over the passions then men.[96] But as Roper argues in her book *Oedipus and the Devil*, to properly understand this history of mass persecution it is important to look beyond images of witches dancing on the sabbath, riding brooms and making pacts with the Devil, as well as beyond straightforward explanations centred on misogyny and gender-role stereotyping. Digging deeper into the 'bizarre and irrational' elements of witchcraft trials, Roper uses the psychoanalytic approach introduced above to unpack the complex emotions and accusations involved in a series of historical cases featuring female and child witches. She shows that anxieties around motherhood and breastfeeding, infantile experiences of the body and sexuality, and fears about child raising, death and unbearable illness all play a role in the behaviours and accusations exhibited in these legal cases. Exploring feelings of envy in historical sources, for example, can help to explain why female members of a community who were seen as barren, lacking fertility or resources, were often feared rather than pitied – because of the potential that they might resent and thus seek to punish those who had goods, animals, or potency. Roper concludes that digging deeper into such cases often reveals psychic conflicts not so dissimilar from our own ways of thinking, even if we would prefer to see ourselves as modern, rational subjects.[97]

Studies such as *Oedipus* have been highly influential in demonstrating both the significance of the emotions and of psychoanalytic approaches for the history of gender and sexuality.[98] And although some scholars criticize the application of theoretical perspectives – not just psychoanalysis, but also Marxist, feminist and queer approaches – to periods that precede the emergence of those theories themselves, I agree with Roper that to neglect such insights risks condemning us to all-too-superficial 'common-sense' models of people and their ways of thinking and feeling in the past.[99] Such irrational and deep-seated feelings as envy, Roper reminds us, 'are pretty fundamental to human existence', even as their forms and society's attitudes towards them have changed profoundly over time.[100]

Paying attention to emotions and psychic processes can also help us to understand the role of sexuality in trials surrounding so-called 'child-witches', which continued through to the beginnings of the modern era. Legal testimony from a wave of such prosecutions in early eighteenth-century

Augsburg, in southern Germany, reveals a strong emphasis on oral and anal bodily functions such as excrement, and the child 'witches' were also pursued for attacking the sexual relationships of their parents and step-parents. The evidence presented at trial included reports of the Devil 'tickling' one girl in her lower body, or of children dropping trousers and raising shirts. In deciphering such evidence, psychoanalytic theories of the 'polymorphous' sexuality of infants and small children, developed by Freud and others such as Melanie Klein in the early twentieth century, can again help us to arrive at a deeper understanding of what is going on. In particular, they remind us that in early childhood, erotic fantasies and pleasures are often not (yet) connected with the genitals or ideas of reproduction, but tend to take more ambiguous forms – which can, in turn, be confronting for adults reluctant to recognize children as sexual beings.[101]

The growing concern with child witches by the late-Reformation was also indicative of broader shifts in attitudes towards children's sexual ideas and behaviours. Children's upbringing became a central theme for eighteenth-century intellectuals such as French philosopher Jean-Jacques Rousseau, who in *Emile: Or Treatise on Education* (1763) reflected on the philosophy and practice of education from the perspective of Emile's tutor. Ideas about how to best raise children were moving out of the realm of religious authority into more secular contexts, and this shift was accompanied by growing fears about children's masturbation and sexual precocity.[102] In 1758 Swiss physician Samuel-Auguste Tissot published his study of *Onania* in French, appearing in German in 1785. Tissot did not hold back in his panicky accounts of the 'danger' to those addicted to this alleged vice. The masturbator, he argued, was likely to undergo

> a general wasting of the whole machine; an enfeeblement of all the corporal senses and of all the faculties of the soul; loss of imagination and memory; imbecillity; contempt; shame; the ignominy such viciousness drags after it; all the functions of life disturbed, suspended, or painfully executed ....[103]

Tissot's treatise on the diseases of mind and body allegedly caused by children's self-pleasure was at once a work of medicine and moral theology, depicting onanism as both a vicious kind of lust and a moral crime against God and nature. Influential across Europe, his anti-onanism tract built on a much broader seventeenth-century literature on the 'sin' of masturbation, popular especially among German Pietists and Swiss Calvinists. In the German-speaking world, Tissot's treatise spurred widespread intellectual debates linking themes of childhood, excess and the imagination.[104] Such concerns also resonated across Europe, especially in relation to institutionalized settings such as boarding schools, but increasingly also implicating the bourgeois family. As Michel Foucault and others have argued, the sexuality of children and teenagers was becoming a problem seen as requiring medical and pedagogical intervention, and as a result, the middle-class family 'became a locus of the psychiatrization of sex'.[105] Chapter 2 explores further how this focus on children's sexuality became couched in the language of science and medicine during the late nineteenth century.

Same-sex relations and nonconforming genders

Same-sex and gender nonconforming behaviours have a long and difficult history of persecution, but also a rich and varied history of expression that scholars have traced from antiquity into the present. Much of what we know of medieval same-sex sexualities centres on ideas of criminality and punishment, for the sources that remain stem largely from legal trials and prosecutions. We have relatively little evidence of everyday 'queer' lives or relationships that may have been tolerated or relatively uncontroversial at particular times and places – and yet, as historians of queer lives frequently remind us, it is important to listen precisely for the silences and omissions in the archives when it comes to writing the histories of socially marginalized people and groups.[106]

In Germany the first known executions of so-called 'sodomites' took place towards the end of the medieval period, in the fourteenth century. This timing was typical of Western Europe more broadly: famous late medieval Italian poet Dante Alighieri placed sodomites in the highest level of purgatory, condemning them to suffer in the afterlife. But the crime of sodomy, or *scelus sodomiditicum*, was already a familiar charge by the early Middle Ages, including in monastic settings.[107] The term was at times used as a 'medieval catch-all' for all manner of non-marital and non-reproductive sexual relations, from bestiality to blasphemy and treason – and not necessarily only by men, as we have seen with Maiden Heinrich. It was not unusual for anti-sodomy laws to resort to ambiguous phrases such as 'damned, forbidden copulation' or transgressions 'against nature'.[108] Yet we should also not go too far in insisting on the inability to pin down this term, which was most commonly understood to refer to same-sex relations, generally between men. 'What sodomy means in certain contexts is all too knowable,' Helmut Puff observes, with seventeenth-century court records clearly distinguishing between *sodomia* (homosexual acts) and *bestialitas* (sex with animals). Puff contrasts the paradoxically 'loud' prescriptions of 'silence' in theological texts on this supposedly 'unmentionable vice' with the rather more explicit approach of secular authorities, who were quite willing to name the sin when it suited their political purposes. Even so, by the seventeenth century capital punishment for this 'crime' had become less common, with sodomy trials now largely shrouded in silence: city governments feared that well-publicized trials might encourage the kind of acts that the laws set out to suppress.[109]

Legal trials were not the only arena in which same-sex acts left historical traces. During the Reformation, images of Sodom were used by Protestant Reformers to attack Rome and the papacy. Woodcut-based pamphlets of the kind we have seen in Figure 1.2 helped to popularize these religious and political tussles. Fiercely pro-marriage and condemnatory of same-sex relations, they broke with a certain politeness and silence that had surrounded many older representations of sodomy. At the same time, a degree of vagueness entered Reformist discussions of same-sex and other non-normative sexual practices. As the focus of normative sexual expression turned towards marriage, the distinction between legitimate and illegitimate or 'impure' sexual activities was increasingly aligned with the boundaries of that institution.[110]

Gender is a crucial category of analysis when it comes to the history of sodomy, with medieval and early modern punishments closely tied up with social expectations of masculinity and femininity. For repeat offenders, punishment amounted to no less than literal destruction of their very being: execution, often followed by burning. The significance of gender in such trials becomes clear in the interrogation in 1530s Augsburg of homosexual acts between the weaver Michel Will, who was married, and various male sexual partners, including several fellow craftsmen and a priest. The legal authorities insisted on finding out details such as whether anal penetration had taken place, and thus the extent to which Will had contravened perceptions of the (dominant) male sexual role. In investigating this case, they thus showed themselves to be as much concerned with the perceived overturning of the gendered division of household labour – and, by extension, civic structures, for the household lay at the core of the guild structure – as with the morality of the acts themselves. 'Both literally and metaphorically, male homosexual acts ... undermined the hierarchies of the household and the boundaries between male and female.'[111]

During the Enlightenment, meanwhile, sodomy discussions shifted towards the natural world. Rejecting the idea that religion should determine law, Enlightenment thinkers viewed male homosexuality as a crime against nature, sometimes accusing men who had sex with men of being 'women-haters' or 'anti-physiques' for neglecting the biological sexual drive. Despite their strong language, this represented a relatively tolerant stance compared to earlier eras, for they also argued that the Church should not interfere in such cases. Instead, 'Nature' would inevitably solve the problem by 'defending her rights'.[112]

In the first volume of his *History of Sexuality*, Foucault famously pinpointed the second half of the nineteenth century as the point at which a change took place from focusing on same-sex acts and behaviours under labels such as 'sodomy' to conceiving of 'the homosexual' as an identity or type of person:

Homosexuality appeared as one of the forms of sexuality when it was transposed from the practice of sodomy onto a kind of interior androgyny, a hermaphrodism of the soul. The sodomite had been a temporary aberration; the homosexual was now a species.[113]

This 'acts versus identities' narrative has been very widely cited, and continues to be a powerful reference point for historians working on the centuries since 1800. As Chapter 2 explores, German legal and medical thinkers played a crucial role in these developments. Yet research on medieval and early modern same-sex sexualities has also led historians to argue that we need to take a closer look at these arguments, especially when it comes to gender. Queer theorist Eve Kosofsky Sedgwick astutely observes that, when we look at the past, 'there can't be an a priori decision about how far it will make sense to conceptualize lesbian and gay male identities together. Or separately.'[114] Demonstrating this, historians have traced very different patterns of criminalization and toleration surrounding female and male same-sex relations at different times. In doing so, they also point to very different understandings of the sexual body itself in the premodern period.

The modern 'lesbian' is generally considered to have made an appearance as a social construct well after the male 'homosexual', only acquiring an unambiguous meaning towards the end of the nineteenth century – and only becoming widely recognized in popular culture during the twentieth.[115] As Judith Brown points out in her study of a 'lesbian' nun in Renaissance Italy, 'Lesbian sexuality did not exist. Neither, for that matter did lesbians,' at least not in a twentieth- or twenty-first-century sense.[116] Yet earlier categories such as 'tribade' were in play from at least the second half of the eighteenth century, and literary traces of female homoeroticism far predate this chronology. Some scholars even suggest there was a 'renaissance' of lesbianism from the late sixteenth century.[117] While 'lesbians' may not have existed in today's sense, though, ideas about what female same-sex behaviours looked like and how they might challenge social norms certainly did. In order to account for a range of experiences without assuming that they neatly aligned with modern conceptions of 'gay', 'lesbian' or 'queer' identities, scholars have suggested more flexible terms such as 'lesbian-like', aimed at capturing a wider spectrum of non-normative sexualities.[118]

We know, for example, that early modern societies regularly punished same-sex acts between women as 'female sodomy' – one of the crimes attributed to 'Maiden Heinrich'. Although penalties for mutual masturbation, buggery, tribadism (rubbing together the female genitals) or self-pollution among women tended to be less severe than for men, at times they also extended to the ultimate penalty of capital punishment. Katherina Hetzeldorfer was the first known woman, or possibly transman, to be executed for female sodomy in Germany in 1477, drowned in the Rhine river in the city of Speyer. Rather like Heinrich, Hetzeldorfer had arrived in Speyer in men's clothing and in the company of a woman whom one witness claimed she had 'abducted', presenting her as a 'sister'. Rumours soon abounded about the nature of their relationship, with one witness claiming Hetzeldorfer 'had deflowered her [sister] and had been making love to her for two years'. Court documents intricately recount Hetzeldorfer's sexual role-play with various female partners, including their use of 'an instrument [made] with a red piece of leather, at the front filled with cotton, and a wooden stick stuck into it'. This appendage had apparently enabled Hetzeldorfer to pass as a man with her various sexual partners until the case came to court. There, assuming a male gender role was just as important as Hetzeldorfer's sexual transgressions in the judges' decision to condemn them to death.[119]

Such acknowledgement of the 'topsy-turvy' ways in which people in the past understood their bodies and desires means not only considering different kinds of same-sex sexual encounter, but also how these intersected with gender variance.[120] In European societies since at least the medieval period, we can trace a rich and varied history of ritualized 'gender-bending' and sexual imposture. These ranged from the carnivalesque processions of the season preceding Lent to the antics of the seventeenth-century theatrical stage. Such rituals of inversion, constrained in time and place, permitted the social world to be temporarily turned upside-down, challenging not only gender expectations, but also social roles determined by occupation or class: a peasant and husband might briefly become a priest, or a cottager a queen.[121] Beyond such authorized masquerades, though, we find plentiful evidence of more permanent forms of non-binary gendered and sexual embodiments. The archives reveal traces of many hundreds of individuals assigned female at birth who, like 'Maiden Heinrich', successfully lived as men for years or decades on end, working in male occupations, fighting as soldiers, and marrying, sometimes repeatedly. In many cases, these individuals' gender-nonconforming biographies were only 'discovered' after death – even as the very notion of 'discovery' threatens to undermine how they chose to present the truth of their gender to the world.[122]

Just as there exists a long history of nonconforming gender embodiments, we can find evidence of competing models of biological sexual difference in circulation since at least the Middle Ages. Premodern German folklore points to numerous stories of changing sex – known as *Geschlechtswechsel* (sex change) or *Geschlechtsverwandlung* (sex transformation) – some more fantastical than others. By the early modern period, the concept of 'hermaphroditism' was also familiar in both elite and more popular circles, whether under medicalized labels such as *Hermaphrodit* or *Androgynus*, or in the more popular arenas of fairground displays and freak shows, where terms such as *Zwitter*, *Zwey-Dorn* or *Mann-Weib* (man-woman) were more common. These labels were also used for animals seen to house two sexes in one body, such as eels. Equally, religious symbols such as the biblical figure of Adam and the Jewish legend of the Golem point to a long history of cultural representations of 'two-sexed beings'.[123]

Several decades ago, historian Thomas Laqueur influentially suggested that during the eighteenth century, a major shift took place in how Europeans thought about sex. He posits a move from an older 'one-sex' model – with femininity and female anatomy viewed as an inverted, inferior version of masculinity, whereby the ovaries were understood as female testes and the vagina as an inside-out penis – to a 'two-sex' model, that viewed the sexes as fundamentally distinct.[124] While this theory has had considerable uptake among Renaissance and modern historians, it has also been criticized by scholars of earlier periods, who point out that even if many medical commentators and natural philosophers accepted the single-sex idea, 'it is by no means clear that a larger public shared this notion'.[125] Even as it remains contested, Laqueur's hypothesis serves as a useful reminder of the very different ways in which gender norms have been conceptualized over time – and that non-binary understandings of sex and gender have a long ancestry.

The decades around 1800 mark a further notable moment in the history of queer relations in the German-speaking world. Tropes of effusive, 'romantic' friendships between men and between women, often expressed through passionate letters, found a firm place in the literary canon via prominent figures such as Goethe, whose travels to Italy opened his eyes to a world of male-male love. Writing to Duke Karl August in late 1787, he added the following voyeuristic postscript to an otherwise more sober account of his trip to the south:

> After this contribution to the statistical knowledge of the land you will ascertain how tight our situation is and will understand a remarkable phenomenon that I have seen nowhere as strong as here, it is the love of men amongst themselves.[126]

During these years, Goethe – far from straightforwardly 'gay' in a modern sense – penned lines that nonetheless strike us today as decidedly 'queer', and that blurred understandings of friendship and romantic intimacy, as Robert Tobin has explored. He wrote verses, for example, describing 'Boys I have also loved,/But I prefer girls;/If I'm tired of her as a girl,/She can serve me as a boy as well.'[127] Such sources prompt us to think beyond narrow twentieth-century definitions of homosexuality and heterosexuality to consider notions of 'love', 'friendship' and 'brotherhood' in more expansive ways – as relationships that may or may not have involved intimate sexual encounters, but which certainly held homoerotic overtones.

German tropes of masculine friendship and brotherly love from these decades had their roots in earlier centuries, deriving from the male collectivities promoted by the medieval system of guilds, peasant assemblies and militias, as well as the bonds that developed between men in the sixteenth-century evangelical movement.[128] By the eighteenth-century, though, scholars identify something that possibly went a little further than 'brotherly' feelings: the awakenings of 'a queer proto-identity'.[129] Such passionate male-male friendship characterizes letters exchanged between soldier-poet Ewald of Kleist and poet Johann Wilhelm Ludwig Gleim, for example, examined by Helmut Walser Smith. Kleist and Gleim's correspondence and poems move beyond the gushing emotions typical of the letter-writing genre favoured by Goethe and others to suggest more explicitly a relationship defined by same-sex love. As Kleist wrote to Gleim: 'I think constantly about you and charmingly imagine you as a lover imagines his distant beauty,' adding that 'I constantly want to sleep with you.'[130] At the same time, they point to a growing sense of Prussian nationalism at the time of the Seven Years War (1756–63), aligning with patriotic ideals of masculinity and soldierly sacrifice: 'And so was through the courage of the two friends,' Kleist writes in his short epic poem *Cissides and Paches* (1758), 'the destruction of the Fatherland avoided'.[131]

Women also engaged in 'romantic' friendships during this era, and indeed well into the nineteenth century in Germany and elsewhere. Carroll Smith-Rosenberg has argued that it 'fundamentally distorts the nature of these women's emotional interaction' to insist on classifying such friendships in either-or categories of 'normal' or 'deviant', 'heterosexual' or 'homosexual', or in ways that neatly separate sexual from platonic love. To do so, she insists, 'is alien to the emotions and attitudes of the nineteenth century'.[132] Illustrating this is another correspondent of Gleim's, the poet Anna Louisa Karsch. Karsch is an unusual figure in German literary history not only on the grounds of her sex, but also due to her relative lack of education and peasant background. Karsch attracted widespread admiration for her writing, and Gleim even dubbed her the 'Prussian Sappho'. This was a role she self-consciously embraced in developing a public literary persona, although unlike her ancient Greek namesake, her works focused not so much on female same-sex love as, in a more eighteenth-century style, the celebration of nature and tender feminine sentiment.[133]

Female friendships have historically been permitted greater leniency in the expression of affection, both verbal and physical, without this necessarily being deemed inappropriately sexual. Among men, on the other hand, such relations came to be increasingly policed and frowned upon in the era of modern masculinity and the building of nation-states, as Enlightenment-era norms of intimate male friendship were reduced to a rather more aromantic model. As George Mosse argued in his influential *Nationalism and Sexuality* (1985), the growth of ideas of nations and nationalisms in early nineteenth-century Europe aligned with new ideas about proper social and gendered behaviour, including an emphasis on controlling sexual passions to meet new expectations of bourgeois respectability, and a view that marriage formed the only respectable sexual relationship. Youthful passions were aligned with patriotic feelings, and distinctions were drawn between insiders and outsiders, between 'virile' masculinity and the 'feminine' passions and weaknesses, and between the 'normal' and the 'abnormal'.[134] It is to this imperialist, nationalist period of German history that the next chapter of this book will turn.

* * *

This chapter has examined the centuries leading to the formal unification of Germany as a nation-state in 1871. It has shown how ideas about marriage, divorce, sexual transgression, prostitution and same-sex relations at the dawning of the modern era built on many centuries of debates and developments, which do not always fit easily into narratives of sexual progress and liberation. We have seen how the religious Penitentials dictating the timing and scope of medieval marital sex, for example, gave way to a reimagining of sex as spiritual union by Reformers in the sixteenth century, when marriage and divorce became a central site of conflict between Catholics and Protestants. This central institution governing the sexual expression of the majority of the population then underwent further transformations during the age of Enlightenment, with a sharper polarization of the expectations placed on husband and wife.

We have also seen how focusing on norms and transgressions can be used to compare very different experiences of sexual regulation and persecution, and how these intersected with ideas about gender. The expulsion of prostitutes from town centres during the Reformation highlights how sex work no longer aligned with spiritualized ideals of marriage during the transition to 'respectable' civil society. The persecution of prostitutes, 'witches', nuns and monks points to abiding social anxieties surrounding those deemed sexually 'other', and a need to police those who fall outside of society's norms. So, too, do the many taboos and punishments that have surrounded same-sex relationships and gender-diverse embodiments over the centuries – even as traditions such as Carnival or folkloric tales of sex changes hint at a pervasive fascination with precisely such transgressions. More broadly, representations of witches or gender-nonconforming priests demonstrate how such figures have served as a cultural projection screen for working through all manner of personal and social challenges that go beyond the obviously sexual, from the political upheavals of the wars of religion, to an individual's identity as a wife, father, husband or mother.

Chapter 2 picks up on this *longue durée* exploration of shifting sexual norms to home in on the role of sex in shaping concerns about bodies, populations and desires within the framework of the modern nation state. It considers how the specific conditions of modernity, including industrialization, urbanization and the growing influence of the middle-classes, enabled new kinds of ideas about sexuality to develop in an era of European imperialism and colonization. These included new ways of thinking about sexual identity and politics through a lens of 'human rights', a burgeoning feminist and sex reform movement, and newly 'scientific' ways of articulating sexual practices and desires.

2

Sexual modernity and nationhood: 1871–1918

The only forms of present-day sexuality that are officially recognized by the state are marriage and regulated prostitution. If marriage has the intrinsic goal of regulating human sexual intercourse, then one can say that today in any case it no longer fulfills this goal, for the great majority of human sexual intercourse (at least among the educated classes or our nations of culture) plays out outside of marriage.

- SEXOLOGIST AND PACIFICIST DR. HELENE STÖCKER, 1905.[1]

In the first decade of the twentieth century, radical new left-wing, feminist and human rights groups, including Helene Stöcker's League for Maternal Protection (*Bund für Mutterschutz*), founded in 1905, loudly contested bourgeois ideals of morality, female sexuality and family. In the pamphlet-style book quoted here, published as part of a series on 'Modern Questions of our Times', Stöcker set out the reasons why modern society needed to take a very different approach to sexual morality. Here and elsewhere, she demanded a 'new ethics' that encompassed sexual freedom for both women and men, 'free' marriage (that is, unions outside of the state's purview), greater access to divorce, abortion and sex education, and protections for single mothers. Perhaps the most radical aspect of Stöcker's new ethics was its call for women's sexual empowerment and liberation from strictly gendered 'sex roles'. Hers was one of many voices that formed a growing sex reform movement from the late Wilhelmine era, gaining steam around the turn of the century. Whereas the 'old ethics' had fixated on ideas of sin – tending to view the sex drive as 'evil' – Stöcker's new ethics aimed to expand norms of sexual morality to 'establish this life, our life, as if it were valuable'.[2] Yet even as it was radically progressive in some senses, Stöcker's reference to 'nations of culture' (*Kulturstaaten*) also reveals how the turn of the century sex reform movement was very much of its time, entrenched in matter-of-fact ways of thinking about European nationalism and cultural exceptionalism in an era of imperialism and colonial domination.

As this example highlights, a sense of living in distinctly 'modern' times pervades historical sources from this period, creating a backdrop for shifting ideas about sexuality, personhood and sexual rights. This chapter spans the period from the late 1860s through to the end of the First World War, from Germany's unification as a federalized nation-state in 1871 to the violence and upheaval of revolutions and a world war. These decades transformed the ethnically and linguistically diverse Austro-Hungarian and Prussian Empires of the nineteenth century into the democratic nation states of the twentieth, and during this era of political change and imperialist expansion, ideas about sex heavily shaped concerns about what it meant to live in modern Germany. Anxieties about population reproduction and health, whether conceived at the level of the individual, the nation or in a broader, imperial sense, were negotiated through public debates about military strength, prostitution and urban degeneration. Sex shaped moral purity campaigns, religious protests and high-profile scandals, and it was central to representations of pleasure and eroticism in art, literature and popular culture. While heterosexual monogamy between people of similar class backgrounds remained the dominant norm of sexual expression, alternatives were loudly propagated and debated, while ideas of whiteness and Europeanness played a growing role in defining acceptable sexual encounters.

Ideas about sex during this period were fundamentally shaped by new, 'scientific' way of thinking about sexual practices, bodies, genders and desires. Where once religion had been crucial to defining sexual norms, now doctors and scientists set about cataloguing 'normal' as well as 'abnormal' or 'deviant' sexualities. In arriving at new kinds of diagnoses and therapies by examining individuals' bodies and sexual histories, their work at times supported and at other times intrusively intervened in the lives of people whose sexual behaviours and desires conflicted with norms of heterosexuality and binary gender. In response to such new, decidedly modern and scientific ways of thinking about sexuality, but also in response to the newly united Germany's strict laws governing things like male same-sex behaviours and gender non-conforming dress, new political and social movements began to emerge. Their spokespeople made claims to recognition and rights as citizens in a modern German state that would include sexually and gender-diverse people. In many respects, they represent the forerunners of late twentieth-century LGBTIQ identity politics.

As we examine shifts in thinking that took place around the same time as Germany's transformation into a modern nation state, it is crucial to maintain a critical perspective on ideas of 'Germanness' itself. As noted in the introduction, this concept crossed national boundaries, encompassing 'a broader linguistic and cultural community that included Austrians, German-speaking Swiss, and "ethnically" German inhabitants of Russia, Italy, France, and Hungary,' but also, through emigration and colonialism, Germans in areas of Africa, North America and the Pacific.[3] At the same time, ideas of Germanness were couched in an increasingly pervasive 'European' identity that connected large swathes of the continent in the decades before the First World War, especially among the more elite political, economic and cultural classes.[4]

Rather than following a strictly conventional chronology that begins with the unification of German states in 1871, a focus on sexuality compels us to start with a series of intellectual, legal and scientific developments during the 1860s that prompted new ways of thinking about sexuality, and especially same-sex desires. This chapter traces the rise of a modern, scientific language of human sexuality and how this intersected with movements for social reform including the early women's, gay and trans rights movements. It then turns to the larger contexts of nationalism, class and political privilege within and against which this new language of sexuality was situated, examining ideas of bourgeois respectability, moral purity campaigns, feminist arguments and media sex scandals. Finally, the chapter steps back from Germany's new national borders to consider how norms of sexuality were negotiated against the transnational backdrops of European colonialism and world war.

The German 'invention' of sexuality and identity politics

Scholars have often described these final decades of the nineteenth century and early decades of the twentieth as the period during which modern sexuality was 'invented' or 'discovered' – when it came to be understood as a crucial aspect of human identity.[5] As we have already seen, historians of premodern periods productively question this tendency to view sexuality and subjectivity purely as concepts borne of the modern era.[6] But there is also widespread agreement that from the late nineteenth century, sexuality began to be spoken about in different ways, in what has sometimes been summarized as an era of 'sexual modernity'.[7] German-speaking writers, doctors, lawyers, scientists and activists were all key to this process, and their writings shifted discussions about sexuality not only within but also well beyond the German-speaking world.

Those seeking legal reforms enabling greater freedom to express their sexual desires and gender within the terms of modern German citizenship – which during these decades was still sharply delimited by class – seized upon new scientific categories such as the 'invert', 'homosexual' and 'transvestite'. They articulated political platforms and created social organizations that, for the first time, were framed around distinct sex-gender 'identities'. Using a language of human rights and democratic citizenship, they fought against the criminalization of male homosexuality under Germany's notoriously harsh Paragraph 175 and advocated for things like the right to change one's name to align with gender identity.

These late nineteenth-century developments had a number of intellectual and scientific precursors. During the 1830s, German-speaking Swiss milliner Heinrich Hössli had penned a two-volume study on male-male love among the ancient Greeks, *Eros*. At a time when legal codes condemned sodomy as a 'crime against nature', Hössli used ideas about nature and biology to sketch a decidedly modern conception of same-sex desire as a fixed, natural and immutable identity: 'male love is true nature, a law of nature.'[8] These ideas later influenced Hannover lawyer Karl Heinrich Ulrichs as he penned a series of legal treatises on homosexual rights. In 1844, Viennese physician Heinrich Kaan also foreshadowed later developments when he penned a study on the sexual 'perversions' under the title *Psychopathia sexualis*, pre-empting psychiatrist Richard von Krafft-Ebing's influential catalogue of the same name by more than forty years.[9]

In the decades that followed, various factors contributed to this push to think about sex in more modern, scientific ways. For Michel Foucault, the 'birth' of the modern homosexual was closely related to an essay penned by German psychiatrist Carl von Westphal on 'contrary sexual sensibility' in the late 1860s.[10] But this is a little too narrow – we might equally look to the political manifestos and writings of figures such as Ulrichs or Austro-Hungarian literary critic Karl Maria Kertbeny during this decade. In 1886, the German-born, Austrian-based Krafft-Ebing published his own mammoth *Psychopathia sexualis*, a textbook for colleagues that brought together all known and various newly diagnosed sexual disorders, with the sauciest passages written up in Latin.[11] Such developments set the scene for up-and-coming sexologist, physician and homosexual and trans rights advocate Magnus Hirschfeld to establish the first scientific journal dedicated to the study of sex-gender variance in 1899, the Yearbook of Sexual Intermediaries (*Jahrbuch für sexuelle Zwischenstufen*). Not long after, Viennese neurologist Sigmund Freud published *Three Essays on the Theory of Sexuality* (1905), signalling a new, 'psychoanalytic' way of interpreting sexual desires and disorders, often with reference to early childhood development.[12] In 1908, the journal *Zeitschrift für Sexualwissenschaft* (Journal of sexual science) appeared, showing how a new generation of sexologists was starting to carve out space for themselves as representatives of a distinct medical-scientific discipline.[13] Taken together, such efforts drew on medico-scientific language to produce new forms of knowledge: 'a conflicted sometimes self-contradictory complex that can be thought of as the conception of "sexuality"'.[14]

It is no accident that the wave of publications focusing on male same-sex desire and sex-gender nonconformity from the 1860s onwards aligned roughly chronologically with Germany's move towards becoming a modern nation-state. Whereas countries such as France had abolished sodomy laws following the Revolution of the late eighteenth century, the newly unified German Empire's adoption of a large amount of Prussian legislation in 1871 provided a more punitive foundation for sexual regulation. This in turn helped to stimulate the 'evolution of the world's most expansive science of homosexuality', as well as all manner of legal writings on the topic.[15]

Kertbeny, who spent much of his adult life in Germany, penned two political tracts during the years leading up to unification, concerned about the proposed adoption of Prussia's harsh anti-gay laws. Coining the term 'homosexual', Kertbeny referenced Enlightenment traditions to argue that modern justice required significant legal reform. He demanded that the state acknowledge the right to 'one's own life, with which one may do as one pleases ... as long as the rights of other individuals of society or of the state are not injured by those actions'.[16] During these same years, the lawyer Ulrichs, writing under the pseudonym Numa Numantius, penned a series of political pamphlets such as *The Riddle of 'Man-Manly' Love*, also strongly criticizing the new German state's move to carry over older anti-homosexual laws.[17] Examining same-sex love from legal, philosophical and scientific perspectives, Ulrichs developed his own theory of same-sex attraction, and advocated for homosexual rights through public lectures and letters to doctors, lawyers, political allies and opponents. Coining the terms *Urning* (often translated as 'Uranian') for a same-sex desiring man and *Urninden* for women (he used *Dioninge* to designate heterosexuals), Ulrichs argued that gender inversion was a central feature of same-sex desire. He used embryological theories to argue that even though some homosexuals could be quite masculine, all bore traces of an original hermaphroditic state. The urning, he wrote, possesses 'a female soul in a male body' (*anima mulierbris virile corpore inclusa*) and reveals this through 'unimistakably feminine' gestures and behaviours.[18] Ulrichs's influence was considerable, and in recent years he has been described as everything from the 'grandfather' of gay liberation to 'the first gay man of modern times'; he has also been recognized for his 'proto-trans' arguments.[19]

Kertbeny and Ulrichs not only sought to position same-sex desires in terms of an interior, 'natural' essence, similar to identities of gender or race, but also to position 'homosexuals' or 'Urnings' themselves as a distinct minority community within a larger heterosexual society.[20] This kind of argument was familiar from nineteenth-century Jewish emancipation movements. Jews had long faced restrictions on their citizenship within German society, and historians have characterized this population as a crucial 'testing grounds' for Enlightenment ideals such as using merit and education rather than birth or religion to determine social rights.[21] By 1871 there were over half a million Jews living within the boundaries of unified Germany, around 1.25 per cent of the population. While the revolution of 1848 had helped to mark the long shift towards emancipation, the 1860s brought full legal and civil equality for Jews in most German states, accompanied by strong movement into the professions and higher education, which had previously been largely inaccessible. In such ways, Jewish mobility emulated the larger emergence of nineteenth-century bourgeois society, while also providing a model for other minorities seeking greater rights and recognition, as Robert Tobin and others have examined.[22] This minority model resonates in Ulrichs's writings, such as when he declared that 'several thousand urnings are living in the cities and the countryside of the lands called "Germany"'.[23] Kertbeny, too, aligned homosexual minority politics with the position of other minorities, although for him the reference was Hungarian nationalism in the context of the Habsburg Empire.[24]

Subsequent activists and scholars built on Ulrichs's insistence that because nature had made them that way, homosexuals should enjoy equal rights within society.[25] In 1897, sexologist and reformer Hirschfeld joined Leipzig publisher Max Spohr and ministerial official Erich Oberg to found the Scientific Humanitarian Committee (*Wissenschaftlich-humanitäres Komitee*, hereafter WhK), a political lobbying group set up to petition the Reichstag to abolish Paragraph 175. For a few years, the movement made steady progress, as leaders drew on scientific studies to underline their arguments for abolition, and attracted many prominent signatories, including a young Albert Einstein. It hit a snag, however, with a series of media scandals from 1906 involving the Kaiser's inner circle, to which we will return.[26]

Thinking sex scientifically

In the decades around 1900 German physicians and psychiatrists went to great efforts to categorize and develop medical guidelines for treating individuals exhibiting sex-gender behaviours and characteristics that did not conform to dominant norms of binary gender and heterosexuality. They did so in a context of heightened nationalism, with politicians and intellectuals increasingly turning their attention to biopolitical priorities of national strength, underpinned by a healthy population and birth rate. Against this backdrop, observes historian Harry Cocks, 'whether someone behaved "normally" in sexual terms became a matter of pressing social concern'.[27] As Ulrichs's thinking reveals, different forms of sex-gender variance were often seen as coexisting, signalled by diagnoses such as 'sexual inversion'. Doctors and scientists who described themselves as 'sexual scientists' or 'sexologists' (*Sexualwissenschaftler/innen*) spent considerable time describing figures such as the 'effeminate' male homosexual or 'masculine' lesbian, forms of 'hermaphroditism' (intersex conditions) and gender-diverse – what we would now call trans or non-binary – identities. They drew on late nineteenth-century forensic medicine and psychiatry, including Westphal's aforementioned study of 'contrary sexual feeling'. The focus of such earlier studies had been very much on sexual acts: doctors giving testimony in cases of sodomy or rape were instructed on how to examine 'sodomites' for evidence of anal penetration, such as tapered penises and funnel-shaped anuses.[28]

One of the most important studies addressing homosexuality among many other sexual 'pathologies' during these decades was Krafft-Ebing's *Psychopathia sexualis* (1886). Krafft-Ebing distinguished between two forms of 'contrary sexual feeling': that which was inborn or hereditary, and that which could be acquired in places such as same-sex boarding schools or prisons. In subsequent editions of this bestselling textbook, Krafft-Ebing introduced more precise breakdowns of these categories, based on case studies compiled from patients and other informants – many of whom had shown agency in writing to him seeking answers about their seemingly peculiar sexual desires. He explored same-sex desires and gender variance in both women and men, arguing that 'androgyny' (in women) and 'gynandry' (in men) represented the most extreme forms of 'contrary sexual feeling', sometimes accompanied by signs of physical inversion.[29] Krafft-Ebing's textbook demonstrates the ways in which early German sexual science or *Sexualwissenschaft* looked beyond the natural and medical sciences to encompass interdisciplinary approaches, from cultural history to literature, as he drew on the literary works of Austrian writer Leopold von Sacher-Masoch and the French Marquis de Sade to illustrate new labels such as 'sadism' and 'masochism'.[30] Krafft-Ebing describes how one of his patients, 'Mr X', reported coming across the works of Sacher-Masoch, which he 'devoured … with desire, despite the fact that many of the bloodthirsty scenes far exceeded my own desire'.[31] As Chris Waters observes, it was during these years that a modern language of perversion and sexual abnormality came into being.[32]

Other prominent sexologists of these decades broadly agreed with Krafft-Ebing's taxonomies of sex and gender variation, although some placed more weight on environment, and some more on heredity. Berlin-based dermatologist and sexologist Iwan Bloch (the two specializations often went hand in hand, as dermatologists had traditionally treated venereal diseases) was in the former camp, arguing that most cases of same-sex love were caused by 'external, occasional factors' such as a disagreeable marriage, excessive masturbation or fears of sexually transmitted infections, rather than biology.[33] Hirschfeld, meanwhile, favoured congenital models in developing a spectrum model of 'sexual intermediaries'. According to this model, 'male' and 'female' were merely ideal theoretical endpoints on a continuous scale of in-between types, with every heterosexual man possessing some feminine characteristics and *vice versa*; homosexuals, 'transvestites' and 'hermaphrodites', sometimes collectively described as the 'third sex', were located towards the middle of the spectrum.[34] This model also had similarities to that of Viennese philosophy student Otto Weininger, although he framed his ideas in a more antisemitic, misogynistic and homophobic manner in his 1903 treatise *Sex and Character*. According to Weininger, '*A female genius … is a contradiction in terms,* for … genius

[i]s nothing but an intensified, fully developed, higher, universally conscious kind of masculinity' (emphasis in original).[35]

Hirschfeld was a vocal advocate for the rights of sex-gender minorities. His professional motto was 'Justice through Science' – also the motto of the Institute for Sexual Science he founded in 1919 in Berlin. He drew on scientific arguments to expand ideas of what was 'normal' or 'natural', arguing that gays, lesbians and transpeople are congenitally predisposed to sex-gender variance. Hirschfeld thus built on the work of Ulrichs and others to establish a new model of sexual identity politics. Homosexuality, he argued, was 'not a misfortune in itself, but rather made so by … unjust prejudice', and thus he recommended that doctors focus on practical advice on how gay patients could 'adapt' or 'assimilate' to their environment.[36] This congenital model continues to be influential today, as illustrated by 'born this way' or 'gay gene' arguments.[37] In 1904 Hirschfeld published a study of Berlin's sexual subcultures, *Berlin's Third Sex*, showing off his familiarity with the local scene, including queer tea dances, cabarets and gay beats. The short book offered readers voyeuristic insights into the lives of hustlers, cross-dressers and intimate relations between male army officers and their same-sex partners around the barracks of the Prussian capital. While not publicly 'out', in Berlin's queer scene Hirschfeld was known as 'Tante (Aunt) Magnesia', frequenting locations with his male lover.[38] Hirschfeld described the strategies that gay men developed to disguise such relationships from social stigma, such as 'transform[ing] a male character into a female when reporting romantic adventures to their companions, just as some translators of the writers of antiquity do'.[39] He also dwelt on the threat of extortion, especially following sexual activities with rent boys, with blackmail a very real concern for same-sex desiring men living in the shadow of Paragraph 175 – particularly those with money and a reputation to lose. Lay sociologist and avid chronicler of Berlin's underworlds, Hans Ostwald, also described this situation in his 1906 study *Männliche Prostitution im kaiserlichen Berlin* (Male prostitution in imperial Berlin), with chapters on 'blackmail letters' and 'prostitution markets' as well as numerous 'confessions from male prostitutes'.[40]

Ideas of trans identity, gender-nonconformity and intersex conditions also crystallized in new ways during this period. Hirschfeld coined the terms 'transvestite' (*Transvestit/in*) and 'transvestism' (*Transvestitismus*) in around 1910, defining these in broadly similar ways to 'trans' or 'transgender' today. He followed this up with an illustrated volume in 1912, co-authored with Berlin artist Max Tilke. This included some images that Hirschfeld and Tilke had collected over the years, as well as others that people in the emerging trans and gender diverse community had sent in after reading Hirschfeld's 1910 work *Die Transvestiten* (Figure 2.1). Hirschfeld's new names for gender expressions and identities were taken up by quite a few gender-nonconforming people, although some turned

FIGURE 2.1 *Images from Hirschfeld and Tilke, Die Transvestiten (illustrated volume, 1912/2nd ed. 1927). Original captions: 'A transvestite from the case studies, in their own women's clothing' (plate XX); 'A married couple from the last Boer war. The woman as warrior' (plate XXV); 'Two young Levantine transvestites from Constantinople' (plate XXIV).*

Source: Deutsche Nationalbibliothek, Leipzig, Signatur: 1925 A 6684 – ill.Teil.

to other labels: British sexologist Havelock Ellis suggested the term 'Eonist' (after cross-dressing eighteenth-century French spy, the Chevalier d'Eon), while German anthropologist Ferdinand Karsch-Haack suggested 'Transmutist' – partly to get away from the implicit focus on clothing (Latin *vestis*) in Hirschfeld's terms.[41]

The boundaries between the categories of 'homosexual' and 'transvestite' were rarely as neat as the scientists might have liked, especially when it came to people who had been assigned female at birth. But as early as the late nineteenth century, Hirschfeld and colleagues such as Bloch had also begun collaborating with police and gender-nonconforming individuals to certify gender-appropriate ID documents known as *Transvestitenscheine* or 'transvestite passes'. Figure 2.2 shows Gert Katter's pass from 1928, which he could produce as required to avoid arrest on charges such as 'gross mischief' or causing a 'public nuisance'.[42] Research into intersex conditions also gained speed, including Franz Ludwig von Neugebauer's *Hermaphroditismus beim Menschen* (Hermaphroditism in humans, 1908). Applying heteronormative and binary gender expectations in restrictive ways, doctors subjected intersex people to what were often unwanted medical interventions. Innovations in antiseptics and anaesthesia meant that surgery was increasingly used on infants born with ambiguous genitalia from the 1890s, for both diagnosis and treatment. One effect of such interventions was to regulate, without the possibility of consent, an individual's future sexual relations. Medical examinations were also required in cases such as Katter's, where an individual applied to legally change their sex.[43]

FIGURE 2.2 *Gerd Katter's* Transvestitenschein *from the Berlin Police, 1928.*
Source: © Magnus-Hirschfeld-Gesellschaft e.V.

Scholars have often criticized sexologists and psychiatrists of this era for using their authority over their patients to pathologize and intervene in their patients' sexual lives, and with some justification.[44] But doctor-patient relationships could also offer a liberating space for some people to finally tell their own sex-gender truths in a space other than the religious confessional.[45] While some turned to the consulting rooms of sexologists such as Hirschfeld and Bloch, others sought affirmation and self-discovery from an even newer branch of the human sciences, psychoanalysis. Developed by the Viennese-based Sigmund Freud and his followers around the turn of the century, psychoanalysis prompted doctors and scientists to pay much more attention to early childhood development in working towards diagnoses and therapies for sexual conditions. In 1905 Freud's groundbreaking *Three Essays on the Theory of Sexuality* offered a wide-ranging explanation of 'normal' development during childhood and puberty. Practices such as thumbsucking or fascination with stool movements, he argued, were examples of the 'polymorphous perverse' eroticism of infancy. Freud also theorized how this development could veer off to become 'sexual aberrations' such as inversion, fetishism or masochism.[46]

Psychoanalysis also brought new perspectives to the study of female sexuality, often given second fiddle in scientific studies of this period. Doctors had often assumed that women were naturally less sexually 'excitable' or more 'frigid' than men, and nineteenth-century medicine was divided on whether a woman's sexual arousal and orgasm were necessary to conceive a child. Krafft-Ebing and Otto Adler were among those to argue that women were less interested in sex, whereas Bloch questioned assumptions of female coldness, suggesting that often, a husband's lack of erotic creativity might be the real cause of his wife's 'sexual anaesthesia'.[47] Freud, meanwhile, saw female frigidity as the result of a harmfully strict upbringing that led some women to resist their 'marital duties' and seek refuge in neuroses. Freud's theory, observes historian Ute Frevert, 'found a chink in the armour of bourgeois sexual morality', recognizing sexuality as a basic human need while condemning the strict double standard that dictated that women remain virgins until marriage, while men were allowed to 'sow their wild oats'.[48]

Psychoanalysts explained same-sex desires and cross-gendered identifications as resulting from incomplete processes of 'normal' development. As Freud declared, the 'pervert' is someone who 'exhibits a certain stage of inhibited development'.[49] Due to statements such as this, but also because of the conservative direction taken by much post-Second World War psychoanalysis, Freudian theory has often been criticized as homophobic.[50] A closer look at early patient cases, though, reveals that at least some practitioners took a sympathetic approach towards their homosexual-identifying patients (most of whom were men).[51] The following exchange between a patient and early Viennese analyst Isidor Sadger, for example, is characterized by careful listening:

[Patient:] I was thinking about the analysis again and believe that I've now understood you somewhat. I think that analysis aims to dissect the human psyche, like a surgeon takes to the body with his scalpel, to uncover the source of the suffering, and remove it if possible.

[Sadger:] On the one hand. I would still like to know from what you are seeking relief, why did you undertake the analysis?

[Patient:] Really to rid myself of the inclination towards loving men.

[Sadger:] Why is that something from which you wish to be freed?

[Patient:] Because it sometimes comes into conflict with my broader outlook on life and my religious convictions, and that sometimes makes me unhappy.[52]

Working carefully with patients across many months, analysts sought to untangle their 'resistances', fantasies and dreams and offer therapeutic relief. While Sadger hoped that psychoanalysis could fully 'cure' homosexuality, Freud later modified his opinion on this: in 1935 her wrote to an 'American mother' of a male homosexual that the goal of psychoanalysis was above all to support patients: 'If he is unhappy, neurotic, torn by conflicts, inhibited in his social life, analysis may bring him harmony, peace of mind, full efficiency whether he remains a homosexual or gets changed.'[53] Psychoanalytic accounts thus offered a counterpoint to the more congenital models of sexologists such as Hirschfeld.[54]

Many early proponents of German sexual science and psychoanalysis were from Jewish backgrounds. This was no accident: within a heavily antisemitic medical profession, sexual medicine, dermatology and psychiatry were regarded as less prestigious and thus more accessible specializations for individuals from non-Christian backgrounds.[55] Many sexologists also leant towards the left of the political spectrum, taking an often progressive approach to sex-gender variance, oriented less towards religious ideas of sin or morality than the scientific urge to sort and diagnose. Yet even though many experienced discrimination in their own professional careers, the writings of both Jewish and non-Jewish German sexologists and psychoanalysts of this era present a complicated legacy. Often, we find racializing and ableist ideas about eugenics, social hygiene and 'degeneration' intertwined with social reform principles such as free love or homosexual rights.[56] Hirschfeld is a good example of this. Because of his LGBTIQ rights advocacy, he has frequently been 'lionized', as Jennifer Evans observes, 'as the guiding light of a rational, scientifically driven human rights movement for sexual toleration'.[57] He was also a concerted anti-racist, and himself a victim of antisemitic attacks. Yet recent studies have complicated this picture, showing how deeply implicated even Hirschfeld's left-wing, liberal writings were in racializing, eugenicist and imperialist assumptions about European superiority vis-à-vis cultural 'Others'.[58]

By naming sexuality and its variants in a newly scientific manner that commanded social authority, German sexologists and psychoanalysts provided a foundation for broader political movements for LGBTIQ rights and sex reform in subsequent decades. Some practitioners, such as Hirschfeld and Stöcker, combined their scholarship and activism to become vocal political advocates. These scientific ways of thinking about sexual difference formed a different kind of basis for social norms of sexual behaviour. They soon began to be reproduced and affirmed in new and creative ways, including through literary texts.

Culture meets science in turn-of-the-century queer literature

Ulrichs's studies of urnings and the writings of Hirschfeld, Krafft-Ebing, Freud and others on 'inversion' and 'homosexuality' were accompanied by a veritable wave of queer literature in the early twentieth century. Thomas

Mann's *Death in Venice* (1912), Robert Musil's *The Confusions of Young Törless* (1906) and the homoerotic poetry of Stefan George all engaged with male same-sex desire in ways that both referenced and challenged scientific ways of talking about sex-gender difference.[59] Similarly, Aimée Duc's 1901 novel *Are These Women?* depicted the adventures in life and love of a cosmopolitan group of emancipated 'new women' university students in Zurich, at a time when women's access to Germany's universities was heavily restricted.[60] These characters refer to themselves as members of a 'third sex' and 'belonging to the ranks of the "Krafft-Ebing types",' and as per sexological models of inversion, embrace masculinized clothing and practices such as smoking. Notably, though, the novel also challenges sexological attempts to cleanly distinguish between 'congenital', masculine female inverts and more feminine, 'pseudohomosexual' women, by depicting characters that combine traditionally feminine traits such as 'coquettishness' or a 'curvaceous' body with more masculine-coded characteristics such as a 'strong and well-built' physicality.[61]

What we might describe as trans or intersex identities are also evident in fiction and life writing from these decades. In 1907, the fictionalized memoirs of 'N.O. Body' (a pseudonym for Martha/Karl Baer) were published, later translated into English as *Memoirs of a Man's Maiden Years*. This work tells the life story of an individual assigned female at birth and raised as a girl, but who enters adulthood as a man. Body recalls encounters with the sexological profession, and the influence of sexual scientific thought is evident in the way Body self-diagnoses an inadequacy in performing 'feminine' tasks such as knitting ('my unskilled hands couldn't hold the needles'). Yet their semi-fictional memoir also opens up room for thinking about gendered identity and erotic pleasures in ways that go beyond medical frameworks, such as when Body reflects on how 'I lay in bed and beautiful women with brown hair and dark eyes leant over me.'[62] Similarly, the 1907 biography 'Diary of a Male Bride' was allegedly based on the diaries of an individual assigned male who 'passed' as a female South American aristocrat and swept across the Berlin queer scene before moving to Breslau (today Wrocław in Poland) and becoming engaged to a (male) teacher, but who then killed themselves out of fear of disclosure.[63] In such ways, cultural texts could open up alternative spaces of queer, trans and intersex visibility to sexual science, even as they engaged with sexual scientific knowledge in thoughtful ways.

The decades around 1900 also saw the rise of what has sometimes been dubbed a 'masculinist' or 'Greek' approach to male same-sex love. Authors such as Adolf Brand, Benedict Friedlaender and Hans Blüher drew on thinkers like Friedrich Nietzsche to challenge the congenital views of homosexuality developed by Ulrichs, Hirschfeld and others, looking instead to classical antiquity for models of brotherly companionship and love between older men and younger boys, and seeking aesthetic rather than scientific ways of expressing male-male desire.[64] This culturally elitist approach to thinking about same-sex desires was strongly evident in Brand's magazine *Der Eigene* (1896–1932), whose title has been variously translated as 'The Special', 'The Autonomous', or 'The Self-Owned'.[65] This magazine, heralded as likely the oldest periodical dedicated to male-male homoerotic desire, celebrated 'masculine culture' through poems, stories, illustrations and photographs by artists including Wilhelm von Gloeden, Sascha Schneider and Elisar von Kupffer.[66] Photographs of scantily dressed boys in laurel wreaths and loin cloths re-enacting an imagined classical past proved popular, as did photographs of male nudes in natural settings such as lakes and forests, evoking the popular *Lebensreform* naturist and body culture movements of the Wilhelmine era.[67] Overtones of right-wing nationalism and Aryan ideals of muscular beauty became increasingly prominent over the journal's several decades of publication, culminating in a Weimar-era series on 'Deutsche Rasse' (German Race) celebrating a hypervirile, blonde, Germanic masculinity. 'Never', one scholar goes so far as to declare, 'would homoeroticism and nationalism be so plainly linked'.[68] Such racialized erotica worked to reaffirm a decidedly white, Germanic norm of same-sex desire – one that also resonated in colonial contexts, as we will see later in this chapter.

Between respectability and reform: Moralists, feminists and scandals

As Germany became a modern nation state with unification in 1871, its sense of nationhood and Empire both shaped and was shaped by ideas of sexuality – from debates about reproductive politics, morality and prostitution, to the rights and responsibilities of men and women towards one another and society. Rapid urbanization and industrialization produced growing fears about degeneration and declining population health. The population expanded rapidly during these decades, from 41 million in 1871 to 65 million by 1910. This growth was felt particularly in the cities, as many people moved out of agricultural employment into often very cramped urban living spaces. At the same time, there were significant improvements to the infant mortality rate, which fell almost 30 per cent in the first year of life between 1871 and 1910, as well as increases to life expectancy across the board. Marriage became more widespread especially among younger Germans, even as the number of children per family decreased. Family sizes remained higher in rural than in urban areas, and among Catholics than Protestants, followed by Jews.[69]

In these conditions of urbanized modernity, bourgeois conservatives were concerned that the 'red threat' of an increasingly organized industrial working class might endanger the social order and their middle-class privilege. Quite a few turned to nationalist politics, which went hand in hand with a larger program of imperialist expansion and colonial acquisitions.[70] Such class-based fears were compounded by gendered and sexualized anxieties, including a perceived crisis of middle-class masculinity, a sense that 'feminizing' nervous disorders were on the rise, a series of prominent homosexual scandals and the growing influence of the women's movement. The next sections of this chapter examine how these developments variously challenged, broadened and reinforced norms of sexuality in the age of German Empire, including through unlikely alliances between branches of the moral purity movement, feminists and socialists.[71] The ways they approached these questions both referenced and moved beyond the parameters of sexual science.

Bourgeois respectability and morality campaigns

Bourgeois ideas about sexuality, morality and respectability shaped Wilhelmine public discourse in significant ways. While sexual scientists were turning their attention to classifying and explaining normal and deviant behaviours, theologians, politicians and pedagogues were proclaiming at length on matters ranging from impotence and frigidity to the dangers of masturbation – examples of what has been dubbed the 'discursive explosion' around sex in the modern era.[72] During the decades after unification, a wave of morality campaigns peopled largely by religious and political conservatives propelled debates around prostitution and venereal disease, birth control, divorce and the rights of single mothers. These prompted responses from left-wing reformers and a growing women's movement, which in turn soon split into a more conservative 'bourgeois' and a more radical, 'socialist' wing.

At the heart of the bourgeoisie's political and social presence in German society stood marriage and the family, 'a model through which [... it] was able to generalize its outlook and values within the larger society'.[73] 'Concepts of sexuality', argues George Mosse of this period, 'haunted bourgeois society and nationalism, to be acknowledged yet curbed'.[74] The bourgeoisie was an influential but also socially divided class, and marriages generally took place within established social groups: children of businessmen and entrepreneurs married into other entrepreneurial families, while the children of educated public servants and academics married into others from the *Bildungsbürgertum*. In many cases, these were 'affairs less of the heart than of the purse-strings', helping to cement political and economic alliances.[75] Wives were responsible for leading the domestic household, which in wealthier families involved coordinating servants to keep up an appearance of prosperity and respectability. This was a model that the less well-off and 'new middle classes' of white-collar workers and public officials also sought to emulate, although with varying degrees of success.[76] Even so, in Germany as elsewhere in Europe and many other parts of the world by around 1900, marriage was less of a life sentence than it had once been. While it still filled familiar functions related to inheritance, property and the raising of children, it was increasingly viewed as a contract that should not only have its basis in love – an earlier development, as we have seen – but should also be a partnership between equals, as Stöcker's writings emphasize, and one that could be dissolved if necessary.[77]

Proletarian autobiographies of this era offer further evidence that, even if dominant, bourgeois norms of family and marriage were never the only available model. These writings reveal an increasingly self-aware working-class resistance to bourgeois portrayals of workers as immoral, tainted by incest, premarital sex, illegitimacy and prostitution. They also highlight the particular vulnerability of working-class women – and occasionally men – to sexual harassment from bourgeois employers. Twenty-one-year-old male servant Heinrich Holek wrote of his experiences with a bourgeois female employer, to whom he was suspected of prostituting himself: 'Madame used to lie in bed every day until noon and I had to bring the letters to her bedroom. ... And now I was supposed to live with their suspicion that I was selling myself to a woman? That very same day I packed my things.'[78] Proletarian marriages and sexual norms were subject to quite different structural expectations than their bourgeois counterparts, and when and under what conditions one married could also look very different for an urban factory worker and a rural labourer. In the countryside, there was often a long transitional phase between childhood and marriage, as children of cottagers and labourers were sent into service – girls in rural Bavaria were sent to work as maidservants from as young as thirteen – and needed time to assemble the necessary skills, funds and status to establish a household of their own.[79] Those in service, meanwhile, had to contend with poor wages and often rough treatment – Elizabeth Jones has examined legal disputes between female servants and employers to show that at least some working-class women used legal channels to file complaints of abuse and sexual harassment.[80]

From the 1880s a powerful conservative morality movement (*Sittlichkeitsbewegung*) began to emerge. It started with organizations of Protestant men in the Rhineland and Berlin, and was followed around a decade later by Catholic groups centred in Cologne. Around the turn of the century some groups allied themselves with conservative religious and women's organizations, although many male morality campaigners were hostile to women's engagement. The rise of such groups has been linked to a sense of German masculinity, and gender roles more broadly, being in 'crisis' – an anxiety surrounding shifting gender norms that crossed confessional lines.[81] The Protestant moral movement particularly condemned prostitution, seeing this as a crime in which the government was complicit with its system of state regulation and brothels. But its targets went well beyond brothels, as leaders objected to contraception, abortion, illegitimacy and divorce, to new forms of popular entertainment such as variety shows and late-night cafes, to sensationalism and violence in the press and popular literature, to the illicit pornography trade (which since the 1860s was booming in Germany as elsewhere in Europe[82]) and to perceived immorality in the arts such as nude painting, sculpture or dance. The churches often backed the efforts of these moral purity organizations, such as when in 1904 the Royal Consistory of Brandenburg directed its church officials to fight against 'the sins of immorality that destroy the body's power and health, do terrible damage to mental and emotional life ... and as a result bring about temporal and eternal destruction'.[83] New movements for gay rights, birth control (the 'neo-Malthusian' movement) and sex reform were all seen as evidence of the country's spiritual and moral decline, in a prudishness that at times verged on the hysterical.[84]

The rise of the moral purity organizations aligned with a broadened policing of vice crimes since unification. This was not just a reaction to shifting sexual norms; rather, sexuality represented a focal point for anxieties about the very pace and upheavals of modernity itself. Along with sexual assaults such as rape, 'vice' included reproductive 'offences' such as abortion or crimes against public decency. Policing linked sexual order to larger questions of political organization and nationhood, as regulating reproductive and sexual behaviours became 'one focus of intense concern for modern states'.[85] The moral purity organizations also strongly supported censorship. Liberals, by contrast, often saw this as an attack on the freedom of the arts and expression. Yet not all views on this topic can be neatly aligned on a scale of liberal and conservative; for prostitution campaigner Anna Pappritz, for example, censorship created its own risks, causing people to 'suspect every form of nudity and naturalness of being indecent'.[86]

Although the morality organizations were populated primarily from the ranks of the bourgeoisie (and especially the educated *Bildungsbürgertum*), bourgeois sexuality was not without contradictions. This class was among the first to deliberately employ birth control to restrict family size and increase the well-being of children and mothers, significantly reducing infant mortality between the 1870s and 1900s. Among the working classes, meanwhile, mortality rates remained shockingly high, as did deaths from illegal abortions, even though proletarian families also used contraception, especially *coitus interruptus* (the withdrawal method).[87] The assimilated Jewish middle classes also saw a declining birth rate. Families of more than two children were a rarity, and Jewish wives of professionals were often not only more highly educated than their non-Jewish counterparts, but also more likely to devote themselves to community affairs, charities and social welfare. The Jewish Women's Federation became an early member of the Federation of German's Women's Associations (*Bund Deutscher Frauenvereine*, BDF) when this was created in 1894 as an umbrella organization for women's associations across Germany.[88] Even as it was populated largely by middle-class women, this growing women's movement would soon be a key site for challenging as well as affirming inherited bourgeois sexual norms.

Feminism and prostitution campaigns

By the beginning of the First World War, the BDF had risen to cater to around half a million German women, and it formed a powerful voice in turn-of-the-century debates around the so-called 'woman question' and prostitution. The 'woman question' was in fact a series of questions centred on women's political participation, access to education and contributions to society, as well as more explicitly sexual issues such as prostitution regulation.[89] As Ann Taylor Allen observes, women in Germany around the turn of the twentieth century, as in many other places in the world, began to organize *en masse* for inclusion in areas of public life as wide-ranging as work, politics and education;

> artists, scientists, and moralists challenged traditional norms of manhood and womanhood; and both men and women experimented with new sexual moralities and gender identities. When we include this colorful story, we highlight upheaval rather than continuity, and change rather than stability.[90]

A radical minority within the BDF pursued a strategy of equal rights feminism, but political moderates including Gertrud Bäumer (BDF chair from 1910–19), Alice Salomon and Helene Lange were more likely to emphasize essential gender differences and separate roles for men and women. They promoted an idea of 'spiritual motherhood', arguing for women's increasing involvement in the public sphere based on their unique capacity to nurture and educate. Women would complement public life, they argued, not only as wives and mothers, but in maternal roles such as teachers, nurses and social workers.

In the first decade of the new century more radical left-wing groups such as Helene Stöcker's League for Maternal Protection became a vocal presence in the women's movement. Founded in 1905, it soon parted ways with the BDF over what it saw as the latter's restrictive bourgeois ideals of morality, female sexuality and family, instead demanding the 'new ethics' and liberation from restrictive gender roles outlined at the beginning of this chapter. Stöcker's organization had strong links to the German Society for the Struggle against Venereal Diseases (*Deutsche Geselleschaft zur Bekämpfung der Geschlechtskrankheiten*), and formed a leading voice in the growing sex reform movement in the late Wilhelmine and into the Weimar eras.[91] While only a few women of this era had access to medical or scientific training, many contributed as activists and intellectuals.

Stöcker, for example, who was among the first German women to receive a doctorate, regularly published in the new sexological journals, drawing specific attention to questions of female sexuality and gendered inequalities.[92]

A key date for the bourgeois women's movement was the year 1908, when a new law regulating who could join what type of organization, the *Reichsvereinsgesetz*, finally allowed women to join political parties. Before this point, it had been relatively easy to brush over internal differences and argue that organizations were fighting for women in ways above party political divisions.[93] In the years immediately before 1914, however, increasingly nationalist and right-wing tendencies began to divide the movement, especially when it was joined by large conservative women's groups including the German Protestant Women's League.[94] Some radical feminists during these years, such as Käthe Schirmacher, also turned from liberal progressivism to a much more avid nationalism in the context of rising militaristic sentiment, showing that sexual emancipation arguments could sometimes go hand in hand with regressive and even reactionary tendencies.[95] We see here a good example of what Geoff Eley has described as the 'tangle of Germany modernity' – a set of 'shifting coordinates of political agency and political subjectivity' that shaped individuals' capacity to think and act as citizens in the new nation state.[96] Edward Dickinson emphasizes that what was at stake was based on a logic of pluralization: 'not the flattening out of difference, not the progressive articulation and imposition of norms and normalcy, but the progressive articulation, organization, and politicization of difference.'[97]

Working-class women were an important part of this politicization of difference, increasingly organizing to fight gender and class oppression in ways that we would today describe as 'intersectional' – 'hand in hand with the male portion of the working class', as August Bebel declared in a bestselling study of women and socialism. But they also shared concerns with their bourgeois counterparts, such as access to the vote and education. Like bourgeois feminists, socialist leaders such as Clara Zetkin sought a greater voice for women in public life, and they, too, were sometimes invested in models of gender difference that emphasized motherhood as women's unique calling. They differed, though, in calling more loudly for welfare-based activism, and in the anti-capitalist framing of their arguments, with Zetkin seeking no less than 'a complete social reversal of present-day society'.[98]

Both conservative and radical branches of the bourgeois women's movement joined socialist feminists in critiquing outdated marriage and divorce laws, especially when the Civil Code (*Bürgerliches Gesetzbuch*) introduced in 1900 reinforced notions of the obedient wife and patriarchal husband. Socialist Lily Braun wrote in 1905 that '[o]nce the female has turned into a human being, that is, an individual personality, with views, judgements and life-goals of her own, then she has been spoiled for the average marriage'.[99] Instead, feminists advocated for more modern models of 'companionate' marriage between equally placed partners – a shift away from the polarized gender ideals that had characterized the nineteenth-century bourgeois household.[100]

Prostitution represented a burning issue for feminist activists and morality campaigners alike, especially in the major cities, where many feared that degeneration and sexual vice were rife. Feminist campaigners known as 'abolitionists' fought to abolish a system of state regulation of prostitution ostensibly aimed at containing the spread of venereal diseases, arguing that this tacitly condoned the bourgeois double standard of applying different sexual morality expectations to men and women. Indeed, visiting a prostitute was something of a rite of passage for young middle-class men, who embraced freedoms afforded them by both gender and class.[101] Abolitionist movements existed not just in Germany, but also Great Britain, France, Russia and the Habsburg Empire, and they strongly critiqued the requirement placed on female prostitutes to register with the police, work out of brothels and be subjected to regular hygienic controls to check for STIs, sometimes as often as twice a week. Prostitutes also faced restrictions on their place of residence, dress, behaviour and access to public places like parks and theatres – while their male clients were free to do as they pleased. Before unification, sex work had been regulated on a local basis by town and city authorities, but after 1871 police-controlled brothels were made illegal, even as the police stepped up the regulation system in the name of public order. This created a paradoxical, two-tiered system: registered sex workers were under tight control, while up to five or ten times as many 'clandestine' street walkers remained outside the system. By 1913, the Munich police oversaw 184 so-called *Kontrollmädchen* or 'girls under police control', but estimated that there were a further 3000 'clandestines' working the streets.[102]

Many bourgeois feminist campaigners shared with members of the conservative moral purity movements the ideal that both women and men should control their sexual urges and restrict these to marriage – another example of how sexual norms could at times be reproduced from very different political standpoints. For radical feminists and socialists, meanwhile, police control of prostitution was typical of the wider undemocratic approach of the nation's elite, disproportionately restricting proletarian sexual practices at a time when working-class women's wages were seldom sufficient to survive on.[103] Anti-vice campaigns were strongly driven by middle-class attempts to 'save the sexually violated'.[104] Although the sexual outcasts to be saved were generally assumed to be from the working classes, fears that the moral turpitude facing young women in major European cities might also cross class lines are evident in contemporary works such as Margarete Böhme's *Diary of a Lost Girl* (*Tagebuch einer Verlorenen*, 1905), an allegedly 'true-life' story of a young bourgeois woman forced into sex slavery.[105] Drawing attention to sexual violence and gendered power inequities, these issues galvanized the women's movement in the final decades of the century. They also highlighted the very different risks that entering urban spaces, places 'traditionally imagined as the site of exchange and erotic activity', posed for women and men.[106]

Another issue that brought together sometimes surprising coalitions of left-leaning reformers, sexologists and feminists was eugenics, as sexual norms were increasingly oriented towards modern biopolitical ideas of population health. Imperialist-era assumptions about racial 'purity' and fears of its 'pollution' coincided with Darwinist ideas about evolution and degeneration, and with nationalist ideas of strength and patriotism.[107] Eugenicist thinking can be found even among the most socially progressive actors of these decades, from Hirschfeld and Stöcker in Germany to prominent British birth control activist Mary Stopes.[108] Sex reformers generally promoted what is sometimes described as 'positive' eugenics aimed at improving population health, such as premarital counselling to ensure the health of potential offspring. They were supported by the work of contemporaries such as physician Max Nordau, who warned of the dangers of degeneration that might result from less-than-ideal sexual pairings such as with homosexuals or alcoholics: 'We distinguish the healthy from the diseased impulse,' he wrote in his 1892 work *Degeneration* (*Entartung*), 'and demand that the latter be combated.'[109] 'Degenerate' conditions, it was feared, could be passed down between generations, adversely affecting the wider health of the nation. Such eugenicist arguments were not yet tied to the genocidal logics of National Socialism, but nor were they without sinister and exclusionary effects. Rather, ideas of health and purity were, observes Kirsten Leng, 'emancipating for some, inhibiting for others', and often outright ableist in their attitudes to disability.[110]

Movements for moral purity, a 'new' ethics, and expanded citizenship rights for women point to various ways in which established norms of sexual behaviour and gender roles were at once contested and defended in Wilhelmine German society. Another notable space for the contestation of norms was a series of highly publicized sex scandals in the decades immediately before the war. These scandals not only highlight new ways of publicly discussing sexual questions through the rapidly expanding print media, but also new ways of conceptualizing sexual identity in general, and homosexual subjectivity, in particular, during Germany's first decades as a modern nation state.

Scandals and sensations

The biggest sex scandal of the Wilhelmine era involved none less than the Emperor himself. Between 1907 and 1909, in a series of protracted legal trials, the young Kaiser Wilhelm II became embroiled by association with accusations of homosexuality directed at members of his inner circle. This was known as the 'Liebenberg roundtable' because the group regularly met for hunting and social gatherings at the Liebenberg country estate of his friend Prince Philipp zu Eulenburg-Hertefeld. Members cultivated a romanticized atmosphere of male friendship, including tender nicknames – soon to be harshly satirized in the German and international press – like 'Phili' (for Eulenburg), 'Tutu' (for military commander of Berlin, Kuno von Moltke) and 'Liebchen' or 'Darling' for the Kaiser himself.[111] This group was suspected of having an undue influence on the Kaiser, in everything from the dismissal of Chancellor Bismarck in 1890 to the generally pacifist direction of German foreign policy. Scandal erupted in 1906 when journalist Maximilian Harden, who published the weekly news magazine *Die Zukunft* (The Future), used his magazine to put pressure on Eulenburg to leave Berlin and thus reduce his political influence. Eulenburg left for a Swiss spa resort, but when he returned in 1907 to receive a prestigious nomination, Harden again took up the attack with a sharp editorial declaiming that things were already 'warm enough' in the Liebenberg circle – with 'warm' well-known German slang for homosexual. Learning of the slander, the Kaiser demanded Eulenburg's (and also Moltke's) accountability, declaring that he must either go into exile or 'make an unambiguous declaration to me and then confront Harden'.[112] This could either take the form of a duel – a still popular form of reckoning accounts between men of the officer and upper classes, despite having been outlawed at unification – or a legal challenge for libel.[113]

Opting for the latter, the Moltke-Harden trial began in October 1907 and attracted huge attention from the national and international press, comparable to the Dreyfus affair in France.[114] Moltke argued that Harden had falsely claimed he was homosexual, which Harden then had to disprove. Rather than offering evidence of actual homosexual activity, Harden's defence took a more novel route, attempting to convince the court of Moltke's homosexual 'disposition'. The case thus turned on feelings rather than acts, with Harden arguing that Moltke harboured 'abnormal sexual feelings'. Among those called by the defence were Moltke's ex-wife, Lilly von Elbe, who reported on her husband's misogyny, and the sexologist Hirschfeld, who sharply distinguished between 'friendship' and 'love'. Presenting his view of homosexuality as an inborn disposition, Hirschfeld argued that Moltke displayed an 'unconscious homosexuality' and that engagement in actual same-sex behaviours was 'irrelevant from a scientific perspective'.[115] Harden was acquitted, the judge agreeing with Hirschfeld. The Kaiser suffered a nervous breakdown, and the Prussian attorney general announced an appeal. The scandal dragged on until 1909, with others such as masculinist Adolf Brand weighing in on the action (and attracting his own libel suit from Chancellor Bülow). Meanwhile, Eulenburg was accused of perjury and only avoided a full trial due to his ongoing ill-health.

This scandal offers a vivid illustration of the changing politics of homosexual visibility in the years before the First World War. Journalists used the mass media to 'out' and savage the reputations of prominent figures in Wilhelmine politics. Bringing together 'an exuberant popular medium – the German daily and political press – with the new sexology of naming homosexuality' these trials popularized a distinct notion of homosexual identity.[116] This is vividly illustrated by a poem by Bavarian satirist Ludwig Thoma from the journal *Simplicissimus* in 1907, in which the narrator puts to readers a series of provocative questions soon to be placed for judgement before a court, such as whether an (unnamed) 'he' is 'homo or hetero' or whether he is 'up to scratch in the marriage bed'.[117] Satirical cartoons and commentaries helped to cement these stereotypes in the eyes of a larger German and European public, as seen in the suggestion for a 'New Prussian Coat of Arms' featuring two cooing men with the features of Philipp Eulenburg and Kuno Moltke (Figure 2.3). The French started referring to the 'German vice' (*vice allemande*), the Italians described homosexuals as 'Berlinese', and the English now referred to the 'German custom'.[118]

The impact of the 'German scandal' thus moved beyond more platonic eighteenth-century understandings of sentimental male-male friendship to solidify homosexuality as a distinct brand of sexual identity.[119] The Eulenburg case was a product of the particular political and media landscape of early twentieth-century modernity. The new visibility of homosexual practices had both emancipatory and homophobic effects. While same-sex desires became thinkable for more people than ever before, some feared it would undermine the very foundations of German masculinity, militarism and nationalism in these crucial years where war seemed on the horizon. Historian Norman Domeier even suggests that the symbolic 'castration' of German imperial prestige fed the nation's appetite for a war that might, as one newspaper put it, act as a 'purifying thunderstorm', re-virilizing a country supposedly languishing in decadence.[120]

The scandal also highlights the significance of the press in shaping Wilhelmine public opinion, at a time when full political participation was limited by the lack of female suffrage and the Prussian three-class franchise system.[121] The Eulenburg press coverage built on that surrounding earlier scandals involving homosexual blackmail of prominent figures, such as Breslau (now Wrocław) judge August Kasse or Berlin department store owner Hermann Israel. The Berlin police had even renamed its investigative unit the Department of Homosexuals and Blackmailers, reflecting the frequency with which male prostitution was linked to extortion. The scandal also perpetuated the earlier media flurry around international cases such as the Oscar Wilde trials in 1890s Britain, or closer to home, that of wealthy industrialist Friedrich Alfred Krupp, who likely committed suicide in 1902 after newspapers accused him of having sex with male minors in

FIGURE 2.3 *'New Prussian Coat of Arms', published in* Jugend: *Münchner illustrierte Wochenschrift für Kunst und Leben, 4 November 1907, p. 1032.*

Source: Public domain.[122]

Italy and Berlin. That story was one that Social Democratic publications such as *Vorwärts*, despite being generally sympathetic to the gay rights cause, had reported on with relish for its capacity to bring down a class enemy.[123] This again highlights the limits of looking at sexual history only from the perspective of progress or liberation, for as we will see time and again, greater freedom for some groups – in this case, the working classes – has often been claimed at the expense of tighter policing for others.

The Eulenburg affair contributed to a broader reactionary tightening of norms of masculine behaviour and friendship in the Imperial era, and laid a foundation for subsequent moral panics. One of these surrounded the bourgeois youth movement on the eve of the First World War, when a radical minority called for emancipation from adult control and the creation of an autonomous *Jugendkultur* (youth culture). This fuelled conservative concerns about the alleged licentiousness and rebellion of adolescent sexuality, which had been popularized in risqué fin-de-siècle cultural works such as Franz Wedekind's play *Spring Awakening* (1891). It also coincided with new discussions of youthful homoeroticism, such as Hans Blüher's 1913 book on the hiking movement, *The German Wandervogel Movement as an Erotic Phenomenon*.[124] In such ways, the genre of the scandal helped to firmly mark male homosexuality in the German public consciousness in the first decade of the new century.

This also had implications for female same-sex relations. Only male-male 'intercourse-like' acts were criminalized under Paragraph 175, although female homosexuality had been subject to the death penalty in Prussia until 1794, and in Austria continued to be outlawed. In a backlash against the homosexual scandals outlined above, and amidst a wider current of legal reform, a new draft German Criminal Code in 1909, intended to replace the Prussian-dominated code of 1871, proposed both harsher penalties for male homosexuality and the inclusion of female same-sex acts under a new Paragraph 250. Although its adoption was ultimately interrupted by the war, the proposal provoked pushback from homosexual rights activists, physicians, lawyers and feminists – albeit not always along queer-friendly lines. Prominent feminist Anna Pappritz argued against the new Paragraph, even as she rejected homosexuality as 'just as reprehensible, unpleasant, and revolting' in women as men. Despite her liberal 'new ethics', Stöcker, too, described female homosexuality as inferior to 'normal love, that is the love between man and woman'.[125] Others feared that the law might unwittingly implicate the many single women who lived together for economic and social reasons.[126]

Some sought more concertedly to expand the space of sexual morality to include same-sex relations. Anna Rüling, for example, aligned female homosexuality with ideas of 'rational' female masculinity, and sharply critiqued the women's movement's widespread rejection of women who loved other women. In a 1904 speech to the WhK she argued that female homosexuals constitute a distinct third sex, 'the natural and obvious link between men and women', and 'inherently similar' to the 'average man' in intellect, behaviour and appearance.[127] Here, we see a conservative gender politics invested in masculine superiority being mapped onto a more radical call for homosexual emancipation. In a different vein, feminist writer-activist and sexologist Johanna Elberskirchen advocated a much more feminine model of female same-sex subjectivities whereby 'both love in the other the same sex – the feminine, not the masculine'.[128] In the end, the difficulties in defining the female homosexual – her 'unnameability' in the terms of Wilhelmine medicine, law and politics – lent this figure a certain immunity.[129]

Even so, the public appetite for scandal did not leave female homosexuality unscathed, especially when the minor Berlin weekly paper *Große Glocke* (Great Bell, 1906–22) decided to publish a series of reports of women's transgressive sexual behaviour. Along with abortion and 'free love', a series on female homosexuality 'navigated the line between tabloid titillation and preaching moral purity', as Marti Lybeck observes.[130] One 1908 report told of a Berlin landlady shocked to find that her nineteen-year-old tenant had invited six women to her apartment where they drank, smoke and engaged in 'a sickening orgy'; in turn, one of the women semi-pseudonymously named in that report, Frl. T. (Miss T), penned a detailed denial, acknowledging the homosexuality of some of the women present, but insisting that 'no such activities took place. There were not even any exaggerated caresses in a distasteful form.' Notable in this report is Frl. T.'s use of the word 'homosexual' to describe herself, even as she sought to defend publicly her own middle-class respectability.[131] Such moves suggest a more visible space for female same-sex desire in the immediate pre-First World War period, even as claims to a respectable version of lesbianism were pitted against a campaign of shaming and intimidation, complete with butch female pimps, lesbian clubs and other 'orgies', by the paper's editors.[132]

These cases both generated and reflected an enormous public appetite for scandal and sensation, and help us to uncover a different kind of history of modernity. There may, argues Scott Spector, be more productive ways of reading moral panics than as examples of modern urban decadence or a straightforward 'othering' of marginalized figures such as the Jew, the homosexual, the criminal or the prostitute. The cultural meanings surrounding media events such as homosexual scandals or serial and ritual murder cases sat in tension with more obviously 'modern' ideals of science and emancipation, and rather than being mutually exclusive, Spector argues, such apparently conflicting ideas of modern society and sexuality were 'strongly and simultaneously present in the self image many urban central Europeans had about the lives they were living'.[133] As the final section of this chapter explores, such tensions, mediated by the press and popular culture, also surrounded discussions of sexuality in the decidedly imperialist contexts of German colonialism and world war.

Empire, colonial imaginings and war

Colonialism was a crucial, but often implicit rather than explicit reference point for Wilhelmine-era discussions of sexuality. Against this backdrop, commentators negotiated and at times challenged sexual norms in ways that foregrounded ideas of race, nation and empire. During the 1880s, the German Empire actively pursued acquisitions in Africa, the South Pacific and China, including German Southwest Africa (now Namibia), German East Africa (now Burundi, Rwanda and Tanzania), Togo, Cameroon, numerous Pacific islands including Samoa and a section of Papua New Guinea and the Chinese enclave of Tsingtao. Both economic and non-economic motives played a role – colonial possessions brought raw materials and new markets for German goods and capital, but they were also a status symbol for European powers, an outlet for German settlers and missionaries, and a resource for scientific research, helping to create new university subdisciplines in fields such as botany.[134] 'This burst of colonial activity', observes Robert Tobin, 'coincided with the explosion of modern discourses concerning sexuality', overlaying existing entanglements of sex, race and nation already discussed, for example, in relation to celebrations of 'Greek' classical ideals of male homosexuality.[135] Although Germany's colonies were often less economically beneficial than politicians had hoped, stories about colonial subjects and possessions helped to propel 'colonial fantasies' into the sexual domain.[136] They reinforced the political dominance of the white, male German citizen, while producing new anxieties around race, reproduction and sexual encounter. 'One could', one scholar has recently noted, 'write a history of Europe's mental engagement with the colonial world in terms of sexualized images'.[137] Thinking about Germany's new colonial 'subjects' helped to expand and problematize who qualified as 'German' and as 'citizens' – terms far from synonymous during this period – and the ways in which both of these ideas were shaped by sex.[138]

In the early phase of colonization, 'imperial patriarchs' such as adventurer Carl Peters (1856–1918), who created the colony of German East Africa, treated the 'natives' as clearly inferior, and valued their own sexual autonomy over local women above all else. As Lora Wildenthal argues, 'German colonial rule rested not only on superior firepower, economic domination, and strategic diplomacy, but also on the sexual coercion' of female colonial subjects – and often also rape. A series of colonial scandals in the 1890s involving Peters, Heinrich Leist and others in accusations of sexual violence and forced prostitution of women of colour raised concerns both in Germany and its overseas territories about whether German men were really spreading 'civilization' or themselves becoming irreparably brutish. This prompted a push for more German women to settle in the colonies and convey a 'civilizing' influence.[139] The Herero and Nama wars and Maji Maji uprising further fuelled German fears around colonial sexual and racial transgressions.[140] Shortly before the First World War, the so-called Rechenberg scandal raised a different kind of fear about how to maintain European authority among the colonized African population when the governor of German East Africa was accused of maintaining sexual relations with a male servant. Repeatedly, the ideology of European colonialism as a civilizing mission overseen by white men and supported by white women conflicted with a sense of the colonies as a space of sexual freedoms for straights and queers alike, far away from the strict norms of German bourgeois society.[141]

Laws around intermarriage and ideas of racial purity (*Rassenreinheit*) were a key focus of colonial anxieties. 'Sex ... became racialized and a defining feature of German civilization. In sexual relations it meant that the partner had to be not only of the opposite sex but also white.'[142] Colonialist women and men were involved on both sides of debates around 'race mixing' (*Rassenmischung*) – especially when it came to marriages between a newer generation of 'liberal nationalist' settler men and local women organized along relatively equitable, companionate lines.[143] Concerns about racial mixing ultimately led to bans on intermarriage in many jurisdictions, although these had a shaky basis, for race was not a formal category in federal German law until the Nazi era.[144] Mixed marriages were banned in German Southwest Africa in 1905, German East Africa in 1906 and in 1912 in Samoa, even as the arguments presented for either side differed significantly by location. In German Southwest Africa, some missionaries supported intermarriage to protect Christian African women from exploitation, while opponents feared that it would damage German authority and lead to inferior children.[145] That colony had very low rates of intermarriage (although prostitution and concubinage were widespread), but in Samoa, the practice was widely accepted among both colonialists and locals, particularly between German men and elite, propertied local women – German-Samoan diarist Frieda Zieschank even wrote that she 'got the impression that these mixed marriages were encouraged by those in charge'.[146] This relative acceptance was underlined by German beliefs about Samoa as a kind of Edenic paradise, and by ideas about the racial purity and beauty of the Samoans themselves, even though the practice was ultimately banned by the central Colonial Office.[147]

German women in the colonies assumed various symbolic functions – as protectors of racial purity, hardworking partners of German men and standard bearers of German culture.[148] 'Only the German woman is to be our culture-bearer' (*Kulturträgerin*), declared one opponent of race mixing in 1912; others warned of German men being 'ruined' by keeping house with 'base colored wenches'.[149] German colonialist women viewed themselves as central to protecting the German race, and by extension, nation. As Tina Campt observes, making white female bodies available to German colonists was seen as an important counter 'to the dangerous temptations of nonwhite, indigenous female sexuality', with nonwhite women seen as conduits of pollution and contamination.[150] Recently, some historians have also begun turning their attention beyond such 'mixed' marriages and encounters to gender and sexual relations among the colonized population. Ulrike Schaper examines, for example, how differing norms around things like a woman's age at marriage or bride price caused problems for German colonial rulers in Cameroon, as different legal cultures came into conflict during attempts to 'integrate differing ideas about marriage, gender roles and the regulation of sexuality in order to keep the colony governable'.[151]

Numerous feminists supported the colonial project, including bourgeois feminist leaders Gertrud Bäumer and Minna Cauer, promoting romanticized images of the courageous and patriotic *Farmersfrau*, and even seeing the colonies as spaces of feminist opportunity. As Cauer declared, '[w]omen must immediately count as equal-born, equally enfranchised members in the churches, schools, and municipalities that are just now springing up from new beginnings.'[152] While arguing for women's rights and autonomy, such demands relied on a logic of racial exclusion, with whiteness invoked as a naturalized collectivity to justify women's entry into the public sphere.[153] Bourgeois German ideals of domesticity and gender roles also helped to cement boundaries between Germans and colonial subjects. Even such quotidian practices as pride in keeping a well-stocked cupboard of white linens helped to reinforce ideas of German superiority, creating an 'imagined community of German housewives'.[154]

The colonial experience also impacted the scientific study of non-normative sexualities, and the language of early German homosexual rights movements, which reproduced a similar logic of racial exclusion.[155] Anthropologist Ferdinand Karsch-Haack used the 'same-sex life of primitive peoples' (*Das gleichgeschlechtliche Leben der Naturvölker*), for example, to argue for the natural existence of sexual variation, and colleagues like Bloch and Hirschfeld followed suit – at once celebrating sexual diversity and affirming European superiority.[156] Respectable science was also used to couch the voyeuristic public appetite for tales and images of exotic, forbidden sexualities, both straight and queer. Bare-breasted Samoan women and tattooed men frequently featured on postcards and in *Völkerschauen* (exhibitions of native peoples in the European metropole), and photographs of beautiful exotic youth dotted the pages of homoeroticist journal *Der Eigene*, suggesting the seductive potential of interracial and often intergenerational eroticism away from the tight mores of European Christianity.[157] While images of sexually available colonized women aligned with fantasies of European colonial domination, Tobin finds that things got more complicated when it came to Samoan men, whom a homoerotic colonial gaze viewed as at once feminized and highly sexed.[158] Racialized ideas of gender and sexuality thus fuelled Germany's 'colonial fantasies' in contradictory ways, although almost always underscoring discourses of German nationhood and superiority, and of colonized peoples as 'other'.

War, sex and violence

Concerns about the health and strength of the German 'race' illuminated in colonial contexts gained further impetus as the nation, and soon much of the world, went to war in 1914. At first the war was welcomed by many, with Emperor Wilhelm II describing it as a necessary 'war of nerves' that would put paid to the increasing frivolity and weakness of industrialized German society. Commentators across the political spectrum echoed these sentiments; left-wing sex reformer Henriette Fürth declared in 1915 that, although eleven months of conflict had created new social problems relating to women's marriage prospects and single motherhood, it had also begun to heal the population: 'The physically weak were strengthened by the unaccustomed exertions of military service and endured these with aplomb. Imagined neuroses disappeared in the trenches.'[159]

Such optimism did not last long. It was soon replaced by fears that bourgeois morality and established gender roles would collapse as millions of men went to the front, women moved into more public roles as nurses, tram drivers and factory workers, and couples were separated for months or even years on end. By the end of the conflict, 85 per cent of eligible German males had served in the army, mostly aged between twenty and forty, and many of them married.[160] Hopes for 'steeling' German masculinity faded fast – in his 1920 memoir *In Stahlgewittern* (Storm of Steel), soldier author Ernst Jünger vividly described his experience of shock following a shell hit, when he collapsed into 'convulsive sobbing' followed by 'extreme indifference'.[161] Rather than steel the nation for modernity, industrialized warfare, observes Andreas Killen, produced nervous breakdown on an industrial scale. Troops were sent back from the front with catastrophic war injuries and psychological traumas, and doctors interested in sexual medicine turned their attention to conditions such as war-related impotence and shellshock.[162]

Civil and military authorities invested considerable efforts into policing Germans' wartime sexual expression, as the conflict underlined biopolitical imperatives such as maintaining a strong birth rate.[163] Anxieties about public health centred on the spread of venereal disease (VD), which threatened reproductive potential, and on collapsing marriage and birth rates at a time when the family and children would be sorely needed for postwar regeneration. Conservatives in particular feared 'that a decline in fertility would also mean a decline in industrial and military power'.[164] A new genre of 'social hygiene' films warned troops against the dangers of VD using graphic images of syphilitics or deformed children.[165] Prostitution regulation continued, but was fraught with contradictions. Army authorities feared the spread of VD among soldiers, and distributed condoms to recruits, but they also set up an extensive system of brothels to promote morale. As a result, regulation of sex workers gained in intensity, and would become a major focus of Weimar-era sex reform.[166]

Female sexuality on the home front was a hot topic and source of moral panics in the courts and media, propelled by images of war wives cavorting with the enemy. Many women were prosecuted and publicly shamed for having sexual relations with prisoners of war, with whom many were now working cheek-by-jowl in agricultural and other industries. Seen as threatening the war effort, women were condemned for even minor missteps, such as having 'push[ed] too closely toward the prisoners in an undignified way', and occasionally, even for simple flirtations or letter writing.[167] In Bischofswerda in Saxony, the acting magistrate sentenced two young girls to ten days in prison for flirting with imprisoned French officers, while three others received eight months each for exchanging letters with prisoners in Nuremberg. The German press leapt on such tales of female infidelities, stressing these women's failure to fulfil their citizenship duties based on older bourgeois expectations of female purity and the idealized German *Hausfrau*.[168]

Just as perceptions of wayward women highlight the extent to which gender and sexuality were at the heart of German self-conception in wartime, so too do representations of traumatized, homosexual or gender-diverse soldiers. Jason Crouthamel has examined the 'intimate' histories of life at the front, using letters, diaries and press records to explore how ordinary soldiers experienced their masculinity and sexuality during the war years. He finds that these sources at times reinforced, but at other times challenged norms of the tough, masculine warrior, as men sought spaces of intimacy with women or other men through correspondence, compassion and nurturing. While male-male intimacy sometimes fell under the patriotic guise of 'comradeship', at times it was more obviously sexual.[169] In etchings and paintings of scenes of the 'soldiers' bath' by artists Max Beckmann or Ernst Ludwig Kirchner (see Figure 2.4), soldiers lay aside their uniforms and gather for communal showers, relaxed and stretching in a relief from the physicality and dirt, seemingly enjoying the presence of the naked male bodies around them.[170]

Some people questioned the suitability of homosexual and gender-nonconforming individuals for military service. A few conscripts turned up for mustering dressed in feminine clothing, demanding to fulfil their patriotic duty in other, more gender-appropriate ways such as nursing or the ambulance service, including famous female imitator 'Voo Doo'.[171] Sexologists Ernst Burchard and Magnus Hirschfeld defended the right of 'transvestites' and 'hermaphrodites' to be excluded from military service, not because they were less patriotic, but because of the risk of shaming and other problems in communal military contexts. For many 'transvestites', Burchard declared, reluctance to be engaged in active service 'is not at all a fear of danger or exertions, but rather the feeling of utter unsuitability for continuous life as a man'. On the other hand, he noted that female-to-male transvestites often actively sought out combat roles that affirmed their masculinity.[172] Some homosexual soldiers, on the other hand, insisted that their same-sex leanings made them superior warriors to their heterosexual counterparts. Even the pacifist Hirschfeld defended queer soldiers, noting the enthusiasm of many gay men to commit themselves to the 'higher cause'

FIGURE 2.4 *Ernst Ludwig Kirchner,* Das Soldatenbad, *1915. Public Domain.*
Source: www.smk.dk/Wikimedia Commons.

of national community: 'homosexuality in and of itself thus must by no means determine suitability for military and war service.'[173] During the war, the quarterly reports of the WhK, the homosexual advocacy group that was by now several decades old, emphasized the unique contributions of homosexual combatants. They published homoerotic poems mourning male lovers, stories celebrating newfound relationships and reports of individuals assigned female at birth who had been discovered 'passing' as male soldiers in places as far afield as Turkey and the United States.[174]

Cross-dressing was also tolerated by the authorities to what might today seem a surprising extent. It formed a popular means of entertainment behind the front lines and in prisoner-of-war camps, accepted by military leaders as 'a temporary act of relief from the stress of war'.[175] Most of the people who participated in these performances identified as neither homosexual nor transvestite, but for some who did, they provided much more than temporary 'relief'. Years later, trans author Emi Wolters reflected on how transvestite performers were so appreciated by the men that they even received special privileges: 'Yes, one went so far as to allow these mock women (*Scheindamen*) to dress as women even off the stage.'[176] Such sources point to the unique contributions of trans and queer subjects both on and behind the front line.

The impact of more than four years of violent conflict on gender roles and sexual identities and relationships extended beyond the end of the war and fall of the German Empire in the November Revolution of 1918. In the early Weimar years, doctors would warn of an epidemic of sexual disorders and violence among the millions of returning soldiers, traumatized by the violence of what they had seen and been forced to do.[177] Allegedly promiscuous war wives were attacked for having contributed to the mythical 'stab in the back' of Germany's troops by a disloyal home front, supported by communists and Jews. Women's greater public visibility, meanwhile, fundamentally shifted discussions around the family, marriage and emancipation at the dawning of Germany's first democracy – subjects central to Chapter 3.

* * *

Stöcker's comments at the start of this chapter point to a society not only grappling with the challenges of modernity, but that saw sexual relations as absolutely at the heart of that process. As doctors, scientists, lawyers, feminists and sex reformers started to articulate new ways of thinking about sexual relationships and gender identities, the stability of older institutions and traditions like marriage and regulated prostitution started to waver, as did the bourgeois structures that these had helped to support. Examining the history of sexuality from Germany's unification in 1871 through to the end of the First World War, this chapter has spanned almost five decades of enormous social, political and cultural change: from the rise of the modern industrialized workplace to the growth of a vocal and multifaceted feminist movement, and from late nineteenth-century calls for gay and trans rights to the negotiation of sexual relations and gender norms against the backdrop of colonialism, conscription and war.

Even as monogamous heterosexuality structured around conventional gendered divisions of labour continued to represent the core means by which adult Germans of the Imperial era, particularly those belonging to the middle classes, were expected to express themselves sexually, various factors contributed to a social landscape in which alternatives to inherited norms of bourgeois morality and binary gender became both more visible and more thinkable. Mass population movement from the countryside to the cities, the rise of industrialized workplaces, sex reform and feminist movements and newly 'scientific' ways of thinking about sex and gender created spaces in which older norms could be questioned. Feminists and sex reformers began advocating for heterosexual relations based in a sense of equal partnership, while queer and trans people started to make explicit claims to legal recognition and respectability, often drawing on the authority of medical science. Such developments were crucial to expanding ideas of 'normal' and 'natural' sexual behaviour for heterosexual Germans as well as for an early generation of LGBTIQ activists, even as they remained deeply implicated in Wilhelmine structures privileging the middle over the working classes, white Germans over colonial and racialized subjects, and men over women. In the years after the First World War, they formed the groundwork for wide-ranging debates around sexual norms, rights and respectability in the newly democratized Weimar Republic.

3

Babylon Berlin? Liberation, violence and politics in the Weimar Republic, 1918–33

Walking along the streets of Weimar Berlin, recollected young queer writer and intellectual Klaus Mann – son of one of Germany's most iconic early twentieth-century novelists, Thomas Mann – a street worker bearing a 'supple cane' one evening leered in his direction. She then issued a whispered invitation into his ear, of a kind only possible during the hyperinflation of the nation's currency during the economic crisis year of 1923: 'Want to be my slave? Costs only six billions and a cigarette. A bargain!'[1] This provocative summons could, in turn, easily be imagined as the soundtrack for artist Otto Dix's famous triptych painting 'Metropolis' (*Großstadt*) from 1927 (Figure 3.1). On the left-hand panel, a crippled war veteran in a natty old uniform, downtrodden and likely living on the streets, chats up a lady of the night on one of Berlin's cobbled streets – her profession evident from her exaggerated make up, gaudy yet underdressed attire and flashy mink stole. To the right, another gaudy yet stone-faced woman dressed in bright pastel colours and shapes suspiciously reminiscent of female genitalia stands among other war veterans. Overwhelming modern architectural structures locate these figures firmly in urban space, reminding us, perhaps, of the groundbreaking sci-fi depiction of modernity in Fritz Lang's film *Metropolis* of the same year, in which a cyborg named Maria fires up the underground workers to revolt against the elitism and hedonism of those above ground. Meanwhile, the central panel of the triptych features an energetic jazz band – with a Black instrumentalist underlining the group's American credentials and cosmopolitanism – playing to a well-dressed, wealthy crowd. The viewer's eye is quickly drawn to the figure of an unmistakeable 'New Woman' to the centre-right. Complete with cropped hair, straight-lined and above-the-knee dress, and pink feather fan, she

FIGURE 3.1 *Otto Dix, 'Metropolis' (Triptych), 1927/28.*

Source: © Otto Dix. Verwertungsgesellschaft Bild-Kunst [VG Bild-Kunst]/Copyright Agency, 2022 / akg-images

sashays across the dance floor with no need of a partner, fully aware of her audience.

This image snappily captures the mythos of the city of Berlin as 'whore of Babylon', an urban mishmash of late-night-cabarets and sexual freedoms, always teetering on the brink of degeneration. 'The woman', social commentator Hans Ostwald had declared in 1911, 'is indeed certainly the embodiment of the singular ways of the city', exemplifying how Berlin itself was becoming conflated 'with an image of a sexually voracious and devouring female who comes to symbolize the city's modernity'.[2] Yet while Weimar culture is often presented as a complex collage of optimism and destruction, hedonism and desperation, with sexuality front and centre, this is also a picture that demands critical interrogation. Dix's painting shows the class-specific ways in which female sexuality was commodified, with low and high-class prostitutes framing the middle-class women displaying themselves on the metropolitan marriage market. According to a much-rehearsed cliché, Weimar Berlin was a city 'dancing on the edge of the volcano' until the National Socialist rise to power in early 1933 put the country on a very different, and much more sexually repressive, path.[3]

This mythos has proved enduringly fascinating for audiences over the century since, who look not only to such Weimar-era *femme fatales* as Lola Lola (Marlene Dietrich) in *The Blue Angel* (1930, dir. von Sternberg) or Lulu (Louise Brooks) in *Pandora's Box* (1929, dir. Pabst), but also to iconic reimaginings of this period. Among the most famous is the 1975 Bob Fosse film *Cabaret* starring Liza Minelli as Sally Bowles, which recast Anglo-American novelist Christopher Isherwood's 1930s semi-autobiographical Berlin diaries (in which he famously declared that 'Berlin meant boys'[4]) for a Cold War climate. More recently, record-breaking German television series *Babylon Berlin* (2017–) goes to the heart of the myth, exhilarating in postmodernist samplings of Expressionist aesthetics and Bauhaus architecture, and juxtaposing modern policing technologies with working-class poverty, queer nightclubs, lively youth culture and frenzied cabaret performances. Through central protagonist Charlotte Ritter – new woman, detective, sex worker, partygoer and working-class sister and daughter – today's audiences glimpse a rich array of experiences shaped by sex and gender: from life-threatening backyard abortions to the struggles of intimacy in crowded tenement flats, from hard-working communist doctors defying the strictures of anti-abortion Paragraph 218, to gay men living their lives in tension between greater social openness and ongoing legal constraints, and from women on minimal wages supporting their families through sex work to young people taking weekend trips to the Wannsee for outdoor tête-à-têtes away from the prying eyes of families.

It is important to look beyond simplistic narratives of 'crisis' and resist viewing this period merely from the perspective of the horrors of the Third Reich. As Eric Weitz observes, the Weimar Republic was characterized as much by 'promise' as by 'tragedy':

> The destructiveness of total war and the creativity of revolution ... propelled the work and thinking of Weimar's protagonists, whether they were visionary artists and architects, political reformers and revolutionaries on the left, or thoughtful, authoritarian-minded intellectuals on the conservative right. They were also animated by something deeper ... the recognition that they were living amid the throes of modernity.[5]

A zeal for political and cultural transformation was evident across traditional lines of class, religion and ethnicity – from vegetarians and nudists to flappers and sex reformers. Feminists, social democrats and eugenicists made use of newfound political freedoms to campaign for changes to abortion laws, expand the rights of single mothers, deregulate prostitution and plan a family in a way that suited one's circumstances. As they did, they took the pursuit of modern scientific knowledge about sex out of the clinics, medical journals and consulting rooms of the prewar era and onto the streets.[6]

These are some of the rich landscapes of Weimar sexual modernity and citizenship that shape this chapter. The first section situates us at the birth of the Republic, interrogating the popular icon known as the 'New Woman', shifting ideas of masculinity and heterosexuality, including in the nudist and youth movements, and the flourishing of queer and trans identity politics and cultural scenes within the newly democratic state. The second section turns to the wider sex reform movement that coalesced during these years especially around reproductive questions of birth control and abortion, but also prostitution. Examining these debates reveals the eugenic underpinnings of much of Germany's sexual politics of this era, from nationalist concerns about the declining birth rate through to more 'rationalized' and feminist calls for sex reform based in modern science – developments introduced in Chapter 2. The final section turns to contemporary debates among historians around the extent to which Weimar 'hedonism', tolerance and sexual reforms might be blamed for a conservative 'backlash' that supported the rise of the Nazis. It considers what is at stake for the history of sexuality in making such claims, and how such debates use sexuality to challenge conventional narratives of German history and its major events.

Embracing modern sexual citizenship

Following the long years of conflict, one of the most iconic images associated with the birth of Germany's Weimar Republic is that of Social Democrat Phillip Scheidemann stepping out onto a balcony of the Reichstag in Berlin to declare that the future government of the country should be 'for the people, by the people'. This ushering in of Germany's first democracy was formalized by vote two months later, in January 1919 – although only after thousands lost their lives in the civil strife that had engulfed the country following war's end, including Communist leaders Rosa Luxemburg and Karl Liebknecht. The upheaval culminated in the November Revolution at the end of 1918 that saw the German monarchy overthrown.[7] These are powerful images and momentous events. But in telling the history of this period through the lens of sexuality, we might choose a different moment, from just a few hundred meters up the road, and mere months after Scheidemann stepped out onto that balcony. On 6 July 1919, the world's first Institute for Sexual Science was ceremoniously opened at the central Berlin address In den Zelten 9a and 10 in the suburb of Tiergarten, next to the Spree river and on the site of today's arts and cultural centre *Haus der Kulturen der Welt* (HKW). Overseen by prominent sexologist Magnus Hirschfeld – after whom the HKW bar is now named, as is the embankment across the river – the Institute housed and oversaw exhibitions, education and museum spaces, marital and birth control counselling and advice for queer and trans-identified people. It supported a permanent medical and scientific staff who undertook cutting-edge research and clinical consultations.[8] Both the optimistic programme of scientifically informed sex reform and the violent demise of this Institute in 1933 are indicative of the tension between promise and anxiety that surrounded much Weimar-era discussion of sexuality.

The end of the First World War brought massive demographic shifts to German society, including much talk of a 'surplus of women' (*Frauenüberschuss*) of marriageable age following the millions of male war deaths: between 1.7 and 1.8 million German men had lost their lives in the war, and by 1925 the census counted around two million more women than men aged between twenty and forty.[9] With the birth of the Republic, women gained the right, for the first time, to vote and stand for public office. Many women moved out of more traditional employment as domestic servants or in agriculture during these years into different kinds of work, first in the war industries, and later into factory or low-paid office work. While the visibility of working women gave some the impression that Germans were among the most modern people in the world, 'a closer look reveals that those women remained in the least-unionized, worst-paid, and most-exploited jobs'.[10] This was made worse by 'demobilization' decrees that compelled married women to leave their jobs to make way for returning men.[11] As a result, many women stayed single in order to keep their jobs in teaching or the civil service.[12]

Meanwhile, millions of men had returned home broken, in body, mind or both, having experienced unspeakable violence in the trenches. Much has been said about the brutalizing effects of the war on German men's sexual practices, from the rise of serial murderers such as Peter Kürten to the spate of *Lustmord* or sex murder imagery in the works of prominent Weimar artists such as Dix and George Grosz. Yet alongside narratives of war-induced violence, the sexual history of this period was characterized by hope, experimentation and a sense of emancipation from old bourgeois norms of heterosexual monogamy and nuclear families, where wives were expected to be firmly under the thumbs of their husbands. A distinctly modern approach to sexual relations could be seen in everything from the rise of youth movements to popular tropes of the sexually and financially liberated 'New Woman', well-dressed male 'dandies' and gender-bending cabaret shows.

After almost a half-century of unification under imperial rule, Germany's Weimar Republic marked the nation's first experiment with democracy and the beginnings of a modern welfare state. This swift democratization fuelled the rise of parties across the spectrum, from extreme left to hard right, as citizenship was suddenly expanded to new segments of the population. With the abolition of the Prussian three-class suffrage system and the extension of voting rights to women, 'citizenship emerged as a new political imaginary'.[13] This far-reaching shift in thinking about who could claim a place within the modern German state was crucial for gay and trans rights activism, as earlier models of sexual minority politics (see Chapter 2) combined with a burgeoning queer subculture. Berlin alone boasted an estimated 100 gay, lesbian and trans or gender-diverse clubs by the early 1920s.[14] There was widespread optimism about who could have a political voice in this new Germany. Yet many conservatives were dismayed by the rise of the left, fearing a threat to their old cultural dominance and middle-class comforts – privileges shattered for many with the hyperinflation of 1923, when many lost their life savings.[15] Considerable population movement from the provinces into the cities and into industrialized employment contributed to a sense of rapid modernization. Many people felt older barriers of class, gender and sexuality being challenged in new ways – even as these social categories, along with ideas of race, religion and ability, continued to restrict and shape people's mobility and life choices.

New woman, men and shifting heterosexual ideals

Images of the 'New Woman', so prominently foregrounded in Dix's *Metropolis*, were a regular feature of the Weimar press, films and novels. She was celebrated and reviled alike for modelling a version of sexually emancipated womanhood, freed from the bonds of children and domestic responsibility, earning her own wage and thus able to invest in (at least off-the-shelf versions of) the latest fashions. Often accused of adopting a 'masculinized' look – short haircuts and straight-waisted styles – she soon became a focus of larger cultural anxieties. Whether the emphasis was on the shifting nature of modern heterosexual relations or perceptions of urban degeneration and decline, there was a strong sense that 'gender itself was at the root of Weimar's crisis'.[16] Satirical cartoons showed the genders 'merging' and women competing with men – and often coming out on top – everywhere from the sporting field to the workplace (see Figure 3.2).

'This New Woman', as Atina Grossmann astutely observed in a key early study of this sociocultural phenomenon, 'was not merely a media myth or a demographer's paranoid fantasy, but a social reality. ... She existed in office and factory, bedroom and kitchen, just as surely as in café, cabaret and film.'[17] Such cultural icons and questioning of female gender norms, Jochen Hung has more recently pointed out, 'are not passively consumed, but co-constructed by the audience at which they are aimed'.[18] We need to take seriously both real and perceived shifts in gender and sexual relations: the ways in which they impacted on how people structured their intimate lives and relationships, and the often quite deliberate ways in which social actors intervened in dominant social norms.

The New Woman was a sexually contested figure, in ways that intersected with ideas of class, religion, race and nation. For conservatives, she was closely bound up with biopolitical fears that Germany's women, especially since the war's end, had forgotten their obligations to reproduce for the health of the nation and *Volk*. In contrast, progressives situated changing gender ideals in relation to recent events such as the Russian Revolution of 1917, issuing in new Soviet ideals of marriage and sexuality, including free unions, instant divorce and legal abortion – ideals that heavily influenced the German Communist party (KPD) during these years.[19] Conservative fears were compounded by moralizing debates around prostitution, pornography and the spread of VD, especially syphilis and gonorrhoea, known to cause infertility and birth defects.[20] Overtones of homophobia and antisemitism fed into these tropes of gender and morality in crisis, and

FIGURE 3.2 *'What Do You Say about Fräulein Mia?'* Berliner Illustrirte Zeitung, *13 November 1927.*

Source: Staatsbibliothek zu Berlin – Preußischer Kulturbesitz, Signatur: 2" Ad 600

contributed to a 'stab in the back' legend that blamed women, Jews and other groups for allegedly undermining the sacrifice of German men at the front by joining revolutionary movements and indulging in the freedoms of the home front. This myth conveniently overlooked the thousands of Jewish soldiers and female workers who had also served the war effort.[21] Popular culture images, meanwhile, frequently suggested that this New Woman had turned her attentions away from men altogether and preferred the company of her girlfriends, or linked her to stereotypical tropes of Jewishness such as dark, curly hair, intellectualism and the nervous condition of 'neurasthenia' seen to haunt urban 'degenerates'.[22] At the same time, Jewish women themselves engaged with this new model of femininity in self-reflexive ways, consciously putting not only their bodies and sexualities, but also often their Jewishness, on display, 'by choosing not to pass, or by covering Jewish-coded traits only in certain situations'.[23]

Clichés of sexual emancipation among Germany's young women had some grounding in shifting social realities. In 1932 the Frankfurt Institute for Sociology interviewed a range of medical specialists, who overwhelmingly believed that women across all classes – and not just the proletariat, long viewed as having more relaxed views – were demonstrating more matter-of-fact, positive attitudes towards premarital sex.[24] Such attitudes were a long way from the 'double standard' that had dominated nineteenth-century bourgeois models of sexuality. Sometimes they even shocked older women's rights activities and sex reformers, marking something of a generational split between the perceived 'old-fashioned spinsters' of the bourgeois women's movement on the one hand, who were more concerned with improving the rights of married and career women, and younger 'unpolitical, consumerist, and media-mad' sisters, on the other.[25] Jill Suzanne Smith points to the common 'playful' confusion between prostitutes and 'respectable' women in Weimar popular culture, her work demonstrating that the boundaries around female sexual behaviour were changing fast.[26] At the same time, the growing economic insecurity of working-class women, especially during the inflation crisis of 1923 and following the financial collapse in 1929, meant that occasional sex work to supplement income was a reality rather than a game for many women – and for quite a few men and gender-diverse people as well.[27] This included many women from rural areas – by 1925, almost 60 per cent of Berlin's regulated prostitutes or *Kontrollmädchen* were from small towns and the provinces.[28]

Images of men and masculinity were similarly changing at speed. Some representations were decidedly negative, as commentators linked a perceived increase in male sexual brutality – vividly captured in the aforementioned sex murder images – to the violence experienced during the war. For commentators such as Hirschfeld or criminologist Eric Wulffen, war neuroses manifested themselves in men trying to replicate the violence of the front in postwar domestic life, while Sigmund Freud added the 'death instinct' as a central psychoanalytic concept during these years.[29] Some historians have also argued that the 'exaggerated' virility of Weimar-era militaristic groups such as the right-wing *Freikorps* and early National Socialists was not only a response to the war defeat, but also to widespread sexual problems and a weakness of the male ego.[30]

But this doesn't tell the whole story about either Weimar or wartime masculinity. For many men, their experience of the conflict had been shaped by a more domesticated sense of soldierly brotherhood and camaraderie, as a 'warm niche' of intimacy provided an emotional bulwark against the 'coldness of the technologized war of mass destruction'.[31] This was evidenced in letters and diaries from the front, but also in postwar reflections on the war years, which complicated ideas of 'manliness' reliant on steely emotional and physical hardness. As Thomas Kühne points out: 'The language of intimacy and the pathos of tenderness, care, empathy, and even love that permeate the evocation of comradeship in testimonies and recollections of former soldiers cloud the emotional and moral ambiguity of manliness.'[32] Meanwhile, a younger generation of men coming of age in the Weimar years was often depicted as softened or 'feminized' and satirized in images of the monocled, fashion-conscious male dandy or the listless urban flâneur – a quiet but pervasive counterpart to the widespread discussion of the 'masculinization' of women.[33]

Media depictions of the Weimar heterosexual couple explored what such upheavals of gender might look like for modern sexual relations. Photographs and cartoons visualized both a sense of optimism about growing equality between the sexes, and anxiety about a softening gender binary, with men and women shown in identical haircuts, outfits and expectations. Such images could evoke a giggle, but also provided readers a focus for thinking through their own views on marriage and heterosexual attraction.[34] The Weimar press thus both reflected and shaped popular ideas about femininity, masculinity and heterosexuality.

Nudism, youth and censorship

These ideas were explored by a younger generation particularly in the context of the nudist or 'free body culture' (*Freikörperkultur*) and hiking movements, and offer telling examples of how the appeal of new types of social organization intersected with 'rationalized' ideas about gender and sexuality in early twentieth-century Germany. Socialist nudists, in particular, had much in common with the sex reform movement, as they argued that the turn towards nature, which 'stands above morality ... and is the sole foundation of health', was a way of helping industrial workers overcome the irrational human sex drive to become healthy and eugenically purposeful members of society.[35] Such statements reveal how the language of eugenics had filtered into even left-wing reformist rhetoric, as we already saw happening in Chapter 2. Not yet overshadowed by the legacy of Nazi genocide, eugenics ideas were promoted everywhere from trade union journals to the travelling exhibitions of the Dresden-based German Hygiene Museum.[36] Yet *Freikörperkultur* was also popular among some nationalist, right-wing groups, in ways that foreshadowed Nazi ideology with their focus on the physical strength and renewal of the racial body by turning to sunlight and nature.[37] As nudism grew into a something like a mass movement, antinudist rhetoric also increased. The town newspaper in one small Bavarian town in 1925, learning that a bourgeois nudist group was meeting nearby, warned readers 'energetically and in public against the further dirtying of our shelters and mountains. Our nation sees this public "naked culture" as pure swinishness.'[38] Opposition like this came particularly from Catholic morality organizations, but also from the ultraconservative press associated with the German National People's Party.

If nudism could be used to argue both for and against nationalist ideas, it could also be used both to contest and shore up norms of gender appearance. While often celebrated as promoting a more emancipatory relationship to the body freed from the compulsions of clothing, scholars influenced by Michel Foucault's writings on discipline also point to ways in which public nudity could reflect an internalization of norms around sexual control and visibility. From this perspective, promoting an open gaze on the body and its movements during activities such as gymnastics – promoted in long-running journals such as *Schönheit* (Beauty) – could function as a normalizing technology, as individuals judged themselves against perceived ideals of physical strength and beauty.[39] But the nudist movement also bolstered ideas of gender merging and equality: 'Men and women are becoming more similar to each other,' declared one 1923 issue of body culture magazine *Licht-Luft-Leben* (Light-air-life).[40]

Hiking similarly brought together the celebration of youth and physical strength with mixed ideas about national renewal, degeneration and homoeroticism. The 'pesky' adolescent sex drive was considered a chief culprit of teenage irrationality. Hiking, it was hoped, would divert young people's physical energies towards the cultivation of discipline, patriotism and connection to nature.[41] Psychologists and sociologists turned their attention to 'youth studies' (*Jugendkunde*), and middle-class activists towards the youth cultivation or *Jugendpflege* movement. They expanded older notions of youth welfare into a vision of cultivating respectable adult citizens, and their work spanned the political spectrum, from Social Democratic to conservative-militarist groups.[42]

In the later years of the Republic, the youth movement became embroiled in heated censorship debates around the *Schund und Schmutz* ('filth and trash') legislation of 1926 ostensibly aimed at protecting Germany's youth from devious influences, particularly pornographic or 'obscene' books and films.[43] The cinema was of particular concern as a wildly popular new form of entertainment, with over 300 theatres in Berlin alone by the early 1920s. Between late 1918 and May 1920 around 150 'social hygiene' and 'sex enlightenment' films had been screened across the country, offering titillating takes on themes such as VD prevention, prostitution, abortion and homosexuality under a loose guise of public health education.[44] It was no accident that the cinema was among the first targets of the reintroduction of censorship in 1920, amidst an uproar around the first film in the world to directly address questions of gay rights, *Anders als die Andern* (Different from the Others, 1919, dir. Oswald). Later, the attention of *Schund und Schmutz* campaigners shifted to pornography.[45] The late-Weimar censorship panic also helped to propel the youth movement's program of social order and moral decency, as the state invested in 'social-hygienic and youth welfare work in an attempt to get young men, uprooted by the war, back on the right track'.[46]

Yet the hiking and youth movements also opened up new spaces of sexual exploration, especially when it came to same-sex desire. In 1912, Hans Blüher's book *The German Wandervogel Movement as an Erotic Phenomenon* provocatively theorized the homoerotic attraction between (male) teenage 'ramblers' and their adult male leaders, in a movement that emphasized youth leading youth.[47] And even though these back-to-nature movements have sometimes been taken as evidence of an 'antimodernist' reaction to an increasingly urbanized and rationalized society, seeking a return to a premodern ideals of an imagined, provincial German *Heimat*, recent scholarship has shown that they were in fact 'far more ambivalent spaces of experiment and reform' – spaces in which *'acceptance* of the modern became negotiated and embraced', including new ways of behaving, of relating to the environment and of relating sexually to one another.'[48]

While Blüher celebrated the hiking and youth movements as spaces of male-male eros, he argued against all-female leagues, believing that Eros could not exist in the same way between women. His antifeminist stance was contradicted by the high numbers of girls and young women in these movements, which only increased following the war years. As in male groups, the movement provided spaces for celebrating female intimate friendships, particularly via ideas of a 'pedagogical Eros' between older and younger women. Viennese psychologist Charlotte Bühler described this as combining self-control, self-education, sacrifice and an absence of sexual feelings with the cultivation of femininity and love, all within a safe space of respectability and discipline.[49]

Although female same-sex sexuality remained relatively taboo in the writings of women associated with the movement, it was not unusual for girls to talk about their 'crushes' on other girls.[50] Such 'schwärmen' was immortalized in the infatuation of schoolgirl Manuela for teacher Elisabeth von Bernburg in the 1931 film *Girls in Uniform* (*Mädchen in Uniform*, dir. Leontine Sagan). Bourgeois feminist leader Gertrud Bäumer (who lived in a 'romantic friendship' with fellow feminist Helene Lange) later reminisced about the *Schwärmerei* shared by a number of schoolgirls for their gym teacher: 'for three years she was the centre of our being. Not an hour went by – literally – that you did not think of her; you never crossed the street without cherishing the silent hope of meeting her.'[51] Yet such youthful female same-sex desires were rarely treated with much earnestness. Some even considered them impossible – one theologian bluntly dismissed female homosexuality as 'generally out of the question'. Youth psychologists also paid more attention to boys than girls, observes Javier Sampier Vendrell in his studies of Weimar adolescent sexuality, and tended to trivialize both female homosexuality in particular, and adolescent homosexuality in general as temporary psychological 'perversities' rather than permanent congenital conditions.[52] In Weimar's consolidating queer scene, on the other hand, images of gender variance and same-sex attraction provided very different kinds of spaces for experimenting with non-normative appearances, relationships and forms of belonging.

Queer and trans identity politics, Weimar style

During the interwar years the fledgling LGBTIQ political and cultural movements of the early twentieth century underwent rapid expansion, dramatically widening visions of sexual citizenship in the context of German modernity and democracy. Joining prewar groups such as the Scientific Humanitarian Committee (WhK) and Adolf Brand's masculinist 'Community of the Special/Autonomous' (Gemeinschaft der Eigenen, GdE) were several new national 'friendship' associations: the League for Human Rights (Bund für Menschenrechte, BfM) and the German Friendship Alliance (Deutscher Freundschafts-Verband, DFV). Despite ideological differences – the WhK took a liberal and scientific stance; the GdE a nationalist tone focused on 'masculinist' culture, while the new friendship associations adopted a broadly liberal platform – all had their sights on the social discrimination stemming from Germany's anti-sodomy laws embedded in Paragraph 175. At the same time, the new friendship organizations embraced a much broader, mass membership than either the WhK or GdE, forming grassroots branches across the country, and combining political and educational platforms with organized social groups. By the mid-1920s, all major German cities had at least one such group, and despite internal conflicts over direction and structure, these organizations could boast an estimated 48,000 members by the end of the decade. Most members were middle-class or lower-middle-class white-collar workers, but quite a few also came from the trades and working classes. One 1926 survey showed that members came from all political affiliations, with as many as 30 per cent identifying with right-wing, *völkisch* views, alongside many who held more predictably left-wing, social democratic or communist allegiances.[53]

Reduced censorship, new mass media possibilities and an expanded sense of citizenship rights all fuelled this expansion of queer culture and politics. The experience of the First World War had also played a role, having offered gay men, in particular, new models of masculine comradeship and a chance to prove their commitment to higher, collective ideals: 'the fact that gay men sacrificed themselves alongside heterosexual men, and shared the spiritual bond of "comradeship," gave them the confidence and credibility to "come out" in Weimar society as legitimate, and equal, members of the nation'.[54] A key figure in this scene was Berlin businessman, gay rights activist and publisher Friedrich Radszuweit, who initiated the establishment of the BfM in 1923 as an offshoot and competitor of the DFV.[55] This group was significant, observes Glenn Ramsay, for the way it signalled a move away from earlier divisions between 'the scientific-effeminate and cultural-masculinist poles of the debate over rights'.[56] The BfM both embraced and actively produced a decidedly commercial queer culture, from bars and balls to subscription-based magazines. One important scene leader was Lotte (sometimes Lothar) Hahm, who led BfM divisions for female homosexuals and transvestites (see Figure 3.3).

Hahm ran their own club and cabaret shows as 'an energetic master of ceremonies at balls, president of the Ladies' Club Violetta, and "captain" of the annual steamboat trip on the Spree river' at which partygoers could, Hahm promised, 'dance the night away until 5 a. m.' A snappy dresser and

FIGURE 3.3 *Lotte Hahm in* Die Freundin, *1929.*

Source: Staatsbibliothek zu Berlin – Preußischer Kulturbesitz, Signatur: 4" Kd 1300/374

sharp political voice, Hahm represented a positive 'figure of identification and emulation', as Marti Lybeck points out, for both women and gender nonconforming people experimenting with gender-variant styles and queer desires.[57]

The new Weimar constitution of 1919 had boldly declared that 'censorship does not take place'.[58] Although in practice there were limitations to this principle – as the banning of *Anders als die Andern* had shown – this provided an important legal basis for a dramatically enlarged queer publishing scene during the 1920s.[59] An impressive range of queer publications was produced and publicly sold and marketed at newsstands during this decade – around thirty in total – even if many occasionally came into conflict with the censor's knife, especially following the *Schund und Schmutz* laws of 1926.[60] One example was weekly magazine *Die Freundschaft* (Friendship), established by Karl Schultz in Berlin in 1919, which targeted (unusually during this period) both gay women and men from all social classes with its combination of fiction, poems, essays and advice. With an initial print run of 20,000 it far outdid Brand's *Der Eigene*, and continued with only a short hiatus during the 1923 inflation until February 1933. Other magazines aimed primarily at men soon followed, such as the hugely popular entertainment magazine *Die Insel* (The Island), with its penchant for sparsely dressed boy models, and the more literary *Uranus* (1921–3). *Die Freundin* (Girlfriend, 1924–33) and *Frauenliebe* (Womanly Love, later *Garçonne*) were among several papers aimed at women.[61]

A development worthy of particular emphasis is that for the first time in the world, a number of magazines and supplements were produced during this decade specifically targeting a trans or gender-diverse identified readership. These adopted Hirschfeld's terminology, with names such as *Der Transvestit* (Transvestite), *Welt der Transvestiten* (Transvestites' World) and *Das 3. Geschlecht* (The Third Sex), but their content extended well beyond the clinic to address legal and social injustices, offer advice on topics such as dressing appropriately or avoiding run-ins with the police and summarize the latest research on gender and hormones. They published many autobiographical pieces, often sent in by readers of the magazines, exploring the process of coming out as gender diverse or trans:

> Every sincere transvestite knows what they are: the first 'misunderstood' childhood inclination, the failed 'first' 'true' love, the first doubt, the horrible awakening and – the struggles, the hot, bitter, secret, lonely struggles, and if all goes well … the final secret, conscious confession to oneself![62]

The queer and trans magazines used a subscriber as well as newsstand system to reach thousands of readers outside of Germany's major cities and the Berlin queer scene that had produced them. After all, not everyone could spend their after-work freedoms whiling away the hours at clubs such as lesbian hotspot Die Zauberflöte (The Magic Flute), which as scene chronicler Ruth Roellig observed, fostered a distinction 'between "Boys" (Bubis) – the masculine – and "Girls" (Mädis) – the feminine women' via its well-known 'bell dance', in which the 'Bubis all received bells to ring in their Mädis.' The transvestite club 'Eldorado', meanwhile, was also popular with tourists from the provinces of all sexual persuasions.[63] These clubs found a sympathetic visual chronicler in artist Jeanne Mammen, whose images such as 'In the Ladies' Club' or 'Transvestite Bar' frequently appeared in the Weimar press. This queer underworld was also celebrated in Berlin's cabaret culture. Marlene Dietrich had a successful stage number with Margo Lion singing a song about 'best girlfriends' who liked to go shopping and more, while the popular 'Lila Lied' (Lavender Song) playfully celebrated a sense of queer pride: 'We *are* different from the others/Who only love while marching in step with morality.'[64]

The classifieds pages of the queer publications reveal the sense of an imagined queer and gender-diverse community that soon expanded not only across Germany, but beyond its borders as well. People wrote in letters and posted advertisements seeking erotic partners or paid employment – including transwomen seeking work in domestic service – from as far afield as Celle, Kiel, Switzerland, Italy and the United States. The personal ads often subtly signalled class preferences through terms such as 'educated' or 'well situated', underlining the Weimar queer media's overwhelmingly middle-class orientation. 'Frankfurt a.M. Where can a lady, 28 years old, find social contacts with similarly well situated ladies or a small social circle?,' asked one advertisement; another submitted by a 'Transvestite living according to their predisposition as a lady … longs for exchange of ideas only with an educated, understanding, internally mature lady or transvestite with the goal of later marriage.'[65] Short stories in the magazines offered further demonstration of how important such ads could be in enabling queer connections: in one tale in Die Freundin, two women working in the same pub are attracted to each other but fear rejection due to social stigma. Each sends off personal ads to the very magazine in which this story was published, resulting in a fortuitous exchange of letters, a first date, a mutual coming out and ultimately, the two becoming a happy couple.[66]

This new media landscape thus actively created a sense of queer belonging in Weimar Germany, even if that sense of belonging largely affirmed middle-class ideals of citizenship and respectability. The development of a new norm of queer respectability was reproduced in visual form as well, through photographs of neatly dressed boyish female Garçonnes (the name of another homosexual women's magazine) in suits and ties, or of transwomen donning low-key, modern feminine styles. Editors and contributors repeatedly urged readers to learn how to 'pass' or at least not stand out in public to avoid awkward encounters. White, middle-class boundaries of queer visibility were also policed via pieces ostracizing individuals involved in sex work or criminal activity, and by the relative absence of contributions from working-class queers or queers and transpeople of colour.[67] In 1929, such emphasis on queer respectability would be central to the most significant gay rights development of the late-Weimar period: the almost-successful bid to dramatically curtail Paragraph 175. This action is discussed in more detail below, as we turn from the specifics of queer and trans identity politics to the broader Weimar sex reform movement.

Coalitions, conflicts and compromise: Sex reform in the welfare state

Debates around population politics and the spread of venereal disease took a central stage in the new era of Weimar democracy, helping to shape the relationship between individual citizens and the welfare state. Shifting expectations of gender and sexual equality and citizenship fuelled a burgeoning sex reform movement, as interwar activists and commentators actively renegotiated norms around heterosexual activity and reproduction inside and outside of marriage. Together, they formed a broad, often coalitional but at times deeply conflicted movement advocating for a 'rationalized' modern sexuality. While rationalization was a concept coming out of modern, mechanized production processes, it could also apply to very different aspects of life during the 1920s, from the organization of the modern household through labour-saving devices to urban planning, and from education reform to the aesthetic of 'New Sobriety' (*Neue Sachlichkeit*) – a cool, pragmatic, pared-back approach to art and life alike. Rationalizing sexuality meant challenging old taboos and restrictions, and drawing on 'enlightened', scientific ideas about individual and public health. It involved feminists, socialists, educators, doctors, representatives of government agencies, morality campaigners and pharmaceutical company advocates, and crossed party-political lines.[68] 'What happened inside the home', remarks historian Geoff Eley, was now 'vital to the public interest'.[69]

Sex reform was, observed one Berlin gynaecologist in 1932, in many ways a 'people's movement' for birth control and sex education; it was also linked to the international birth control movement and figures such as Margaret Sanger.[70] Activities ranged from courses for teachers on sexual ethics and pedagogy to public screenings of *Aufklärungsfilme*: films aimed at educating young people on sexual questions and dangers, as well as campaigning around issues such as abortion, prostitution, marriage and maternal health. Demands for a rational, modern approach to sex reform were closely related to Germany's recent history. The war years and mass migration to the cities had propelled rising rates of venereal disease and a declining birth rate – already a source of panic for nationalist politicians and moral campaigners before the war, as we saw in Chapter 2. The bitter war defeat and 2.4 million casualties only heightened concerns about the future of the family as the basis of a strong postwar society.[71] Notably, these fears contrasted with the concerns about *over*population that had dominated earlier European debates, famously charted in Thomas Malthus's *Essays on the Principles of Population* (1798). Between 1800 and 1900 the German population had more than doubled from around 25 to 56 million, but by the turn of the century, the fertility rate was dropping sharply. That abortion and contraception were also widely practiced in the countryside and smaller towns is evident from the declining difference in the birth rate between cities and rural areas.[72]

Many doctors viewed such population trends through a lens of 'social hygiene', the understanding that medicine had a broader social role to play in fostering the physical and moral health of the family and wider community, and not just that of the individual.[73] Similarly, while some reformers prioritized individual well-being and freedoms, including women's right to control their fertility, others emphasized the health of the larger population. More often, though, these arguments about individual and collective responsibility merged, in what Atina Grossmann describes as a 'motherhood-eugenics consensus' running through the larger movement: 'Across a wide political spectrum, they [sex reformers] shared a vision of a "healthy" modern society in which access to legal abortion, contraception, eugenic sex education, and general social welfare would assure a new "rational" social order that was both stable and humane.'[74] The movement emphasized sexual duties rather than rights, the desirability and naturalness of motherhood – including a need to protect vulnerable unmarried mothers – and the importance to society of healthy offspring. Fertility had become a collective concern, and as Annette Timm observes, these goals were seen as legitimate grounds for state and welfare intervention. Despite all manner of political divisions, there was agreement that 'because of its implications for the future of the German family and nation, sexual decision making was too important to be left entirely up to the individual'.[75] The Weimar sex reform movement called for sexual relations based on equality between the sexes, the freedom to choose the size of one's family and make decisions about one's own body, and ways to promote the quality, and not just the quantity, of Germany's next generation.

Marriage and birth control

After the war, while many young people still got married, they were tending to have far fewer children – certainly not enough to compensate for war-time losses. Together with fears of an abortion 'scourge', this contributed to popular ideas of Germany as a *Volk ohne Jugend*, or 'people without a youth'. By the end of the Republic in 1933, the birth rate had declined from a postwar peak of 25.9 per 1000 to 14.7, the lowest in Europe, and was especially low in the cities (9.4 per 1000 in Berlin), reinforcing stereotypes of these as 'corrupt' or 'degenerate' spaces.[76] It is not surprising, then, that marriage and reproduction became important topics of reformist and feminist energy.

Whereas the earlier German Civil Code of 1900 had given husbands the final word, Article 119 of the Weimar Constitution now declared that marriage, as the basis of the family and the nation, should be founded on gender equality.[77] This was an example of using the law to encourage progressive shifts in gender norms and heterosexual relations. And even if there is always significant wriggle room between official decrees and how people actually structured their relationships, popular marriage manuals also reflected growing expectations that marriage should be erotically satisfying for both parties, and that this was a topic that could be (reasonably) openly discussed. Dutchman Th. Van de Velde's *The Ideal Marriage* (*Die vollkommene Ehe*) provided young couples with detailed advice on 'physiology and technique' when it appeared in German in 1926, following in the vein of other internationally successful books on marriage and family planning such as Marie Stopes' *Married Love* (1918).[78] Such books, scholars have shown, formed part of a larger project of securing heterosexual ideals such as simultaneous orgasm as 'normal' and 'natural' in the early twentieth century.[79] Marriage and sex education manuals and new journals such as *Sexual-Hygiene* were especially important in bringing information about modern contraception methods to working-class couples, including those in the countryside who might previously have had to put their trust in travelling salespeople.[80]

Some couples during this period took up the idea of 'companionate marriage', which involved consciously rejecting older patriarchal ideals and committing to live together and trial their compatibility before formalizing their relationship or having children. This model, described by American judge Ben Lindsey in his book *Companionate Marriage*, was explained by one commentator in the German press in 1929 as follows:

> If the first rush of love has passed and the young people have been disappointed in their expectations, the companionate marriage can be dissolved quite easily. All that is required for divorce is a simple, mutual agreement. Nor is there any obligation of support, since they have no responsibility for children and the wife has continued in her occupation.[81]

Many couples – whether or not they viewed their relationship as 'companionate' – used contraception to avoid reproduction altogether: by 1933, around a third of marriages in Berlin and Hamburg were childless.[82] Compared to the nineteenth century, families were becoming smaller, children being born later and women younger when they completed their childbearing. Conservatives lamented these trends, but they had benefits for women's health and careers, with less time spend on reproductive labour.[83] Some chose not to marry at all. In particular, some intellectual and professional women, as well as some committed to working-class politics – for the Left had by this stage developed forceful critiques of marriage as an institution – preferred to live in non-state-sanctioned 'marriage-like' arrangements with so-called 'life companions' or *Lebensgefährten*.[84]

Across the country during the later Weimar years, a wave of sexual and birth control counselling centres was set up to support these ideas of rationalized sexuality and family planning. Often the doctors and staff working at these centres drew on eugenic or 'racial hygiene' ideas in promoting the health of any offspring.[85] As early as 1907, Helene Stöcker's League for Maternal Protection, introduced in Chapter 2, had proposed that couples contemplating marriage obtain a statement attesting to their fitness before they could wed. This was supported by various morality leagues and pronatalist groups, even though it would have actively discriminated against the mentally ill and those suffering hereditary diseases.[86] While the government of the time did not support the League's proposal, the Interior Minister did agree in 1921 that all couples should be given a leaflet outlining the dangers of venereal and other forms of disease, and this was followed in 1926 by the foundation of locally run marriage guidance clinics.[87] Over 100 were established that year, rising to around 200 by 1933, including quite a few in rural areas and small towns. They particularly targeted working-class clients, following the motto that it was 'better to prevent than to abort'.[88]

Historians are somewhat divided on the goals and success of these clinics. Grossmann argues that they were set up as an official alternative to the birth control clinics being established by other, non-state organizations, and that the people who visited the centres generally had pragmatic reasons for doing so, being 'more interested in safe inexpensive contraceptives and general sex advice than in premarital health certificates or testing their physical fitness for marriage and procreation'.[89] Cornelie Usborne suggests that the Prussian clinics attracted only a 'derisively small number of clients', whereas Paul Weindling sees them as important forerunners to the Nazis' 'racial health' clinics, helping to transform eugenics into a mainstream concern.[90] Certainly, the clinics' embrace of eugenic ideas was based on troubling racializing and ableist assumptions. As welfare measures to support society's most vulnerable gained speed under the often left-leaning governments of the Republic, some also feared that measures such as support for adequate housing, the unemployed, single mothers and young people would work against Social Darwinist principles of natural selection and promote weaker, less 'gifted' offspring.[91] It is important to remember, though, that such eugenic ideas were shared by many left-wing reformers, feminists, Social Democrats and Communists as well as nationalist conservatives, and were not yet thoroughly infused by their blatant abuse by the National Socialists after 1933 – who ultimately introduced a certificate of the kind Stöcker had earlier proposed.[92] We must also recognize the genuinely emancipatory impetus of much Weimar-era sex reform, and the extent to which Nazi social policy represented 'a radical break' with these trends.[93]

While the new sex and marital counselling centres improved access to birth control across class divides, contraception and abortion remained highly regulated and contested. Advertising contraceptives was in something of a grey legal area. As early as the 1880s, manufacturers had circulated cheap mail-order pamphlets disguised as Neo-Malthusian literature: a movement that, as the name suggests, was worried that overpopulation would diminish population health.[94] The obscenity clause of the 1900 Penal Code subsequently banned the advertising of 'objects intended for indecent use', and Chancellor von Bülow even proposed banning contraception and abortifacient devices altogether in the years before the war, although this was ultimately rejected.[95] After the war, and before censorship restrictions were sharpened in 1926, ads for 'rubberwares' or cures for 'women's troubles' were not unusual.[96] By the early 1930s, as socialist doctor and sex educator Max Hodann declared to his audience at the World League for Sexual Reform conference in London, contraceptives could be sold and openly discussed in Germany, but the '*advertising* of these remedies, such as in window displays of drugstores and pharmacies, is forbidden on the grounds of creating a "public nuisance"!' This, he noted, might be hard to understand for 'our friends in English-speaking countries', where the birth control movement had made significant inroads into public opinion.[97]

Condoms were exempted from restrictions on contraception because of their perceived role in battling VD (and during the war had been made readily available to soldiers).[98] They were also a massively profitable business. The Berlin-based Fromms company produced the world's first branded condom, selling around 24 million annually and becoming a household name: 'Wenn's euch packt, nehmt Fromms Act' ('When you're aroused, look to Fromms'), sang the cabarettists of the late 1920s.[99] The most popular form of contraception, though, remained the withdrawal method, *coitus interruptus*. While this relied on agreement among couples and was criticized by some doctors as leading to nervous exhaustion or 'neurasthenia', it was practical in that it didn't require visiting a doctor and easily avoided legal sanctions.[100]

Abortion campaigns and working-class voices

Sex reformers campaigned vigorously against the heavy legal penalties prohibiting abortion under Paragraph 218 of the Criminal Code of 1871, which pushed many women into unsafe procedures. The years before the war had already seen an inquiry into what many considered the alarming medical treatment of 'miscarriages' and whether these were being facilitated by physicians; in 1915 the trial of Munich doctor and abortion campaigner Hope Bridges Adams-Lehmann showcased the relative ease with which women could obtain surgical abortions at that time – despite it being a criminal offence. Prewar studies by Berlin sexologist Max Marcuse had also shown the extent to which working-class women relied on abortion to regulate family size, as an alternative to contraception, with female networks helping to facilitate backyard procedures. Abortions increased during the Weimar years, and so did the pushback against what many considered a highly punitive and dangerous law, especially during the final years of the Republic. In the early 1930s a concerted parliamentary and mass campaign to reform or abolish Paragraph 218 saw feminists join forces with women and socialist doctors in the fight for safe, legal abortions. In 1930, 356 of 476 female doctors in Berlin signed a petition to the Reichstag to fully repeal the abortion law.[101]

A regular topic in communist papers such as *Die Rote Fahne* (Red Flag), the daily tragedies caused by the punitive law were also thematized in popular culture, including the play *Cyankali* (Cyanide) by socialist doctor and playwright Friedrich Wolf (Figure 3.4). In 1931 Wolf was arrested for assisting with medical abortions, along with fellow socialist doctor Else Kienle, who united feminist and socialist principles in demanding: 'What use is suffrage to women if they are to remain helpless baby machines?'[102] Kienle began a hunger strike from prison in protest, which the *Rote Fahne* declared 'must serve as an alarm for the working population to be even more decisive in fighting the battle against the paragraph of shame 218'.[103]

Wolf's play gained international attention, telling the tragic tale of twenty-year-old pregnant Hete, who together with her boyfriend Paul is suddenly made unemployed, their families unable to contemplate an extra mouth to feed – a situation that had already driven a neighbour to suicide. The play contrasted the relative ease with which the rich could access abortions with the often life-threatening conditions under which working-class women underwent these procedures – and the complicity of middle-class doctors in facilitating this situation. When Hete's physician Dr Moeller refuses to help, even while acknowledging that 'over ten thousand German mothers die yearly of such inexpert treatment by non-doctors', she retorts in a desperate rage: 'There are so many of you doctors in Germany ... thousands of doctors ... and this is how you leave people to die?' After a botched attempt at inducing abortion herself, Hete accidentally takes an overdose of the abortifacient and deadly poison cyanide, and her mother and boyfriend are arrested for assisting with this 'crime'.[104]

The hardship caused by Paragraph 218 also featured in the strongly Communist-influenced 1932 film *Kuhle Wampe oder Wem gehört die Welt?* (Kuhle Wampe or who does the world belong to?), directed by Slatan Dudow with a script co-written by Bertolt Brecht. It shows a lower middle-class family, the Bönikes, fall into financial straits during the Depression, with daughter Anni suddenly finding herself pregnant and opting for termination. This choice enables her to escape a shotgun engagement and find a sense

FIGURE 3.4 *Cover of Friedrich Wolf's play,* Cyankali, *1929.*

Source: Staatsbibliothek zu Berlin – Preußischer Kulturbesitz, Abteilung Historische Drucke, Signatur: 19 ZZ 9994.

of purpose through communist sporting clubs and workers groups.[105] Such popular culture representations reflect the growing political voice of Germany's working classes – particularly amidst the tragic economic realities of the late Weimar era, with left-wing parties gaining over a third of the total vote in the November 1932 elections. They also depict a new common-sense approach to women's rights to make decisions about their own bodies, sexual relationships and their consequences. In such ways, two groups who had only recently gained access to citizenship rights in the context of Weimar democracy and modernity – women and workers – put pressure on older normative expectations of maternal femininity.

Moral panics, religion and race

While rationalized, class-conscious understandings of sexuality were gaining strength, religion continued to play a significant – and often underestimated – role for many citizens of the new Republic. Churches and religiously affiliated organizations, including Catholic, Protestant and Jewish branches of the women's movement, heavily influenced public discussions of reproduction and sexuality. Although industrialization processes had reduced the churches' traditional influence, and the Weimar Constitution had declared an official separation of church and state, the churches remained wealthy, powerful forces shaping social policy and influencing many people's individual decision-making. Sexuality and the family were areas in which, as Cornelie Usborne observes, these institutions especially chose to (re)affirm this public influence. The ways in which they did so was not always straightforwardly reactionary or repressive, but could also 'offer a genuine alternative to the new rationalised life-style promoted by the Left'.[106] The influence of the churches was further strengthened by ties to centre and right-wing political parties, the morality leagues, and to the large Christian women's associations, which far outnumbered their secular feminist counterparts with almost two million members.[107]

Religious arguments on sex took on different hues in different parts of Germany, with debates on abortion or censorship much sterner in Catholic-dominated areas such as rural Bavaria or the Rhineland than in Protestant areas such as Saxony and Prussia. The Catholic Church founded its own network of marriage counselling centres, promoting an ideal of large families rather than facilitating access to contraception: primate Cardinal Bertram saw their goal in no uncertain terms as being to 'counteract the pollution of the moral fabric of family life'.[108] The Church's welfare arm, the *Caritasverband*, forthrightly opposed the secularization of welfare services, arguing for the importance of spiritual guidance as well as material support, representing a conflict of values between church and state.[109] Jewish women's organizations, too, had an important voice in shaping views on family and reproduction, with confessional organizations such as The League of Jewish Women (*Jüdischer Frauenbund*) providing an important space of community and identity.[110]

The BDF, as the mainstay umbrella of the bourgeois women's movement, remained a strong supporter of traditional family values during the Weimar era. Somewhat counter-intuitively from a present-day feminist perspective, it campaigned against legalized abortion and contraception advertising. Middle-class women's organizations were particularly vocal in one early Weimar moral panic that also had distinctly racialized overtones. After Germany's war defeat and the signing of the Treaty of Versailles, panicked cries about the 'Black shame on the Rhine' quickly arose in the press and a series of organized propaganda campaigns responding to the presence of French foreign troops stationed in the Rhineland, many of them men of colour from northern Africa and Senegal. The exaggerated, racist language of these campaigns is evident in pamphlets published by the Rhenish Women's League, for example, which declared its 'deepest horror' to have 'learned of the shameful and unbearable suffering to which German women and children are subjected by the coloured occupation troops'. Fusing imagery of sexual victimization with nationalist and racial overtones, the League was careful to omit from its materials 'passages that hinted at the possibility that Rhenish women may have invited African soldiers' sexual advances'.[111] Other groups were even more explicitly racist, describing 'the bestial rapes of German girls, women and old ladies ... and the unnatural sexual abuse of boys' as a result of 'the black horror, committed against white German women!'[112] Even where relations between black French soldiers and white German women appear to have been consensual, they were often interpreted through a language of sexual violence and miscegenation, framed as a threat to German national honour and racial purity.[113]

The racist language of this campaign against 'mulattoization' drew heavily on older fears cultivated through Germany's prewar colonial contacts – colonies 'lost' with the war defeat.[114] Black male soldiers were demonized as sexually rapacious, infectious and uncivilized, even as their service in the occupying forces suggested a racial equality that situated them as a direct threat to white men. As Tina Campt explains, 'racial parity threatened to emasculate the white German male'.[115] The 'Negro', declared one blatantly racist attack in a Hamburg newspaper in 1921, was now 'systematically being trained to desire that which was formerly unreachable for him – the white woman!'[116] The figure of the 'Rhineland Bastard', meanwhile, a derogatory term for children of Black soldiers and white German women, was held up as a potent symbol of this threat to German purity, with the children sometimes even depicted as carriers of STIs.[117]

Fears around racial mixing were also an obsession of late-Weimar Nazi propaganda paper *Der Stürmer*, which deployed extreme antisemitic imagery of hook-nosed, lecherous Jewish doctors and pimps 'trading' in white German girls as part of an alleged international conspiracy.[118] It also singled out Magnus Hirschfeld as one of the most prominent Weimar-era representatives of the sex reform and homosexual rights movements, declaring him 'a shameless and horrible poisoner of our people' (Figure 3.5). Such attacks continued a long line of violent assaults against Hirschfeld's person that stretched back to 1920, when he was beaten and left for dead by right-wing hooligans after giving a lecture in Munich.[119]

Moral panics of this kind point to the sensationalist, racialized ways in which the policing and defence of white women's sexuality played out at the expense of the rights and dignity of other minority groups. Even purportedly feminist goals were at times pitted against the rights of Jews or Blacks in ways that undermine accounts of Weimar sexual and gender politics as straightforwardly emancipatory.

FIGURE 3.5 *'Dr. Magnus Hirschfeld', cover image of* Der Stürmer, *4 February 1929.*

Source: Deutsche Nationalbibliothek, Leipzig, Signatur: B 1986, ZDB

Prostitution reform, gay rights and political compromise

Debates about whether the state should deregulate prostitution represent a further important example of how Weimar sexual politics cut across traditional lines of religion, party politics and feminism. The passing in 1927 of the Law to Combat Venereal Diseases made medical treatment compulsory for people infected with STIs – with potential prison sentences for those who knowingly infected others. This shifted a significant onus of legal proof and regulation away from prostitutes and onto *anyone* with a sexually transmitted infection. As we saw in Chapter 2, while prostitution was officially illegal under the 1871 Criminal Code, it had long been tolerated by police, subject to a system of state regulation that included frequent medical exams and restrictions on prostitutes' movements. The new law, which was supported by a broad coalition of bourgeois parties including the Catholic Centre Party, as well as the right-wing German People's Party and the left-wing Social Democrats, contained a clause that repealed state regulation of prostitution and decriminalized the practice in larger towns. This represented a compromise for socialist and bourgeois feminists, who had advocated for unconditional decriminalization, but who agreed to the watered-down reform in order to win conservative support.[120] Both contemporary feminists and historians since have tended to herald this law as a major achievement for the interwar women's movement: a 'victory of those ideas, for which the leaders of the German women's movement have fought bravely, selflessly, persistently, and undeterred despite all the attacks on them for thirty years,' declared liberal feminist Marie Elisabeth Lüders.[121] In particular, the law broke with the 'blatant sexual double standard' that had seen the policing of female sex workers, but not their male clients.[122] Prostitution debates were no longer simply about moral panics or straightforward regulation; instead, they entailed 'frank, productive discussions about sexuality, ones that defied the double standard in order to contemplate potential nonmarital outlets for women's desire'.[123]

The compromise by left-wing feminists was typical of a larger trend in Weimar sexual politics of which we have already seen several examples: more radical reforms were curtailed in order to enable moderate changes that conformed more easily to social norms and ideas of respectability. Historian Laurie Marhoefer dubs this the 'Weimar settlement on sexual politics'.[124] This settlement was 'an interrelated set of compromises that most of the parties could live with in relative calm': a politics of toleration rather than outright liberation. The rights and freedoms of majority groups increased, often with cross-party consensus, but at the expense of heavier policing or ostracizing of minority groups, whose non-normative sexual practices were to remain firmly outside of the public eye. Marhoefer identifies this compromise at work in debates around prostitution, the age of consent and Paragraph 175. The abortion debate, they note, was an unusual example of 'failed compromise', in that it led many to lend support to the Communist Party.[125] Such emphasis on compromise and respectability as the guiding principles of Weimar sexual politics offers an important challenge to clichés of Weimar hedonism and liberation. As Marhoefer declares in no uncertain terms, such 'narratives of decadence and amorality rest on ahistorical premises'.[126]

Compromise politics were perhaps most vividly on display in contests over homosexual rights. Here the rights of male prostitutes came into conflict with the respectability arguments of homosexual emancipationists, leading to a sharp split in the movement. It even led founding member Hirschfeld to resign from the WhK, a group of which he had been a founding member in 1897, and that during the Weimar years had continued its lobbying of the Reichstag for reform of Paragraph 175. At least some in the movement, including Hirschfeld, feared that the anti-gay law both heightened the demand for commercial sex, and left gay men vulnerable to extortion.[127] Berlin already had a strong reputation for 'soldier' prostitution and male cruising during the nineteenth century, but the population of male prostitutes rose rapidly after the war in the face of economic instability and demobilization.[128] Male prostitution was not as regulated as female sex work had been for decades, but the market was growing, and was being filled especially by boys from lower-class backgrounds, as a study by Hirschfeld's younger colleague Richard Linsert showed.[129]

In 1929, gay rights activists came very close to succeeding with a major proposal to reform Paragraph 175. Perhaps surprisingly, this was supported by a Reichstag committee that spanned the political spectrum, including Communists, Social Democrats, but also fierce conservatives. Penal Code Committee chairman Dr. Wilhelm Kahl, for example, opposed the law not because he supported homosexual emancipation, but because of the way it encouraged the 'tragedy of blackmail' while catching only a very small minority of offenders; he also hoped that the reform would quieten activists, and 'stop the unrestrained agitation and propaganda in favor of homosexuality'.[130] The goal, he declared, was 'not to liberate male-male-sex; it was rather to restrict criminality only to forms of male-male sex that truly threatened society'.[131] Rather than banish Paragraph 175 altogether, the Committee proposed to replace it with a new Paragraph 297 that would criminalize male same-sex sex if one party was under twenty-one, if undue influence was used or if the relationship involved money.[132] Some scholars describe the conservative support for reform as an 'unqualified victory for the homosexual rights movement', noting that Hirschfeld and colleagues including media mogul Friedrich Radszuweit supported the compromise.[133] But the WhK's new leaders, Kurt Hiller and Richard Linsert, objected to the way it leveraged these reforms by, firstly, instituting a higher age of consent for men than for women, and secondly, by criminalizing male prostitution – amendments that punished the financially vulnerable and limited an individual's right over their own body.[134]

The question, observes Marhoefer, boiled down to one that would also face later generations of gay activists: 'was the liberation of respectable homosexual men at the expense of male prostitutes an acceptable settlement?'[135] For Linsert and Hiller, it was not, and following Hirschfeld's resignation they took the WhK in a more radical direction. The reform proposal coincided with the growing sense of crisis that besieged the final years of the Republic, as the collapse of the last Weimar coalition aligned with global economic depression and the rapid rise of right-wing nationalism.

In the end it was never formalized into law; instead, Paragraph 175 was sharpened under the subsequent Nazi regime.[136] The debate also highlights the role of science in consolidating the battle lines of Weimar sexual politics, for Hirschfeld continued to use biological arguments to argue for 'justice through science' for homosexual men (and to a lesser extent, women), whereas Linsert, Hiller and Radszuweit favoured a less essentializing language of self-determination, citizenship and human rights.[137]

Sexology, psychoanalysis and sex reform

Weimar-era sex reform politics and sexual science were deeply intertwined, with science used to variously challenge and police social norms around sexuality. Sexologists numbered among the enthusiastic campaigners for abortion rights, sex education and sex counselling, and as we saw in Chapter 2, vocally advocated for same-sex desiring and gender-diverse people. Germany was already internationally recognized as the leading light of international sex research by the turn of the century, but in 1919, this reputation was underscored by the founding of Hirschfeld's Institute in a former mansion on the Spree, financially supported by the city's Social Democratic government and an endowed foundation of 30,000 marks.

The Institute provided a home for Hirschfeld's rich library and collections of photographs of 'sexual intermediacy', in addition to the clinical and public initiatives outlined earlier: research laboratories, consulting rooms, spaces for public exhibits and lectures, and a dedicated sexual counselling service. In its first year alone, the Institute attracted 1500 medical doctors and students and a further 2000 'lay' visitors, of whom 30 per cent reportedly identified as belonging to the 'intersexual variant' – people with same-sex, transgendered or intersex identifications.[138] It oversaw some of the world's first sex confirmation surgeries and pioneered new hormone treatments, at a time when there was still only very limited wider social and scientific understanding of trans identifications.[139] Hirschfeld and his medical colleague Max Hodann, who had a sex advice column in the birth control journal *Sexual-Hygiene*, allied themselves with socialist and communist reformers and doctors, as well as with Stöcker's League.[140] Over the years, the Institute attracted long-term residents, domestic staff and international guests including novelist Christopher Isherwood and English archaeologist Francis Turville-Petre; Isherwood later recalled how Francis and his servant Ervin Hansen would regularly 'bring ... one or more boys from Berlin's bars' back to their temporary home'.[141]

The Institute became something of a tourist destination, seen to characterize the liberal spirit of Weimar Berlin and chronicled in popular guides of the metropolis. In 1921 it hosted what was retrospectively declared the first meeting of the World League for Sex Reform in Berlin, which over the next decade became a lively model of coalitional activism that included doctors, psychoanalysts, sex and birth control campaigners and feminist activists from across Europe, North America and parts of Asia.[142] Even though it suffered financially with the hyperinflation of 1923, the Institute continued to play a strong role in legal reform, public education and the treatment of individual patients, providing free advice for low-income earners.[143] Yet even as it was progressive in many respects, the Institute also pursued a science deeply implicated in eugenic concerns. Like the state-based marriage counselling clinics, the service at Hirschfeld's Institute sought to achieve 'the highest possible quality of offspring'.[144] At weekly public Q and A sessions in the Institute's Ernst Haeckel Hall, Hirschfeld and colleagues fielded questions from visitors such as 'How long do condoms last?' or 'What is the best way to have sex without making a baby?'[145] The hall's name was no coincidence: zoologist Ernst Haeckel had been responsible for popularizing Darwin's theories in Germany, and his writings informed the popular movement known as 'Monism', which promoted Social Darwinist ideologies as a kind of scientific replacement for religion.[146]

Even as old religious and moral norms and gender roles were being questioned, the turn to science, as prominent Weimar historian Detlev Peukert has argued, could be 'just as rigid as the old norms and taboos, albeit in a different way', legitimizing new ways of regulating 'what was natural, normal and healthy in the most intimate areas of life'.[147] Yet what exactly constituted the 'natural' or the 'normal' was up for debate. Were so-called 'abnormal' conditions such as homosexuality inborn and incurable, or did the 'normal' and 'perverse' constitute a flexible spectrum of possibility across the span of a human life?[148] Many sexologists – Hirschfeld in particular – took a strongly biological approach, as we have seen, arguing that homosexuality and gender-variance were congenital, lifelong conditions. This commitment to biological explanations helped to fan a wave of new sex hormone research, spearheaded by endocrinologist Eugen Steinach and his team at Vienna's Institute for Experimental Biology. Experimenting with cross-sexed organ transplants in guinea pigs and rats, Steinach's team also pioneered a wildly popular – although ultimately discredited – 'rejuvenation' procedure, dubbed the 'Steinach operation', which many men around the globe underwent in the hope that it would cure all manner of ailments, from lack of sex drive to cancer. Female variants such as oophorectomy (removal of the ovaries) and x-ray therapies were also trialled, but with less enthusiasm or apparent success. Some researchers even provocatively suggested that methods such as castration and testicle transplants from 'normal' (heterosexual) men might 'cure' male homosexuality and effeminacy.[149]

Such procedures were popularized via a documentary called *The Steinach Film* (1922/23, dir. Kaufmann and Thomalla), tickets to which sold out for weeks on end at the Ufa-Palast Cinema at Berlin Zoo. The film soon screened across the world, voyeuristically explaining the actions of the 'inner secretions' on gender characteristics and sexual desires through footage of prancing peacocks, caveman courtship rituals, bearded ladies and effeminate gay men.[150] It also inspired some people to write to sex researchers such as Hirschfeld volunteering themselves for experimental hormone and surgical therapies. 'Would it not', wrote one young correspondent who had been assigned male at birth, 'perhaps be possible to remove my testicles and in their place insert an ovary, and then in this fashion I could become a complete woman?' Another person to approach Hirschfeld's Institute seeking gender confirmation surgery was apprentice builder Gerd Katter, introduced in Chapter 2. Katter had been assigned female at birth, and had attempted a self-mastectomy before being granted a transvestite pass by the Berlin police.[151]

Other researchers were convinced that a combination of environmental and congenital factors needed to be considered in approaching sex on a scientific basis. Freudian explanations of sexual development rapidly gained credibility in both professional and popular circles during these years, when psychoanalysts also became more active in public outreach. In 1920 the Berlin Psychoanalytic Institute was established as both a psychoanalytic training facility and a means for low-income earners to access free treatment, including on sexual questions.[152] In both sexology and psychoanalysis during these years, meanwhile, women were making important inroads and developing more woman-centred approaches to sex research. Sexologist Mathilde Vaerting developed distinctly feminist analyses of male and female psychology, arguing that differences resulted from social rather than biological inequalities. 'The differences shown to exist between [women and men] are just as likely to depend upon sociological causes, and to be the outcome of the reciprocal position of the sexes, as to be due to the congenital divergencies.'[153]

Psychoanalysts Helene Deutsch and Karen Horney developed highly original analyses of female 'frigidity' and homosexuality, and made a strong case for involving women doctors and analysts in the treatment of female sexual complaints. Whereas Freud had described female same-sex desires in terms of masculine (over)identification, Deutsch argued that far more significant was the 'pre-Oedipal', early childhood phase of maternal connection between mother and daughter. She steered clear of the problematic claims of some male colleagues that psychoanalysis might 'cure' homosexuality, arguing instead that analytic methods were best applied to relieve patients' 'neurotic' symptoms – she happily reported on meeting one of her same-sex desiring female patients a year after the analysis to find a 'flourishing, radiant human being'.[154] Horney, meanwhile, insisted that explaining female 'frigidity' had to take into account post-First World War gender relations – the problem, she declared, was not so much a rejection of sexual intimacy as an (unconscious) rejection of the female role in a society that consistently undervalued women's perspectives: 'It is, after all, well known that our culture is a masculine culture.'[155] Horney also provocatively challenged Freudian theories of 'penis envy', suggesting that a larger problem might be men's envy of the female womb.[156] Sofie

Lazarsfeld, working in the school of individual psychology developed by Viennese doctor Alfred Adler, also challenged orthodox accounts of sexual difference. Drawing on hormone research, she affirmed that 'it is possible to change a woman almost completely into a male or a man into a female, at least theoretically'.[157] In such ways, observes Kirsten Leng, interwar women sexologists responded to the challenges of their era, including 'revised gender roles, strained heterosexual relations, and ongoing biopolitical concerns', interrogating sexual difference while insisting on the importance of social and cultural influences in shaping sexual life.[158]

Ideas of race, religion and ethnicity further shaped interwar sex research in ways that tended to exploit cultural otherness in the name of enlightenment or emancipation for white, European subjects. Even before the war, sexologists such as Hirschfeld and Iwan Bloch had begun looking to other cultures to situate homosexuality and transvestism as 'universal' phenomena that should be protected by law.[159] Freud, too, drew on ideas about 'savages' versus 'civilized' peoples in forging universalizing theories about the cultural – and sexual – significance of systems of 'totem' and 'taboo'.[160] Such invocations of cultural anthropology, even where they represented genuine attempts to expand the scope of research into human sexuality beyond national and cultural boundaries, remained deeply entwined in the racist, colonialist and nationalist assumptions of their day.[161]

Life is a cabaret? Weimar sexuality and the rise of the Nazis

In Christopher Isherwood's Berlin diaries, captured in his semi-fictionalized work *Goodbye to Berlin*, the protagonist describes a visit to the rather disappointing nightclub 'Salomé' with German friend Fritz Wendel as part of a tour of 'the dives'. Such slumming tours were popularized by contemporary guidebooks such as Curt Moreck's *Guide to 'Depraved' Berlin* (*Führer durch das 'lasterhafte' Berlin*, 1931), offering tourists from the provinces or abroad glimpses into the city's club and 'vice' scenes, from crossdressing performances to streetwalkers. 'Sensation is a need for the modern human being. He needs it as a whip on the nerves, he needs it like the addict needs his jab,' Moreck's guide declared.[162] This 'need' is palpable in Isherwood's novel, with Fritz disparagingly noting that the management of the Salomé club 'run it entirely for the benefit of provincial sightseers' – 'respectable middle-aged tradesman and their families'.[163] On the way out, the two men encounter a group of drunk American youths:

> Their leader was a small stocky young man in pince-nez, with an annoyingly prominent jaw.
> 'Say,' he asked Fritz, 'what's on here?'
> 'Men dressed as women,' Fritz grinned.

The little American simply couldn't believe it.
'Men dressed as *women*? As *women* hey? Do you mean they're *queer*?'
'Eventually we're all queer,' drawled Fritz solemnly, in lugubrious
tones.[164]

Isherwood was only one of many international 'sex tourists' who came to
Berlin seeking erotic adventures, and who with their hard foreign currency
could live a fairly charmed existence, especially in the early years of inflation
until 1923, or in the years of economic depression from late 1929.[165] But
how have such images shaped the way we view Weimar's sexual history?
Could delving into them challenge grander narratives of Weimar's rise and
demise?

It has sometimes been argued that the rise of the Nazis resulted at least
partly from a 'backlash' against Weimar sexual immorality, especially
following changes to the VD law and regulation of prostitution in the late
1920s. 'Theories of how sex helped to bring down the Weimar Republic,'
observes Marhoefer, 'are almost as old as the Weimar Republic itself.'[166] Yet
this is also a narrative which, Marhoefer rightly points out, historians of
sexuality have a special responsibility to interrogate, given its implication
in one of the most important questions for twentieth-century German
historiography: how the Nazis came to power, and maintained that power
over the course of a devastating twelve-year dictatorship. Popular films such
as *Cabaret*, mentioned at the beginning of this chapter, have contributed to
a widely shared cultural understanding that sex was a cornerstone of both
Nazi disquiet and Weimar modernity. Anxieties around sexual expressions,
scholars and commentators of this period have argued, merged with
much wider disquiet surrounding the rapid pace of change and perceived
'degeneracy' of the Republic itself.

Yet to pin the Nazi ascension to power too tightly to a moral backlash
may well mean assuming that sexual morality was more controversial and
omnipresent in Weimar political debate than was actually the case. This is
certainly Marhoefer's conclusion, as they examine election records to find
that sexual politics did *not* noticeably attract voters to the Nazi Party in
the early 1930s. Marhoefer finds that conservative complaints about the
venereal disease law in fact remained quite limited and specific during these
years. They show that prostitution was simply not such a major concern for
conservatives, and more importantly, that Weimar-era sexual politics were
not the most significant factor in driving votes towards the NSDAP, especially
for voters located more towards the Centre of the political spectrum. For this
demographic, far more pressing were factors such as economic hardship,
fears of Communist revolution and general disgruntlement with the Weimar
political system. This is not to say that morality and sexual politics were not
discussed, but rather that they may not have played the key causal role in
ushering in the Nazis that has sometimes been assumed.[167]

Even as such conclusions remain open to further interrogation and contest by future researchers, Marhoefer's rebuttal of the 'backlash thesis' has inspired a robust exchange with other historians of Weimar who have argued more forcefully for the impact of legal reforms around sexuality and perceptions of increasing immorality in precipitating the fall of the Republic.[168] On the one hand, Marhoefer acknowledges the difficulty of proving a historical case that involves arguing in the negative: 'It is difficult to prove that something did not happen. My argument depends on searching for evidence of backlash in likely places and demonstrating that although sexual politics were important and were up for debate, they did not undermined (sic) democracy.'[169] Julia Roos, in contrast, argues in her study of Weimar prostitution that 'the liberalization of legal and public attitudes' did indeed cause 'a powerful conservative backlash that contributed in fateful ways to the destruction of Weimar democracy'. Roos positions conflicts over gender and sexuality – and in particular, the 'right-wing backlash' against the 'fragile political compromise' represented by the 1927 Venereal Disease law – as just as crucial to the 'crisis and ultimate demise of the Weimar Republic' as class antagonism or left-right political struggles.[170] Edward Dickinson agrees with Roos that 'there absolutely was a "backlash"', but he nonetheless finds convincing 'Marhoefer's careful, concrete, and detailed delineation of the relatively unimportant role of sexual politics in the decisive political turning points of the early 1930s'. Dickinson suggests that 'the simple yes/no, either/or logic of the question may militate against developing a model of causation that better does justice to the complexity of Weimar politics, culture, and society'.[171]

This, in my view, represents the most productive approach, in that it emphasizes how questioning of commonplace narratives such as the 'backlash' thesis, of the kind Marhoefer undertakes, can open us up to deeper explanation of the actual sources and debates surrounding sexuality in the final years of the Republic. Such questioning pushes us to look for continuities as well as change through the ruptures of 1933 into the years of National Socialism, for even as some things did change, sexuality was not simply repressed from one moment to the next with the Nazi seizure of power. The Weimar 'backlash' debate, in short, raises key questions for historians of sexuality, highlighting both the potential and limits of taking sexual politics as an explanation for the big questions of twentieth-century history.

* * *

The fourteen years of Germany's first democracy, with its rapidly liberalizing public sphere and booming print media freed up by a relative absence of censorship, provided a fertile backdrop against which individuals and groups could start organizing in force around categories of sex, gender and human rights to demand recognition by the German state. Norms of gender were troubled and played around with during this interwar period, not least through popular discussions of women becoming 'masculinized' and men becoming 'effeminate' – discussions that helped to focus more amorphous concerns about the pace of modernity itself onto the embodied and knowable. Youth, nudist and body culture movements all opened up new spaces for sexual exploration and same-sex homoeroticism, and the new frameworks of Weimar citizenship opened up spaces not only for articulating queer and trans rights, but for a flourishing queer media and club scene, especially in the larger cities.

Highly politicized and at times surprising coalitions of movements and actors made up the vibrant landscape of Weimar sex reform, seeking to establish more rationalized, 'modern' sexual norms, and to contest restrictive legislation inherited from the prewar period constraining sexual choices around abortion, prostitution, and contraception. Norms were also negotiated and reinforced among wider publics via the framework of scientific sex research during these years. Films brought themes as varied as the dangers of venereal disease to the workings of the sex hormones to a wide Weimar audience of cinemagoers, while female sexologists and psychoanalysts vocally questioned older 'scientific' ideas of female sexuality.

This chapter has particularly emphasized the centrality of ideas of compromise and middle-class respectability as factors framing Weimar sexual politics, showing how in various debates, from gay and trans law reform to prostitution deregulation, claims for greater rights for some members of society were made at the expense of other, minority groups. Finally, we considered the role of sexuality in wider historiographical debates about the Weimar Republic as immediate precursor to the Third Reich – with historians divided over the extent to which a sexual 'backlash' contributed to this dire political development. Chapter 4 picks up this thread of analysis, seeking out continuities as well as breaks with Weimar norms of sexuality, gender and intimacy into the Nazi era. 1933 did not represent a straightforward rupture when it came to sexual politics; instead, looking at sexuality can help us to problematize even well-established periodizations. Nazi ideology and 'racial hygiene' policies built in important ways on what had come before. This included a sense of living in an era of scientific modernity, and the idea that it was appropriate to intervene into citizens' intimate lives, as modelled by Weimar-era sex reformers.

4

Pronatalism to persecution: Sex in Nazi Germany, 1933–45

On the morning of 6 May – several days before the famous bonfire of blacklisted books by Nazi students at Berlin's central Bebelplatz – around 100 students rolled up in vans to sexologist Magnus Hirschfeld's Institute for Sexual Science at In den Zelten, complete with a brass band to jolly along proceedings. An eye-witness recalled the scenes that followed:

> The students tried to gain entry to all the rooms; when these were locked – for example, the ground-floor display rooms and the former and present office of the World League for Sexual Reform – they smashed down the doors. ... They took off what struck them as suspicious, keeping mainly to the so-called 'black list.' But at the same time they pilfered other books, such as a large work on Tutankhamen and many art magazines from the private library of the secretary, Giese. Then they removed from the archive the large boards with representations of intersexual cases .... They tore most of the other pictures, photographs of important persons, from the walls and played football with them, so that large piles of ruined pictures and broken glass were left behind. When one student objected that the material was of a *medical* nature, another replied that the real point, their real concern, was not to seize a few books and pictures but to *destroy the institute.*[1]

The burgeoning Weimar sex reform movement had, as Chapter 3 has shown, vocally supported homosexual rights and legal access to abortion and contraception. When the Nazis came to power, its activities and organizations were among the earliest victims of the new regime. The situation was not helped by the strong left-wing and Jewish affiliations of many leading Weimar-era reformers, including Hirschfeld. The Gestapo, or Nazi secret police, compiled a 'Liquidation' file to document the destruction of the lay sex reform organizations between February and June of 1933.

During the twelve years that followed, many activists and scholars whose work had centred on the science and politics of sexuality found themselves confronting unenviable fates. Some were arrested, some went into exile and others faced suicide and in some cases, death in the notorious concentration camps.[2]

The history of sexuality offers a crucial lens on one of the biggest questions in German history: How could an ostensibly 'civilized' nation – a term itself carrying considerable imperialist baggage – oversee one of the most horrific and organized genocides the world has ever seen? In the early 2000s historian Elizabeth Heineman pointed to sexuality and Nazism as the 'doubly unspeakable'.[3] She put a finger on the way that sex in the so-called Third Reich was for decades a 'virtual terra incognita' for historians, threatening to offer an inappropriately titillating or trivializing take on what was, without any doubt, a brutally destructive regime.[4] In particular, scholars hesitated to explore evidence of pleasure that conflicted with the exclusionary official ideology of reproductive heterosexuality oriented towards the expansion of a racially 'pure' and 'Aryan' *Volk*.[5] In recent decades, though, historians have begun confronting such taboos: they have carefully unpacked the tensions, hypocrisies and contradictions surrounding the history of sexuality during this period, and questioned taken-for-granted assumptions that it was overwhelmingly experienced as repressive. 'We simply cannot understand why Nazism was so attractive to so many people if we focus only on its sexually repressive aspects,' observes Dagmar Herzog, even as she notes the particular difficulty of fitting analyses of gender and sexuality during the Holocaust into available frameworks.[6] Similarly, Jennifer Evans emphasizes that we must consider how both the repressive and the pleasurable contributed to the 'appeal, successes and failures' of the Nazi regime.[7] Scholars have also worked to reconcile the pervasive view of the Third Reich as 'repressive' or 'sex-hostile' with popular culture representations of this period as 'lurid and salacious', such as fetishized images of female SS guards in jack boots.[8] Although exploring this past involves dealing with material that is often painful or traumatic, including brutal histories of sexual violence, these scholars remind us that it is crucial to make pleasure and desire part of how we narrate this difficult period.[9]

Homing in on sexuality under Nazism not only challenges wider historical narratives of the liberalization of sexual norms in modernity, but also pushes us to question clear-cut categories of 'victimhood' and 'persecution' to instead consider more layered pictures of how people perceived and enacted their sexual desires and identities under authoritarian rule. How did people negotiate consent from clearly uneven positions of authority? How might we build a picture of sexuality under Nazism that brings together both the sexual freedoms and abuses suffered in movements such the League of German Girls? How might we approach the Nazi regime's celebration of certain norms of sexuality – family-oriented, heteronormative, based around clearly gendered roles of soldierly masculinity and domestic motherhood – with the brutal repression of those seen not to conform, such as Jews, disabled or queer and trans people?

In many ways, what counted as 'normal' sexuality remained similar to what had come before. Longstanding social and cultural expectations of heterosexual monogamy, marriage and procreation were still the core framework of acceptable sexual expression, even as many people – including in the Nazi Party itself – desired and behaved in ways that fell outside of those norms. Yet other things changed, most notably, the long reach of the Nazi state into people's intimate lives. Much more obviously than in earlier periods, the regime's biopolitical concerns put pressure on individuals to align their sexuality with the explicitly racialized ideals of a white, 'Aryan', able-bodied *Volkskörper* (body of the people or nation). Nazi leaders saw population growth and social stability as necessary to meet the Party's goals of an unashamedly expansionist German state – the megalomania of which was reflected in the imperialist terminology of the 'Third Reich'.[10] They actively promoted some forms of sexual and gender expression – marriage, motherhood, lots of children and clear-cut gender roles – as long as the people involved met the criteria for healthy, 'Aryan' citizenship. At the same time, new ideas about 'deviant' sexual expression evolved to reflect the regime's overwhelming eugenic emphasis on 'racial hygiene'. Expressed via new categories such as 'asocial', the sexual activities of so-called 'inferior' groups – Jews, Afro-Germans, queer and trans folk, physically or mentally disabled people and promiscuous women – became explicit targets of Nazi sexual persecution, even as that persecution remained uneven.

'One struggles', observe the editors of one recent collection, 'to find other dictatorial regimes in the twentieth century that made so much' of pleasure and sexuality, noting the Party's programmatic emphasis on *Kraft durch Freude* or 'strength through joy'. The Nazis promoted leisure, entertainment and consumption, aware that pleasurable activities like smoking, travel and visits to the cinema, dance halls or cabaret could be more effective at shoring up social stability and conformity than direct indoctrination.[11] As Elizabeth Harvey et al. argue in a recent study of private life under Nazism, Nazi leaders recognized the benefit of enabling 'private self-optimization' and mobilizing the same 'not just to change the political system but also to revolutionise German lifestyles'.[12] At the same time, they created a heavily racist system in which private life was particularly precarious: 'the regime destroyed the private lives of those who did not conform to National Socialist norms, before eradicating their very existence.'[13] Such attention to the nuances of pleasure and power, private and public, and liberation and repression has propelled some historians of sexuality towards microhistories of individuals, everyday interactions and emotions – especially to gain access to situations far removed from our own everyday reality, such as life in the concentration camps. Thinking about sexuality in such contexts is not always easy, but it is crucial work, not least because it was precisely 'the asymmetries in those everyday power relations that were instrumental in producing the Holocaust'.[14]

This chapter explores these questions of sexuality under fascism, tracing continuities and ruptures between the liberatory gains of the Weimar period in areas such as abortion and contraception reform, women's emancipation and queer rights, and the racially oriented policies of eugenics, sterilization and the policing of minority groups under National Socialism. It turns firstly to Nazi ideologies and cultural representations of gender and marriage, before teasing out the regime's dual-edged racializing logic of pronatalist and antinatalist policy. It then examines the contradictions and nuances shaping the experiences of queer and gender-diverse people under Nazism, showing that even while the regime oversaw a violent history of intervention into LGBTIQ lives, it did not completely shut down possibilities for queer expression. Finally, it considers patterns of sexual violence and barter that emerged in the context of war, occupation and the concentration camps.

Conflicted norms: Nazi ideologies of sex, gender and family

According to Nazi ideology, the main place for sex was in marriage, and the main purpose to produce as many racially 'pure' children as possible. These future soldiers, workers and mothers would build an increasingly powerful 'Aryan' state, justifying new geographic conquests to provide that body politic with the necessary *Lebensraum*, literally 'living space'. Party leaders echoed earlier generations of conservative nationalists in bemoaning the rapidly decreasing birth rate, which had fallen from 25.9 per 1000 population in 1920 to 14.7 per 1000 in 1933, the lowest rates in all of Europe.[15] As well as promoting 'an immense venture in reproductive engineering', Nazi sexual ideology took to new extremes a racially driven eugenic programme informed by the latest science and medicine.[16]

The Party seized on the conservative, middle-class attitudes to sexuality that had prevailed among wide swathes of the population into the 1920s and 1930s, despite the radicalizing impulses of the Weimar era. These were reinforced by church teachings and had been fuelled by the polarizing debates around abortion in the early 1930s. At the same time, many Nazi leaders were themselves known to be highly promiscuous, and some even embraced a pro-sex stance that involved attacking the Christian churches for foreclosing 'healthy Germanic instincts'.[17] A few, such as SA leader Ernst Röhm (more on him below), were even rumoured to prefer the company of men. The Nazi emphasis on marriage and sexual morality brought together, at times in paradoxical ways, legacies of bourgeois nineteenth-century domesticity, racial hygiene and social Darwinism with a racially 'pure' version of modern sexual liberalism.[18] This at times led to surprising positions, such as official support for 'Aryan' single mothers. But it was far from a situation of anything goes, as Heineman concludes: 'Rather, it was a coherent whole that simultaneously rejected Victorian prudery and the "degenerate" sexuality associated with Weimar in favour of a "clean" but distinctly sexual life.'[19]

This ideology upheld some older sex-gender norms while radically disrupting others. The state was conceived as an organism made up of smaller 'cells', of which the family was the most important. Wilhelm Frick, Reich Minister of the Interior, declared as much in a national broadcast in May 1934: 'The family is the primordial cell of the Volk, that is why the National Socialist state places it at the centre of its policy.'[20] The Party leadership developed policies to confront the falling birth rate. This was often blamed retrospectively on the selfishness and hedonism of the Republic – for even if the role of Weimar sexual liberalism in precipitating the rise of the Nazis remains under debate, as we saw in Chapter 3, it became part of an established Nazi narrative under fascist rule.[21] Leaders used organic language to describe decreasing family sizes as evidence of a 'cancer' or degeneration at the level of the nation. Such concerns were used to justify pronatalist, or pro-birth, policies and interventions – it was now declared the 'patriotic duty' of doctors, medical officers, judges and social workers to insert themselves into family planning decisions in the name of public health.[22] Although some within the Party disagreed with placing the family on a pedastal, arguing that the Party's *Männerbünde* or men's organizations should be the main priority, most considered the nuclear family the primary unit of the German state, and its protection a primary responsibility of the *Volk*.[23]

This racialized pronatalist agenda aligned with increasingly polarized gender expectations. Men were to serve their duty on the battlefield, and women as mothers.[24] A popular handbook for young mothers made this comparison in forthright terms: 'At every time becoming a mother has been compared with the highest virtues of the man, who in the days of utmost hardship defends *Volk* and homeland with his own life.'[25] Eugenicist A. Mayer declared in 1938 that 'The worth of a nation is shown in the preparedness of its women to become valuable mothers .... Germany must once again become a fertile land of mothers and children.'[26] Women were split into two categories: healthy, racially pure 'Aryans' whose primarily goal in life was to serve the nation through reproduction, and those deemed racially 'other' or 'inferior': Jews, Gypsies and other so-called 'asocials'.[27] National Socialism institutionalized racism, in short, in ways that were absolutely tied up with gender, situating race and gender as 'the two paramount and immutable categories of human nature'.[28]

In some areas of public life, though, Nazi ideologies of women as mothers and homemakers and men as soldiers and patriarchs gave way to the continuation of more diverse gender practices and erotic imagery. For one thing, the more muscular female physicality, shorter haircuts and rationalized clothing styles that had attracted such attention in the Weimar media did not simply disappear. Popular magazines or films such as Leni Riefenstahl's *Olympia* (1938) show that a modern, if Nazified, fascist gender aesthetic still had room to celebrate female athleticism and non-eroticized heterosexual sporting 'camaraderie'.[29] Weimar-inspired sexual iconography continued to influence both popular and more avant-garde cultural spheres, from the Germanicized 'Hiller Girls' (a Nazi version of the 1920s British dance troupe sensation, the Tiller Girls), to the inclusion of expressionist dancers in the 1936 Olympics opening night ceremony.[30] During the 1940s, women's fashion magazines saw a re-emergence of masculine styles, now taking on a distinctly militaristic look in line with the renewed wartime climate.[31] Among men, meanwhile, Nazi ideals of soldierly virility were contested by some homosexual veterans from the First World War, who claimed access to both 'masculinity' and a role in the *Volksgemeinschaft* (people's community) that encompassed same-sex desires.[32] Yet even such diversity could subtly support the Nazi regime. For rather than representing a turn away from modernity, such cultural representations underscore the image of the Nazi state as distinctly modern, with leaders quite ready to appeal to a sense of sexual progressiveness 'to fortify the otherwise restrictive sexual politics of the state'.[33]

'Strength through Joy' in the nudist and youth movements

The nudist (FKK), life reform and youth movements inherited from the Wilhelmine and Weimar eras, traditionally quite sexually liberal spaces, were an important space for the negotiation of norms of gender and sexual morality under National Socialism. During this period, these movements adopted more binary gender ideals, celebrating manly, muscular men and physically healthy and robust, yet decidedly feminine women. Socialist branches of the naturist movement were shut down, and even more right-wing groups underwent a thoroughgoing *Gleichschaltung*, the process of forced conformity to Nazi ideology.[34] The movement's leading journal, *Deutsche Leibeszucht* (German Body Culture) published images of nude 'Aryan' women, men and children relaxing, posing and weightlifting against a backdrop of forests and lakes, and articles on public and nude bathing alongside poems celebrating 'Der Führer', the fatherland and the German worker, as part of an increasingly Germanicized aesthetic (see Figure 4.1).

In such ways, it connected to the wider 'strength through joy' movement, which also now oversaw the workers' hiking groups popular since the Weimar era. Nazi leaders viewed the movement in ways that ranged 'from

FIGURE 4.1 *Cover,* Deutsche Leibeszucht *(German Body Culture), 4 March 1940.*
Source: Staatsbibliothek zu Berlin, Preußischer Kulturbesitz, Signatur Zsn 75923.

demonization to guarded acceptance.[35] In 1933 Interior Minister Hermann Göring declared the FKK movement 'one of the greatest dangers to German culture and morality', and others similarly denounced it as an un-Germanic 'eroticization and Bolshevization of public life'. Ten years later, though, the 1942 'Police Ordinance for the Regulation of Bathing' signalled a position of 'tacit tolerance'.[36] Catholic leaders were certainly disappointed with what they saw as the Nazis' defence of both nudist culture and extramarital sex, lamenting a prevailing 'spirit of uncleanness' and loosening of sexual morality.[37]

Seemingly contradictory sexual and moral positions also characterize the sexual politics of the official Party youth groups, the Hitler Youth (HJ) for boys and the League of German Girls (BDM), although these positions cohered around the regime's racial goals. Nazi youth leader Baldur Shirach declared that 'girls will willingly approach their future destiny as mothers of the new generation'.[38] In this vein, the BDM strongly promoted physical fitness and hygiene in preparation for girls' future roles as mothers of the *Volk*. Leaders also warned of the dangers of sexually transmitted diseases and 'cultural poisoning' resulting from sexual relations with non-Aryans. Yet the League was plagued by horror stories of girls returning from BDM camps either pregnant or infected with STIs, and lewd jokes abounded about the BDM acronym, variously said to stand for *Bund deutscher Milchkühe* (League of German Cows), *Bald deutsche Mütter* (German mothers-to-be) or the directly subversive *Baldur drück mich* (Baldur, take me).[39] Although both the HJ and BDM promoted non-sexual camaraderie, offering 'fresh, clean, clear German air' as an alternative to explicit sexual education, a 'good deal of flirting during youth group activities' took place, and there were many reports of girls having sexual relationships with soldiers or SS officers. While celebrated as pure and honourable with their blonde braids and uniforms, 'Aryan' girls and women, Patricia Szobar observes, 'could not be completely relied upon to devote their energies to producing healthy and racially pure offspring for the *Volk*'.[40] In such ways, Nazi youth organizations simultaneously provided spaces of sexual experimentation while also reinforcing the regime's exclusionary racial politics.

Marriage, pronatalism and motherhood

A core area in which policymakers sought to promote the Nazis' racializing sex-gender ideology was in regulating marriage and divorce.[41] One Nazi policymaker declared marriage

> the lasting life-long union of two genetically healthy persons of the same race and of different sexes, which has been approved by the national community, and is based on mutual ties of loyalty, love and respect. Its purpose is the maintenance and furtherance of the common good through harmonious cooperation, the procreation of genetically healthy children of the same race, and the education of them to become hard-working national comrades.[42]

Hitler had considered the institution important enough to discuss it in his notorious Weimar-era memoir, *Mein Kampf* (1925). He described the need to raise the status of marriage to 'give it the consecration of an institution which is called upon to produce images of the Lord', but his messaging also veered from traditional Christian to more social Darwinist concerns as he stressed early marriage as a prerequisite for 'healthy and resistant offspring'.[43] Marriage, in short, constituted a fundamental duty to the National Socialist state. A 1934 document outlining the 'Ten Commandments for the Choice of a Spouse' reflected the dual emphasis of Nazi racial hygiene on increasing the quantity and quality of the *Volk*: among other things, it prodded the nation's youth to 'remember that you are a German' (commandment 1); that 'if you are genetically healthy you should not remain unmarried' (commandment 2); that it was imperative 'in choosing a spouse [to] ask about his ancestors' (commandment 6); and that one 'should want to have as many children as possible' (commandment 10).[44] Sexual activity was to be directed towards 'the maintenance of the nation and not the enjoyment of the individual' – although, assuming sufficient healthy children had been produced, 'then, from the point of view of the nation, there is no objection to further satisfaction of the sexual urge'.[45]

To promote this normative vision and discourage anyone from straying from the straight and narrow, the regime devised a series of carrot and stick measures, including a system of marriage permissions, prohibitions and loans. Couples wishing to marry first had to apply for an official permit certifying their genetic compatibility to reproduce, according to the Law for the Protection of the Hereditary Health of the German People, sometimes referred to as the Marriage Health Law, which came into power on 18 October 1935. 'The only right thing to do', declared one advice manual to young mothers, 'is of course to gain certainty about this vital question before marriage'.[46] The requirement for local health authorities to issue couples with a 'certificate of fitness to marry' put considerable strain on doctors (particularly after the Nazis banned Jewish doctors from practicing), especially as the couple intending to marry did not have to pay for the requisite health checks.[47] In practice, the requirement for premarital certificates was deployed unevenly, and was never made mandatory across the board.[48] Marriage could, however, be restricted on numerous grounds: along with infectious or hereditary disease these included a legal declaration of incompetence, psychological illness, Jewish ancestry or the vague category of 'asocialism'. Having a record of crime or reformatory school, promiscuity (especially for women), alcoholism, 'feeble-mindedness' or being 'workshy' could all bar an individual from marrying a fertile and eugenically 'desirable' German.[49]

One woman denied marriage on this basis was Else K., who not only failed her 'intelligence test', but was forcibly sterilized when the assessment process revealed information about her deceased brother, who had been hospitalized in an asylum for schizophrenia – the sharply antinatalist flipside of the National Socialist promotion of 'healthy' marriage and offspring, discussed below.[50] Sometimes, though, permissions were granted even to those deemed hereditarily 'unfit', because of the perceived benefits in maintaining social stability or preventing the spread of genetic diseases. Factory worker and father of five Johannes in 1940 applied to marry his beloved Susanna, who had five illegitimate children of her own and had been sterilized. He made a case that she could take good care of his household, and the health department agreed, the Reich Minister of the interior condoning the marriage as 'desirable' because of the way it provided a home for the many children involved, without threatening to produce more.[51]

Marriage pamphlets and counselling helped to reproduce the racialized norms underlying Nazi sexual policy. They advised would-be couples to visit family doctors for eugenic approval before marriage, and to carefully research their future spouse's family histories. In Nazi marriage law, 'you do not marry your partner alone, rather to an extent you marry his ancestors [as well].'[52] The Nazis took up and adopted popular sex advice formats from the Weimar era, even as the kinds of sex and marriage counselling centres that had flourished as part of 1920s sex reform were now attacked for serving 'Bolshevik cultural leanings' and fostering female solidarity in their promotion of birth control – contraception was actively frowned upon and access restricted by the new regime. 'What must be fought against with all force,' advised one guide for mothers, 'is the *arbitrary prevention of hereditarily healthy offspring*, which became such a shocking matter of course in the period following the First World War'.[53]

Starting in May 1933, the Prussian Minister of the Interior forced the closure of many such centres and the seizure of their records. Others were brought under the wing of the National Socialist People's Welfare Organization (NSV), to provide 'systematic, responsible education for future German fathers and mothers'.[54] This was less an outright rejection of a rationalized, modern brand of sex reform than a turning of this project away from the social welfare goals of the Weimar era in what Geoff Eley describes as 'a radicalized and more concerted direction, powered by the machinery of a centralized and coercive state, freed from the earlier restraints of professional ethics, constitutional democracy, and liberal precepts of the rule of law'.[55] In line with Nazi population politics, in 1941 Heinrich Himmler ordered that all contraceptives except for condoms be banned (the latter were still freely distributed to soldiers to protect against STIs).[56] Yet such policy measures must also be weighed against lived realities and the ongoing influence of 'rationalizing' expectations around family planning: 'Most women avoided the "mother cult" by limiting their family size and managing their homes just as they had in earlier eras,' as Michelle Mouton points out.[57] Rather than eradicating birth control, Nazi policy simply pushed it underground.[58]

Financial incentives were another carrot used to underscore Nazi ideals of marriage directed towards reproduction. In 1935, a marriage loans scheme was introduced to encourage healthy couples to marry younger and have more children. Those who could comply with the strict medical and racial guidelines were offered loans of up to 1000 Reichsmark, payable in coupons, to help them set up a household. Low repayments were reducible by 25 per cent per child born to the couple.[59] Initially, loans were contingent on the female partner giving up paid work, as the program formed part of the Law to Reduce Unemployment and targeted so-called 'double earners'. Later, though, as the state found itself faced with a shortage of labour in the context of a rearmament boom, this requirement was dropped – a fairly typical example of the regime flexibly adjusting its policies to suit its changing circumstances.[60] The scheme proved popular – at the 1936 Party Rally the Secretary of State boasted that around 620,000 marriages had already been assisted by the loans, with 425,000 children born to those marriages.[61] Yet the marriage loans scheme was only somewhat successful as population policy, with the uptake most prevalent among lower-income earners who had delayed marriage during the Depression.[62] Other carrots and sticks took the form of tax incentives and levies: from 1938, childless couples joined unmarried men in being compelled to pay 10 per cent of their income in additional taxes, as punishment for their 'refusal to multiply' (*Fortpflanzungsverweigerung*), while unmarried women faced accusations of 'racial desertion'.[63] Parents of six children, on the other hand, paid no personal income tax, and each child represented a 15 per cent income tax deduction even for smaller families.[64]

While some pronatalist policies worked to increase the status of fathers, such as the payment of family allowances, many focused on promoting mothers.[65] Those who had borne multiple children were awarded with everything from free theatre tickets to national recognition in the form of the Honour Cross – bronze, silver or gold, depending on the number of healthy biological children one had borne. The Nazis also appropriated the older Mothers' Day tradition, turning this into a racialized and nationalistic celebration of the 'German family'.[66] One promotional poster proclaimed: 'The care of mothers and children is the holiest duty of the entire German Volk,' while the declaration of Mothers' Day as a national holiday was aimed, as head of the Mothers' Day Reich Committee Dr Rudolf Knauer declared, to 'awaken motherly responsibility towards the Volk in the souls of German women'.[67] Such emphasis on fertility as the overriding goal of 'healthy' women's sexuality worked, argues Annette Timm, to desexualize 'ordinary' women, even as those deemed 'outsiders', such as prostitutes and other 'asocials' were hypersexualized and strictly surveilled.[68]

The state carefully supervised 'valuable' pregnant women via social workers and midwives. It offered rest homes and aid programs, and provided practical advice and assistance through the 'Mother and Child' section of the National Socialist People's Welfare Organization (NSV). This ran courses in modern childcare at its approximately 25,000 advice centres, which around 1.7 million German women had attended by March 1939.[69] Motherhood was also at the centre of the National Socialist women's organizations, overseen by the *Deutsches Frauenwerk*, with 'Mothers' Schools' offering training in household and maternal skills.[70] The popular handbook 'The German Mother and Her First Child', written by 'housewife, mother, and doctor' Johanna Haarer (the order of attributes is telling) at the Munich Mothers' School, and issued in multiple editions from 1934, exemplifies the Nazi approach to motherhood: 'No other event in the life of a woman wrests her so thoroughly from her individual fate and inserts her into the great event of the life of peoples (*Völkerleben*) as this walk to the front of the mothers of our *Volk*' (see Figure 4.2).[71] Nazi pronatalist policies, as Claudia Koonz argues, merged nineteenth-century social norms of domesticity with twentieth-century welfare and state incentives – but she reminds us, too, that statistics alone cannot tell us why Germans married, nor why newlyweds were not producing more children than during the 'decadent' Weimar era. Some non-Nazi parents likely sought to avoid bringing children into a Nazi society.[72] Others weighed up the financial incentives of the loans scheme against the long-term costs of having several children and decided against it.[73]

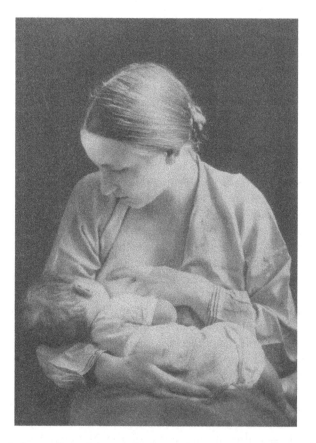

FIGURE 4.2 *Image from Johanna Haarer, 'The German Mother and Her First Child', 1934.*

Source: Staatsbibliothek zu Berlin, Preußischer Kulturbesitz, Signatur: Ke 1660.

In a move that defies assumptions of outright sexual and moral policing under the Nazis, the Party's support for mothers also extended to unmarried women, provided they met the requisite racial criteria. Those who did not were likely to be branded 'asocial' or 'promiscuous'.[74] A striking example of this was the Lebensborn 'Fount of Life' Association. Established by the SS under Himmler in 1936, this network of care homes aimed to enable single women deemed eugenically valuable to bear children in a discrete, safe and comfortable environment. During the war, Himmler even envisaged the program as an opportunity to make such women available for impregnation by SS men, to be adopted by healthy families.[75] In private at least, he was quite free with his view 'that any young woman who is alone and longs for a child can turn to *Lebensborn* with perfect confidence. I would sponsor the child and provide for its education'.[76] Such views did not necessarily represent the mainstream Party view. Here there was greater sympathy for more moderate calls by the likes of Deputy Führer Rudolf Hess to improve the situation of unwed mothers and illegitimate children, such as a pregnant woman whose fiancé had died at the front: 'What would it help if a people were victorious but became extinct through the sacrifice for the victory?'[77] Himmler, meanwhile, found himself having to fend off rumours that the Lebensborn program encouraged illegitimacy. He did so by emphasizing that a woman's role as a mother must come first, 'since she is, during and after her pregnancy, not a married or an unmarried woman but a mother', and by positioning the program as a counter to the 'scourge of abortion' which saw a loss to the 'German nation' of up to 600,000 children annually.[78]

Further exemplifying the complex tensions between liberalizing and repressive tendencies was the tendency for at least some Nazi policy to resonate with earlier feminist demands. From 1937, unmarried mothers could insist on a degree of respect by being addressed as 'Frau' rather than 'Fräulein' in all official business – 'ironically', remarks Jill Stephenson, 'this was exactly what the radical feminists had long demanded'.[79] Nazi support of single mothers also resonated with earlier calls by socialists and feminists such as Helene Stöcker to end legal discrimination – although whereas Stöcker had focused on women's needs, in Nazi ideology it was a woman's obligation to the *Volk* that was the central concern.[80] The Nazis were by no means a feminist organization, though. Germany's major feminist organization, the BDF, clearly saw the writing on the wall when in May 1933 it elected to dissolve itself rather than conform to *Gleichschaltung*. With the Party's success in the 1932 state elections, observes Ann Taylor Allen, 'the feminist leaders had begun to realize the danger to women's rights of the party's highly misogynist program,' and by June 1933 the BDF magazine *Die Frau* was already under official control.[81]

While wide-reaching, and at times quite radical in their intervention into individuals' sexual and reproductive choices, these measures did not amount to 'forced' or 'compulsory' motherhood – a topic that has been much debated by historians of women's experiences under Nazism.[82] Generally, scholars agree that women were not actually forced to have children against their will. Rather, couples faced considerable social pressure to have children soon after marriage, and this was promoted by the kinds of pronatalist policies outlined above: 'the "valuable" were tiresomely persuaded and cajoled in reproductive matters, but not coerced in the way that the "worthless" routinely were.'[83] As Jewish socialist doctor Käte Frankenthal explained after herself leaving Germany in 1933, 'German women are too enlightened. For such a law (extending beyond Paragraph 218 [the anti-abortion law]) not even Hitler could achieve obedience.'[84] Historian Gisela Bock concludes, in an exhaustive examination of this question, that National Socialism, despite all the rhetoric, did not achieve a *Gebärzwang* (compulsion to give birth) above and beyond that which had already existed.[85] Instead, she finds that the German 'population miracle' of the 1930s – for there was a definite rise in the birth rate after 1933 – can be explained primarily by economic factors. Germany was the first and only country to achieve full employment during these years, following a period of extreme and often enforced childlessness during the Depression, and contemporary studies from the United States showed a close correlation between rising employment and birth rates.[86] The relationship to Nazi pronatalism, Bock insists, was temporal rather than causal. It is also important to view the increase in births – from under 1.1 million live births in 1931 to over 1.4 million in 1939 – against increasing rates of marriage, which meant that couples were actually choosing to have smaller families, on average 1.8 children in 1940 versus 2.3 in 1920.[87] The norms of marriage and reproduction were changing, but not always in ways that the Nazi government could regulate to its liking. And exemplifying the limits of Nazi marriage and pronatalist policy to enact normative change were marriages between partners deemed by the Nazis to be of 'mixed' races – in particular, Jewish and non-Jewish Germans – as well as liberalizing attitudes towards divorce.

The limits of marriage: Mixed marriages, antisemitism and divorce

The central limitation imposed by Nazi marriage policy was along lines of race. The Law for the Protection of German Blood and Honour, one of the so-called 'Nuremberg Laws' from 15 September 1935, prohibited marriages and sexual relationships between Jews and 'Aryans', which had been legal for decades.[88] The Nuremberg Laws also created new categories of *Mischlinge* to designate children with both Jewish and non-Jewish descent – 'first-degree *Mischlinge*' were those who did not practice the Jewish religion and had no Jewish spouse but two Jewish grandparents, while 'second-degree *Mischlinge*' had one Jewish grandparent. The laws restricted whom one was permitted to marry: 'Aryans' could marry only 'second-degree *Mischlinge*', and the latter were prohibited from marrying 'full Jews'. As Marion A. Kaplan notes, '[b]oth groups had to observe strict marriage restrictions, but in general the "*Mischlinge*" would be spared the expropriation, ghettoization, and destruction reserved for Jews.'[89] This law was soon expanded to prohibit marriages between the 'healthy' and hereditarily ill – even though definitions of 'Jewish' and 'unhealthy' remained ambiguous.[90] The ambivalence surrounding the Jewish *Mischlinge* also, Tina Campt points out, 'came to include and ascribe an equally ambivalent status to Afro-Germans', whose mixed-race children were described as 'bastards', as well as Sinti and Roma.[91]

'Aryans' who had relationships with Jews or other groups now deemed 'alien' were vulnerable to denunciation for committing *Rassenschande* – sexual relations with a member of an 'inferior' race.[92] Even before the 1935 Law was introduced, 'mixed' couples faced harassment and persecution: 'Aryan' women with Jewish lovers might be shoved around by local SA members, or forced to parade the streets bearing signs such as 'I fornicate with Jews'.[93] That year the wildly antisemitic paper *Der Stürmer* published a list of 'recent mixed marriages', with full personal details, advising local party members to look into the affairs of these 'race defilers'.[94] (Evidence suggests that the actual motivations of individuals denouncing their neighbours were more likely to be personal self-protection from a violent ex, disgruntlement or revenge rather than loyalty to the regime.[95]) Such state-endorsed antisemitism led to a divorce boom among Jewish-Gentile couples, with mixed marriages dropping from around 35,000 in 1933 to 20,000 in 1939 and a mere 12,487 by 1944 – the result not only of marital separations, but also emigration, exile, deportation and death.[96]

Yet even in these highly strained circumstances, an impressive number of mixed marriages remained intact – estimates suggest around 80–90 per cent – in testament to the bravery of both partners in the face of Nazi intimidation.[97] Verena Groth, daughter of a part-Jewish father and 'Aryan' mother, later recalled: 'My mother would never have divorced [my father], even in what was an unhappy marriage, and especially not after she knew it would be his downfall.'[98] In 1943, a week-long protest took place in the Rosenstrasse in Berlin, where around two thousand Jews with non-Jewish spouses and children had been locked up. Those protesting, mostly the wives of those imprisoned, returned each day despite threats by the police and SS, chanting 'Give us back our husbands'.[99] These events are movingly recounted in Margarethe von Trotta's 2003 film *Rosenstraße*, and show how at least some non-Jewish partners, 'through noncompliance and protest', demonstrated courage in defending their Jewish spouses. Their ultimate success also points to marriage as offering a level of protection against the state's institutionalized racial persecution, as those protesting appealed to Nazi ideals of family.[100]

While persecution of 'mixed' couples reflects the brutality of Nazi antisemitism, changes to divorce legislation in 1938 with the new Marriage

Law for Greater Germany (*Großdeutsches Ehegesetz, GEG*) offer insight into the more contradictory logics of Nazi sexual morality. The Party at once sought to develop a progressive divorce policy that allowed people to leave unsatisfactory unions, while skewing that policy firmly towards its population and racial priorities.[101] Some aspects of the new law aligned with earlier calls by social progressives for no-fault divorce for couples whose relationship had irreparably broken down and who had lived apart for three years.[102] But the underlying logic was to free individuals up for new marriages and children. In deciding whether a divorce was 'morally justified', judges were expected to interpret this with a view to the needs of *Volk*.[103] For such reasons, some historians argue that the contradictions in Nazi sexual policy were at best 'apparent' (*Scheinwidersprüche*): a closer look reveals that they overwhelmingly aligned with the priorities of Nazi racial hygiene.[104]

Nazi pronatalism was reflected in the divorce reforms via a new clause providing that a marriage could be dissolved on the basis of premature infertility (other new health grounds included mental disorder and contagious illness). This applied only where no 'hereditarily healthy' children had ensued; equally, a partner could sue for divorce if the other had tried illegally to prevent a birth (abortion), or refused without good cause to have children.[105] On the flipside, they could be prevented from divorce if the couple already had healthy children, either biological or adopted.[106] Alimony expectations also shifted – 'guilty' husbands had to support their wives in the manner to which they were accustomed, reflecting the Nazi expectation that women devote themselves to home life. If, however, a man remarried and had further children, payments could be reduced, leaving some divorced single mothers vulnerable and disgruntled.[107]

Nazi divorce reform went beyond what was possible elsewhere in Europe, and resulted in 62,000 divorces in 1939 alone, the first full year of operation. Officials assumed that many who had previously not had legal grounds for divorce now took advantage of the law change, as around half of these marriages were at least twenty years old.[108] Adultery remained grounds for divorce under certain circumstances.[109] The law raised the ire of church groups, and was also criticized by some Nazi politicians, who pointed to the Party's emphasis on the traditional family, as well as the cost of having more divorced wives and their children reliant on the state. In Austria, meanwhile – which was covered by the legal reform following Hitler's 1938 annexation of his country of birth into the greater 'German Reich' – the dominance of the Catholic church meant that previously, access to divorce had been exceedingly rare; consequently, many now welcomed the Nazi reforms.[110] While divorce laws point to the limits of Nazi ideals of marriage and family, in tension between liberalizing reforms and *völkisch* priorities, a comprehensive program of anti-natalism represented the punitive flipside of the regime's racialized sexual policy.

Nazi eugenics, anti-natalism, and institutionalized racism

It is impossible to discuss the pronatalist and pro-marriage policies of the Nazis without also examining their antinatalist counterparts.[111] These followed a much more sinister form of eugenic logic, aimed at policing and prohibiting the births of 'unhealthy' or racially 'polluted' children. Some schemes, such as the aforementioned marriage loans, had a double-edged function, used both to promote and police Nazi sexual ideology. For some unlucky applicants, the required medical checks to access the loan coupons not only denied them permission to marry, but also recommended them for sterilization. Understandably, some Germans stopped applying for the loans, or abandoned their marriage plans altogether.[112]

Abortion was another example of this two-sided approach. Terminating pregnancies continued to be banned for the healthy, 'Aryan' population. Convictions under §218 rose by 50 per cent between 1934 and 1938, and older Paragraphs 219 and 220 were reintroduced, penalizing the advertising or provision of abortion services. Violations could even attract the death penalty from 1943 'if the perpetrator through such deeds continuously impairs the vitality of the German *Volk*'.[113] Despite this, the Gestapo estimated that there were between half a million to a million illicit abortions a year during the late 1930s (probably linked to greater difficulty obtaining contraceptives).[114] Contemporaries accused women seeking an abortion of 'degeneration, complacency, and selfishness'.[115] As Edward Dickinson shows, after 1935 the number of women convicted of abortion offences 'skyrocketed'.[116] From 1936 the policing of abortion was overseen by the Reich Central Office for the Fight Against Homosexuality and Abortions. As the name suggests, this office lumped together various forms of 'deviant' behaviour and 'public morality' issues.[117] Homosexual men, in particular, were viewed as 'population policy zeros' due to their unlikelihood to reproduce.[118]

Yet revisions to the abortion law also *required* that some pregnancies be forcibly terminated for 'eugenic, racial, and ethnic reasons'.[119] In this respect, abortion was conceptually linked to the regime's T4 euthanasia program, which murdered many sick and disabled people, including children with Down's syndrome. Medical experts played an important role: 'the Reich Committee began to exterminate "undesirable" children even before birth, refining and modernizing euthanasia'.[120] Abortion was also enforced in so-called 'pregnancies of defiance' among women deemed 'unfit', but who fell pregnant before they could be sterilized (sometimes with the explicit support of the Catholic Church).[121] Terminations were legally permissible for Jews from 1938, for Polish or other Eastern European workers from 1943, and for 'Aryan' women where pregnancy posed a serious threat to the life of the mother.[122] In such cases the decision was to be made, as one contemporary motherhood guide explained, not by an individual, 'but rather a special commission of doctors. In this way all errors and abuse are ruled out.'[123]

Overseeing forced sterilization of the hereditarily 'unfit' or 'unworthy' was the 1933 Law to Prevent Hereditarily Sick Offspring (*Gesetz zur Verhütung erbkranken Nachwuchses*). The regime saw this as complementing the aforementioned Marriage Health Law and the Law for the Protection of German Blood and Honour. While pronatalist policies targeted women and mothers, anti-natalist policy had a wider reach, targeting anyone believed to be carrying 'unworthy' genes.[124] In 1934, 205 special eugenic courts were established to decide on the 'worth' of individuals to have children, and within a year social workers had forwarded 100,000 applications 'on behalf' of their clients.[125] Between 1934 and 1945 a total of 300,000 to 400,000 people, or around 1 per cent of the population aged between 16 and 50, were sterilized according to this law.[126] It covered nine broadly defined 'diseases': 'congenital feeblemindedness, schizophrenia, manic depression, hereditary epilepsy, Huntington's chorea, hereditary blindness, hereditary deafness, serious physical deformities, and chronic alcoholism'.[127] Yet the interpretation of these categories – especially 'feeblemindedness' – was decidedly elastic and influenced by class and gender prejudices: working-class mothers and families reliant on welfare were especially vulnerable, and women were much more likely than men to be sterilized for allegedly 'loose morals' or having borne illegitimate children.[128] Mathilde M., mother of seven, protested at the unfairness of being nominated for sterilization, challenging the imposition of 'intelligence' questions testing her ability to calculate interest or lottery winnings:

> one should be able to understand that a rural woman like me ... does not gain an exceptional social intelligence working with children and on a farm. ... The experience I had with the intelligence test, someone else would have had with questions about agricultural farming or preparing fodder, so this cannot possibly be based in feeblemindedness.[129]

Like Mathilde M., around two thirds of those sterilized were women. Other groups targeted by this law included psychiatric asylum residents and members of ethnic minorities, including Sinti and Roma – frequently denounced in derogatory terms as 'Gypsies' in ways that combined ideas of the 'racially alien' and 'asocial'.[130]

The idea of sterilization was not new – during the Weimar period there had also been some talk of voluntary sterilization of the 'degenerate', with eugenicists pointing to the costs of keeping disabled people in hospitals and asylums. Such thinking can be traced back to nineteenth-century social Darwinism and, in Germany, the writings of zoologist Ernst Haeckel.[131] Fears of miscegenation had also fuelled earlier calls to sterilize the Rhineland children of Black soldiers and white German mothers (see Chapter 3), who were now approaching adulthood. In 1933 the Nazis commissioned new research to support the compulsory sterilization of these Afro-German children, aware that this stood on shaky legal ground; in practice it was carried out on a semi-voluntary basis, with parental permission and medical evaluations required.[132] Yet we must be careful, cautions Atina Grossmann, not to overemphasize continuities between Weimar social regulation and Nazi eugenics, with the path from Weimar sex reform a 'convoluted and highly contested route', and the Nazi seizure of power 'a radical break' for campaigners for abortion, birth control and sexual counselling.[133] What was new about the Third Reich, observes Lisa Pine, 'was not only the fact that these ideas had a much wider currency, but that they were radicalized and actualized by the regime with the help of the medical profession'.[134] Other nations during these decades, including the United States and Denmark, also pursued sterilization programs for mentally disabled people – in the United States from as early as 1909. Yet the scale was vastly different. Although US eugenicists had hoped to sterilize up to 14 million people out of a total population of 125 million in estimates of 1932, the real number was closer to 29,000 between 1933 and 1945. On a per capita basis, the figure in Germany during this period was thirty times higher, although numbers decreased after 1937, after working through the pool of patients in mental hospitals.[135]

Supporters of Nazi eugenics argued that the sterilization operation was 'basically risk-free' and did not affect one's psychological life or ability to have intercourse: 'Making a person infertile, or sterilisation, does not mean making them sexless, *castration*.'[136] The reality was rather more sinister: the official risk of death stood at 0.5 per cent for women and 0.1 per cent for men, while the specialist medical press reported female mortality rates of up to 5 per cent, and shocking surgical conditions.[137] News of these deaths made this an unpopular law, and increasing public resistance led to fewer operations on women, as well as a move towards 'unbloody' sterilization by x-ray radiation from 1936 – practiced particularly widely in the concentration camps after 1939.[138]

Religion was an important factor determining responses to the regime's anti-natalism. Some Catholic nuns refused to identify candidates for sterilization, although they did so without the explicit support of the Church, which had reached a broad agreement (Concordat) between Pope Pius XI and the Nazi regime, whereby Hitler agreed to defend Catholic rights while the Vatican agreed to support the dictatorship. As Koonz notes, the Nazi leaders shrewdly waited until celebrations about this agreement had subsided before passing the sterilization law, which put Catholics in a conflict of conscience. During the subsequent decade church leaders tended to take a conciliatory approach, agreeing with the authorities that voluntary sterilization might sometimes be acceptable.[139] While Protestant women had for some decades been more supportive than Catholics of birth control, and sometimes also abortion and divorce, Jewish women's organizations tended to be more critical of abortion, but open to birth control. They cautioned, however, against the links between Nazi misogyny and antisemitism, and after 1933 many felt betrayed by the silence of larger women's organizations at the treatment of their Jewish 'sisters'.[140] In later years, racial hygiene policies developed by the Nazi regime fed directly into the wider program of genocide that especially targeted Europe's Jewish population – events commonly known as the Holocaust or Shoah.

The racializing logic underlying Nazi anti-natalist and pronatalist policy offers, as we have already seen, a way of working through the apparent contradictions surrounding sexuality under Nazism. From this perspective, just as it was no coincidence that the same Office that policed abortion oversaw anti-homosexual regulation, it was common for the regime to group together female prostitutes, single mothers and lesbians as 'deviant' or 'asocial' because of their perceived role in spreading STIs and failing to contribute to the birth rate. Hitler sensationally declared the fight against syphilis and prostitution 'one of the colossal tasks of humanity ... for here the sickening of the body is just the result of the sickening of the moral, social and racial instincts'.[141] From 1933, the Law for the Protection of the People and the State allowed police to arrest known prostitutes and made soliciting an offense. Policing was uneven, though, and often left up to local health or social service departments. These could variously lump sex workers as 'asocials' together with those considered vagabonds or mentally ill, earmark them for sterilization or even send them to concentration camps.[142] Especially vulnerable to police regulation were women considered 'asocial' for having passed on STIs to soldiers – often orphaned or neglected teenage girls near military barracks. Quite a few women not engaged in sex work also found themselves caught up in police raids and forced to undergo medical checks – including, embarrassingly, some wives and daughters of Nazi party officials.[143]

The policing of 'asocials' was thus riven with hypocrisy and gendered double standards. Men were more likely to be assigned this classification based on criminality or chronic unemployment than sexual behaviour, while the Nazis stigmatized female prostitutes even as they condoned state-regulated brothels and sex services for soldiers and camp guards.[144] This double standard had high-level support: Party heavyweight Himmler feared that not allowing prostitution would produce homosexuality, weaker soldiers and reduced productivity. A similar logic justified setting up brothels for 'ordinary' Germans and, by 1942, even for some forced labourers and concentration camp prisoners. Sex with prostitutes was carefully rationed – in Auschwitz, military personnel could visit the downtown brothel twice a week on Mondays and Wednesdays. Even as leaders held up the chaste Aryan family as its gold standard, Annette Timm points out, they supported extramarital sex in various forms: they authorized sexual crimes committed under military oversight or in the camps; they oversaw the Lebensborn program; and they condoned prostitution.[145] Despite contravening Nazi ideals of monogamous marriage and racially pure families, such positions nonetheless reflect the underlying goal 'of a racially sanitized state with the power to rule Europe and beyond'.[146]

Persecution, consent, desire: Queer and trans lives under Nazism

Much of the queer political and social scene that had flourished during the Weimar years, especially in larger cities such as Berlin and Hamburg was, along with Hirschfeld's Institute, quashed with the Nazi seizure of power. Queer and trans magazines, activist groups and social organizations began to be forcibly shut down as early as the spring of 1933.[147] This happened with little warning: the last issue of queer women's magazine *Die Freundin* (Girlfriend), published on 8 March, proffered an optimistic invitation to new subscribers alongside its regular love poems, short stories, and a light-hearted instalment of its 'Tranvestites' World' column on 'fashion follies'. There is little sign of the imminent political threat, or even the kind of fierce commentary that had greeted earlier censorship attacks under the Weimar authorities. Following a year-long ban in 1929, for example, the magazine's cover had sported a provocative image of scene leader Lotte Hahm (Figure 3.3) holding up a poster with the words: 'Hurray! *Die Freundin* is back again!,' along with articles criticizing the discriminatory effects of the Weimar 'trash and filth' laws.[148] By 1933, though, the situation for queer Germans, and the possibilities of responding politically to that situation, were changing quickly, drastically and often in unpredictable ways.

The years after 1933 saw a marked, but uneven, rise in legal punishments and violence against queer and trans people. The 'Night of Long Knives' in 1934, described below, marked an early turning point in Nazi attitudes to nonnormative sexualities, yet the very mixed experiences of queer and gender-diverse individuals during these years also force us to think critically about what exactly constituted 'persecution' on the grounds of sex or gender. The evidence also prompts difficult questions about sexual consent – how might we do historical justice, for example, to a same-sex relationship between a concentration camp guard and inmate, clearly based on uneven positions of power, yet not wholly explicable in those terms? Aside from some early forerunners, it was not until the 1990s that historians turned concerted attention to questions of 'outsider' sexualities in Nazi Germany, prompted by developments in feminist and gay history.[149] Since then, the history of queer and trans experiences under Nazism has become a theoretically sophisticated subfield. A first wave of research, especially by German-based historians and activists, focused on making visible LGBTIQ stories once hidden and taboo. Recent work has demonstrated how attention to individual experiences can challenge often unproductive hierarchies of victimhood and suffering.

This rich historiography has important implications beyond the history of sexuality, offering new ways of thinking about how we represent and remember lives lived and lost under Nazi rule.

The Night of Long Knives

On the evening of 30 June 1934, the leader of the Nazi paramilitary *Sturmabteilung* (SA), or Storm Troopers, Ernst Röhm, was arrested and, two days later, murdered, after being handed a pistol and offered the opportunity to kill himself. Three days of bloody massacre followed, in which many leading figures within this organization, including quite a number known to have regularly engaged in same-sex activity, were also killed. Historians have repeatedly returned to Röhm and the SA as examples of how ideas of militarized masculinity and comradeship could combine with homosexuality and nationalist racial politics – much as Adolf Brand's earlier magazine *Der Eigene* had done.[150] The regime's homosexual 'purge' of its own ranks became known as the 'Röhm purge' or 'Night of Long Knives', as behaviours that had been widely known and tolerated began to be viewed as a political threat.

These events cannot be straightforwardly explained in terms of homophobia. Evidence suggests that while Hitler had a range of powerful motives for getting rid of Röhm (Figure 4.3) and the SA, 'homophobia was not one of his major obsessions'.[151] The SA, a militarized, revolutionary force with left-leaning economic sympathies, had been very useful to Hitler in the years before the Nazi seizure of power, but now posed an increasing threat. In justifying the purge, Hitler chose to believe the advice of openly homophobic SS (*Schutzstaffel*) commander Himmler, among others, that Röhm was planning a revolutionary coup. Hitler ordered Röhm and the SA to take a month-long vacation and then launched the attack with the assistance of the SS and army. There is doubt about whether Röhm actually was plotting a coup, and in ordering the attacks, it is quite possible that Hitler went against his own appraisal of Röhm's loyalty. The consequences of these decisions, however, were very real: at least eighty-five people murdered, and possibly many more, many but not all of them stormtroopers.[152]

Beyond its immediate victims, the purge represented a significant shift in rhetoric, as Hitler and his inner circle justified the killings as necessary for the defence of the Nazi state and the moral reputation of the Party.[153] Propaganda minister Joseph Goebbels declared the events a 'storm of purification' against the SA's 'unparalleled debauchery', with Röhm and his fellows coming 'close to tainting the entire leadership with their shameful and disgusting sexual aberrations'.[154] Hitler made it clear that where homosexuality in the SA might previously have been quietly tolerated, that was no longer the case. He issued a set of orders referencing the anti-homosexual laws, demanding that 'all SA leaders exactingly punish all

FIGURE 4.3 *Ernst Röhm, 1924.*

Source: US National Archives NARA 242-HF-0376 001. Public domain/Wikimedia Commons.

offenses against P175 with immediate expulsion'.[155] A newly caustic tone is evident from his public address to the Reichstag shortly afterwards, in which he declared: 'I gave the order to shoot the ringleaders in this treason, and I further gave the order to cauterize down to the raw flesh the ulcers poisoning the wells of our domestic life.'[156] Hitler's use of such moral panic arguments tapped into earlier stereotypes about homosexual cliques in the highest level of government fostered during the Eulenburg affair in the years before the First World War (Chapter 2).[157] They also aligned with a growing emphasis on homosexuality as a 'disease' within the logics of Nazi racial hygiene, and homosexuals as 'degenerates' who corrupted ideal masculine comradeship. Homophobic official propaganda also bolstered ordinary citizens to denounce neighbours on sexual grounds – mostly men, but also some women.[158]

Coming to stand for a distinctly fascist brand of male homoeroticism, the cultural appeal of 'gay Nazis' has been an enduring topic of historical critique over the decades since. In the 1970s, cultural critic Susan Sontag famously reflected on the psychology of 'fascinating fascism', while more recently, Dagmar Herzog and Jack Halberstam explore and challenge the significance of Nazi queer eroticism as much more than just the Party's abject 'other'. (Even the elite SS, despite Himmler's openly homophobic stance, had a handful of homosexual cases per year – a number Himmler hoped to minimize by sending offenders to concentration camps.[159]) In interrogating the persistent 'gay Nazi' myth, scholars note that there is no evidence that same-sex behaviours were more or less prevalent than in the broader population. Instead, they urge us to decouple gay sex from left-wing political radicalism – 'there is no guarantee as to what form the political will take when it comes to sex,' insists Halberstam[160] – and think instead through the 'uncomfortable, unsettling' ways in which homoerotic imagery and behaviours were tangled up with a fascist political agenda.[161]

With the Night of Long Knives, we also need to question whether homosexuality was really the main driving concern. Laurie Marhoefer examines an earlier scandal surrounding Röhm and a brawl in the Reichstag in 1931–2, before the Nazis came to power, and shows that the NSDAP actually weathered this without much trouble, with Hitler standing by his right-hand man, and the late-Weimar media showing constraint in reporting on letters alleging Röhm's homosexuality. That scandal had been spurred along by the left-wing Social Democrats – despite that party's support for homosexual rights. The letters turned out to be fakes, but rumours about Röhm's sexual orientation persisted, and other, more dangerous letters turned out to be real. By 1934, the fragile NSDAP stance of quiet tolerance was no longer deemed sustainable, and plots to remove Röhm increased, culminating in the Night of Long Knives. In the years that followed, moves to eradicate homosexuality and its perceived threat to the *Volkskörper* intensified. Even so, such moments of Nazi tolerance as well as left-wing homophobia should give us pause in viewing Nazi-era sexuality purely through a lens of repression and rupture.[162] They illustrate how claims to sexual morality are often made less out of commitment to sexual norms than the strategic fuelling of political arguments.

Cracking down on homosexuality

Almost exactly one year later after the purge, on 28 June 1935, the regime extended the much-maligned Paragraph 175 criminalizing male homosexuality. Its more punitive version went beyond coitus-like acts to include a wide array of same-sex behaviours such as hugs or simultaneous masturbation. Men engaging in same-sex sex were not only vulnerable to blackmail and imprisonment, as they had been in the Weimar era, but could now be convicted for years of 'preventive' imprisonment in concentration camps. The burden of evidence was also significantly lowered: men were now vulnerable to prosecution 'objectively when a general sense of shame is harmed and subjectively when there exists the lustful intention to excite either of the two men or a third party'.[163] As Edward Dickinson shows, the Nazis managed to swiftly undo many of the reform achievements of the Weimar era, with arrests under Paragraph 175 increasing tenfold between 1933 and 1938, from 857 to 8559 per year. There were significant leaps in convictions in 1936 and 1937 following the revision to the legislation widening the definition of 'unnatural indecency', and mass, coordinated raids on venues that gay men were known to frequent.[164]

Overseeing such operations, and compiling lists of suspected active homosexuals, was the Special Commission for Homosexuality in Berlin, established by the Gestapo in late 1934. From 1936 this morphed into the aforementioned Reich Central Office for the Fight Against Homosexuality and Abortions, which organized a nation-wide crackdown of homosexual gathering places that same year, raiding and closing down gay bars, and placing suspected restaurants, public toilets and beats under surveillance. Indictments of gay men under Paragraph 175 shot up from 948 in 1934 to over 5000 by 1936, with many trials carried out in 'expedited fashion', with little opportunity for legal defence. The reach of these indictments spread beyond the trials themselves, as even those not arrested remained vulnerable to efforts to 'cleanse' workplaces of gay male employees.[165]

During the twelve years of fascist rule, these sharpened legal measures led to many queer and trans individuals being arrested and sent to concentration camps: of around 100,000 prosecutions for same-sex activities, approximately 50,000 gay men were sentenced by Nazi judges, and around 5000 were shipped to the camps between 1933 and 1945. There they were forced to wear the pink triangle emblem on their camp uniforms (see Figure 4.4) – a symbol later reclaimed by gay activists internationally as a reminder of long histories of LGBTIQ persecution. These inmates included a number of gender-diverse and trans individuals officially categorized as homosexual. In a sinister twist on earlier explorations by sexologists and psychoanalysts into a homosexual 'cure', Buchenwald physician Carl Varnet oversaw a frequently lethal program of interventions on homosexual men: hormonal implants, horrific surgical experiments and forced castrations, and even murder.[166]

Some survived to tell their stories. The documentary *Paragraph 175* (dir. Rob Epstein and Jeffrey Friedman, 2000), charts the experiences of several gay men and one lesbian under fascist rule, including resistance fighter and refugee helper Gad Beck, who survived the Nazi era living illegally in Berlin

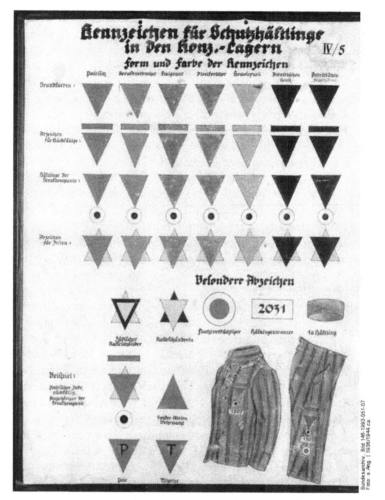

FIGURE 4.4 *Chart of prisoner markings in concentration camps, including the pink triangle (third from right), for prisoners marked 'homosexuell'.*

Source: Bundesarchiv Bild 146-1993-051-07. Public domain/Wikimedia Commons.

and whose memoir *An Underground Life: Memoirs of a Gay Jew in Nazi Berlin* offers a valuable queer eyewitness account. Beck describes how his negotiation of same-sex relationships during these years was shaped as much by a need for a roof over his head as by desire, as well as the creative strategies he and his comrades used to disguise taboo encounters. One of his relationships was with Paul Dreyer, who worked for the Bell chemical company and surprises Beck with 'how forthright' he is in his sexual demands. Dreyer lived with his mother, and would tell her that he was off to the company for air raid duty when actually he came over to Beck's with bread and ham 'expecting love duties' (*Liebesdienste*). Beck recalls that 'honestly, sexually he didn't suit me at all' – for despite his good looks and 'typical German sentimentality', Dreyer 'was always too intense (*heftig*) for me, too much a man'. Nonetheless, the day-to-day realities of underground existence won out: 'I played along with the game, because I did find him congenial after all – and we needed the apartment!'[167] Several eyewitness accounts also exist from queer women who lived through this period, especially thanks to oral histories collected by historian Claudia Schoppmann: Jewish artist Gertrud Sandmann, for example, survived underground in Berlin with the help of her lover Hedwig, while fellow Jewish lesbian Annette Eick just missed being sent to the death camps thanks to the assistance of a police chief's wife: 'If I'd missed the postman, I'd have landed in Auschwitz.'[168]

Everyday queer intimacies and 'heterogeneous' persecution

As accounts such as Beck's and Eick's show, Nazi attempts to 'eradicate' queers did not equate to the outright elimination of anyone who did not conform. Instead, they encompassed a diverse range of persecutions and discriminations – and occasionally, even relative tolerance – often aimed at 're-educating' and integrating non-conforming individuals into Nazi society.[169] Understandably, during these years many people chose to live less visibly queer lives for the sake of safety and self-preservation. Some lesbians and gay men married one another to avoid discrimination and protect their jobs. Although being compelled to adapt to the regime's repressive heteronormativity for the sake of everyday survival was very different to being arrested or imprisoned, such measures could also have lasting negative psychological effects.[170] Yet certain aspects of the queer scene survived well into the Nazi era, either quietly tolerated or pushed underground. As late as April 1940, Gestapo investigators reported on a gathering of the queer 'bowling club *Lustige Neun*' at the Concordia ballrooms in Berlin. The event had attracted, the police reported, around 300 lesbians (*Lesbierinnen*), who engaged in dancing, drinking and 'displays of affection'. The Gestapo had been watching over club activities since 1935, but on this as on other occasions, did not feel it necessary – or even within their legal purview – to intervene. Instead, they merely observed that 'nothing special was noted'.[171]

Such anecdotes highlight the ambiguous situation of queer women, who faced increased social discrimination and surveillance during these years, but did not fall under the legal framework of Paragraph 175. (Austria was an exception: female homosexuality remained illegal even following the annexation of that country by the Nazis in 1938.) Examining the experiences of same-sex desiring women and transmasculine and transfeminine people requires us to look closely at and through conventional sources such as court cases. The Nazis' differentiated approach to male and female homosexuality remained in place throughout the dictatorship, despite some discussion on whether to extend the law to women. By and large, though, officials 'considered it superfluous to criminalize lesbians', concerned that this might 'seduce' heterosexual women into otherwise unknown same-sex behaviours, or endanger the 'naturally' more tender relations among women.[172] 'Lesbians were not taken seriously,' observes Birthe Kundrus, both because they were considered sexually passive but also because they could still conceive children.[173] This ambiguous legal position did not make queer women immune to imprisonment, though – in many cases, their sexuality almost certainly contributed to their arrest ostensibly on other grounds. Some also faced the sadistic punishment of being forced to work in Nazi-run brothels, sometimes servicing male homosexuals undergoing 'reeducation'.[174]

The genderqueer Lotte Hahm mentioned earlier offers a good example of how a simple lens of 'persecution' cannot always capture the experience of queer people under Nazism. Certainly, Hahm was a victim of the regime, imprisoned in Moringen concentration camp in 1935 after being accused of 'seducing' an under-age woman – likely a false charge brought by the woman's father. Reports from fellow prisoners suggest Hahm had been tricked by a Gestapo agent into watching over his suitcase at Alexanderplatz, which was subsequently found to be filled with illegal communist materials. Hahm was later released – probably in 1938, when the Moringen camp was dissolved – and returned to Berlin where they again began organizing queer events. These were generally short-lived, but highlight continuities of queer subculture even under this most authoritarian of regimes. After 1945 Hahm started up a new women's club and was active in human rights circles.[175]

That Hahm's arrest was most likely justified on grounds of communist sympathizing rather than sexuality represents a familiar pattern in the histories of queer women and trans people. While gay man faced sporadic 'purges' and imprisonment, and were forced to wear the notorious pink triangle, gay women were more likely to be locked up on charges of being communists, prostitutes or Jews. As a result, they often wore the red insignia of political prisoners, or the black triangle assigned to 'asocials'.[176] In attempting to unpack what Nazi persecution of queer women and trans people actually looked like, recent studies have shown how important it is to move beyond labels like 'lesbian' or 'persecution' to examine how specific, contextualized reactions to same-sex behaviours were influenced by factors such as Jewishness, age, risk, consent and violence.[177] Samuel Huneke suggests the phrase 'heterogeneous persecution' to describe the wide range of oppressions faced by queer women, including the kind of 'guarded tolerance' shown by the Gestapo surveillance of the *Lustige neun*. Ingeborg Boxhammer and Christiane Leidinger use queer feminist approaches to examine intersections of misogyny, heteronormativity and enforced gender binaries.[178] Marhoefer, meanwhile, takes a microhistory lens to the case of Ilse Totzke – someone who, like Hahm, might today identify as 'queer' or 'transmasculine' given her same-sex desires and masculine self-presentation.[179]

Totzke was aged thirty when she climbed over a fence on the German-Swiss border with twenty-seven-year-old Jewish kindergarten teacher Ruth Basinski, after helping Basinski escape detention in Berlin. Examining her subsequent custody by the Gestapo in Würzburg and the allegations that preceded her arrest, Marhoefer shows that what at first appears as a 'motley collection of seemingly unrelated accusations' takes on a 'unifying theme' when viewed through the lens of gender-fuelled suspicion[180]:

> Though not the subjects of an official state persecution, gender-nonconforming women, transvestites, and women who drew negative attention because of their lesbianism ran a clear, pronounced risk of provoking anxiety in neighbors, acquaintances, and state officials, and that anxiety could, ultimately, inspire the kind of state violence that Totzke suffered.[181]

Even as the Gestapo refrained from direct statements about Totzke's gender presentation or sexuality, Marhoefer's close reading of repeated references to her purported lesbianism or masculinity in the accounts of her denouncers suggest that these were almost certainly factors in her arrest.[182]

Photographs can open up particularly rich layers of historical analysis in such cases. Jennifer Evans and Elissa Mailänder examine police mugshots of Fritz Kitzing, picked up for street solicitation in women's clothing in Berlin's Augsburgerstrasse in late 1933, and later transferred into a series of workhouses and concentration camps. They show that the charges laid against Kitzing defied the 'normal' application of the prostitution law, for the state applied a statute usually reserved for public lasciviousness in women, and thus, perhaps surprisingly, 'seems to have recognized Kitzing's assumed gender and not his biological sex' (see Figure 4.5).[183] Other individuals who defied gender norms often found themselves pushed into categories not of their choosing. Fifty-year-old Erna K was taken into custody for allegedly 'endangering public security and order' by wearing men's clothing (despite having been previously issued with a transvestite pass) and was briefly sent to Lichtenburg concentration camp – only to later receive an official Gestapo permit to wear men's clothing, provided they not use public toilets or baths when doing so. Postal worker Gerd W. petitioned the police to have their cross-dressing permit officially restored – a process that required a medical examination and denial of any 'homosexual' relations. They were ultimately successful in gaining permission to wear men's clothing, although they were refused a new permit.[184] Some people were still applying for transvestite passes as late as 1938, suggesting an ongoing tolerance of certain, regulated expressions of gender diversity.[185]

When it came to intersex people, there were continuities but also breaks with Weimar-era practices. German registry offices were familiar, albeit rarely well-practiced, with provisionally registering intersex infants, at least until a permanent assignment of sex and name could be made, since 'the

FIGURE 4.5 *Kitzing police mugshots.*
Source: Landesarchiv Berlin, A Pr. Br. Rep. 030-02-05, Nr. 169

civil code knew only two sexes'.[186] But Ulrike Klöppel points to how Nazi eugenic principles were also deployed to police anatomical nonconformity, often in ways that drew politicized and highly questionable connections between intersex conditions, Jewishness and leftist and feminist politics. A key goal was to prevent intersex people from marrying, or in some cases, enforce sterilization to avoid the production of 'degenerate' offspring.[187]

Recent scholarship has further deepened our picture of queer experience during these years by showing how meaningful spaces of agency and sexual barter could exist even in the notorious concentration camps. Anna Hájková examines the relationship between camp guard Anneliese Kohlmann and Czech Jewish prisoner Lotte Winterova at Bergen Belsen, showing that while their relationship may or may not have been physical, it did involve Kohlmann, known by the masculine nickname 'Bubi', organizing her postings to follow the attractive Winterova from one camp to another. Winterova, meanwhile, knowingly engaged in barter to make the camp experience less dreadful for herself and her family. Examining such 'ambivalent' interactions is crucial to constructing more inclusive histories, argues Hájková, especially given the scarcity of queer victim voices even within the very large archives of Jewish survivor narratives such as the USC Shoah Foundation Visual History Archive.[188]

Beyond the camps, too, 'queer' experiences of asymmetrical power relations and sexual economies could shape intimate relationships. Gad Beck's memoirs reveal a complex set of negotiations of consent and sexual barter as he tells of how his lover Dreyer sexually exploited Ukrainian forced labourers at his company:

> Among the workers it soon got around what the price of a bath at Dreyer's was. Today it's maybe hard to imagine, but back then during the war, when the workers couldn't wash themselves after the dirty grind and apart from that weren't having any sex, because there weren't any women, they did tend to go along with it.[189]

Attending to the wide-ranging experiences of queer and gender-diverse people under Nazism forces us to think critically about what 'persecution' looked like, and how it was shaped by factors such as race, class or political allegiance. Similar considerations shape recent scholarship on the experience of Black Germans under Nazism, even as sources suggest that official attitudes to this group were not directly comparable with Nazi attitudes towards Germany's Jewish population, but rather much more localized and differentiated – highly dependent on the whims of local officers and the uneven application of regulations often originally intended for other groups such as gay men or those of 'inferior' stock.[190] Crucially, such intersectional histories of nonconformity and sex-gender diversity during the Nazi era remind us of the need to embrace complexity and tell plural, multi-layered stories that encompass violence and persecution, but also longing, eroticism and desire.

Everyday sexuality in wartime: Marriage, barter, violence

Following the declaration of war against Poland in 1939, Nazi pronatalist and anti-natalist policy continued to shape the everyday lives, relationships and gender expectations of Germans, as did older inherited sexual norms of heterosexual monogamy. But a number of things also changed. That year saw couples rush to the altar, as strict health and eugenic requirements were relaxed to bolster morale. 'War marriages' enabled couples to marry even at different times and locations while the man was at the front.[191] The rising marriage rate, observes Heineman, 'suggest[s] a backlog of couples who had previously been unable to marry', with the looser regulations benefitting socially 'undesirable' individuals as much as those considered 'desirable'.[192] Soon, though, couples across the country faced new pressures, as millions of men aged between eighteen and forty-five were called up into the military and long periods of separation ensued. Conflicts during home leave were inflamed by fears of wives having extramarital relations while their partners were away. This represented a continuation of the gendered double standard, for as we have seen, the army provided soldiers with access to brothels, even as women at home were held to a higher moral bar including in divorce cases. Public opinion was more divided, though, with many sympathetic to the plight of adulterous women left alone for extended periods.[193]

Declining marriage rates saw some creative policy and initiatives. One decree enabled women, generally single mothers, to enter into a 'postmortem' marriage with a deceased soldier – popularly dubbed 'corpse marriages'. This allowed them to access benefits and legitimize their children, in

> a concession to reality: It made widows out of unmarried Aryan mothers who had conceived children when their engagement was firm: women whose illegitimate children did not indicate their asociability. ... They and their children would remain part of the *Volksgemeinschaft*.[194]

Around 18,000 women entered such marriages by 1945. And while this caused problems, such as when there was more than once potential 'fiancée', or where the marriage caused the soldier's parents to lose welfare benefits, they were hugely important to a generation of wartime women who 'had a deep personal stake in the institution and entitlements of marriage without ever having experienced routine married life'.[195] Such investment was also reflected in the efforts of organizations such as the National Association of the German Family, which oversaw letter-writing centres to encourage postal romances between German women and soldiers at the front.[196]

More controversially, many German women entered into liaisons with foreign – especially Polish – workers and prisoners of war (POWs).[197] Over seven million foreigners were living in the 'Greater German Reich' by late 1944, including 1.9 million POWs and 5.7 million forced labourers.[198] Hamburg social worker Dr Käthe Petersen warned of a rapid moral decline among soldiers' wives, linking this to the new economic and social realities:

> Many previously respectable wives have been alerted to the existence of other men through going out to work. In many firms – the tram company is a particularly good example – the male workers seem to have acquired the habit of going after the soldiers' wives. ... Women who previously devoted themselves to their household chores, and were good mothers, have been led by such influences to neglect their housework and children, and to interest themselves only in night-time adventures and the quest for male company.[199]

Often, such 'fraternizing with the enemy' fell under the purview of Nazi race laws, with the Office of Racial Policy warning in 1940 of the 'extraordinary threat of contamination and pollution this concentration of foreign workers poses ... to our German lineage'.[200] Penalties for contravening these laws varied according to gender and racial status. A German man who had sex with a female foreign worker was as likely to face public approval as be sent to a concentration camp. In contrast, German women with foreign lovers might by publicly humiliated by local vigilantes, who would shave the heads of accused women and parade them down the street bearing placards; some were then sent to prison or a concentration camp. Their foreign lovers most often faced execution.[201] Such penalties again highlight the need to view race and gender intersectionally in the history of sexuality. 'National Socialist racism was never gender-neutral', but imposed different roles, expectations and limits on women and men – particularly when it came to sexual encounters.[202]

In 1942 a new crime, 'insulting husbands at the front', was introduced. This allowed married soldiers whose wives had had affairs to sue those wives' lovers – while the marriage remained intact, at least in a legal sense. Adulterous women risked having their state benefits removed on the grounds of 'immoral conduct'. From 1943 they could even face 'postmortem divorce' proceedings, instituted by the state against war widows seen to be damaging their fallen husband's honour, 'not to mention the damage done to the state treasury, which paid a widow's pension'.[203] This applied particularly to German women who had relations with 'racially inferior' POWs, especially Slavs. Yet although they faced censure, many women later recalled such encounters in ways that emphasized romantic love and sexual pleasure.[204] Andrea Bartl, convicted to over a year's penal servitude by a Nazi Special Court for having an affair with a French POW, later remembered giving her lover, Beaulieu, a silver bracelet as a 'keepsake' of the 'intimate nature' of their relationship.[205] The war years also saw increased Gestapo pressure on 'Aryan' women in mixed marriages to divorce Jewish husbands, as 'persecution of the Jews now took priority over all other aspects of Nazi racial policy'.[206]

While these are examples of how Nazi officials policed sexual relationships between Germans and foreigners that were often at least semi-consensual, non-consensual sexual violence and rape were used both by and against the regime to underscore relationships of power. Feminist historians have also demonstrated how rape functioned as an overt strategy of war: 'For most nations during the Second World War, the victorious power's sexual "occupation" of the "body" of another nation symbolized both the military defeat of the enemy nation and the humiliation of its male population.'[207] On the German side, Nazi soldiers and officials committed widespread rape in occupied territories, and as noted above, forced women into work in military and concentration camp brothels.[208] Elissa Mailänder has undertaken a close reading of a 'rape-joke trophy selfie' photograph, in which around fifteen German soldiers at the Eastern Front stand around laughing as one of their number mimics penetrative sex with a woman who may be either alive or dead, and who may or may not have been subjected to gang rape. Mailänder shows how the performative mimicry at work in this image draws attention to the self-aware masculine arrogance, agency and subjugation of women deemed racially inferior – as well as the importance of engaging with the 'ambiguous and contradictory meanings' of fragmentary sources.[209] Such work supports Regina Mühlhäuser's influential analysis of the diverse motives for sexual violence among Wehrmacht (German army) soldiers, which shows that the military created structures that actively enabled licentiousness and violence.[210]

During the final weeks of war and following the liberation of the country by the Allied forces, rape also became a frighteningly everyday occurrence for millions of German women. In the southwest, the French command condoned mass rape and plunder following the occupation of Freudenstadt – long hushed over in the interests of postwar German-French 'friendship'.[211] Most notoriously, the liberation of East Prussia and Berlin by the Soviet Red Army involved the rape of hundreds of thousands of women – estimates suggest at least 110,000 women were victims of one or more rapes in April and May alone, and as many as one in three women, or 500,000 of the 1.5 million women living in the largely female city of Berlin at the close of the war, ultimately endured attacks – often on multiple occasions and by multiple abusers. These had serious consequences: suicide, STIs, abortions and unwanted pregnancies. Many women also felt compelled to engage in semi-prostitution with a single Russian 'protector' to guard against further attacks, or in exchange for food or money in a city largely in rubble and cut off from supplies.[212] Journalist Marta Hillers described this collective experience of sexual violence and barter in her diary of April and May 1945: 'I need a wolf here who will keep the wolves away from me. An officer, as high as possible, Kommandant, General, whatever I can get.'[213] Despite Hillers' pragmatic tone, the traumatic legacy of the attacks haunted the postwar decades, showcased in the 1992 documentary *Liberators Take Liberties: War, Rapes, Children (BeFreier und BeFreite)* by feminist historians and filmmakers Helke Sanders and Barbara Johr. The Red Army rapes have been central to discussions around women's victimhood and sexual agency during these years, feeding into wider debates about whether and how it is possible to discuss 'German' suffering or victimhood in the context of the Holocaust.[214]

The extremes of Nazi racial policy, and the regime's persecution of Jewish, Sinti, Roma, Black, homosexual, disabled and other marginalized groups, were most fully realized within the genocidal framework of the concentration camps. Yet even here, as we saw in the context of queer experience, historians of sexuality and the Holocaust insist that we move beyond black-and-white polarizations of victimhood and persecution to focus instead on categories such as 'guilt', 'barter' or 'redress'. Sexual violence did play a pivotal and traumatic role in the camp experience of many: men and boys as well as women and girls.[215] It was also part of the experience of many whose gender or sexual expression fell outside of social norms. Yet sexual relationships could also be shaped by intimacy, eroticism and degrees of consent and negotiation, as well as by intersections of race, gender, class and ability.[216] The 'range of sexual barter was wide and varied, from bringing dainties to a virginal teenage girlfriend, to being a functionary's lover for protection from transports, to the straightforward exchange of intercourse for food'.[217] We write better histories when we acknowledge such gradations of agency and the complexity of interpersonal relationships rather than assuming that we can always map victimhood and persecution neatly onto sexual encounters.[218]

* * *

The Third Reich's traumatic and violent legacies are closely bound up with sexuality – an entanglement vividly symbolized by the storming of Hirschfeld's Institute in 1933. The logics of Nazi racial hygiene were fundamental to its pronatalist and anti-natalist policies around marriage, abortion, birth control and divorce. These areas of normative policy and policing were crucial to underpinning the regime's power over even the most intimate aspects of the lives of everyday Germans. Sexuality is central, too, to the history of war and genocide that characterized the later years of National Socialism: the violence of the mass rapes; the homophobic, transphobic and misogynistic persecution of 'deviants' and 'asocials'; the sexual abuse and uneven relationships of exchange in the concentration camps; and the racist and ableist legacies of Nazi eugenics.[219] This period, which has presented many challenges for historians of sexuality, shows us time and again the importance of challenging easy categorizations of identity, victimhood and persecution.

Part of the problem in thinking about how to memorialize the sexual history of this period, Jennifer Evans observes, has been our reluctance to look to the past for 'erotic subjectivities that don't easily graft onto our own'.[220] Scholars have carved out productive paths of inquiry by emphasizing the need to look beyond the 'unspeakable' to attend not just to violent histories of persecution, but to how these coexisted alongside more optimistic and emancipatory experiences of pleasure and desire. The sexual history of German modernity under fascist rule pushes us to look more closely at everyday intimacies and intersections between gendered, classed, racialized and other social positionings which variously challenged and affirmed older norms. It opens up crucial questions around how we remember traumatic pasts, and how we might do justice to the role of intimacy in shaping human experience even under the strict conditions of life in an authoritarian state. The next two chapters consider the long legacies of this period into the postwar decades.

5

Love, sex and marriage in the divided Germanies

At the latest in the 1970s the citizens in the GDR started to defy all kinds of possible constrictions with respect to their partner- and sexual behavior. They became FKK-fans. They birthed illegitimate children in droves. They handed in divorce papers when love had faded. They casually got involved with a coworker if they felt like it. At some point kissing couples lay on the grass in Leipzig's Clara-Zetkin-Park or female students sunbathed naked, and no police intervened. ... This process was also combined with a more positive valuation of sexuality ... very connected with family and with love. So: somehow a romantic ideal.[1]

The rose-tinted glasses with which East German sexologist Kurt Starke here looks back on shifts in the changing sexual culture of the German Democratic Republic (GDR) were by no means unique. The East German state and the many sex educators and counsellors it employed prided themselves on offering 'better' conditions for sex and intimacy than the capitalist West. A 1963 youth memorandum (*Jugendkommuniqué*) by the dominant Socialist Unity Party (SED) – formed from a forced merger of the Communist Party (KPD) and Social Democratic Party (SPD) in 1946 – underlined this official support for premarital sex, stating that 'every true love between two young people deserves candid respect' and that 'true love belongs to young people like young people belong to socialism'.[2] GDR sexologists wrote at length about female orgasm, while strong female employment, parental leave and childcare arrangements helped to dissolve taboos around single motherhood and promote women's sexual as well as financial independence. But did women really have better sex under socialism, as one bestselling recent history has claimed?[3] Was the German Democratic Republic a haven of liberated sexuality, nudist culture and gender equality, or as others have suggested, a much more stifling period of forced conformity of love and relationships to the economic priorities of state socialism?

Equally, how accurate is the frequently repeated narrative of progressive liberation for the history of sexuality in the Federal Republic of Germany (FRG) or West Germany during these decades, moving from postwar baby boom and 1950s domesticity to a 'revolution' of 'sex as spectator sport', as loudly proclaimed by leading news magazine *Der Spiegel* in 1966, fuelled by radical student and counterculture movements?[4] What were the conditions enabling young Luftwaffe transport pilot and war widow Beate Uhse to move from penning a small guidebook on the rhythm method of contraception to mail-order sex aid business, to eventually overseeing the largest commercialized erotica business in the world?[5] What led a new generation of feminists in West Germany of the 1970s to declare that 'sexuality is the lynchpin of the women's question', at once 'mirror and instrument of the oppression of women in all spheres of life', and how much did they have in common with their sisters in the East?[6]

The postwar history of the two Germanies is one that begins in the crisis years of the 'zero hour' of levelled cities and liberation by the Allies. Occupying forces from Britain, France and the United States strongly shaped the developing political climate in the West, while the East established itself as a socialist state under Soviet oversight. These authorities faced numerous challenges in the initial aftermath: clearing the rubble left from years of bombing campaigns, re-establishing services and infrastructure and denazifying the population were front and centre, but also 'the more elusive and abstract hope of returning some semblance of normalcy to everyday life' – a reconstruction that was emotional as much as material.[7] Four years of occupation rule transformed into the division and formation of the two German states in 1949, although the formal military occupation continued until the mid-1950s, and there was still considerable movement between East and West until the erection of the Berlin Wall in the summer of 1961.[8] This chapter takes us from these immediate postwar years, when women known as *Trümmerfrauen* were clearing away the rubble to begin the long process of rebuilding, and 'Bahnhof boys' lined up alongside 'loose women' selling sex from Berlin's railway stations.[9] It then homes in on shifting norms of intimacy during the four decades of political division when Germany was at the very epicentre of the Cold War, until the fall of the Berlin Wall in 1989. The focus is on ideas of 'normal' love and marriage within and across these two political contexts, including how these were reflected and problematized via shifting divorce patterns and laws, and in diverging cultures of sex education, advice and media, from popular magazines to pornography. It examines how ideas of sex and marriage overlapped and diverged across the very different political, economic and social structures of western capitalist democracy and eastern state socialism. More broadly, it continues this book's larger task of challenging straightforward narratives of sexual emancipation by highlighting the ongoing tensions between sexual freedoms and normative restrictions that shaped sexual life during this period, and continuities as well as breaks with sexual developments during the Weimar and Nazi eras.

The sexual history of the GDR and FRG during these decades has often been treated separately, although a number of studies have begun to present what Jennifer Evans describes as a more 'entangled' picture of cross-border encounter and intersecting developments in matters ranging from policing and law reform to the history of the Pill, and transnational networks of pornography and erotica.[10] Historians of West Germany have produced excellent studies on postwar marriage, single motherhood, youth cultures and the widely touted 'sexual revolution', while those focusing on the East have examined socialist family policy, marriage and divorce, sex education, pornography and Cold War sexual politics. Chapters 5 and 6 emphasize the productive comparisons that emerge from examining German-German sexual cultures through a comparative, entangled lens. In a study of youth cultures across East and West, Uta Poiger emphasizes that such a comparative approach requires us to 'employ concepts that make meaningful comparisons possible, concepts that allow us to think about fundamental differences between the two Cold War enemies as well as similarities between them'. She suggests, and I agree, that categories of 'norms', 'normality' and 'identity' work particularly well for this purpose.[11]

While this chapter focuses especially on more normative and state-sanctioned forms of sexual expression, homing in on dominant ideas of marriage, family and sex education, with a particular focus on the earlier postwar decades, Chapter 6 represents the counterpart of this history, examining various waves of radical and oppositional thought and activism, from 1950s youth movements, when trends in fashions, music and sexual attitudes often crossed the new German-German border, through to 1980s AIDS activism. There the particular focus is on the period often heralded as one of sexual 'revolution' from the late 1960s, when debates around abortion, contraception, feminism, LGBTIQ rights and identities, and public sexual cultures and pornography – sometimes dubbed a *Sexwelle* (sex wave) – took off amidst a heady climate of student, left-wing and feminist activism. There is, of course, significant cross-over between these two chapters: the evolution in sex education guides and marriage manuals discussed below, for example, formed part and parcel of the critiques of established gender roles, ideas of sexual emancipation and burgeoning sexual print cultures examined in Chapter 6, as did shifting attitudes to marriage and divorce. What this thematic focus aims to achieve is a deeper comparative perspective of the intertwined sexual history of these decades: the parallels as well as very real differences in how sex and intimacy were experienced across the German-German divide.

Love in the rubble: The years of occupation (1945–9)

Images of *Trümmerfrauen* digging through the rubble to keep their families going in the absence of husbands and restore a semblance of everyday life have often come to symbolize a widespread sense of 'crisis' in the immediate aftermath of 1945 – the 'zero hour' of defeat and liberation from the years of Nazi rule and genocide. The 'Aryan' family propaganda of the Nazis lay in tatters, with many German families torn apart, and many households headed by war widows or divorcees. As one Berlin journalist declared in 1946: 'The family fragment dominates the hour.'[12] Many of the men who had managed to return from the war were physically and emotionally damaged, at times unable to work altogether; others returned only years later from prisoner-of-war camps. During this time, families contended with severe rations and shortages. Noting the impact this had on intimate relations and traditional family forms, historians have described the 'fragility of heterosexuality' of these postwar years.[13]

Compounding this fragility was the widespread sexual violence that characterized the end of the war and first months of liberation, with mass rapes of German women by occupying soldiers in both East and West, as seen in Chapter 4. Jewish survivors of the Holocaust faced particular challenges in the wake of the horrors of the Nazi era, with the trauma of that experience to last for generations. Displaced persons, including from the former German territory of East Prussia, found themselves without a home and needing to re-establish themselves within Germany's much tighter national borders. As one contemporary observer remarked, Berlin's 'morals as well as its buildings (lay) in ruins, its families shattered as well as its houses'.[14] Germans across the political spectrum found themselves confronted with the reality of their most recent past, even as many, especially in the first postwar decades, tended to view themselves as victims rather than victimizers of Hitler's Germany: in 1950 philosopher Hannah Arendt scathingly diagnosed 'a deep-rooted, stubborn, and at times vicious refusal to come to terms with what really happened'.[15]

Examining these years of upheaval, occupation and crisis, Jennifer Evans argues that we must take seriously the many blurrings and overlaps of sexual activity and exchange. Importantly, her 'entangled' approach involves viewing men and women, queer, straight and trans, as part of an overlapping landscape of sexual practices and cultures – one defined not only by violence and trauma, but also by eroticism, desire and excitement. As we saw in Chapter 4 in relation to intimacy in the concentration camps or underground, it is important to acknowledge this multilayered experience of sexuality even in spaces in which agency and mobility were significantly limited. During the later war months, Evans finds that the communities that developed in the air raid bunkers were similarly 'highly charged places of social interaction'.[16]

As people gathered under the sound of bombs to cook, seek shelter, gossip, comfort and annoy one another, they shared stories and flirtatious glances, at times 'breaking down established social, class, age, and racial boundaries' in ways that, while often boring or terrifying, could also 'yield a host of erotic possibilities'.[17] In the years that followed, too, these massive spaces took on a variety of functions that at times had distinctly sexual overtones – a shelter for many of Berlin's orphaned or homeless street youth, in particular, the bunkers 'provided emotional relief from the quotidian challenges of life after Hitler with black marketeers, rent boys, and fallen women camping out together in subterranean cliques and gangs'.[18]

The first postwar decade saw a rapid rise in prostitution. In the immediate postwar years, an estimated 100,000 women in Berlin were either registered, professional or amateur prostitutes – around 7 per cent of the entire female population.[19] STI rates were rising rapidly – as they also had after the First World War – and syphilis and gonorrhoea again became widespread problems. Fears of sinking moral standards among Germany's postwar population tapped into and implicitly reproduced Nazi-era attacks on 'immoral' women who slept with prisoners of war or had affairs while their husbands were at the front.[20] In both East and West occupied zones there was a very fine line between prostitution and promiscuity, and this blurring continued into the era of division. In the East, the label 'hwG' (*häufig wechselnder Geschlechtsverkehr*, or frequently changing sexual partners) came to be used interchangeably with prostitution, especially in official contexts.[21] In the western zones in particular, young German women seen to be 'fraternizing' with American GIs attracted dismissive labels suggestive of immorality or prostitution such as '*Amiliebchen*' (Ami-lover) or 'Veronika' – sexualized and gendered attacks explored in more detail in the context of new youth cultures in Chapter 6.

The entanglements of sexual practices and spaces that Evans describes were particularly evident amidst the rubble of the capital, Berlin, where 'boy and girl prostitutes often worked the same spaces', even if they were policed under very different laws.[22] Increasing numbers of children and young people were now among the city's sex workers, often desperate to earn money for food or shelter.[23] Making up another sizable minority of sex workers, male prostitutes continued to be policed in the immediate occupation years as they had been during the Nazi era, under the 1935 version of the anti-homosexual Paragraph 175. And while this was somewhat relaxed in the East in 1950, following the establishment of the GDR a year earlier, laws against buying sex or sex with minors remained firmly in place in the name of youth protection. In the West, the full force of Paragraph 175 continued to apply well into the late 1960s (see Chapter 6).[24] Yet at least in the early years of occupation and the frequent crossing of zones for work, entertainment, or sex before the building of Wall, 'the homosocial mapping of the city's male sex trade resisted the rigidity of ideological borders': police in the Soviet zone often arrested West Berliners who had come over for sex, and boys frequently travelled in the other direction to service wealthy men in the west.[25] Police across the zones also cooperated in policing rent boys. Eighteen-year-old Horst D. from the western working-class district of Neukölln was arrested in 1948 during a raid on Zoo station in the British zone and questioned for being in a 'known hangout for homosexuals and rent boys', before being pinned down on previous charges of assault in the Soviet zone. 'With little fanfare or opposition', Evans notes, 'he was promptly sent eastward for questioning'.[26]

In 1949 two new Republics were formed, and with this formal political and economic split along heavily ideological lines, the foundations were laid for distinct sexual cultures to emerge in the decades that followed. Politicians and intellectuals across East and West positioned marriage and the family as central building blocks of postwar reconstruction, but that reconstruction was oriented towards the divergent goals of socialism and democracy.[27] Before homing in on questions of marriage and divorce, let us turn firstly to larger narratives that have surrounded the history of sexuality in East and West in the 1950s and early 1960s – images of an at times stultifying sexual conservatism and emphasis on traditional gender roles in the newly formed FRG, and of attempts to integrate sex into a more positive, forward-looking version of state socialism in the East. As we will see, in both contexts older norms of binary and heterosexual monogamy continued to play a key role.

Embracing domesticity in the Federal Republic

In West Germany in the early years of division, economic improvement was soon strongly in evidence – the beginnings of the much-proclaimed 1950s 'Economic miracle', fuelled by the US Marshall plan. The black market had already largely disappeared following the currency reform of 20 June 1948, and the FRG began to establish itself among western powers as an important democratic partner in the battle against communism, especially with the foundation in April 1949 of the North Atlantic Treaty Organization.[28] Amidst these postwar transitions there was considerable emphasis in the media and politics on instituting a return to 'normal' – even as what constituted 'normal' life had fundamentally changed. In particular women's status and the place of the family became important domestic political issues. Women vastly outnumbered men: in 1950, there were 1400 women for every 1000 men aged between twenty-five and thirty-nine. Many households were headed by women, and the divorce rate continued to grow until the early 1950s as a result of long separations and radically disrupted partnerships.[29] The West German Basic Law (*Grundgesetz*) adopted in 1949 stated that 'men and women have the same rights'. This went further than the Weimar-era promise that equality was 'fundamentally' guaranteed, and reacted against the Nazis' marginalization of women's rights, recognizing women's contributions during the war and immediate postwar years. But it was only pushed through in the face of opposition from the conservative Christian Democratic and Christian Social Unions (CDU and CSU).[30]

The gender equality enshrined in the Basic Law did not prevent many women and men alike embracing, or seeking to return to, traditional models of marriage and family life in the unsettled climate of the 1950s. 'In practice,' observes Annette Timm, 'focusing on women's "needs" meant preserving older conceptions of the patriarchal, bourgeois family in which women's economic dependence was a function of their role as mothers, and pro-natalist sentiments were enshrined in public policy.'[31] Scholars frequently describe this as an era of intense sexual conservatism, when people were 'desperately seeking normality'.[32] The core reference point for what Robert Moeller has dubbed the 'political reconstruction of the family' during these years, as Christopher Neumaier examines in his new *longue durée* history of the family in modern Germany, was that inherited from the nineteenth century: 'the ideal of the Christian bourgeois nuclear family, whose interior space was protected from state intervention'.[33] This ideal marked a decisive rejection of the kind of Nazi-era intervention into family structures and reproduction seen in Chapter 4. The emphasis on non-working mothers, meanwhile, represented a rejection of the socialist expectations of women's paid work in evidence in the Soviet occupied zone, which only increased in the GDR. In such ways, West German leaders drew on the traditional ideal of the bourgeois nuclear family and old-fashioned gender roles to shore up the self-image of the Cold War-era Federal Republic.[34]

Nineteenth-century norms of gender complementarity were celebrated in politics and the media, and reproduced through everyday interactions with friends, family and the wider community. A number of factors helped to underscore this conservative gender and family ideal. Elizabeth Heineman observes that some women whose husbands had returned from the war found that their menfolk, now recovering from wounds both physical and emotional, proved more pleasant companions than they had once been. Post-Marshall Plan economic stability also encouraged female dependence on husbands in ways that some viewed as appealing: 'a male wage enabled a level of material comfort inaccessible to women living on their own'.[35] At the same time, subtle shifts such as a reduced age gap between husband and wife upon marriage point to the long reach of more egalitarian models of partnership, such as the 'companionate marriage' embraced by many during the Weimar years. In a large sociological study of families in and around the regional city of Darmstadt in Hesse during the 1950s, Gerhard Baumert found that whereas interwar marriages had had a typical age gap of five to ten years, this had reduced to three to five – and while this did not necessarily affect the gendered division of labour within those marriages, it did impact on the nature of the partnership itself, including a 'very significant loosening up of previously rigid notions and models'.[36] While this was partly due to longer-term transformations, it was also a consequence of the Second World War. Baumert also found that the urban/rural difference had decreased, with rural inhabitants now only marginally more conservative in outlook than those in the cities, and similarly marginal differences between Catholics and Protestants, and men and women. As Neumaier observes, Baumert showed 'that the traditional socio-structural distinguishing characteristics had significantly lost meaning in the postwar period'.[37]

Many women who had rejected marriage during the war and occupation years now embraced this long-standing institution. On average, West German women began to marry and have children at a younger age, to divorce less frequently and, where financially possible, to move away from paid work. The appeal of the hearth and private realm, summarized by the traditional 'three Ks' of children, kitchen and church (*Kinder, Küche, Kirche*) so celebrated by the Nazis, regained – or retained – significant appeal.[38] Factors like lack of childcare meant that many women in the West who worked outside of the home did so out of economic necessity rather than for career reasons, and they tended to remain in part-time or much lower paid work than men.[39] They also faced social ostracism: conservatives saw working mothers as a threat to traditional marriage and family, their independence preventing a return to normality. Such political views did not always reflect reality in direct ways, however. West Germany's 'economic miracle' also led many women into paid work, and by 1950, married mothers made up around 13 per cent of the workforce. By 1960, this figure had more than doubled.[40]

Pointing to continuities in sexual attitudes across the major political rupture of 1945, sexual conservatism was particularly evident in church and political campaigns aimed at protecting children and teenagers from explicit imagery. These continued in the vein of earlier moral purity movements, as authorities elected to retain Nazi-era laws restricting the advertisement of most contraceptive methods. In 1953, the West German parliament introduced a new anti-smut *Schund und Schmutz* law restricting the sale and display of pornography, the Law on the Distribution of Youth-Endangering Publications. This was strongly reminiscent of late-Weimar censorship in the name of youth protection, and continued rather than broke with Nazi-era policing of materials deemed 'immoral' (see Figure 5.1).[41]

Other signs of a more restrictive moral climate – one that was also more overtly Christianized than either Weimar or Nazi public debate – include the thwarting of attempts to liberalize abortion laws by coalitions of left- and right-wing Christian intellectuals and politicians, and the renewed persecution of male homosexuality after a momentary period of tolerance in the immediate postwar years.[42] That such shifts were not just at the level of political debate, but were also personally experienced, at least in hindsight, as more repressive is evident in comments such as New Left writer Ulf

FIGURE 5.1 *Braunschweig students throwing 'youth endangering' comics into rubbish trucks to swap against 'good youth books.'*

Source: © Ullstein Bild, Image No. 00823522.

Preuss-Lausitz's later description of his 1950s adolescence: 'The postwar child was *surrounded ... with the prohibitions and injunctions ...* . The postwar German family (or what was left of it) was fixated on conformity, on not standing out.'[43] And while such memories are always coloured by the later development of collective forms of historical remembering, notably the pervasive rhetoric of 'sexual revolution' that has come to characterize the period since the late 1960s, and in which the New Left played a prominent role, the atmosphere of social conservatism and Cold War liberal consensus was firmly underscored at a political level with the establishment of a 'Grand

Coalition' government between CDU and SPD in 1966 – soon to become a target of the student radical movements.[44] At an official level at least, the moral purity campaigns of this decade dominated public discussions of sex in the Federal Republic.[45]

Emphasizing moral 'cleanliness' (*Sauberkeit*) was not simply about sex. Even as 1950s sexual conservatism had many continuities with the recent Nazi past, it also represents a way in which West German authorities sought to draw a line between that past and their own postwar state. Dagmar Herzog has argued that this formed

> a core element in securing West German Christianity's antifascist moral authority, for during the Third Reich sexual matters had formed a main focus of conflict between the Nazis and the Catholic Church in particular and Nazis had continually ridiculed Christian prudery and opposition to premarital heterosexuality.[46]

This dedicated 're-Christianization' in the 1950s, Herzog argues, represented a strategic and self-affirming method of shifting focus away from the mass murder of the Holocaust, whether in domestic debates, relationships with occupying forces or in international relations.[47] In this view, withdrawal into the private sphere was an understandable response to the invasion of private life during the Nazi era, reinforced by the desire to avoid directly confronting the larger, national responsibility for mass murder and world war. The urge to repair marriages and rebuild families after the deprivations of war also fulfilled deeply personal needs.[48] As Sybille Steinbacher observes, while Herzog with this argument does not question larger narratives of postwar sexual history as moving from a more repressive to a more liberal phase, her psychoanalytically informed analysis of this conservatism as a direct reaction to Nazi sexual politics adds an important angle to the historiography.[49] It also complements the studies by Moeller and others outlined above regarding the decidedly political implications of the 'reconstruction' of the postwar West German family.

But the sexual history of this initial postwar period in the Federal Republic cannot be told purely through a lens of conservatism. The plural and at times radical sexual cultures that coexisted during these years are highlighted by scholarship such as Evans's study of Berlin's sexual subcultures, or Heineman's work on postwar marriage and its limits, as well as by the burgeoning number of queer histories of this decade.[50] It is also important to recognize generational differences, for there was, observes Evans, 'something new about this generation of pleasure-hungry youth, thirsting for adventure amidst the graying ashes of the broken cityscape'.[51] Things were no less complex in the East during these decades, even as the political rhetoric and economic priorities of state socialism provided very different frameworks for discussing sexual matters. There, too, the postwar decades witnessed a combination of challenges to and affirmations of established binary gender roles, heterosexual monogamy and ideas of moral cleanliness. At the same time these were increasingly skewed towards the ways in which loving relationships and families might support the goals of the 'workers' and peasants' state'.

Evolving socialist sex-gender norms: A veneer of equality?

In *Love in the Time of Communism*, historian Josie McLellan poses a fundamental question for historians of sexuality in the GDR: in what ways did and could political repression and sexual liberation coexist? And how, in turn, might we explain trends such as soaring rates of divorce, abortion and births outside marriage, or the enormous popularity of nude bathing in the context of the GDR?[52] One prominent narrative about East German sexuality is that private freedoms provided an important outlet: an escape from the constraints of life under the authoritarian state overseen by the SED. This was effectively the only party in a system that, despite regular elections, deeply undermined democratic participation through measures such as heavy secret police (*Stasi*) surveillance and strong punishments for dissidents. The economic and political goals of the East German state, meanwhile, required a strong and active workforce of women as well as men, and this meant balancing seemingly competing priorities: keeping women in paid work, while also improving the birth rate.[53]

'When the SED looked at women in the early 1950s, they saw (potential) workers,' remarks Donna Harsch in her history of women and family in the GDR.[54] At the same time, the East German government quickly enacted laws and structures that emphasized women's maternal responsibility: the Department of Mother and Child, first part of the Ministry of Labour and later the Ministry of Health, 'suggests that the agency most directly involved with women also saw a (prospective) mother when it looked at women'. In the East as in the West, the massive population devastation caused by the war was keenly felt by leaders, who embraced a firmly pronatalist policy. 'In fact, reproduction ran a close second to production in policy toward women in the 1950s.'[55] In this, SED policy represented a continuity of Nazi-era approaches, as well as older norms of femininity: 'The message about maternity did not have to undo twelve years of Nazi propaganda. It did not have to overcome church teachings.'[56] In contrast to Nazi-era pronatalism, however, marriage, the family and sexual responsibility were now situated in normative terms as moral building blocks of socialist citizenship.

The GDR's Law on the Protection of Mother and Child of 1950 declared that 'a healthy family is one of the fundamental pillars of a democratic society'. As Paul Betts observes, 'the family was to assume its place alongside the workplace as the primary site of socialist personality formation.'[57] Yet the emphasis was clearly on fertility: the 1950 maternal protection law introduced a host of new maternal and child welfare provisions, including maternity leave and infant health centres, while increasing regulations on abortion.[58] This focus on protecting marriage, families and motherhood was underlined in the 1965 Family Law Book, which declared the family the 'smallest cell of society' in the GDR, based on 'mutual love, respect and trust between all family members'.[59] It was further reinforced by the 1968 Constitution: 'Every citizen enjoys the right to the respect, protection and promotion of his/her marriage and family.'[60]

In later decades, and especially from the early 1970s, this vision was given political heft via vastly improved maternity leave provisions, access to contraception and abortion on demand. Yet while this focus on maternity and reproduction resonated with West German policy of this era, GDR state socialism differed from the West in its attitudes to sexual practices and morality. Party leaders took an increasingly permissive attitude towards youth and premarital sexuality, from an earlier point in time than in the West. The state began promoting itself as 'a world leader in the heart and the bedroom' rather than a punitive moral force. Such permissiveness feeds into what is sometimes dubbed the 'romantic' narrative of socialist sexual attitudes – captured in actor Katharina Thalbach's nostalgic reflection that in the GDR: 'We had more sex, and we had more to laugh about.'[61] McLellan reminds us, though, that such romanticized memories sat in tension with pervasive political repression, with Thalbach herself an opponent of the communist regime who left the East along with many other intellectuals and artists in the late 1970s. The reality, McLellan points out, was an 'uneasy mixture of prudishness and pragmatism': condoned sex under state socialism remained firmly directed towards heterosexual, loving and monogamous relationships.[62]

Redefining norms surrounding women's work and equality were central to these Cold War struggles between the two Germanies about which system provided its citizens with a better – and in some cases, more decisively 'modern' – way of life. In the East, women's equality with men was taken for granted, and merged with understandings of women's work.[63] In 1950, GDR President Otto Grotewohl defended women's integration in the workplace by declaring that 'one can impose nothing more dishonourable on a woman than to expect her to be her husband's unpaid maid'.[64] East German leaders promoted an image of hard-working male labourers and efficient and inventive female workers and homemakers, and historians broadly concur with Robert Moeller that the family and women's status 'clearly emerged as symbols of the distance between the two Germany's (sic)'.[65] Even so, as Neumaier points out, the structure of the bourgeois family remained remarkably stable in the socialist GDR, where one might have expected a 'radical break' given the significance of the political transformations since 1945.[66]

The SED ran campaigns aimed explicitly at countering established gender roles and hierarchies, and promoting domestic duties as the responsibility of men as well as women. Correspondingly, the 1965 Family Code called on men to take on their share of both childrearing and household chores.[67] East German women also enjoyed greater financial independence and better access to childcare and parental provisions than in the West, even if the new socialist state remained far from a 'female paradise', as Mary Fulbrook points out.[68] Somewhat ironically, this expansion of gender norms could also work to reinforce old double standards, as women's financial independence freed some East German men to sleep around. Serial adulterer and Berlin doctor Herr J. happily declared that 'women are independent; in the GDR they all had equal rights after all,' in an interview reflecting on his own promiscuous life choices.[69] Such men no longer needed to worry too much about child support or alimony, confident that the state would step in.

As such anecdotes suggest, GDR rhetoric of gender equality had definite limits. Advertising campaigns did not simply change what men did on the home front – even as they may have prompted some couples towards discussions about household labour that they may not otherwise have had – and nor did formal gender equality stop people judging each other on the basis of how they conducted their sexual relationships or structured their families.[70] The state was much more concerned with finding ways for women to combine work and domestic tasks, and thus contribute to wider economic productivity, than on overturning long-standing inequalities in the gendered division of labour – even as it hoped that such a modern approach could help win over the hearts and minds of younger demographics, in particular.[71] It is also important to note that a double burden of labour was felt by men and women in different ways under state socialism. For if women were supposed to be homemakers as well as good socialist workers, men were expected to be DIY experts and car mechanics, and both sexes were encouraged to undertake volunteer work for Party organizations in addition to paid labour and domestic responsibilities. There were also distinct limits to women's widely touted emancipation in the realms of work and finances, for even where women did work alongside men in manual labour occupations conventionally gendered masculine, such as welding or in smelting plants, their contribution in those jobs tended to be viewed as lesser: they were more poorly paid, and remained at the lower ranks of their professions.[72] 'For the most part, women work in offices whereas men do back-breaking work,' reported male interviewees in one 1980s interview collection.[73] Such discrepancies caused disgruntlement across gender lines.

Nonetheless, scholars agree that there were real differences between East and West when it came to gender roles and family. GDR leaders celebrated socialism as enabling 'better' sex than in the West, whose highly commodified sexual culture was strongly criticized, even as they echoed their counterparts in the FRG in strongly prioritizing heterosexual, monogamous intimacy and the family as the building blocks of a strong socialist society. This stance led them to veer between socially and politically conservative and more liberal standpoints, particularly on topics such as youth sexuality. GDR sexual culture also differed from other eastern European countries during the postwar decades. East German men, known for being comfortable with housework, nappies and strong women, enjoyed a very different image to the 'socialist machismo' of some other Soviet bloc states. Prostitution was far less common in the GDR than in Poland or Hungary, and the treatment of gay men, including by the church, was more liberal than in the Soviet Union, Poland or Romania. Trends such as nudism, examined in Chapter 6, also drew on distinctly German FKK trends that stretched back to the early twentieth century.[74] It is crucial to recognize these distinctions between the very different political, religious and cultural landscapes of countries like Poland, Hungary and Czechoslovakia during these decades, which too often have been viewed through a reductive Iron Curtain lens.[75] At the same time, in both East and West, shifting sexual norms were always caught in tension between older conservative ideas about gender and morality and more progressive attempts to rethink how bodies and individuals might relate to one another in the conditions of late modernity. 'Although East and West Germany sought a return to traditional gender norms and sexual practices,' Evans argues, 'often the very institutions designed to impart these messages and correct behavior were unable to do so given a host of organizational and economic constraints.'[76]

Within the repressive structures of East German socialism, some scholars have argued, sexual relationships and the family became a sacred locus of privacy and escape from public life. Herzog is one proponent of this view: 'sex eventually became a crucial free space in this otherwise profoundly unfree society.'[77] In contrast, others describe the family much more damningly as merely the 'instrumentalized life sphere' of state control. 'The truth,' Paul Betts observes, 'is naturally somewhere in between': while GDR family members may have often had less time to spend with one another than their Western counterparts due to different expectations and provisions around childcare, work and schooling, the family and private realms were nonetheless important spaces of love and intimacy.[78] Certainly, changing political realities and increased restrictions on free speech – restrictions that in some respects resonated with those of the Nazi era – provided a context in which individuals and groups not only could, but needed to reimagine the possibilities for sexual expression, intimacy and activism. But sexuality was not purely a space of private escape; it was also fundamental to the East German state's view of socialism as a modern, progressive alternative to the capitalist West, as well as to its pronatalist goals centred on increasing economic productivity. Party elites sought to sell an appealing image of socialist sexual emancipation, grounded in formal gender equality. But they did so in ways that also strongly promoted fertility, 'as concern rose that employed women's natural urge might not be as strong as the state wished'.[79] The next sections of this chapter consider how these tensions between pronatalism and liberalism played out in relation to marriage, divorce and family policy in both East and West, with leaders at times reinforcing political priorities and gender norms familiar from earlier eras, while at other times seeking to draw a line under the Nazi past. As they did, they worked to underscore two decidedly different models of German modernity.

Changing attitudes to marriage, divorce and the family in the FRG

Marriage and the family have been central themes of this book, enduring over centuries as frameworks for socially approved expressions of sexuality, intimacy and raising children. Yet during the postwar decades, attitudes to marriage and divorce began to diverge between East and West, as governments on both sides of the German-German border sought to use this institution to promote different political ideologies around work, communal life and citizenship. For many young people in the East, marriage represented a way out from under their parents' roof: a path to independence, housing and financial stability in the face of severe postwar shortages. In the West, it veered between conservative postwar ideal and target of 1968 student radicals seeking to overthrow the systems of earlier generations.

The West German Basic Law of 1949 placed marriage and family 'under the special protection of the public order'.[80] Yet this did not fundamentally challenge the patriarchal structures that had underpinned family law since the 1900 civil code (*Bürgerliches Gesetzbuch*), and the 'family' continued to be narrowly defined, centred on heterosexual marriage and immediate offspring.[81] For the conservative CDU/CSU coalition that led the FRG from 1949 to 1966, this definition excluded the many single women – unmarried, widowed or divorced – who led households with dependent children or adults. The political leadership was also critical of mothers who entered the workforce, continuing to affirm the norm of male breadwinners.[82]

Debates around the family came to the fore around the 'money for children' (*Kindergeld*) program. The Allies had suspended Nazi-era policies such as marriage loans and supplements for large families because of their racial criteria.[83] After 1948, when the currency stabilized following postwar inflation, pressure to reintroduce payments increased. Debates on this topic raged for several years, with the expectation of family support underpinned by an expectation that mothers could and would reject paid work if possible. This contrasted starkly with measures in the Soviet Occupation Zone, from 1949 the GDR, where women were explicitly encouraged into work.[84]

In 1952 a new Law for the Protection of Mothers was passed by the West German government with cross-party support, removing the Nazis' racially specific criteria. It provided family allowances where the father's salary either did not suffice, or was non-existent, and prohibited employers from firing pregnant women except in exceptional circumstances. This considerably expanded protections for unmarried mothers. In a political climate that clearly favoured male breadwinners and stay-at-home mothers, the law aimed, observes Heineman, 'to improve the health of children born to parents who could not meet this ideal'.[85] In reality, though, the version of the *Kindergeld* provisions finalized in 1954 continued to favour 'complete families' with husbands in work, dependent wives and several children.[86]

Discrimination on the grounds of gender and sexuality coalesced around marital status in multiple ways during these decades. West German women working in the civil service faced particular difficulties: upon marriage they were forced, as they had been during much of the Nazi era, to resign from their positions, ostensibly so that employers could hire demobilized men. For married women, there was strong pressure to stay at home and look after the children, and considerable stigma around placing children in day care – notably, these different expectations of mothers in East and West remained palpable even after reunification in 1989. Despite the name, a new 'Equal Rights Law' (*Gleichberechtigungsgesetz*) passed in 1957 gave fathers the final say on decisions regarding children where spouses disagreed. While it was declared unconstitutional in 1959, 'the ideal of the "housewife marriage" that undergirded marriage, divorce, and family law was not revised completely until 1977'.[87] Sometimes, commentators showed empathy with women's position by acknowledging men's shortcomings, and advising women to compensate for indignities experienced by their husband at work. A woman should put up with it 'when he tells you something, even if it seems boring to you', and 'carefully avoid at all occasions putting your husband in a bad light'.[88] Such statements worked to reinforce woman's place as that of sympathetic supporter of a male breadwinner. And although technically, the FRG had abolished discrimination against illegitimate children, shaming of such children and their mothers remained common.[89] Nonetheless, Heineman points out that left-wing and feminist pressure ensured ongoing discussion of the rights of unwed mothers and their children during these years.[90]

The moral purity emphasis of West German postwar politics was strongly supported by the major churches. The Protestant and Catholic churches backed major campaigns against premarital sex, producing millions of conservative sex advice flyers.[91] Catholics and Protestants actively underscored normative values by promoting women's choice to stay at home as housewives and mothers – sometimes in quite polemical terms, such as when Catholic family minister Franz Josef Wuermling declared in 1953: '*Save our mothers for our families and our children! Their absence there can never be rectified!*'[92] During these years, both the Catholic and Protestant churches reaffirmed decidedly patriarchal understandings of the role of the husband and father as head of the family, with the Catholic church in particular developing an ideal of the nuclear family as the 'church in miniature', centred around the central sacrament of marriage.[93]

Yet FRG divorce statistics present a subtle challenge to such conservative ideals of heteronormative domesticity and traditional gender norms. They also reflect the impact of increasing political and economic stability by the 1950s. In the first years after the war, hundreds of thousands of couples divorced: almost 90,000 West German couples in 1948 alone. This included a considerable backlog that had built up during the later war years. Contemporaries despaired about the stability of wartime marriages, even though the 'divorce boom' of this period was accompanied by a 'marriage boom'.[94] A notable shift during these years was in the number of women filing for divorce – before the war, men were nearly three times more likely to sue for divorce, while by 1949 they were on a par with women. There were also more women who thought twice about marrying altogether. 'I've become skeptical because of the large number of divorces,' declared one young woman, while Berlin women's magazine *Sie* described how many women 'coolly and objectively' consider the question of marriage and family, only to 'say with conviction "no" and are nevertheless happy'.[95] Yet even if there was more space for critical views, this hardly undermined the institution of marriage on a larger scale; 90 per cent of respondents to one 1949 survey of West Germans answered that they considered marriage 'necessary' rather than 'obsolete'.[96]

West German courts stuck with the practice of no-fault divorce that had been introduced during the Nazi era, despite opposition from religious groups. Those who opposed no-fault divorce pointed out that it tended to lump wives who did not wish to divorce with responsibility for the children, but no access to alimony (which required assigning guilt). In contrast, left-wing parties and many feminists stood true to older beliefs that estranged partners should be able to end a union – even if they objected to the racialized ways in which the Nazis had exploited no-fault divorce.[97] Yet during the 1950s, at least, following the initial postwar boom, FRG divorce remained relatively rare. Not only were women expected to tend patiently to their husbands' needs, but it also became more difficult to divorce following a new law passed in 1961.[98] With this legislation, the Bundestag affirmed a series of highly restrictive Supreme Court decisions over the previous decade based on the religious principle of the indissolubility of marriage, meaning that the partner who objected to a divorce was almost always favoured. As a result, many unhappy marriages were forcibly maintained. While the government saw this 'reform' as benefiting women who did not consent to divorce, 'the premise that women who had been betrayed and abandoned by their husbands would in most cases wish to hold on to the broken bond,' Ute Frevert observes, 'lacked any factual foundation' – especially as women were soon suing for divorce twice as often as men.[99]

By the late 1960s, the West German Parliament and judiciary began to rethink the legal situation in the face of a rising divorce rate – up from 103 divorces per 1000 in 1961–5 to 231 a decade later. In 1977 the governing social-liberal coalition finally passed a law establishing breakdown of the marriage as the primary factor in approving divorce. From 1965, a couple could also choose to take the wife's maiden name rather than the husband's as family surname, and marriage and family law reflected a broader shift towards marriages between partners with equal rights, no longer explicitly supporting a gendered division of labour and housework.[100] During these decades, West German divorce courts practiced a more hands-off stance than in the GDR, to which we will now turn.

Marriage and divorce in state socialism

Attitudes to marriage, divorce and the family in the GDR soon began to follow patterns quite different from those on the other side of the German-German border. The 1950s saw a wave of enterprise intended to build up a new socialist society: collectivized farms, moving industries under state ownership, and the centralization of economic planning.[101] Even the wedding ceremony was to be 'socialist', with the state concerned that citizens were still looking to the church rather than the state when it came to major life events like birth and marriage. Regional party groups compiled guidelines for suitably socialist nuptials, including the language of the vows.[102] Some

FIGURE 5.2 *Socialist mass wedding in Wernigerode, Saxony-Anhalt, 5 June 1986.*
Source: © ddrbildarchiv.de/Siegfried Bonitz

towns even oversaw mass weddings tied up with socialist ritual, as shown in Figure 5.2.

Major economic shifts following the division of the two German states were accompanied by an extensive suite of GDR social policy that included state-funded childcare, dedicated monthly 'housework days' for married women and generous maternity leave provisions. These were progressively expanded over the decades that followed, particularly when Erich Honecker took over the reins from Walter Ulbricht as SED First Secretary in 1971, marking the start of a period of less obviously ideological rule. In 1972 Honecker oversaw progressive policies including abortion on demand, maternity grants of up to 1000 marks per child and extensive paid maternity leave.[103]

The East German state was aware that it needed to make it attractive for young mothers and couples to have children in the constrained economic conditions of the postwar GDR. A new marriage loan system provided couples up to 5000 GDR marks at a time when the average monthly income was 814 marks, and that of young people often considerably less. Couples aged under twenty-six on below-average incomes could use the loans to build or furnish a house with a fridge, furniture and a TV. As in the West, such initiatives point to certain continuities between Nazi and postwar marriage and family policy. Like the Nazi-era loans, they incentivized having children by reducing the repayable amount significantly with the birth of each child: 1000 marks with the first child, 1500 after the birth of the second and 2500 after third. They proved incredibly popular, with over 200,000 applications in the first three years.[104] Contemporaries were well aware of the loan scheme's pronatalist intentions: Volker V., 25 when he and his partner Veronika were interviewed in 1974, declared: 'When the new abortion law was created and the birth rate went down significantly, that was perhaps why this loan for young married couples was set up, to put the brakes on the decline in births.'[105] This offsetting of the loan amount by having children even made its way into language in a new verb, known colloquially as 'abkindern', as Anja Schröter has found. By the late 1980s, even older couples aged above thirty could apply for loans, now increased to a maximum of 7000 GDR marks, and the loan was written off after three children.[106]

From 1976, maternity and child welfare provisions were increased with the introduction of the so-called *Babyjahr* (baby year), which increased maternity leave to twenty-six weeks at full pay and a further twenty-six weeks at a lower rate of pay for second and subsequent children.[107] These provisions were soon extended to single or unmarried mothers, leading Heineman to argue that 'if the West German polity defined the housewife as normative and the woman standing alone as problematic, the opposite was true in the East'.[108] East German leaders were clearly more comfortable with unmarried women, who could more straightforwardly contribute to reconstruction efforts than married women, who were in turn less likely to remain in paid employment.[109] Marriage loans, childcare and an increasing weight of social expectation all contributed to a trend towards having children early. As Frau N later recalled, 'in those days, everybody had their children when they were 20.'[110] By 1985 the median age for East German women having their first child was twenty-two, with first-time mothers over thirty quickly becoming a rarity.

The difficult GDR housing situation was another incentive to marry early. Marriage seemed to many a ticket to freedom from their parents' four walls into their own state-subsidized apartment, in a housing system that promoted the nuclear family over share housing or other models.[111] Getting an apartment was much more likely once a couple started having children, so for the first few years, many young couples found themselves with little choice but to live with their parents or in-laws. Even as late as 1974, only around half of new couples were offered somewhere to live in the first year of marriage.[112] As one might imagine, this could cause considerable family and marital conflict, as eighteen-year-old tree nursery worker Anke criticized: 'Why do most people marry at just 18? Because they think: Got to get away from the parents! Got to get a flat! And then they are divorced at 20. The state is doing something wrong there with the encouragement of young marriages.'[113] Another young couple interviewed in 1974 – by two West German researchers curious about the intimate lives of those 'other' Germans behind the Wall – also described the constrained housing situation as a major factor on intimate decisions. Holger S., 21, a steel construction fitter, told of how it could be very hard to find a place without the right (Party) connections:

> you don't get a flat when you're not married. Even when you are married, it can take five years to get a flat. And new builds cost 200 marks. You only get flats here through connections. I scratch your back, you scratch mine – you have to know someone in the housing office.[114]

Together with his partner Ruth W., nineteen, a nurse, Holger described how they had built out the attic in Ruth's parents' flat, and how it was not unusual to hear of 'young people living together' given the long wait before permissions to marriage were granted.[115]

While housing constraints and marriage loans fostered early unions and childbearing, East Germans also fronted up much more readily to the divorce courts than their Western counterparts. Paul Betts argues that much of this shift was spearheaded by women, who by the late 1950s were already more likely than men to file for divorce.[116] While the principle of assigning fault was central to West German divorce law until 1977, the GDR had established no-fault divorce by the mid-1950s – the key factor, as Anja Schröter explains in a recent study, was to establish how 'dysfunctional' or 'shattered' (zerrüttet) the marriage had become. At the same time, the courts were given the responsibility to carefully ascertain whether this was really the case, or whether reconciliation was still possible.[117] In justifying a claim for divorce infidelity was frequently cited, though also common were domestic violence, defamation or men who had driven their family into debt. East German judges insisted that couples seeking divorce first 'attempted reconciliation' via a counselling centre. In this way, courts and social workers took on a role of intimate mediation that continued the work of state-run counselling centres and family doctors from the Weimar and Nazi eras: by 1966 the GDR had around 100 marriage counselling centres, and more than double that by a decade later.[118]

West Germans tended to criticize the GDR legal system in general for intruding too much into private affairs, and blamed the higher divorce rate in particular on the pressure on women to undertake paid work. In contrast, commentators in the GDR were more likely to see divorce as part and parcel of women's emancipation, showing how the same demographic patterns could be used to underscore very different normative ideals – the stay at home mother in the West, and gender equality in the East.[119] Certainly, the East German authorities placed more emphasis than their counterparts in the West on the collective responsibilities of socialist marriage, intended 'as a foundation of communal life'. Disinclination to work, or the affair of a partner inhibiting work capacity, were now key legitimating grounds for divorce.[120] On the other hand, East German citizens were encouraged to intervene in the troubled private lives of friends and colleagues for the sake of saving a marriage and preserving its many ties with wider state systems of childcare, education, youth organizations, housing and employment.[121] In one case, jurists and colleagues visited the home of an alcoholic, abusive husband who was having an affair with a workmate, informing him 'that he must bring some order and cleanliness to his private affairs if he hopes to enjoy the respect of his colleagues at work'.[122]

Sometimes, this pressure to reconcile a broken marriage and undergo counselling before one could file for divorce could sharply disadvantage the female partner. The sense that domestic violence accusations were not taken particularly seriously by the police is a trend that Jane Freeland has found to be prevalent in both East and West Germany during the 1960s and 1970s. When Frau A. from Leipzig reported her husband for assault in 1986, for example, she was told that she would need to get a doctor's certificate – which was refused – and 'had the feeling that at least as far as the two police officers were concerned, whatever took place within a marriage, so long as it didn't disturb the peace in the building or anything, wasn't such a big deal'. Her divorce application was denied, and instead she had to attend two compulsory reconciliation sessions.[123] Freeland's finding of very similar stories of abused women on both sides of the Wall is especially notable given the very different models of gender and family roles promoted by those two Cold War contexts. Overriding political differences, however, was the ongoing expectation in East and West that women would do the lion's share of domestic and childcare duties, and a shared reluctance to listen to women's stories: 'women living with violence struggled to be heard on both sides of the iron curtain.'[124]

Yet shifts were also perceptible that challenged such attempts to protect socialist marriages at all costs. East German judges – many of them women – were more willing than in previous eras to scold husbands for sexist behaviour, and women more readily named sexual problems in seeking to dissolve an unhappy marriage. As one woman complained in 1966, 'we do not understand each other sexually, are never satisfied, and I must say, my nerves suffer because of it.'[125] By the 1960s, women were also more likely to explicitly name their husband's domestic violence or alcoholism as grounds for divorce proceedings.[126] Such intimate grounds took on increasing importance as, over time, the family and private sphere began to assume a greater role within East German life as spaces of emotional fulfilment, distinct from the state-controlled areas of work and education. Journalist Günter Gaus famously dubbed this the 'niche society' of the GDR.[127]

By the 1970s it became even easier to divorce, with the 1975 Socialist Civil Code stating that this could be granted if the domestic community (*Lebensgemeinschaft*) between the spouses was ruined. Divorce requests tumbled in – and could now be processed in as little as three weeks. There was less focus on fault, and a greater willingness by judges to acknowledge the problems of 'everyday socialism' such as housing and material constraints in fuelling marital conflicts. Courts and social workers became more hesitant about intervening in private matters, and by the 1980s, nearly 80 per cent of divorce claims were successful.[128] People also became quite agile at figuring out what kinds of arguments would fly with the courts, and were prepared to 'lay it on a bit thick' if required, as actor Dorothea Reeder recalled.[129] Illegitimate children were also granted strong legal protections under GDR law, even if Starke's comments at the start of this chapter about unmarried mothers birthing children in 'droves' are undoubtedly overblown. As one 1970s legal text declared, 'single mothers enjoy the care and protection of society. Children born outside of marriage in all questions have the same rights as those born within marriage.'[130]

The role of housing constraints in pushing couples not only towards early marriage, but sometimes also early divorce, was a common feature of GDR divorce cases. As one Frau Becker declared: 'Because a new-build flat was only possible as a result of an imminent marriage, the marriage was undertaken.'[131] And while most people in their divorce files claimed to have married out of love, in a few cases more practical reasons played a role, like getting on a shorter waiting list for a car or driving licence. Musician Robert Maler later recalled that in at least one of his marriages, love was 'not so acute' a reason – more important was his girlfriend having come to the top of the driving license waitlist.[132] Reflecting on these shifting attitudes, Betts notes: 'More than anywhere else in the GDR, divorce courts brought the private sphere to public attention, revealing both the hopes and limits of the socialist project ..., as well as the determination on the part of East German citizens to define and defend private life.'[133]

The normalization of divorce worked to normalize serial monogamy and marriage, as increasingly, divorce requests came in from people who had been previously divorced. By the 1980s, East Germans had not turned away from marriage *per se*, but as McLellan points out, 'it was not necessarily seen as a lifelong commitment': 39 per cent of weddings by 1989 featured at least one previously married partner.[134] Cohabitation was common – 'It's a lot simpler if you're not married,' observed aforementioned tree nursery worker Anke.[135] Policy measures initially intended to stabilize or increase the birth rate while allowing women to continue in work thus often had different results from what was intended: 'Parodoxically, the economic independence enjoyed by East German women enabled couples with children to dissolve relationships that were not working.'[136] Divorce became more common, and the norms of 'family' in the GDR expanded to include single-parent households, stepfamilies and co-habiting couples.[137]

Sex in print: Sex education, marriage manuals and pornography

Sex education, marriage manuals and self-help guides, already a feature of the Weimar media landscape, took off in a big way in both GDR and FRG, and offer a particularly telling guide of changing norms surrounding sexual behaviours and relationships. In the East it was common to hear criticisms of the highly commercialized and exploitative nature of West German sexual culture. Socialist leaders, as we have seen above, held up socialist forms of intimacy as more fulfilling, loving, and authentic, and GDR sexologists and educators generally supported this line. In particular, they denounced the so-called 'sex-wave' (*Sexwelle*) or 'sex-flood' of commodified 'sex propaganda' and 'pornography' seen to thoroughly infiltrate Western literature and film, particularly under the influence of 'American amorality'.[138]

That there was, indeed, something of a 'sex boom' in the illustrated West German media of these decades is well established, with prominent article series, reader advice columns and plenty of saucy images boosting cover and advertising sales.[139] While this peaked in the post-1968 era, it had its roots from as early as the 1950s, when despite the overriding political conservatism of the period, the groundbreaking findings of the US Kinsey Reports on the sex lives of 'average' Americans were starting to make their way across the Atlantic. Particularly shocking, on both sides of the pond, was the very high percentage of American men who reported having same-sex encounters at some point in their lives, even if they later identified as sexually 'normal', that is, heterosexual.[140] Media coverage of the Reports was widespread across western Europe and had a big impact on the ways in which many West Germans thought and talked about their intimate lives. 'Sexuality', observes Steinbacher, 'sold decidedly well in West Germany', with the illustrated magazine *Wochenend* (Weekend) in 1949 among the first to disseminate Kinsey's findings to an audience of around two million readers. The long-running *Spiegel* news magazine was not far behind with its explorations of 'German everyday eroticism'.[141]

Even as such public forums for discussing sexual intimacy were perceived by many as new and shocking, marriage and heterosexuality remained at the centre of much of this coverage, as did an emphasis on loving and ethical relationships. 'Satisfying the drives is not everything,' one *Wochenend* report underlined, while others tried to add pizzazz to old institutions by focusing on questions such as how to address 'boredom in marriage'.[142] Broadly speaking, the rise in media attention to sex from the 1950s promoted a more positive discourse of sexual pleasures than the moral purity emphasis of political and religious discussions of marriage and family. At the same time, it fuelled conservative fears about the 'banalization' of sexuality and pornography. Kinsey was accused of 'attacks on human dignity', while Catholic commentators declared this kind of sexual 'mass enlightenment' to be nothing less than 'criminal' – and Kinsey himself an 'enemy to all human order'.[143]

Until the late 1960s, most West German sex education materials and teacher training in this area were strongly infused by the conservative Christian perspectives of the leading political party and major churches. And even as magazines like *Der Spiegel* were starting to celebrate a 'spectator' sex, this was not the reality of all contemporary popular media, with popular magazines for girls often railing against premarital sex.[144] In 1968 the ministry of cultural affairs declared sex education directed towards 'responsible sexual behaviour' a necessary part of education at large and made it a compulsory part of the school curriculum. While this ruling represents an expansion around norms of when and how one might discuss sexual matters compared to earlier eras (although sex education had been an established part of high school education since at least the early twentieth century), it also had clear moral parameters. As well as offering 'objectively founded knowledge', West German sex education was to be aimed towards 'contribut[ing] to young people acknowledging their tasks as man or woman, developing their sense of values and conscience and the necessity of moral decision-making'.[145] By and large, promiscuity and sexual 'deviance' – everything outside of loving heterosexual partnerships – was firmly frowned upon.

A staged educational approach was recommended: children in their first year of class were to learn about sexual difference and the 'facts of motherhood', and by the end of year six they should have learned about developments in puberty and know the basic facts of life. More detailed knowledge on sexual relations, marriage, masturbation, abortion, sexual crimes and homosexuality was to be conveyed by year ten. At the same time, the ministry emphasized that sex education should begin at home – leading generations of parents from the 1950s onwards to turn to the 'flourishing market' of sexual enlightenment publications.[146] These often included illustrations, and by the 1970s, detailed photographs of sexual practices and positions. In one typical photograph from *Zeig mal!* (Show me!), a pictorial sex education book for children and parents, youthful erotic arousal is illustrated by a (presumably) male hand reaching out towards a (presumably) female nipple.[147] Although progressive in their openness to discussing sexual topics, such books continued to emphasize normative approaches to gendered sexual expectations of male activity and female passivity.

By the late 1960s, West Germans had access to a booming commercial sex industry. Key to this development was a groundbreaking 1962 censorship case centred on a translation of French author Jean Genet's *The Lady of Flowers*, which depicted homosexuality in frank terms. Hamburg chief prosecutor Ernst Buchholz successfully argued that 'artistic freedom takes priority over protecting youth'.[148] Following a series of major reforms to the criminal law code, materials that had previously fallen under anti-smut censorship laws now gained a wide audience, as publishing sexually explicit material could be defended on artistic or educational grounds. Soon, magazines began running risqué articles on love, sex education and nudism.[149] Popular publications included the bestselling book *Gruppensex in Deutschland* (Group Sex in Germany, 1968), while entrepreneur Beate Uhse expanded her business from that of travelling saleswoman offering female clients contraceptive advice on the side, to a mail-order business in the small town of Braderup near the Danish border, to a massively successful chain of sex shops spreading right across the FRG (Figure 5.3).[150] This postwar 'sex boom' helped to normalize sexual advertising and pornography: erotica and pornography were increasingly widely available, and billboards and magazines loudly used sex to sell all sorts of products. Pseudoscientific sex 'enlightenment' films such as *Du* (You, 1968) or *Das Wunder der Liebe* (The Miracle of Love, 1967) hit the big screens, depicting 'sexperts' voyeuristically interviewing prostitutes and sex criminals or naked couples poring over their sex lives.[151] Particularly when it came to sexual 'enlightenment' literature aimed at adults, as historian Franz X. Eder wryly observes, the lines between advice, education, eroticism and pornography were increasingly blurred.[152]

In 1969 *Der Spiegel* diagnosed a veritable 'porn wave' (*Porno-Welle*) washing over West German public culture, complete with 'phalli on coloured slides, vaginas in close-up, coitus on card games, pederasty on calendars, lustful moans on records, sadism in dime novels, sodomy in 5-minute films'.[153] Such widely available imagery represented a significant break with the 'gentleman's magazines' of the 1950s and early 1960s: *Er* (He), founded in 1951, and *Die Gondel* (The gondola) had continued in the vein of the pin-up culture of the 1930s and 1940s, evoking the provocative revelations of

FIGURE 5.3 *Entrepreneur Beate Uhse with son Ulrich (left) and company representative Melzer (right) in front of her mail-order company in Flensburg, ca 1970.*

Source: Peter Timm/ullstein bild via Getty Images

the strip tease, but always covering up breasts and pubic areas with skimpy bathers or lingerie.[154] Not only did these transform into more obviously pornographic 'men's magazines' in the early-to-mid 1970s, but they were joined by all manner of weekly sex magazines such as *Sexy* or the famous *Praline*, priced accessibly at 1–2 Marks. Such publications pushed at the limits of what could be represented in print: not just full-frontal female nudity, but a detailed exploration of sexual issues, desires and fears, from impotence and syphilis to forced prostitution. Despite regular run-ins with the censors, for the first time in the FRG 'it became possible to speak of a public, freely available mass market for pornographic publications' – a market helped along by new editions of erotic classics from earlier eras, from works by the Marquis de Sade to the novel *Fanny Hill*.[155]

Some materials also gained a wide audience that in later decades would again become unacceptable: images of naked children or open discussions of child sexuality, for example, 'were for many contemporaries from the end of the 1960s to the start of the 1970s a central aspect of both personal and social "enlightenment" and "emancipation"'.[156] Glossy hardcore porn magazines also became widely available for the first time, at first trickling down from

Sweden and Denmark, who significantly liberalized their pornography laws in the late 1960s. It was not long before the FRG developed into one of the strongest international porn markets, with dozens of hardcore magazines publishing at least six annual issues of between ten and forty thousand copies, and a growing variety of specialist and highly explicit magazines such as *Anal Sex*, *Teenage Sex* or *Sex Bizarre*.[157] As more and more sexually explicit material became readily available for sale at West German sex shops and newsstands, a culture of commercialized sex developed that many in the East saw as underscoring the worst of western capitalism.

In the GDR, meanwhile, strict censorship laws meant that all publications required Ministry of Culture approval. This requirement strongly shaped publicly available representations of sex, whether in educational and advice manuals or popular literature and film. But it did not always equate to a strictly repressive or normative stance: as McLellan has established, 'in some cases the censors actually expressed views that were more forward-thinking than the authors themselves'.[158] By the mid 1960s, the governing SED even began to advocate a more open discussion of sexual acts through culture. As it did, though, it dismissed aesthetic tendencies to 'prudery and prettification', and emphasized that sexual representations had to align with socialist ideals of proper partnership – or at least show how nonconforming characters were punished for their waywardness.[159]

East German sex and marriage manuals generally supported ideas of 'good' socialist sex as an essential part of loving relationships between husbands and wives – the focus was clearly on penetrative heterosexual sex – which in turn represented the ideal foundation for childbearing. 'Life becomes fulfilled only with three children,' wrote Rudolf Neubert in *The New Marriage Manual* (1957).[160] For many years, Harsch observes, this was the only advice book in the East aimed at married couples, and even as it conceded that childish marriage could be 'good', Neubert strongly affirmed that 'children are the root, the happiness, the most beautiful fulfillment of every healthy marriage.'[161] Similar attitudes permeate sex guides from the 1950s right through to the 1980s. But even as they were highly normative in some respects, they also promoted an atmosphere of sexual permissiveness and pleasure, provided this occurred within the limits of heterosexual monogamy. A 1959 sex guide declared sex 'the quintessence of being alive'.[162] Such views and self-understanding that sex might be different under the banner of socialism also impacted the worldview of individual East Germans. As one woman later reflected: 'After all, it was a proletarian society. None of this bourgeois concern with chastity until the wedding night.'[163] Where women in the West were sometimes pitied as mere 'lust object[s] for the man', sex under socialism was promoted as being about 'life-joy' and recognition of 'the capacity for sensual pleasure'.[164]

By the 1970s, GDR sex manuals and other sexological publications, like their western counterparts, became even more open in emphasizing how to achieve mutual sexual pleasure, and some even dabbled in risqué topics like group sex. One particularly popular GDR sexual self-help guide was sexologist Siegfried Schnabl's bestselling 1969 *Mann und Frau Intim* (Man and Woman Intimately), inspired by American works such as William Masters and Virginia Johnson's *Human Sexual Response* (1966).[165] Schnabl found, for example, that women with only primary school education were less likely to experience regular climax:

> As in the GDR the graduates of tertiary and technical colleges don't belong to a privileged population group, this finding also shows that social factors have an influence on sexual disturbances and that the improvement of people's social conditions is suited to minimizing their appearance.[166]

The socialist ideology framing such statistics is evident from Schnabl's relation of orgasm rates to educational levels and occupation. He also made a name for himself via advice columns in popular women's magazines like *Für Dich*, with article titles such as 'Does the Pill quash desire?'[167] By the early 1980s, over 40 per cent of young East German women interviewed in one study claimed to reach orgasm almost every time they had sex.[168] Such high reported rates of female pleasure could take Western scholars by surprise: a 1988 study comparing female students' experiences in East and West found that East German heterosexual women liked sex more than their western sisters, and experienced orgasm more frequently.[169]

While promoting a sex-positive stance for monogamous heterosexual adult couples, GDR sexologists were more mixed about when and under what circumstances young people should start having sex. Neubert's aforementioned marriage manual, hugely popular in the 1950s and 1960s, supported premarital intercourse for young adults (but not younger teenagers), even where this led to pregnancy, provided children were 'conceived and received in love'. In general, though, as in the West, sympathy for premarital sex was tempered by the clear expectation that marriage would follow.[170] Practices less obviously in line with socialist ideals, including homosexuality, promiscuity, prostitution and sadomasochism or kink tended to be relegated to chapters on 'abnormal' sexuality. At best, such practices were viewed as less conducive to 'inner harmony', at worst, they were declared downright 'perverse'.[171]

GDR sex education books for young people broadly followed the tone of this sexological literature, balancing a permissive tone with reinforcing norms of heterosexual monogamy. By the Honecker era of the 1970s, guides for teenagers like the 1975 *Denkst du schon an Liebe?* (Thinking about love already?) provided fairly explicit advice for teenagers 'taking their first steps on the precarious dance floor of love'.[172] Popular magazines underlined the importance of frankness in talking to children about sexual matters – but also the importance of putting love first. 'Love is on the curriculum' declared a report in *Für Dich* on the sex education curriculum of the Erich-Weinert-Oberschule in Hohenmölsen in Saxony-Anhalt, noting with some disdain the difference between this approach and that of educators in the Federal Republic, 'which is even criticized by West German pedagogues': 'In the end our children know all about male testicles and female ovaries. But nothing, absolutely nothing, about love,' the report cites one anonymous West German teacher as saying.[173] More broadly, the SED leadership worked hard to promote itself as pro-youth, and its pro-sex position formed part of this stance. It did so, as Mark Fenemore shows, even as official youth organizations like the FDJ (Free German Youth) or Young Pioneers, with their focus on hiking and campfires, were starting to lose touch with a youth culture that was looking more and more to Western jeans, fashions and music.[174] The age of consent for heterosexual sex in the GDR was fourteen for both sexes (although different for same-sex relations, as we will see), and the age at which young people started having sex grew progressively younger. By the 1970s, many young people were having their first sexual experiences between the ages of sixteen and nineteen.[175] This shift was helped along by increased urbanization, more leisure time and a growing sense of independence: East German teenagers in apprenticeships enjoyed greater capacity than their parents to buy things like radios, tents and mopeds that enabled socializing between the sexes away from the family home.[176]

Popular magazines such as *Das Magazin* and *Für Dich* likewise promoted a progressive image of socialist sex, with plenty of nudity and erotic allusions.[177] But the relatively tame tone of these images was far removed from West German pornography, with its 'nonaverage bombshell bodies'.[178] 'Pornography' charges were also thrown about fairly loosely to police all manner of publications seen to defy the official party stance – whether or not they depicted sexually explicit materials.[179] This is not to say that East Germans were not well aware of changing international cultures of sexual consumerism. Although illegal, West German TV reception spread into wide reaches of the GDR from as early as the mid-1950s, and there was a lively black market traffic of smuggled magazines, books and literature.[180] Amateur pornography and erotica also boomed, in both straight and gay varieties, with new research by Kyle Frackman highlighting the dynamic cultures of amateur, smuggled and recycled pornography that developed in East German gay male communities in the face of official censorship.[181] Chapter 6 examines such countercultural and subcultural sexual movements in greater detail.

* * *

Heterosexuality was seen as foundational to the establishment of strong postwar statehood in both East and West following the wide-scale destruction of the Second World War and years of Allied occupation rule. For political and church leaders and social commentators in each of the postwar Germanies, marriage and the family represented pivotal building blocks of postwar reconstruction. These long-standing institutions also provided many Germans with a space of escape and private refuge – whether from the recent horrors of war and genocide, or from an increasingly interventionist East German state, in which the family represented a rare site beyond immediate political control.

Yet there were also important differences between East and West, especially in relation to gender politics, that shaped how people could express themselves sexually during these decades. In West Germany, a strong emphasis on nuclear families and domesticity placed heavy expectations on women to stay home and bear and care for children while husbands went out to work. The leading Christian conservative parties, and the legislation they oversaw in the FRG in the 1950s and early 1960s, underscored these traditional roles, engaging in moral panics and only gradually supporting reforms to enable people to end unhappy marriages, or the rights of unmarried mothers. In the GDR, a much more concerted rhetoric of gender equality, female independence and provisions for childcare set up a very different basis for marriage and divorce. It became easier to leave miserable unions, and leaders celebrated socialism as a 'better' climate for sex and love – as long as these continued to be framed by monogamy and family. At the same time, material constraints, especially around housing, pushed many young people towards marriage and children at an early age – for some at least, well before they were ready.

Print cultures across East and West bolstered these divergent expectations and ideologies of sexual responsibility, pleasure and intimacy. Censorship laws were much more lenient in the West, despite initial moves to ban 'obscene' publications for the sake of the nation's youth, enabling a thriving culture of commercial pornography from the late 1960s. East German authors, meanwhile, were keenly aware of the censors' knife, and the authorities dismissed pornography as an evil of western consumerism. Yet they also supported the expansion and normalization of other spaces for talking about sex, such as sex education guides and marriage manuals. These, often fairly liberal in tone, especially when it came to young people's sexuality, shored up ideals of socialist sex – heteronormative, monogamous, loving – as superior.

This chapter has highlighted continuities as well as ruptures with the sexual politics of the pre-war era, including the conservative sexual politics of the Nazis. 1945 represented in many respects a radical political, economic and social break in modern German history, but it did not suddenly overturn how most people thought about sex, or how they chose to structure their intimate lives. This happened, as we have seen, in a more gradual fashion across several decades, responding to influences as diverse as the US Kinsey Reports, the material realities of state socialism and an increasingly open discussion of sex in the West German media. We turn now to examine some of the more radical movements that also shaped sex and love during this era: developments that ran parallel to, but often also challenged, the history of state-sanctioned love and marriage charted in this chapter. Chapter 6 homes in on radicals, rebels and revolutionaries, starting with the immediate postwar occupation years, and moving through to 1950s youth gangs, the famed '1968 generation', feminists and LGBTIQ activists of the 1970s and beyond. Together, these two chapters demonstrate how, even as heterosexual monogamy and marriage remained touchstones of postwar German modernity, other norms surrounding sexual behaviours and public cultures were radically expanded during these decades, in both East and West.

6

Sexual evolutions and revolutions: From rock'n'roll to gay liberation

It is with a gentle nostalgia that Charlotte von Mahlsdorf, self-identified transvestite and a major figure in the East German underground queer subculture, recalls her first experience of *Klappensex* or beat sex in a public toilet in a park amidst the rubble of 1949 Berlin: 'It was a wonderful night with my first pick-up, and the next morning after breakfast he pressed my arm and said: "Well darling, I've never had such a charming thing as you. You're the first person who didn't ask immediately for cigarettes or money".'[1] Pointing to the difficulty of seeking out like-minded queers, especially in the early decades of state socialism – 'At that time one couldn't run personal ads, there was no gay subculture with bars – what was one supposed to do, if you didn't want to live like a monk? And I certainly didn't want that!' – Mahlsdorf loudly proclaims a sex-positive stance. Over her own long life this encompassed same-sex and queerly heterosex experiences, decades of gender-variant expression and regular sadomasochism and flagellation. As she declares: 'sexuality can't be repressed, why should one try.'[2]

Mahlsdorf's memoirs position her as something of a loner, happy amidst her painstakingly preserved museum of 1890s *Gründerzeit* (founding period) furniture and antiquities on the outskirts of the city, which she defended over time against raids by the Nazi Gestapo and then the East German secret police, or Stasi. Yet her long life of genderqueer activism also offers a fitting frame for thinking about the history of these postwar decades in a divided Germany in more 'revolutionary' terms. For even as norms of marriage and heteronormative partnership continued to be strongly reinforced during these decades, as the previous chapter explored, there were also many spaces in which normative frameworks of intimacy were radically challenged. During the 1970s, von Mahlsdorf opened up her museum and home – into which she had transported, almost single-handedly, the fit-out and décor of an iconic Weimar-era bar, the *Mulackritze* – as a much-needed base for underground East German

LGBTIQ networks in the face of political and social ostracism and rising suicide rates. As she recalls, '[l]esbian mothers, gay fathers, simple workers, actors, engineers, doctors: everyone met in the Mulackritze.'[3]

Reflecting on the postwar history of sexuality in Germany, Dagmar Herzog writes that '[o]ne of the areas that we still understand the least is the long sexual revolution of the second half of the twentieth century.'[4] Although both GDR and FRG experienced social, political and cultural upheaval in the years around 1968, this was more pronounced, and more sudden, in the West, where student radicals drove a widespread protest movement. Much of the rhetoric of sexual 'revolution' focused on this and other western European student movements erupting in places such as Italy and France.[5] Together with a renewed phase of feminist activism from the late 1960s and 1970s, members of these movements sought to develop new, more democratic forms of self-determination. For many, this included radically reimagining sexual relations, through public discussions of premarital sex, sexual 'enlightenment', same-sex relationships, women's sexual pleasure and pornography. Not only in Europe, but in many places around the world, left-wing and feminist activists made sexual politics part of their intertwined critiques of the state, economic inequalities and patriarchal gender relations, frequently citing the motto: 'The Personal is Political.' Even so, historians warn against viewing this 'revolutionary' moment too narrowly. Franz X. Eder suggests, for example, that it is more accurate to speak of the 'long history' of a sexual revolution in the FRG that lasted from the late 1940s to the 1980s, with clear connections to Weimar and Nazi-era developments. It is necessary, he argues, to think beyond binaries of 'oppression' versus 'emancipation' in considering how individuals experienced themselves sexually during these decades.[6] This position is very much in line with that of this book: time and again, we have seen that it is crucial to look beyond straightforward notions of liberation and instead interrogate how norms were variously reproduced and challenged in specific contexts. Only by embracing this complexity can we do proper justice to the history of sexuality in modern Germany.

In the East, too, it is more accurate to track longer shifts in sexual attitudes than look for a specific, society-changing 'event'. It is also important to recognize where GDR sexual history diverged from its western counterpart. 'There were already in the 1950s notable elements of liberality in East Germany that had no parallel in West Germany,' observes Herzog, arguing that it is more appropriate to think of the sexual history of these decades in the GDR in terms of an 'evolution' rather than 'revolution' of attitudes:

There was no sexual revolution in East Germany. Unlike West Germany, where the mid- to late 1960s saw a liberalization of the social and cultural landscape so dramatic that to many observers it seemed as though it had happened virtually overnight, East Germany experienced a far more gradual evolution of sexual mores.[7]

This chapter homes in on the more radical aspects of this evolution of sexual norms and practices. It traces struggles and rebellions centred on ideas of sexual pleasure, equality and citizenship, from the immediate postwar and 1950s rock'n'roll era with its lively youth culture, 'Marlon Brandos' and 'Veronikas', through to the '1968 generation' and emergence of movements for women's, gay and trans rights. Like Chapter 5, it examines both continuities and ruptures across the East-West divide, and between the Weimar, Nazi and postwar periods. Once again, we see that the history of postwar sexuality was not a straightforward narrative of progress from older norms and moral standards, but rather built on earlier developments and postwar politics and culture in at times unpredictable ways.

Postwar struggles and pleasures: Rioters, Veronikas, prostitutes and nudists

Although they have certainly attracted the most attention in the cultural memory of the late twentieth century, the student and feminist movements of the late 1960s were not the first examples of rebellious youth seeking to carve out new sexual cultures, leisure patterns and fashions in the two postwar-era Germanies. The 1950s saw American music and movies like jazz, westerns and boogie make a significant mark on both East and West youth cultures, producing a less judgemental context for nonmarital sexual encounters than the conservative family ideals of politicians and religious leaders. Pop culture 'young rebel' figures like Marlon Brando's character in *The Wild One* (1953, dir. Benedek) inspired leather jackets, jeans and ducktail haircuts, as well as a youth riot movement across both Germanies in the late 1950s, involving plenty of arrests.[8] On one memorable summer evening in 1955, a West Berlin motorbike gang rode out to the Havel river to a café called Big Window, shocking the patrons with 'provocative skinny-dipping' and general commotion. One West Berlin paper later dubbed them the 'Marlon Brandos',[9] but the press more often used the term *Halbstarke* (hooligans, but literally 'semistrong'). In doing so, they revived a fairly perjorative term first applied to working-class young male rebels in the 1910s.[10]

Most rioters were men, many of them experimenting with different kinds of masculinity through their American-influenced fashions and rebellion. In particular, their styles and behaviours challenged the male gender roles sanctioned by new versions of military service in the context of post-Second World War rearmament and occupation in East and West: the call to be strong and loyal, but not overly militaristic.[11] One West German commentator even called the *Halbstarke* gangs a 'motorbike-SA'. That comparison with the Nazi Storm Troopers revived older associations with homosexuality and the Röhm purge (see Chapter 4), provocatively linking the youth rebels with sexual deviance at a time when male homosexuality remained strictly criminalized under Paragraph 175. While the youth rebel phenomenon was stronger in the West, cinemas along the West Berlin border proved a popular way of exporting *Halbstarken* fashions and music into the East, as well as dance and music rooted in African American culture, like boogie-woogie and rock'n'roll. During 1956 and 1957 it was estimated that around 26,000 East Berliners attended these border theatres daily, with teenagers making up the vast majority. Young East Germans embraced American-style haircuts and jeans, sometimes adapting locally made blue or black pants with rivets to emulate a look that the high West German exchange rate placed out of reach for many in the East. Like their Western counterparts, they listened to American music, and many also rioted.[12] Some gay men also drew on *Halbstarke* machismo styles to hide their sexuality and perceptions of effeminacy during these years: 'I wanted to become like the men in Hemingway's novels,' one recalled.[13] These new youth cultures and consumer trends crossed solidifying political and ideological lines and impacted on how people experienced their gender and sexuality.

As with the male rebels, young women's embrace of 1950s American rock'n'roll and movies was a cause of cultural anxieties in the early post-war decades. Especially in the US occupation zone and then in the Federal Republic, German women caught dancing and 'fraternizing' with American soldiers stationed in the country were accused of promiscuity, selfishness and undermining the authority of German men. Often labelled '*Amiliebchen*' (Ami-lovers) or 'Veronikas', with strong overtones of commercialized sex, American posters for occupying US troops dramatically warned of the dangers of STIs from sex with local women. One billboard featured a woman in a trench coat stamped with the letters 'VD' – an acronym also popularized in the song 'Veronika, Dankeschön'.[14] In the GDR, too, there was public shaming of 'Veronikas', as well as of female fans of bebop and rock'n'roll, who were accused of being sexually wayward. Even male teachers were warned to guard themselves against 'precociously sexual or morally corrupted girls' under their charge – a caution that reflected old gendered double standards, unfairly placing responsibility for upholding ideas of sexual morality on underage girls rather than grown men.[15]

In the areas under US control, the authorities attempted to enact strong restrictions on fraternization, although these didn't last long. Some estimates suggest that around 90 per cent of US soldiers had sexual contact with German 'Fräuleins'. and while marriages between these groups were initially banned, by late 1947 there were already 2300 German-American marriages, and by the mid 1950s this had risen to around 7000.[16] That these encounters could be fun and sexy as well as grounds for social ostracization is evident from Figure 6.1, showing a group of 'Fräuleins' and US soldiers at an intimate beach party at Berlin's Wannsee lake in the summer of 1945.

The emphasis on 'fraternization' highlights strikingly different views on relationships with occupying forces, especially in the western occupied zones between 1945 and 1949, than the focus on rape in the Soviet zone in the

FIGURE 6.1 *'GI's German Girls Enjoy Beach Party' at Wannsee beach, Berlin, 6 July 1945.*

Source: Getty Images.

immediate postwar era. Yet there were also some parallels, as scholars have shown.[17] Certainly, relationships between US soldiers and German women often involved mutual affection and sometimes resulted in marriage. But they also had undeniable economic and barter functions, offering women privileged access to food and consumer goods such as nylon stockings, as well as personal protection.[18] They were, moreover, a focus of intense anxieties, especially when the soldiers involved were African Americans. The popularity of jazz and rock'n'roll in the postwar decades reawakened the long-standing tension of fascination and racism that had surrounded African Americans and Black Germans since at least the Weimar era, especially when it came to white German women who had relationships with Black US soldiers. US and German military authorities also enacted policies that stemmed from fears of miscegenation: even after removing the initial ban on fraternization, it was much harder for mixed-race than all-white couples to gain marriage licences from US military commanders.[19]

Like the issue of 'fraternizing', with its perceived threat to dominant ideals of stable marriage and family, female prostitution attracted considerable political attention in both new German states, albeit in very different ways. In the early 1950s in the FRG, the Bundestag debated a new Law for the Control of Venereal Diseases. Passed in 1953, this decidedly pragmatic law had some parallels with that passed in the late-Weimar period, in that it abolished police regulation of prostitutes. But it also went considerably further: the law decriminalized prostitution, instead emphasizing personal protection and improved welfare measures.[20] Voluntary compliance was now seen as the most effective way of controlling STIs, rather than enforced source tracing of infections in women picked up by the police.[21]

This contrasted with the heavy policing of prostitution in the GDR, where the official emphasis was on having a 'clean state': First Secretary Erich Honecker famously described the need for the socialist state to fight against the Western 'propaganda of immorality'. The governing SED Party took a firm line not only against prostitution, but also pornography, censoring explicit materials and their distribution.[22] Both practices continued to exist, of course, but they were pushed largely underground. Sex workers faced fierce repression, although there were a few exceptions, such as during the biannual business exhibition or *Messe* in Leipzig.[23] During the 1973 World Youth Games, when many thousands of young people flocked to the GDR's capital, Honecker and Stasi chief Erich Mielke oversaw a punitive practice of arbitrary arrest and confinement in psychiatric institutions for prostitutes and other so-called 'asocials' who threatened the 'clean and orderly' image of the event. Those deemed asocial on the basis of recalcitrance or non-conformism – terminology with sinister overtones of Nazi-era practices – were regularly placed under the close watch of Stasi in schools, workplaces and social services. In some cases, the Stasi even pressured individuals to spy on their spouse or neighbours as 'inofficial collaborators', or IMs.[24] Yet just as it made exceptions during the *Messe*, the GDR state was not averse, as Josie McLellan points out, to pragmatically embracing sex as a 'weapon'. Foreign intelligence chief Markus Wolf later brayed in his memoirs of his pride in 'perfecting the use of sex in spying'. Authorities also regularly pressured prostitutes to act as informers or used sexual evidence to coerce individuals under surveillance.[25] The ways in which those with strong Party connections could access paid sex via a phone call, or demand it in exchange for material or political favours, are movingly portrayed in the 2006 film *The Lives of Others* (dir. von Donnersmarck).

If one hallmark of East German sexual culture was the relative absence of commercialized sexual cultures and publicly available prostitution – always with certain exceptions, as we have just seen – another was the relative comfort with public nudity. These two phenomena not only distinguish East from West during these decades, but both contemporaries and historians tend to see them as causally related.[26] Nudist culture (*Freikörperkultur*, FKK) was already an important aspect of the youth and life reform movements of the late Wilhelmine and Weimar eras, before being directed towards an increasingly fascist aesthetic during the Third Reich. In the GDR, however, the practice of gathering nude, especially on beaches or in parks, took on a new set of meanings both personal and political (Figure 6.2). The relationship between nudism and sexuality is, McLellan notes, a troubled one – not strictly a sexual activity, it remains nonetheless 'difficult to break

FIGURE 6.2 *On the FKK beach in Leipzig, ca 1980.*

Source: Alamy Images.

the psychological link between sex and the naked body'.[27] Especially in the early years of communist rule in the GDR, it was widely seen as a practice with sexual connotations, and from the late 1960s, as one of the more obvious aspects of the wider sexual 'revolution'.[28]

At first, the East German state was wary of nudism: in 1954–5 the SED leadership sought to forcibly suppress it as a dangerous sign of Western corruption, and as late as 1960 there were armed police attempts to clear beaches of FKK adherents. During the early 1960s, though, it transitioned into a much more widespread and tolerated activity – we might recall sexologist Kurt Starke's comments at the beginning of Chapter 5 about nude sunbathing students in Leipzig's Clara Zetkin park.[29] It was not uncommon for whole families to walk around naked at home – and often, the same parents who were comfortable with nakedness supported open discussions of sex education with their children.[30] Some historians have described GDR nudism as a little 'niche' of freedom in an otherwise repressive regime, or even as 'a nonviolent means of resistance' against the constricting uniforms and work clothing that symbolized life under socialism.[31] But we must be careful not to take such assessments too far. Nudism was undoubtedly a popular practice, and a campaign of coordinated but peaceful civil disobedience by some pioneering activists led to the overturning of the aforementioned ban in 1954. But resisting the ban was not the same as resisting the regime. On the contrary, McLellan argues that the state's growing tolerance and even co-option of the practice over time as a sign of progressive socialism removed much of its critical capacity. For most, nude bathing was as much about pleasure and recreation as politics. It also held different meanings for different people, from families and neighbours socializing, to gay men cruising, to teenagers embracing experimentation with newfound freedoms.[32]

1968ers, 'sexual revolution' and feminist reproductive activism

If alternative youth cultures, commercialized sex and nudism were long-standing features of the postwar landscape, youth rebellion started to take a different path in the late 1960s, and to look increasingly different in East and West. In the FRG, student radicals began to react fiercely against the social conservatism and Cold War liberal consensus of the postwar decades described in Chapter 5. They challenged their parents' generation – their own parents, but also university professors, politicians and other authority figures – about their activities during the Nazi era, and joined forces with Marxists and pacifists in protesting against capitalism, imperialism, racism and the American war in Vietnam.[33] They experimented with new counter-cultural fashions such as Beatles-style haircuts, delved into left-wing philosophy and challenged what they saw as their parents' stuffy sex-gender politics. Working to articulate self-consciously revolutionary links between anti-capitalism and new forms of sexual expression, they turned to writings by left-wing philosophers and psychoanalysts like Herbert Marcuse and Wilhelm Reich, as well as novels such as Peter Schneider's *Lenz* (1973) and Verena Stefan's *Häutungen* (*Shedding*) (1975), exploring what became known in some quarters as a 'new subjectivity'.[34]

In the GDR, students of this era, particularly those with working-class backgrounds, were more likely to feel grateful to the system for providing different kinds of educational opportunities than their parents had had. In contrast, it was young workers who were more likely to rebel. This was evident in protests following the Prague Spring of 1968, when Soviet troops came in to suppress protests in Czechoslovakia. While East German troops were called in to secure the border, many young workers were busy handing out flyers or more subtly rebelling by playing Western music at parties. The SED saw this as a form of Western attack aimed at 'depoliticizing' socialist youth.[35] But interviews conducted with East Germans about their sexual behaviours and attitudes during these decades demonstrate that people's actual experiences were not simply about political rebellion, and that they were also much more colourful and experimental than state-approved ideology might suggest. Over time, an everyday socialism emerged in which the state made increasing concessions to individualism and the importance of the private sphere, and permitted

FIGURE 6.3 *Still from* Die Legende von Paul und Paula *(1973, GDR, dir. Carow)*

'thaws' and experiments in the cultural sphere.[36] A good example of this is the 1973 film *The Legend of Paul and Paula* (dir. Heiner Carow). With its nods towards flower power, its embrace of gender equality and single motherhood, and its sympathetic account of extramarital affairs and the constraints of married life, the film rang true with audiences in a way that earlier, more ideological film productions by the East German state-owned DEFA studios had not.[37]

A prominent feature of the 1968 counter-cultural movements in both Germanies was an emphasis on new kinds of communal living that broke with conventional structures of marriage and the nuclear family. In the FRG, share houses (WGs) and other communal living arrangements such as squatting were popular aspects of student culture and offered new spaces of sexual experimentation: '[m]embers tried to develop interpersonal and sexual relations unencumbered by traditional social restrictions and made these part of their critique of the overall political and economic system of the Federal Republic.'[38] These trends also influenced youth cultures in the East. While the constrained GDR housing situation, noted in Chapter 5, made share or communal housing a much more difficult proposition, with couples often only eligible for their own place upon marriage or the birth of a child, there were a few notable exceptions, such as the 'Kommune I Ost' experiment in East Berlin from 1969 to 1972, or the Kellnerstrasse commune in Halle. These followed in the mode of the famous Kommune I and II in West Berlin. Such attempts to break from socialist models of the nuclear family were condemned by sex education manuals as immature protests against capitalism, and by senior party officials as pointing to 'a rise in decadent ways of life: young people, particularly Beat fans, try to live in "extended families" or "communes".'[39] At least some regular citizens agreed – for middle-aged married Party members Olga and Fritz K., share housing in the West merely highlighted the limitations of 'a society where you don't feel at home' (Olga), and where whole generations were 'turning away' (Fritz).[40] Others, though, remember communal life in the GDR more warmly, as a time 'filled with work and parties, with flirtations and politics'.[41] And while only some had access to such arrangements, for many young East Germans periods spent in residential hostels or *Internate* during their studies or apprenticeships offered similarly memorable, if sometimes highly regulated, spaces of sexual experimentation away from the parental home.[42]

The 'sexual revolution' is closely associated with the New Left and student movements that gained speed from 1968, but a number of parallel movements contributed to this wider 'revolutionary' atmosphere in crucial ways, particularly when it came to questions of sexual emancipation. Feminist, gay and trans liberation movements all challenged the mainstream version of '68 student politics, which tended to replicate hierarchies not so different to mainstream society and politics in both East and West: most leaders and spokespeople were white, cisgendered, heterosexual men, often from middle-class or reasonably privileged socio-economic backgrounds. The revolutionary atmosphere of the years after 1968 helped to create spaces for alternative ideas about sexual expressions and gender roles, often in ways that radically split ideas of sexuality from reproduction. But somewhat counter-intuitively, as we shall see, even as new movements posed challenges to old hierarchies and norms, they often reaffirmed essentializing models of identity.[43]

Feminism, the Pill and abortion reform

By the early 1970s, many West German women in as well as outside the New Left and student movements were getting fed up with the overbearing male dominance and marginalization of female perspectives. A new 'wave' of feminist activism and culture arose, campaigning around issues ranging from abortion reform to vaginal orgasm. 'Shared feelings of frustration and disillusionment at the way men and male-dominated society limited their life choices created solidarity among women,' Jane Freeland observes, with West German film-maker Helke Sander typical of many when she reflected that 'I married, because I was pregnant, and for economic reasons could not afford to remain unmarried.'[44] Women increasingly expressed feelings of being unfulfilled, unhappy, angry and disillusioned.[45] The urgent need for abortion law reform in the West was particularly important in inspiring a new generation of FRG feminists. They could look back to memories of progressive Weimar-era campaigns against Paragraph 218 'infused with a passionate belief that a new and better world for women and men was not only necessary but also possible'.[46] Anti-capitalist priorities were also prominent in feminist arguments: the group *Brot und Rosen* (Figure 6.4), modelled on the US Bread and Roses, combined anti-consumer culture with anti-patriarchal critique in a fierce attack on the commercialization of women's bodies

FIGURE 6.4 *Women's Handbook Number 1: Abortion, Contraception. Brot und Rosen, 1972.*

Source: Deutsches Hygiene-Museum, Dresden / Friedhelm Hoffmann

by men, including through pornography and advertising: 'Our bodies are being used, in order to sell products with which men make millions.'[47]

Across the FRG, feminist groups were established in most major towns and cities, drawing attention to women's rights in areas such as equal pay and maternity leave. Inspired by the North American women's movement, activities were often creative and mutually affirming, from protests at sex shops and beauty contests to opening independent childcare services, bookstores and domestic violence shelters, and founding consciousness-raising groups or *Quatschgruppen* ('chat groups'). Members protested against sexual violence and economic injustice, and developed new forums for discussing women's sexuality and pleasure – including with other women.[48] The radical liberationist politics of the movement is evident in names of groups such as the Council for the Liberation of Women in West Berlin or the Women's Revolutionary Council in Frankfurt.[49] In 1975 Alice Schwarzer, founder of the long-standing *Emma* magazine (1977–today), published her bestselling *Der 'kleine Unterschied' und seine großen Folgen* (The little difference and its huge consequences), in which she wrote that countless discussions with women about abortion, career and housework had led her to the conclusion 'that sexuality was the linchpin of the woman question', at once 'mirror and instrument of the oppression of women in all spheres of life'.[50] Verena Stefan's aforementioned novel *Shedding*, meanwhile, sold 150,000 copies in three years and soon became known as the 'bible of the women's movement'. Although criticized by some for an essentializing view of the female body, it drew attention through its first-person narrator to women's feelings of bodily alienation and emotional dependency in patriarchal society, while celebrating the possibilities of lesbian love and female community cultivated by groups such as *Brot ♀ Rosen*.[51]

Although there were various splits between West German feminist and lesbian groups, there was also recognition of commonalities. As Freeland finds, 'a shared concern with the body' was a key theme uniting the movement, and often centred on the creation of separate women's spaces, 'both discursive and physical'.[52] Many straight women closely followed debates among lesbians and bisexual women about sexual practices and pleasures, at least sometimes 'hoping to learn from them as they sought to repair what they felt were damaged relationships to their own bodies'.[53] At one memorable meeting at the West Berlin Women's Center in 1973, US feminists Debbie Law and Carol Downer first spoke about the self-help abortion clinic that they had founded in California, before Law took off her clothes from the waist down, got up on a table, inserted a speculum into her vagina and invited the women present to come and take a look. What they saw, as women at the event reported, defied their expectations: 'Not ugly and unappetizing, but beautiful and aesthetic', even 'like an orchid', as Freeland's research reveals.[54]

While many 1970s feminists were critical of the commercialization of sex and women's bodies, consumerism could also be an important way of exploring female sexuality during these decades. Erica Carter points to the importance of bedrooms as spaces in which girls could experiment with makeup, beauty treatments, fashions and fantasies inspired by popular culture.[55] Teen magazine *Bravo*'s advice and sex education segments, including the legendary 'Dr. Sommer' column, were hugely influential for generations of West German adolescents, and quite a few in the East as well, thanks to cross-border smuggling of publications. In the 1970s the editors received around seven thousand letters a week, especially from girls, and the magazine's team of sexperts writing under the 'Dr. Sommer' pseudonym issued advice to the countless young readers who passed around the approximately one million copies printed each week.[56]

Feminism developed in different ways in the East, where gender equality and female employment were taken as largely given. But here too, there was increasing openness about female sexuality, and new spaces for voicing women's sexual (dis)satisfaction. Feminist critiques by authors such as Christa Wolf and Brigitte Reimann echoed Maxie Wander's 1977 oral history collection, *Guten Morgen Du Schöne* (Good morning, beautiful), in which she spoke frankly with nineteen girls and women about their lives, work, relationships and politics.[57] In her introduction to that collection, Wolf declared that the book showed how the 'private life and feelings of many women in the GDR have transformed'.[58] Even if we stick with Herzog's assessment of a sexual 'evolution' rather than revolution in the GDR – which she argues also applied to feminism, on the basis that there was 'no large-and dramatic feminist protest movement or development of a women-centred counterculture' as developed in the West[59] – shifting attitudes around women's rights and sexual expression associated with the post-1968 era clearly resonated across the Iron Curtain.

Although some East German women may not have seen much need for a dedicated feminist movement, their sense of sexual self-determination was nonetheless grounded in a decidedly feminist sense of financial independence, by changes to divorce and abortion laws that improved women's agency in marital and reproductive decision-making, and in some cases, too, by a critical negotiation of West German feminist discussions of sexuality.[60] As one woman later put it, GDR sexuality was in some respects more emancipated than in the West: 'In the East, sex was not for sale.'[61] East German women were more prepared, as we saw in Chapter 5, to leave unsatisfactory relationships, and they were also more likely to cite sexist attitudes or inadequate sexual performance in divorce proceedings. After reunification, some also expressed exasperation at West German heterosexual women who continued to complain at length about male partners and sexual dissatisfaction, rather than just moving on.[62]

In East and West alike, more relaxed and more decidedly feminist attitudes towards premarital sexuality and female pleasure were helped along by the increasing availability of the Pill. In the FRG following its introduction in

1961, the so-called 'Anti-Baby-Pill' helped drive a shift from shame to pride in attitudes to sex outside marriage, as people started having sex at an ever younger age. News magazine *Der Spiegel* declared in 1971 that 'within four to six years, the sexual behavior of German youth has changed as never before in this century'.[63] *Der Stern* described the landing of the Pill as an 'historic day' and 'enormous step forwards', while the tabloid *Bild* called it the 'green bomb', in reference to its green packaging.[64] Teens started to call for the Pill to be widely distributed alongside liberalized sex education, and some handed pills directly to classmates and demanded that schools establish 'love rooms' for upper-level students.[65]

The Catholic Church took a strong stand against this and other 'artificial' contraceptives, reiterating this stance to the disappointment of many German Catholics via the Papal encyclical of 1968. The Protestant Church was also sceptical, but with a 'Memorandum on Questions of Sexual Ethics' published in 1971 ultimately passed moral responsibility for these questions to individuals, rejecting any distinction between 'natural' and 'artificial' methods. Notably, some feminists were also opposed, viewing the Pill as a patriarchal mechanism for pushing all responsibility for family planning onto women with unclear long-term health effects. But by 1972 around 3.8 million West German women were 'on' the Pill – around 30 per cent of all fifteen to forty-five-year-olds. A dramatic drop in the birth rate followed between 1963 and 1975, the so-called *Pillenknick* or 'pill hiccup', although women's improved career and educational mobility almost certainly played a role in individual decisions to delay or reject having children.[66]

In the GDR, the new method was given the gentler name 'Desired Child Pill' (*Wunschkindpille*). That name had been proposed by West German physician Anne-Maria Durand-Wever at the Pro Familia annual conference of 1964, and was soon taken on over the border as a brand name for oral contraceptives in the GDR.[67] Introduced in 1965, despite some concerns about hormonal effects such as weight gain, by 1970 it was part of the daily routine for around one-fifth of East Berlin women of childbearing age, with those elsewhere in the country not far behind. The price was kept low, at around 3.50 GDR marks per month, and it was soon by far the most popular contraceptive. Among one group of Leipzig women surveyed in 1987, 80 per cent of whom reported using contraception, two thirds chose the Pill, while far fewer opted for IUDs and pessaries (around 8 per cent), the rhythm method (5 per cent), condoms (3 per cent) and coitus interruptus (also 3 per cent). By 1990, as many as 90 per cent of GDR women surveyed had previously taken or were still on the Pill.[68] For many, the introduction of this new form of birth control transformed their sense of sexual freedom: 'we all swallow this green pill for breakfast that has given us freedom,' reported one of the interviewees in Wander's collection *Guten Morgen, Du Schöne.*[69] One of McLellan's oral history interviewees, meanwhile – herself a highly religious mother of nine – spoke of the Pill as 'the greatest intervention that there has ever been'. Despite such experiences of the Pill as liberatory, though, in the East as in the West 'the Pill placed the responsibility for contraception firmly at women's feet.'[70]

Even more than contraception, abortion was a focus of postwar feminist activism, especially in the West. In the East during the immediate postwar years, the Soviet zone authorities had taken a liberal approach, largely dismantling the anti-abortion Paragraph 218. This also allowed women to end pregnancies resulting from the large-scale rapes by Red Army troops, with expanded justifications for abortion now including poverty and sexual violence.[71] Soon, though, the GDR's emphasis on population renewal inspired a more conservative turn. The 1950 Law for the Protection of Mother and Child and the Rights of Women introduced more restrictive abortion conditions alongside the more generous maternal and child welfare provisions described in Chapter 5. Abortion was now only possible where there were grave concerns about hereditary illness or the health of the pregnant woman, and had to be assessed by a 'termination commission' consisting of doctors and representatives from the Ministry of Health and Democratic Women's League.[72] The rate of legal abortions dropped dramatically, from 122 per 10,000 births in 1952 to forty-four three years later – one of the lowest rates in the industrialized world, although illegal abortions continued at an estimated rate of 70,000–100,000 per year. Donna Harsch's close examination of GDR abortion policies finds that some nurses and social workers bravely spoke out to blame these figures on poor GDR social conditions and material constraints, as did some of the women requesting abortions.[73] One thirty-four-year-old woman, a teacher and mother of two with an alcoholic and unfaithful Party member husband, who suffered from depression and incontinence, wrote to the authorities in obvious despair: 'Do you really think that women are destined to take on all the burdens of life? I know that my husband will never change his way of life, and that I face terrible years if this application is turned down again.'[74]

During the 1960s, however, liberalizing attitudes coincided with a dramatic increase in the birth rate, from thirteen births per 1000 in 1951 to 17.6 in 1958.[75] Trends towards births outside marriage in the GDR had more in common with several Scandinavian countries than either the FRG or other Eastern European nations, and this was also the case for abortion: while rates trailed significantly behind the USSR, where it had been legalized in 1955 and contraception access was poor, in East Germany abortion was far more common than in West Germany or the UK, and by the 1980s, undertaken at a similar rate to Sweden or Denmark, with around 400 per 1000 live births.[76] First-trimester abortion on demand was legalized on 9 March 1972, which the SED under Honecker claimed as part of a progressive, pro-equality stance.[77] By 1973, 38 per cent of all pregnancies were terminated – a statistic that reflects a lack of good access to contraception as much as a strong desire by GDR women to control their family planning; this figure fell to 27 per cent by 1987.[78] Achieved not least thanks to campaigning by a new generation of female and working-class doctors, East German abortion law reform was, as Harsch emphasizes, part of a global wave of law reform activism that spread across both East and West from the mid-1960s, from Australia to Denmark, and from the United States to Czechoslovakia.[79]

In the West, the emerging women's movement spearheaded changes to women's reproductive rights. The immediate postwar period saw a rapid rise in abortion rates, peaking in 1950. Illegal abortions during subsequent decades were estimated at anywhere between 300,000 and one million per year, with around 10,000 women dying each year as a result.[80] Such figures, and the inequity of bearing the brunt of unwanted pregnancies, propelled many women into activism under the slogan 'My belly belongs to me', storming hearings of male experts, doctors and lawyers on the future of the decades-old Paragraph 218. One strategy promoted by prominent feminist Schwarzer was that of 'self-incrimination', with women encouraged to publicly admit that they had had an abortion, despite the criminal implications. On 6 June 1971, *Stern* magazine published an article with the title 'We Had Abortions', presenting readers with no few than 374 women's experiences of unwanted pregnancies; at another point, 'Schwarzer even attempt[ed] to televise an abortion.'[81] By 1973 surveys showed that 83 per cent of West German women favoured legal abortion, and despite huge opposition from the Catholic Church, in 1974 the social-liberal government succeeded in passing a law allowing for legal abortion funded by health insurance schemes in the first trimester. Although appealed in 1975, in 1976 abortion up to the twelfth (and in some cases, twenty-second) week of pregnancy was confirmed on a range of eugenic, medical, criminological and social grounds, although a requirement for mandatory counselling still applied.[82]

While abortion arguments were often framed in terms of a woman's rights, other justifications were also used. The kind of rationalized approach to birth control and abortion familiar from the Weimar sex reform movement is evident in the comments of Hans Harmsen, honorary president of West German family planning organization Pro Familia. Founded in 1952, Pro Familia was among the first West German organizations to publicly advocate for reform to the abortion law. Harmsen declared in 1980 that 'abortion is *not the cause* of lower fertility rates, but merely *an instrument* to fulfil the wish of restricting the number of one's children.'[83] Harmsen pointed out that the GDR had both a higher abortion and a higher birth rate than the West. Consequently, as Claudia Roesch shows, the Pro Familia organization argued that the Federal Republic should focus on supporting young families rather than restricting access to family planning measures.[84]

In some cases, eugenic considerations also played a role – and as Roesch notes, Harmsen himself was a contested figure given his earlier support of forced sterilization during the Nazi era.[85] Immediately after the war,

Catholic sociologist Werner Schoellgen argued that 'the eugenic idea' was still significant despite 'the abuse in the Third Reich', and 1950s Catholic periodicals encouraged couples to conceive high numbers of 'physically and psychologically valuable offspring'. Such pro-eugenics views were not limited to religious groups.[86] Two decades later, in 1971, West German news magazine *Der Spiegel* was highly dismissive of the 15 per cent of West German doctors who had argued, in the context of debates around 'thalidomide babies' and foetal abnormalities, that 'children should be born against the will of the mother, even if they will come into the world as cripples or mental idiots'.[87] Such language discriminating against disabled individuals was strongly reminiscent of Nazi-era policies, although it also remained common across much of Europe. Indeed, Roesch has found that quite a few women fronting up to crisis pregnancy counselling were in their late thirties and married with children, had become pregnant accidentally, and feared that their age would increase the risk of having a child with a disability.[88] Such concerns point to the naturalization of eugenic norms about reproduction now extricated from Nazi racial hygiene policies, in ways that represent longer lines of continuity with the priorities of late nineteenth- and early twentieth-century sex reform.

Repression to liberation: LGBTIQ movements in East and West

If the feminist movement was spearheading the right to contraception, to make decisions about ones' own body, to experience sexual pleasure and more broadly, a separation of sexuality from reproduction, the postwar re-emergence of gay and trans liberation politics represented different branches of the wider sexual 'revolution'. This multifaceted movement, or rather plural and overlapping movements, took off in Germany and elsewhere around the globe in the years following the Stonewall riots in 1969 in New York City, when transpeople, queens and queers had fought back against police brutality and discrimination near the city's famous Stonewall Inn.[89] As we have seen, this was not Germany's first brush with a gay or trans rights movement – activists in that country could look back on a long history of queer identity politics, from the writings of nineteenth-century activists such as Karl Heinrich Ulrichs to the work of organized lobbying groups such as the Scientific Humanitarian Committee and the thriving gay, lesbian and trans scenes of Weimar Berlin. But these scenes had been almost completely torn apart during the years of Nazi rule. While many after 1945 still remembered the dynamic queer politics and nightlife of yore, many were also deeply traumatized from years spent hiding their sexuality or gender, locked up in concentration camps or living in constant fear of Gestapo surveillance and arrest.

The top priority for gay liberationists was challenging ongoing legal discrimination against male-male sex. After the war, although the Allies had busied themselves dismantling a host of other authoritarian Nazi laws, Paragraph 175 continued to be enforced, even as some courts in the Soviet-occupied eastern zone argued that it should be annulled.[90] After the formal division of GDR and FRG in 1949, the East German Supreme Court of Berlin decided in 1950 to liberalize the legislation, on the basis that the 1935 version of Paragraph 175 was an 'instrument of power for the Nazi state to prepare for war'.[91] Judges and police in the GDR were directed not to prosecute consensual activity between adult men. And while this certainly did not eliminate persecution or social ostracism, the situation contrasted starkly with the police raids and criminalization that dogged gay men in the early days of the FRG. Recent studies by scholars such as Craig Griffiths, Samuel Huneke and Clayton Whisnant have helped to unpack these up-and-down years of postwar gay persecution and liberation, some focusing on the Federal Republic, and others looking at cross-German continuities and ruptures. Notably, this research delves into the implications of gay identity politics with larger Cold War cultures of surveillance and policing.[92]

The GDR government loudly declared itself antifascist and anti-capitalist. This led to celebrating a specifically socialist brand of heterosexual intimacy, as we have seen, but also had a negative flipside of policing sexual deviance, which was often considered by the authorities to go hand in hand with political dissidence. By and large, throughout the forty-year period of the GDR's existence queer people were consistently marginalized, despite broader discourses of sexual liberalism. 'To the bitter end the regime maintained churlish notions of sexual propriety,' observes Evans, especially when it came to gay men, and especially in key institutional spaces such as politics, education, the police and military service.[93] The SED's homophobic stance can be traced back to the Weimar-era Communist Party, when the KPD had joined the attack on SA leader Ernst Röhm as symbolic of a gay Nazi conspiracy.[94] Throughout the postwar decades, the spaces of the GDR gay scene, such as bars, parks and public toilets, remained less visible than in the West. Lesbian culture was even more hidden, and queer magazines and associations were prohibited as non-official forms of organization.[95] The celebrated 'niches' of GDR private life tended to exclude lesbians and gay men even well into the 1970s and 1980s. One woman recalled that 'I have to keep it a secret from my work collective'; another, living in the provinces, noted the 'terrible loneliness [that] starts when your workmates say goodbye each afternoon'.[96] This only began to change during the 1980s, argues Maria Bühner, as lesbian desires that had long been 'invisible, unnamed, and hidden in the private sphere' increasingly found spaces in which they could be discussed, with new activist networks fighting for recognition.[97]

In the FRG, the Nazi version of Paragraph 175 was retained for several more years before being integrated into the new German Criminal Code. This resulted in numerous lengthy court cases during the 1950s and early 1960s, and around 45,000 convictions, peaking in the years 1957 to 1962.[98] The conservative and heteronormative 'Golden Fifties' in West Germany seemed an unlikely context for the rebuilding of gay scenes after the destruction of the Nazi years. Konrad Adenauer's government used the ongoing legal and social stigmatization of gay men to shore up arguments about sexual respectability, family and the protection of youth, even as it parted ways with the racial hygiene arguments of the Nazis.[99] Catholic leaders also loudly lamented the alleged dangers of homosexuality. They drew on scientific and psychoanalytic approaches to frame their opposition in seemingly rational, modern terms, as a contagious condition against which youth required protection, especially 'during the time of their bisexual lability and homosexual receptiveness', as one commentator argued in 1953.[100]

Yet despite the conservative atmosphere, new spaces of queer desire, socializing and politics did re-emerge, especially in larger West German cities like Hamburg, Cologne and West Berlin. In the 1950s FRG, as in much of Western Europe and North America, gay culture tended to reflect the larger mood of respectability and restraint. A new 'homophile' movement emphasized conformity to social norms of gender expression and respectable public behaviour as the cost of social inclusion – though as we have seen, respectability arguments were already a feature of Weimar gay and trans rights politics.[101] Many same-sex desiring men, observes sociologist Martin Dannecker, 'were driven by a burning desire for recognition and the urgent craving to appear normal'. Sometimes, though, this resulted in decidedly exclusionary tactics directed against others who fell outside of heteronormative sex-gender frameworks, including gay men who did not share the homophile movement's ideals of monogamous or platonic male-male love.[102]

One of the most important German-language magazines of the homophile movement of the 1950s and 1960s was *Der Kreis* (The Circle), based in 1943 in Switzerland, but reaching a multilingual, transnational audience of subscribers – by 1959, 700 of the 2000 copies per issue were sent beyond Swiss borders. As reader Johannes Werres recalls, reading the magazine suddenly made homosexuality seem appealing, 'It was truly exciting ... For me this moment was a historic moment in my life that changed everything.'[103] The friendship clubs established by the homophile movement followed in the footsteps of Weimar-era activists, insisting on homosexuality as 'natural' and 'inborn'. As Clayton Whisnant shows in an in-depth study of gay culture during this early postwar period, while many older activists had been part of the Weimar movement, they now found themselves having to rebuild publications and organizations from the ground up following the extensive persecutions of the Nazi era.[104] This traumatic experience had left many seeking a similar stability to many straight Germans of the 1950s – the desire to fit in and lead a quiet life was particularly urgent for many gay men after

years of state surveillance and state-sponsored violence. In seeking to claim
a space of respectable recognition in the new West German state, homophile
activists also drew on the findings of sexual science. They did so, though, in
much more self-affirming ways than religious critics of homosexuality. This
involved deploying similar tactics to those of interwar sex reformers such
as Hirschfeld: as Benno Gammerl shows, they promoted arguments such as
'that the young lad between 15 and 17 is erotically fixed and can no longer
be "seduced" into a homosexual disposition'.[105] Some also drew on the work
of sexologist Hans Giese, who in 1949 established a new Institute for Sexual
Research in Frankfurt. Giese, Whisnant notes, sought to establish himself
as Magnus Hirschfeld's progressive successor, despite notable differences in
their scientific views.[106]

The homophile movement was a largely male phenomenon. While
a few same-sex desiring women were active in the early days, female
homosexuality barely featured in West German public discourse until the
late 1960s, its invisibility in the criminal law contributing to its ongoing
erasure in psychiatry, medicine and sociology as well.[107] Yet gay male
and lesbian scenes also developed in different spaces that challenged the
homophile movement's push for respectability. Public bathrooms and
cruising grounds proved especially important places for gay male sex. In the
context of bombed-out Berlin, Jennifer Evans also explores the role of places
such as the abandoned wartime bunkers, stations and the street for enabling
new spaces of erotic encounter, including the culture of rent boys gathering
around the famed train station Bahnhof Zoo.[108]

Others defied the normative tendencies and respectability politics
of the postwar homophile movement through nonconforming gender
expression. Effeminate *Tunten* (roughly 'queens' or 'sissies'), hypermasculine
leathermen – who, like the *Halbstarken*, borrowed from American popular
culture to experiment with new macho looks – and transpeople all presented
alternative constellations of sexual desire and gender embodiment, and
developed a distinctly gender-diverse scene.[109] The nightspot 'Ellis Bierbar'
in West Berlin was one place that, throughout its long existence that reached
into the late 1980s, attracted such a mixed crowd. As Evans observes, this
Stricherkneipe (rent-boy bar) was owned by a motorcycle lesbian who gave
the place its name, with a fitout that was a throwback to the 'old' Berlin of the
1900s, its multilayered identity exemplifying the 'burgeoning and competing
homosexual subcultures that came back into view after the war'. Despite
being under police surveillance well into the 1960s, the bar 'projected an air
of tolerance among the community itself: hustlers, transvestites, sissy boys, ...
and mannish women [seeking] sanctuary from prying eyes and judgmental
hearts.' Mahlsdorf, too, later recalled evenings out during these years among
'half-naked young men, in fancy evening dresses or in enchanting almost
transparent flimsy garments'.[110] Such spaces, as Evans explores further in
a new book on postwar queer kinship, represented an important but often

overlooked space of coalitional LGBTIQ sociality – the kind of space often celebrated by today's queer theorists and activists.[111]

Law reform, experts and activists

The legal situation for gay men changed dramatically in the late 1960s in both German states. In East Germany, male same-sex sex between consenting adults was decriminalized in 1968, a year earlier than in the West, although a few years after other Eastern European states including Hungary and Czechoslovakia.[112] Paragraph 175 was replaced with Paragraph 151 in the new GDR Criminal Code, and homosexuality was ruled a 'biological problem' rather than an 'illness'. This law continued, though, to prohibit same-sex contact with minors under the age of eighteen, even though the age of consent for heterosexual relations was fourteen. For the first time, it also extended punishment to women. It was only fully repealed in 1988.[113]

Meanwhile, on 25 June 1969, after years of political and legal debate, FRG legislators also significantly reformed West German laws surrounding male homosexuality. Consensual sex between adult males was decriminalized, and by 1982, as Edward Dickinson shows, 'the rate for this crime was less than 4 per cent what it had been at its postwar high in 1959 and one-quarter what it had been in 1882'.[114] Decriminalization had clear limits in the West as well, however. Gay men remained subject to considerably stricter legal constraints on their sex lives than their straight counterparts: homosexual contact with minors under the age of twenty-one was prohibited, male prostitution continued to be outlawed and sex between men aged eighteen to twenty-one could be punished with up to five years jail – a move particularly aimed at restricting homosexuality in the military.[115]

Examining the debates leading up to this significant, if ambivalent, West German law reform, Whisnant emphasizes the legal reform efforts of both the homophile movement and a new generation of progressive lawyers, doctors, theologians and politicians. These, he argues, were more important than pressure from student and New Left radicals, or the newer, burgeoning gay liberation movement, or even the widely touted *Sexwelle*, the public media discussion of sexual themes examined in Chapter 5. While the reform occurred at a highly symbolic time, the year of the Stonewall riots, it had much longer roots – Whisnant finds that already in the late 1950s, many West German intellectuals were turning to scientific arguments favouring decriminalization, and to legal and religious arguments that stressed a separation of law and morality. These findings complicate common understandings of postwar gay liberation as a movement that only really took off in the 1970s. Those supporting more progressive approaches to the 'homosexual question' included liberal Christian thinkers – Protestants and Catholics alike – who feared that taking a negative attitude towards sex *per se* might drive people away from the church altogether.[116] Swiss theologian and marriage counsellor Theodor Bovet was particularly influential in this context. His 1959 book *A Meaningful Way of Being Different* argued that homosexuality was not just about sex, but 'a total difference in an individual's way of being'. In making this argument, Bovet drew on the latest psychological research on inborn and acquired homosexuality, and he insisted that a truly Christian ethics required a more human, nuanced response than outright rejection.[117]

In the GDR, expert opinions on the topic were similarly mixed. On the one hand, many sexologists and educators adhered to the conformist view, shared by SED leaders, that homosexuality undermined the ideal of 'clean' socialist relationships. Not unlike Nazi-era intellectuals, many viewed same-sex relations as pathological, and frequently aligned with criminality. Often, they argued, homosexuality was a result of seduction during youth. Sometimes, an apparently sympathetic tone only barely disguises the normative impetus of such 'expert' opinions. In his popular *Die Geschlechterfage* (The Question of the Sexes), prominent sexologist Rudolf Neubert described homosexuality as a 'deformation of the inner glands' and homosexuals as people 'to be pitied just as much as those born with any other deformation', recommending a range of hormone, surgical and psychotherapy treatments.[118] Kurt Freund in neighbouring Czechoslovakia, meanwhile, argued for Pavlovian-based behavioural 'aversion therapy'. This coercive psychotherapy treatment method not only found its way into GDR clinics, but also well beyond the Eastern bloc during the 1950s and 1960s, as Kate Davison has shown.[119] S/M and kink cultures were also criticized by GDR sex writers, although on more ideological grounds: they argued that such relationships were tied down by structures of capitalist oppression and domination. That such cultures nonetheless existed in the East is evident from Stasi files detailing sadomasochistic practices among nonconformist youth cliques, or in fantasy literature aimed at soldiers.[120] But there were also some East German experts who promoted a more liberal, less medicalizing approach. Outspoken sexologist Rudolf Klimmer, based in Dresden, whose 1958 book *Homosexuality as a Biological-Sociological Problem of the Time* was published in the West due to censorship restrictions, advocated that homosexuals be officially recognized as 'victims of Nazism'.[121] Klimmer, himself a victim of Nazi homophobic persecution, loudly affirmed that '[t]he homosexual is no more asocial or predisposed towards criminal behavior than the heterosexual is.'[122]

Following these key law reforms in East and West, the 1970s in the two Germanies are often portrayed as something of a 'golden age for queers'.[123] Yet even as changes to Paragraph 175 were the backdrop for a liberalized queer scene during this decade, longer cultural developments again played a role – a reminder that narratives of 'liberation' also require historical contextualization. In the East, some artists and intellectuals harked back to earlier socialist utopias of gender and sexual liberation to advocate for a less narrow-minded approach. Playwright Heiner Müller in his play *Zement* (Cement, 1972) showcased the radical sex-gender visions of early Russian revolutionary Alexandra Kollontai, for example, while a 1975 collection of short stories by feminist authors, later released under the title *Sex-Change*, used tropes of biological transformation to critique gender inequality and patriarchal sexual relations.[124] One of the first responses to the decriminalization of male homosexuality in West Germany, meanwhile, was a sharp rise in publications and nightclubs targeting a gay male market. This booming commercial scene soon had tendrils that extended over the border, as many of these publications were smuggled across the Wall to be passed around East German gay networks.[125]

1971 marked another important moment, as filmmaker Rosa von Praunheim premiered his film *It is not the homosexual who is perverse, but the society in which he lives* at the Berlinale film festival. The film depicts a young gay man from the countryside who comes to Berlin and explores urban gay life. It was screened by regional public broadcaster WDR in early 1972, before being sent across the television waves of the entire West Germany via federal broadcaster ARD in 1973. Particularly because it was so accessible to audiences regardless of location, the film made enormous waves across a country in which 'schwul' (gay) was still frequently used as an insult. In making it, von Praunheim worked with aforementioned sociologist Martin Dannecker to criticize what might now be termed 'homonormative' attempts to fit in with the straight world – the approach favoured by the homophile movement. Instead, the film advocates for gays and lesbians reclaiming labels often used against them, like *schwul,* and proclaiming proudly antinormative, anti-bourgeois forms of sex-gender existence. To simply emulate heterosexuals, von Praunheim insisted, was to reject not only one's own homosexuality, but also its counternormative political potential. This involved criticizing the lifestyle choices of many fellow gays: 'Gay people don't want to be gay; instead; they want to live the bourgeois, trashy life of the average citizen'.[126]

Within a month of the film's release, the Homosexual Initiative of West Berlin (*Homosexuelle Aktion Westberlin*, HAW) was founded by young radicals, modelled on New York's Gay Liberation Front (Figure 6.5). This was soon followed by other groups across the FRG, who published newsletters, opened information and counselling centres, promoted queer arts and organized conferences such as 'Homolulu' in Frankfurt in 1979.[127] It wasn't long before frustrations with the male dominance of the gay movement as well as homophobia within the women's movement led to the formation of breakaway lesbian groups as well, such as the *Lesbisches Aktionzentrum Westberlin* (Lesbian Action Centre West Berlin, LAZ).[128]

Despite significant gains, historians caution against reading LGBTIQ history since the 1970s in overly nostalgic or singular terms. They point out that heterosexuality was also experiencing enormous shifts during

FIGURE 6.5 *Homosexuelle Aktion Westberlin, 1973.*
Source: Getty Images/Ullstein Bild.

this decade, and that the growth of the erotic publishing trade, sex work and premarital and non-monogamous sex impacted both queer and straight experience in ways that were deeply 'entangled', to return to Evans's phrase.[129] Celebrations of the gay (male) 1970s also have distinct limits – for one thing, they have often erased female same-sex and lesbian feminist perspectives, which cast critical light on patriarchal as well as heterosexist structures.[130] Black lesbians and feminists were particularly marginalized from mainstream queer debates, even as important new networks of 'quotidian intellectuals' were solidifying around key figures such as Audre Lorde in 1980s Berlin, as Tiffany Florvil shows.[131] Benno Gammerl goes so far as to declare the decidedly normalizing tendencies that continued to shape the LGBTIQ movement during these decades. He notes that even if the 'norms' in question were no longer confined to monogamous respectability, it was nonetheless the case that a decidedly cisgender, masculine aesthetic and politics came to dominate the movement, and that groups including sex workers, effeminate homosexuals and *Tunten*, leather and fetish adherents, and paedophiles were sidelined. This process of scene-internal 'normalization' disrupts ideas of successive sexual liberation, and continued to shape queer culture during the 1980s in the context of safer sex discourses and HIV/AIDS, discussed below.[132]

The gender-normative tone of the dominant gay male movement is evident in one interview with a 'Mr Pohl', who recalls that he had wanted nothing to do with 'shrieking, stupid queens' ('kreischenden, blöden

Tunten'). On the contrary, he felt a need to prove his manhood by signing up for military service.[133] From 1973 to 1975 in West Berlin, such tensions culminated in the so-called *Tuntenstreit* (roughly 'queens' dispute'), with gender non-conforming activists questioning the gay movement's emphasis on masculinity and respectability.[134] Intergenerational sex was another point of contention, for which the two main West German gay magazines, *Du und Ich* (You and me) and *him*, serve as a useful barometer. They move from cautiously distanced interviews with rentboys in the 1970s to silence on the topic by the 1980s – even as increasing numbers of letters from readers criticized the invisibility of intergenerational sex as an 'attack against paedophiles'.[135] As Craig Griffiths argues in a new study, 1970s West German gay liberation was 'shot through with ambiguities and ambivalence', even as it was precisely the tensions created 'by the desire to be "normal" clashing with the affirmation of difference, by hope meeting fear, that lent gay liberation its power and dynamism'.[136]

In the GDR, too, von Praunheim's film made waves. Many East German gays viewed it via (illegal) West German television, while others were alerted to screenings via activists smuggling queer publications across the border.[137] Nineteen years old at the time, Eduard Stapel saw the film and realized that he was not alone, while von Mahlsdorf recalls in her memoirs how it motivated East Berlin gays and lesbians to establish communication centres and cultivate a stronger sense of self-understanding, at a time when queer bars were regularly shut down or under surveillance.[138] Pushed to find underground spaces for cruising and cottaging, East German gay men were frequently exposed to macho gangs, some of whom used good-looking young men as 'honey traps' to lure in victims who might then be robbed, blackmailed or bashed.[139] Homophobia was widespread – 'everybody I knew then despised gays and told jokes about them', recalls one interviewee. It remained hard to meet like-minded people, even when the first organized GDR gay and lesbian groups started to appear in the 1980s under the auspices of church structures.[140] Yet beneath the surface, queer life did persist, including a thriving network of smuggled and amateur erotica and pornography. These documents, as Kyle Frackman shows, offer 'evidence of a clandestine yet joyful sexual culture'.[141] Amateur photographers created gay porn in their living rooms and bedrooms, defying state prohibitions on the distribution of pornographic material and challenging official lines on sexuality 'both for their non-procreative focus and for their homoeroticism, as men were the objects of other men's sexual desires'.[142]

Another important space of queer intimacies during these years, and one often overlooked by historians, was prisons. Andrea Rottmann unpacks some of the complex queer relationships, particularly between women, that developed behind bars in both East and West. These include the experiences of masculine-presenting lesbian or 'Bubi' Rita 'Tommy' Thomas, an East Berlin dog groomer who spent ten months in the early 1950s in the Barnimstraße prison near Berlin's Alexanderplatz for gun possession. Tommy

FIGURE 6.6 *Charlotte von Mahlsdorf in her museum outside Berlin.*
Source: Sueddeutsche Zeitung Photo/Alamy Images

later described the prison as a space in which there were plenty of 'pretty women', including one with whom she celebrated a playful 'engagement', but where she also managed to carve out a space in a single cell for writing and introspection. And as we saw in Chapter 4 in the context of Anna Hájková's work on the concentration camps, these queer networks of desire and exchange could include guards as well as prisoners. Tommy recalls the prisoners giving two of the guards the nicknames 'Tin Tooth Bubi' and 'Miss Fox', language suggesting a decidedly sexualized and queer categorizing of prison hierarchies and relations.[143]

During these years, more than a few East German queers left for what they hoped were the greener pastures of the West. Often they were unable to say goodbye to the communities that had supported them, for fear of risking the escape. As von Mahlsdorf (Figure 6.6) remembers: 'those who emigrated or were deported simply disappeared from one day to the next'.[144] But important pockets of resistance also developed. In an unusual concession by the state, in 1973 British-based gay activist Peter Tatchell was invited to the World Festival Games (*Weltfestspiele*) in East Berlin. He brought along hundreds of smuggled gay liberation flyers and had the opportunity to speak to thousands of assembled youth alongside other left-wing celebrities such as US racial justice campaigner Angela Davis.[145] Six months earlier, the Homosexual Interest Group Berlin (*Homosexuelle Interessengemenschaft Berlin*, HIB), which despite its name, brought together a wide range of gay and lesbian, bisexual and trans activists, had been founded in the Eastern districts of the city to coincide with the screening of von Praunheim's film on West German TV. The group sought to forge a space for gay liberation within socialism by 'educating' the authorities, and through self-help groups and social networks. Von Mahlsdorf offered the group the basement of her museum for meetings, while lesbian activist Ursula Sillge was inspired to organize a women-only event at the museum in Spring 1978, with a secret invitation passed on to 'appropriately interested girl friends' to get around the authorities. Unfortunately, they got wind of it and the approximately 100 women who arrived were sent away by the police. The work of the HIB faded out soon afterwards.[146]

During the 1980s, the Protestant church presented a shelter and organizational base for oppositional voices, including feminist, pacifist and environmentalist organizations as well as queer groups. This partial public sphere was made possible by the Church-State Agreement of 1978. Queer church groups existed in Magdeburg, Dresden and Erfurt, as well as Berlin, and by the middle of the decade, many smaller towns as well. Their significance for individual members was emphasized by Gabriele S. in an interview: 'To be able to gather up the courage to stand up in meetings and say "I am a lesbian woman and live with my girlfriend", to do that in public was very important for me and for building my self-confidence.'[147] This 1980s activism in the East, Maria Bühner emphasizes, combined struggles for queer rights with criticism of the state and the legitimacy of the ruling SED. It was also spurred along by international activism around AIDS and new academic understandings of homosexuality.[148]

Not surprisingly, the Church-based groups were under regular Stasi surveillance, with the Protestant Church well-known as a haven for dissidents. One report suggested that regular events in Leipzig were drawing 70–100 attendees a fortnight, and more for major events. While the GDR queer movement grew rapidly, like its West German counterpart it soon experienced fragmentation. With gay men often dominating the conversation, one group of women formed a separate 'Lesbians in the Church' (Lesben in der Kirche, LiK) group to focus more explicitly on feminist topics. Another secular Berlin group led by Sillge became the foundation of the Sonntags-Club ('Sunday Club'), still in existence today, and focused on assimilating gay men and lesbians into socialist society, including through better housing and positive representations.[149] While McLellan provides an excellent overview of these groups, Bühner's study is notable for its investigation of the role of emotions in groups such as LiK: the GDR's 'repressive emotional regime', she argues, characterized by invisibility and isolation, inspired activists to develop 'their own ideas of what it meant to be a lesbian'.[150]

The LiK's first meeting was in a private apartment, attended by around fifteen women. When the police arrived it was evident that a safer space was required, and the women turned to the Church. A core aspect of their strategy was on 'coming out', claiming sexuality as central to one's personality. They developed consciousness-raising groups not unlike those that emerged in other Western countries as part of the feminist movement during these decades.[151] Other lesbian groups formed elsewhere in the GDR during those years, including a breakaway group from the Arbeitskreis Homosexualität Dresden in 1986, which over the next three years oversaw a heady program of three women's festivals with around 300 guests at each. Groups also formed in Magdeburg, Halle, Jena and Erfurt. The 'Erfurter Lesben' were attached to the Evangelical City Mission of that city, while attempts in Leipzig to break away from Arbeitskreis Homosexualität Leipzig took a little longer, with the lesbian group Lila Pause only formed in 1989. There were, notes Bühner, multiple reasons why lesbians broke away from the mixed homosexual rights groups, even though many continued to engage with broader activist networks. Some felt that there was not enough attention to issues that concerned lesbians, while others wanted to create separate women's spaces. Many of these networks were also connected to the independent women's rights movement, which in turn sometimes hosted lesbian-specific events, including workshops in Dresden and Hanstorf near Rostock in 1988 and 1989.[152]

As we have seen in previous chapters, strategies such as coming out and claiming a space of recognition reflect typical ways of understanding the relationship of sexuality in relation to ideas of subjectivity and citizenship in modernity more broadly. They built on much longer histories across the twentieth as well as the late-nineteenth century of queers making explicit, public claims to visibility and recognition. A further important focus of GDR lesbian and gay activism during this decade was on recognizing homosexuals as victims of Nazism. Gay and lesbian groups visited memorial services at former concentration camps such as Ravensbrück and Sachsenhausen, laid wreaths and wrote in visitors' books. The authorities frequently sought to downplay or foil such actions, including by tearing out the pages signed by queer visitors in memory of homosexual victims of the regime.[153]

While often less visible in groups that tended to organize under labels such as 'homosexual' or 'lesbian', trans, bisexual and intersex activists were a firm and very active part of these movements advocating for greater tolerance and acceptance for sex and gender diversity in the postwar decades, in both East and West. At the same time, it is important to recognize the distinct legal, medical and social struggles of individuals marginalized on the basis of their gender identity or ambiguous birth sex – sometimes even within movements campaigning for other sexual freedoms. While some of the most significant legal changes affecting trans individuals have only come into play in very recent decades, in 1980 West Germany was among the first countries to introduce a Transsexual Law (*Transsexuellengesetz*), which enabled changes of name and identity documents, provided surgical alteration had taken place. (This interventionist condition was later declared unconstitutional and removed in 2011.[154]) The East German government, meanwhile, showed a perhaps surprisingly tolerant view of transsexuality as an inborn, and thus legally defensible condition, when in 1976 the Ministry of Health approved sex confirmation procedures as a 'cure' for this condition.[155] From the early postwar years, trans activists were a crucial part of wider queer networks, including Maria Sabine Augstein and Nora Eckert in West Germany, or von Mahlsdorf in the East.[156] Such activists pushed back on and also actively shaped the work of medical experts working with gender-diverse patients. These included gender confirmation surgery pioneer Harry Benjamin, a German-born émigré who had moved to North America before the First World War, and who in his later work in the postwar United States frequently drew on his earlier contacts with sexologists and researchers such as Eugen Steinach in Vienna and Magnus Hirschfeld in Berlin.[157]

Intersex policy and medicine during these postwar decades were heavily shaped by US-based psychologist John Money at Johns Hopkins Hospital in Baltimore. As Ulrike Klöppel shows, Money was known from the 1950s for his promotion of a psychosocial theory of 'gender identity' rather than notions of biologically determined sex. On this basis, he advocated for cosmetic surgery and hormone treatments in intersex infants and children, at times going against other indicators of biological sex. This combined surgical-hormonal approach was taken up widely in both the FRG and GDR from around 1970. Against the wishes of many German doctors, who argued in favour of genital surgery on intersex infants, the explicit consent of the patient was required, meaning that interventions were only permitted from puberty. These medical debates occurred in the absence of legal or medical recognition of 'third sex' possibilities, and as Klöppel shows, worked to create a medical norm that reinforced the disenfranchisement of intersex people. By the end of the century, it had become clear that Money's wide-ranging experiment on the lives of individuals with ambiguous birth genitalia had failed, even leading in some cases to suicide.[158]

HIV/AIDS and safety as the new 1980s norm

If the 1970s were experienced as 'revolutionary' by many queers as well as straights, East as well as West Germans, the HIV/AIDS epidemic from the 1980s represented a move in a more restrictive direction, as discussions around sexuality and intimacy focused increasingly on safety and protection: 'safer sex' and especially condom use. From the beginning of the epidemic, the media in many countries placed a strong and often highly discriminatory emphasis on the sexual practices of men who had sex with men. The illness was first identified in the West by doctors in Los Angeles and San Francisco in the early 1980s, and the HIV virus was subsequently identified and named by French and German scientists in 1983. Later, though, it was recognized that there had been AIDS patients in Europe since at least the 1970s, as Annette Timm and Joshua Sanborn point out.[159] HIV infections were far more numerous among gay men in the FRG than GDR, where limited freedom of movement and a relative lack of injectable drugs inhibited its spread. Infection demographics spread unevenly elsewhere in Europe, with gay men the main sufferers in West Germany, Denmark and the UK, while in France and Belgium, it was more associated with people – many of them not gay – with links to Central Africa, where AIDS-related disease was spreading rapidly.[160]

In the Federal Republic both before and after the fall of the Berlin Wall in 1989 and unification in 1990, the mainstream media contributed significantly to shaping an image of the illness as intimately connected to sexuality. It did so even as other modes of transmission became increasingly well-known, such as with the so-called 'blood donation scandal' of 1993.[161] Headlines such as the 'Deadly AIDS plague' ('Tödliche Seuche AIDS') gracing the covers of the *Spiegel* and other publications from as early as 1983 resulted, argues Magdalena Beljan, not just in widespread practice of safer sex, but also perceptions of a widespread 'loss of pleasure', with AIDS frequently depicted as a negative consequence of the increasing sexualization of society since the 'revolution'. From the early days of the epidemic, promiscuous homosexual men were blamed as a key conduit: the media persistently portrayed gay sex – and anal sex, in particular – as more dangerous and risky than straight sex, often suggesting, or at least implying, that gay men were to blame for their

FIGURE 6.7 *German ACT-UP initiative, 1990. Sign reads '5300 Crosses, 5300 AIDS Deaths. Stop the Dying! ACT UP.'*

Source: Gamma-Rapho/Getty Images.

'immoderate' sexuality and illness. Not infrequently, dubious statistics were deployed to support blatantly homophobic assumptions.[162]

While many gay sufferers experienced stigmatization and cruelty, in and outside of healthcare settings, this marginalization also motivated a new wave of LGBTIQ activism. A central focus were the community-based *Aidshilfe* or AIDS self-help support and resource networks in cities and towns especially across West Germany, which also saw the establishment of local branches of the deliberately disruptive and radical international Queer Nation and ACT UP movements: the latter had founded thirteen groups across the FRG by 1989. Actions included 'die-ins' on the street, cemetery installations (Figure 6.7), boycotts, organized 'civil disobedience' and a spectacular protest during the notoriously conservative Catholic bishops' conference in Fulda in 1991.[163] After the fall of the Wall, intravenous drug use soared in the GDR and much of Eastern Europe, and HIV infection rates rose there as well. Since the 2000s, heterosexual contact has become much more widely recognized as a source of transmission.[164]

Leading US activist Douglas Crimp later reflected on how the 'AIDS crisis' forced a fundamental rethink of the fragmentation that had come to characterize LGBTIQ movements around the world. The public health catastrophe was especially influential in promoting new political identities and collectivities under the banner of 'queer'. As feminist sociologist Sabine Hark observes, it was a pivotal moment in establishing a new era of coalitional politics:

> In groups like *ACT UP* and *Queer Nation*, for the first time since the 1960s, large numbers of lesbians and gays again worked together ....*ACT UP, Queer Nation* and other groups made the state their addressee and an arena of political dispute on a national, federate state, and communal level, they fought against the state-forced discursifying of AIDS as a "gay plague", and against the intensification of juridical and disciplinary regulation of same-sex desire; at the same time, however, they worked to make the state discharge its duties by demanding better medical and nurse-based care, state-supported prevention campaigns or support for self-help networks.[165]

Ultimately, the struggle against AIDS and associated stigma led to a wider social acceptance of gays, lesbians and trans people across both East and West – many of whom had been active as carers as well as activists. It also led to greater comfort with reporting on bisexual sexual histories, and a greater openness in talking about contraception, condoms and safe sex among straight as well as queer populations. 'Far from marking an end to the sexual revolution,' concludes Herzog, 'the emergence of the disease and the fight to contain it were accompanied by ongoing sexual liberalization.'[166]

* * *

The term 'revolution' evokes images of radical social upheaval and even violence, often centred in a particular city or country over a period of weeks or months. With the oft-cited 'sexual revolution' and *Sexwelle* of the postwar decades this was only partially true – it is more accurate to speak of a series of countercultural movements, coalitions and breaks. These ranged, as we have seen, from the rockers, rebels and 'Veronikas' of the 1950s in East and West, experimenting with new kinds of relationships and gendered styles, to the students and workers of the '68 generation, trialling new forms of communal living and intimacy. They encompassed feminist groups drawing attention to women's sexual pleasure and reproductive rights, and increasingly also gay, lesbian and trans liberation movements, with all their many splinter groups, during the 1970s and 1980s. The latter did not simply spring out of the ether, but built on the foundations of the 1950s and 1960s homophile movement, occasionally referring back to longer histories of Wilhelmine and Weimar sexual identity politics, and Nazi-era persecution.

Through these movements and countermovements, social norms and expectations around how, when and with whom one might engage in intimate sexual relations were radically questioned. Just as von Mahlsdorf's memories of gay beat sex in late 1940s Berlin should give us pause before diagnosing the fundamental conservatism of the early postwar decades, so too should the homophobic media representations of the AIDS 'crisis' prevent any too-swift tales of progress towards a fundamentally liberated present. The history of sexuality in the two postwar Germanies is no neat story from liberation via revolution, but rather one frequently marked by 'ambivalence', as Griffiths has argued of West German gay liberation politics. It was a product of contests between conservative and more liberal voices in religion, politics, science and within the feminist and queer liberation movements themselves. Yet through these contests, helped along by developments such as the Pill and the circulation via commercial and amateur media and networks of sexually explicit materials and political critiques, extramarital and same-sex sexuality were increasingly naturalized as legitimate forms of sexual expression. These developments paved the way for more recent reforms in the post-reunification era, such as the introduction of the so-called 'marriage for all' in 2017 – developments to which this book's conclusion turns.

Conclusion
Political transitions and intimate transformations since the Berlin Wall

The end of four decades of German-German division was also marked by a milestone in the German history of sexuality, and particularly in East German queer history. On the night of 9 November 1989, crowds raced across Berlin to border crossings following an almost accidental announcement by Politbüro member Günter Schabowski – on national TV – that travel restrictions were to be lifted, with immediate effect. This surprised many border guards, who soon caved to the pressure as thousands of East Berliners swept into West Berlin – the much celebrated, and occasionally lamented, 'fall' of the very real Berlin Wall, and with it the metaphoric Iron Curtain that had divided Europe since the war.[1] But it was also a revolutionary night for gay East Germans, as the film *Coming Out* (dir. Heiner Carow, 1989) premiered at the Kino International, telling the story of teacher and father-to-be Philipp who falls in love with Matthias and struggles to come to terms with his identity. It is a moving story that puts the audience into the shoes of its queer protagonists, allowing viewers to share in their longings and desires, but also their sense of isolation and marginalization. As Matthias at one point poignantly asks his lover Philipp: 'Do you know that feeling, when you make your bed in the evening, that feeling that tonight maybe someone will ring the doorbell after all – but no one does?' Filmed at gay bars and hangouts in East Berlin, it featured a cameo by Charlotte von Mahlsdorf, by now an icon of the GDR's LGBTIQ scene. 'As East Germany's first (and last) foray into queer cinema', remarks one scholar, 'Carow's film marked the high point of an increasingly public discussion of "homosexuality" that took place in East Germany during the late 1980s' (see Figure 7.1).[2]

FIGURE 7.1 *Still from* Coming Out *(1989, GDR, dir. Carow).*

During these years of transition, with formal unification between GDR and FRG following a year later in 1990, several 'protocol' or interview-based collections were published examining the lives of GDR gays and lesbians. Kerstin Gutsche's *Ich ahnungsloser Engel* (Innocent Angel) featured twelve lesbians reflecting on queer life in the East – with a strong emphasis on couples and families rather than sex, and a desire to be 'different but normal'. This was the title of Jürgen Lemke's collection of interviews with men of varied ages, sexual identities, professions and classes – a work which, as Katrin Sieg points out, in fact subtly challenged any singular ideas of 'normality', covering long-term gay monogamy, bisexual life in the provinces and an interview with the flamboyant von Mahlsdorf.[3] Between the fall of the Wall and the nation's first free elections, a number of feminist, gay and lesbian organizations sprang up in the East hoping to combine a more open political critique with a 'third path' of democratic socialism (as opposed to being simply folded into Western capitalism). They dreamed of a democratized system in which sex-gender variance might be viewed less as 'deviant', and more as part of a liberalized mainstream.[4]

As the example of *Coming Out* shows, a history of sexuality perspective offers a distinct slant on the narrative of the swift reunification of two fundamentally divergent political and economic systems on 3 October 1990, following four decades of Cold War separation. In a flash, over nine million citizens of the 'really-existing' socialist German Democratic Republic found their country recategorized into the nine 'new states' of the Federal Republic. This conclusion explores how with these changes, certain norms of marriage, family, sexual liberation and identity from the old East and West continued to be reproduced and naturalized in ways that have shaped life in the so-called Berlin Republic into the present. Others, though, have been fundamentally challenged, not least thanks to developments such as legalized gay marriage or 'marriage for all', and trans representation in the German federal parliament.

German unification: A 'marriage' of inequality?

Reunification was frequently portrayed in the German media of the early 1990s in gendered, and often sexual terms, as a 'marriage' between East and West. Unlike the rhetoric of 'divorce' surrounding Brexit in the late 2010s, this marriage metaphor had clearly hierarchical connotations, with a feminized GDR frequently depicted as vanquished, conquered or otherwise more or less forcefully colonized by the macho, overbearing FRG. As one scholar described in the immediate aftermath of events,

> The casting of East and West in the roles of opposite-sex partners, a rhetorical device shared by interlocutors across the ideological spectrum, constructs the moment of unification as heterosexual desire, and the destination of the couple, naturally, as matrimony.[5]

Initial visions of the GDR as a 'virgin' market quickly shifted to more disillusioned visions of a 'despoiled and tainted love object' or 'whore'.[6] Such sexualized metaphors highlighted the very real sense of political, social and legal inequities that went hand in hand with the atmosphere of emancipation and freedom following the fall of the Wall (Figure 7.2).[7]

1989 brought with it a number of other shifts pertinent to the history of sexuality, including a flourish of sexual consumerism. West German sex shop entrepreneur Beate Uhse was quick off the starting blocks, sending truckloads of sex toys and pornography into the 'new' states the day after the Wall came down, with East Germans often queuing for hours to get a chance to browse. Some reflected on a sense of having 'been left out' of the pleasures of commercialized sex; pornography shops rapidly put down roots in the 'new' states.[8] From this perspective, some experienced reunification as a time of sexual emancipation, a time 'which we have dreamed of for 40 years'. Forty-five-year-old Silvia E. reflected in her diary that 'I want to know if there is anything that could help me get more fun out of my sex life' after living in the GDR where 'everything was grey and monotonous'.[9]

But others saw things quite differently, particularly in the former GDR, where many mourned the loss of a uniquely East German stance towards sexuality and the body. Nudist culture, as we saw in Chapter 6, had taken on special significance as a symbol of East German difference. Some West Germans, not without a touch of paternalism, viewed the practice as evidence of a simpler existence on the other side of the Wall, or sometimes as a sign of anti-communist resistance.[10] East Germans, though, tended to embrace FKK

Aber doch nicht so schnell!

FIGURE 7.2 *'But not so fast'. Fritz Behrendt,* Frankfurter Allgemeine Zeitung, *12 December 1989.*

Source: © Fritz Behrendt, courtesy of Baaske Cartoons

as a distinctive feature of their identity and sexual liberalism. They resented West German attempts to demarcate nudist and non-nudist areas on Baltic sea beaches, perceived as a further degree of colonization by the capitalist West and reported on as the 'underpants wars'. As Herr S., one of Josie McLellan's interviewees, declared: 'the Wessis [West Germans] are rather prudish. People then [in the GDR] just lay down beside each other'.[11] This sense of a loss or curtailing of a free practice of nudism was seen as closely related to the rise of sexual consumerism, with many East German women, in particular, no longer feeling secure in their nudity 'now that they were viewed with Western men's "pornographically schooled gaze"'.[12] Many also turned away from Western pornography after the initial rush of excitement, with some from the former East expressing disappointment at its quality, others at its lack of meaningful eroticism – two thirds of the new porn video stores had closed again by 1995.[13]

During these years many East German couples struggled to maintain intimacy and daily life in a context of declining financial security and widespread job losses, often forced to retrain at a late career stage with only tenuous employment prospects. A sense of crisis ensued, as 'couples first clung together despite conflicts and then crashed as they struggled with varying degrees of success to reinvent themselves under new conditions'.[14]

This sense of crisis – exacerbated by anxieties about East German women and men leaving their partners for greener pastures (and beds) in the West – was also a prominent theme in German literature of the *Wende*, as the unification period became commonly known.[15]

Abortion was a further point of contention. East German women were, with good justification, concerned that the ready access to terminations that they had enjoyed since the early 1970s would disappear, while West German feminists hoped that unification might offer a chance to adopt the more liberal GDR regulations – which, in the end, largely turned out to be the case. A compromise law ratified in 1994 allowed all German women access to abortions in the first trimester following pre-abortion counselling, which had been a condition in the West.[16] This was a rare instance in the post-Wall years of East German law and the progressive gains for women in GDR society influencing the shape of the newly reunified Germany. It also complicates pictures of a feminized GDR simply 'colonized' by a rampaging masculine West, even as such stereotypes highlight economic and social inequalities that have continued to prevail to some degree even more than three decades since the events of 1989.

Sexuality identity politics since the Wall: The limits of inclusion

Another significant area of reform and changing social and cultural norms since the *Wende* has been queer and trans politics and rights. Paragraph 175 was abolished in all forms in 1994, ending well over a century of formalized criminalization.[17] The decades since have seen an impressive array of legal reforms expanding the citizenship rights of queer and trans individuals in areas ranging from healthcare to intimate partnerships. In 2017 Germany introduced what was widely hailed as 'marriage for all' (*Ehe für alle*), legalizing same-sex marital unions as part of a wave of similar reforms in countries around the world during the previous two decades. This had been preceded in 2001 by the introduction of registered civil partnerships (*eingetragene Lebenspartnerschaften*) for same-sex couples, a form of legal recognition with more limited rights – and fewer tax benefits – than marriage.[18] Another important reform involved changes to the 'Transsexual law' or *Transsexuellengesetz* in 2011, when the Federal Constitutional Court ruled as unconstitutional an earlier requirement that a person undergo sex confirmation surgery and become permanently infertile before their gender identity and corresponding civil status could be fully recognized in law.[19]

Improvements in formal representation for LGBTIQ citizens – with 'I' increasingly added to the acronym to reflect activism by and for intersex people, and sometimes also '+' or '*' to include a range of other identities – have been reflected in the growing presence of queer and trans politicians.

Berlin mayor Klaus Wowereit (2001–14) – famous for declaring the city 'poor but sexy', also made headlines when he announced before the 2001 election, 'I'm gay, and that's a good thing.' From 2009 to 2011 then-leader of the Free Democratic Party of Germany (FDP), Guido Westerwelle, served as foreign minister in a coalition government with Angela Merkel's CDU/CSU, his same-sex partner Michael Mronz often accompanying him on official state visits.[20] In the most recent federal elections of 2021, two trans women were for the first time elected to Germany's Bundestag, or Federal Parliament, both standing for the left-liberal party Bündnis 90/Die Grünen: Tessa Ganserer in Bavaria (previously a member of the state parliament) and Nyke Slawik in North Rhine-Westphalia.[21]

Yet accompanying these gains in legal and political recognition have been debates that highlight the limits of such recognition. Drawing attention to the cost of inclusion in the social norm, these form part of a much longer fault line in German LGBTIQ politics that we have seen running across the twentieth century, from contestations around queer 'respectability' in the Weimar era to the 'homophilia' of the 1950s and 1960s. Criticism from within the queer scene has centred on the perceived 'homonormativity' of mainstream gay and lesbian politics, which has often prioritized quite socially normative reform agendas: norms of marriage and reproduction have been taken up in queer contexts in the emphasis on rights to marriage and adoption, for example. While important for many, such political priorities centre on achieving inclusion within social norms of sexuality and social life, rather than challenging the heteronormative mainstream.

This is a criticism shared across many countries, especially in North America and Europe, where adopting a 'human rights' focus for LGBTIQ politics has often prioritized certain voices over others – but without interrogating the distinctly racializing and gendered structures of European modernity within which such rights discourses first emerged.[22] Such critiques have dovetailed with attacks on the commercialization and limiting body cultures of major LGBTIQ 'pride' events such as the Christopher Street Day parades held each summer across the country. This led in the late 1990s to mid-2010s to alternative events such as Kreuzberg Pride in Berlin, also known as the Transgenialer CSD (Transgenial CSD), or the 'Wigstöckel' trans festival of the early 2000s – events that celebrated political perspectives, bodies and identities sidelined by the main parades. In 2010, prominent US gender theorist and philosopher Judith Butler drew widespread attention when they refused to accept a 'Civil Courage' award from the Berlin CSD event organizers on the grounds that the event had become too commercial and uncritical of racialized exclusions. 'We experience again and again how single representatives of our gay organizations express themselves in racist terms,' Butler declared to the gathered crowds.[23]

A further fault line palpable not only in Germany but also the United States, UK, Australia and elsewhere in recent years has been between a school of so-called 'gender-critical' public intellectuals and 'TERFS' (trans-exclusionary radical feminists), on the one hand – the term 'gender-critical' or, in German, *Anti-Genderismus,* somewhat counter-intuitively indicates an opposition to gender diversity and critiques that problematize concepts such as 'woman', rather than the opposite – and queer, trans and feminist scholars and activists who advocate for more inclusive and coalitional political approaches, on the other. These debates, which in German have infiltrated mainstream politics in discussions around issues such as transwomen's access to women's sport, have also centred on linguistic issues such as the use of the 'gender star' (*Gendersternchen*) to designate gender-inclusive plural forms – often in deeply harmful, unnecessary and exclusionary ways.[24]

Such contestations highlight the limits of a political stance focused on achieving inclusion within heteronormatively oriented structures of marriage and family, and which has tended to privilege cis, white, able-bodied, middle-class and western perspectives. Recently, several historians of modern German sexuality have given additional weight to such critiques by showing how twenty-first-century sex-gender identity politics are founded on much longer-standing assumptions of the whiteness and able-bodiedness of the modern homosexual or transgender citizen, and deeply rooted in the imperialist and colonialist contexts in which those modern sexual rights discourses first emerged.[25] Asking the provocative question 'Was the homosexual born white?', Laurie Marhoefer argues that

> from the very beginning of gay politics, German thinkers created the homosexual subject as unmarked by race, that is, as deracialised. This allowed for a queer politics that was unconcerned with racism. In addition, it arguably made the homosexual subject implicitly, functionally white.[26]

Such studies show the value of historical research in demonstrating how today's political blind spots are not just a contemporary phenomenon, but can be traced back to the imperializing and racist assumptions underlying Wilhelmine and Weimar-era sexual politics, informing ideas of sexual subjectivity in Germany and beyond throughout much of the modern era.

Traces of exclusionary practices are particularly evident when it comes to attitudes to LGBTIQ Muslims in today's Germany. Jin Haritaworn and Fatima El-Tayeb draw attention to such ongoing racializing exclusions in today's queer activism. They demand that we recognize as political a much wider range of cultural and aesthetic interventions that might not easily conform to western and neoliberal discourses of citizenship, such as safer sex performances by queer of colour activist group Strange Fruit.[27] In the queer scene of Germany's larger cities, popular parties such as 'Gayhane' and 'Turkish Delight' reflect a need for spaces that openly embrace diversity in a subculture often complicit in maintaining highly racialized standards of physical attractiveness, and have been important for an 'out' generation of queer Muslims in shaping alternative visions of cultural belonging.[28] Yet there have also been examples of nasty anti-intellectual backlash within the queer scene. Self-described 'political drag queen' and academic Patsy l'Amour laLove is among those who attack as elitist fellow academics who have used critical Whiteness and intersectional approaches to critique the kinds of exclusions described above. Penning polemical pieces, l'Amour laLove and others seek, somewhat paradoxically, to police the boundaries of queer debate in the name of 'free speech' – even as this sometimes involves promoting Islamophobic and transphobic language.[29]

These questions of who is included within the terms of German sexual citizenship are not unique to LGBTIQ politics. As Dagmar Herzog observes, '[f]rom the late 1990s on, the entire complex of issues surrounding European identities and citizenships began to rest with remarkable frequency on sex-related concerns,' with Europe increasingly viewing itself 'as the defender of "sexual democracy" against what was taken to be a constitutively homophobic and misogynistic European Islam'.[30] Such tendencies are not new. Since the eighteenth century, German armchair anthropologists used the treatment of women to mark out Germany's alleged superiority over nations 'othered' as Oriental.[31] European cultures have also exhibited a long-standing fascination with ideas of polygamy, sensuality and bisexuality often associated with Muslim societies, while downplaying European men's own sexual double standards.[32] Such othering tendencies have been fuelled in a post-9/11 age by fears of terrorism, with German Muslims subjected to persistent racialization and discrimination in the face of frequently exaggerated threats. Popular representations of Germany's largest ethnic minority, Turkish Germans, have often perpetuated gendered and sexualized stereotypes of backwardness: images of forced marriage and 'honour' killings of promiscuous wives or sisters by jealous husbands and brothers. At the same time, the new millennium has seen increasingly diverse portrayals of Turkish-German culture in genres ranging from 'chick lit' to wedding films, helping to diversify ideas around intercultural and same-sex marriage for wider German audiences. As Heather Benbow suggests, such generic takes on modern marriage, while intervening in stereotypes of cultural difference, at times also reflect more normative desires, revealing a yearning within German culture for the kinds of patriarchal and traditional roles and relationships often projected onto a Turkish minority 'Other'.[33]

Yet Germany's legal approach to its Islamic minority has also shifted in more progressive ways that point to expanding norms of social inclusion. In 2000 the country's citizenship laws were dramatically reformed, as the long-held *jus sanguinis* principle of citizenship by heredity was broadened to acknowledge the *jus soli* principle of citizenship by birthplace. This made citizenship far more accessible to the many children or grandchildren of migrants to Germany – in particular, from the waves of mass migration under the 'guest worker' programs of the 1950s and 1960s.[34] More recently,

Germany's understanding of itself as a land of migration has been shaped by the estimated one million asylum seekers, of various religious affiliations, who arrived in Germany escaping conflicts in places such as Syria around the year 2015 – a striking demographic shift famously approached under Chancellor Angela Merkel's pragmatic motto 'We'll make it happen' ('Wir schaffen das').

But other examples of discrimination continue, and frequently, sex is the focus. Some conservative parties reacted to changing citizenship laws in ways that sought to defend 'European' sexual freedoms against a supposedly rampaging Islamic threat, while shoring up the symbolic boundaries of what is sometimes dubbed 'Fortress Europe'. At times, this meant shifting their own positions on sexual morality: conservatives who had formerly taken a decidedly homophobic and traditional gender line now began insisting that citizenship tests include questions that would showcase the applicant's comfort with liberal laws and attitudes towards homosexuality or female sexual independence. Others adopted a purportedly 'feminist' stance in order to contest the wearing of religious coverings such as headscarves and burqas in schools and workplaces. Such developments have resulted, Herzog points out, in a 'novel cultural consensus' surrounding the importance of gender equity, sexual minority rights and sexual freedoms outside marriage, even as they have tended to further anti-Muslim racism.[35] A particular focal point was the New Years' Eve celebrations in Cologne in 2015, during which hundreds of women became the victims of sexual attacks. This resulted in hotly contested discussions in the German media about the end of Germany's 'welcome culture' for asylum seekers, the racialization of sexual violence and police racism, including the pervasive tendency to assume immigrant perpetrators.[36] As Sabine Hark and Paula-Irene Villa observe of the complex layerings of racism, sexism and feminism tied up in public discussions of this event:

> Speaking of 'Cologne' conjures up an allegedly precise, clearly framed event: mass sexual harassment of women in the public sphere of a major German city. Carried out by non-German men, by migrants or foreigners. ... At the same time 'Cologne' is also the name of a notoriously unclear incident, a code circulating through time and space that encompasses a multiplicity of traces of meaning and produces abiding resonances.[37]

Importantly, both Muslim European 'culture brokers' vocally challenging Islamic fundamentalism, and non-Muslims who can see the difference between the majority of European Muslims on the one hand – many of whom advocate the separation of state and religion – and the provocative statements of a fundamentalist minority, on the other, have done much to challenge the polarizing terms of these debates around Islam and sexuality in contemporary Germany.[38]

Contesting norms of memory

Contestations over who is included or excluded from contemporary sex-gender identity politics and citizenship connect in important ways with debates surrounding Holocaust memorialization. These have centred on the visibility, or relative lack thereof, of the suffering and victimhood of different groups during the years of National Socialism. In the context of twenty-first-century German LGBTIQ politics, these memory debates constitute something of a fault line running through activism and scholarship, opening up fractures not only between gay and lesbian activist agendas, but also in relation to trans and gendervariant, ethnic and disabled perspectives.[39] Sometimes, queer historians have found themselves on the firing line for daring to broach these topics.[40] Experiences of Nazi persecution resonate into the present, but the complex experiences of LGBTIQ people during the years of National Socialist dictatorship have left a tricky legacy when it comes to memorializing these events. As Chapter 4 showed, historians of queer experience have pushed back against straightforward descriptors such as 'victimhood' and 'persecution', arguing that these are too clear-cut to describe the reality of many individuals' experiences.

For too long, the focus of queer Holocaust memory politics has been caught up with trying to establish hierarchies of persecution – who was

FIGURE 7.3 Homo-Mahnmal: *The memorial to LGBTIQ victims of the Holocaust in Berlin's Tiergarten.*

Source: Author, 2022

truly a victim of the Nazis, and which groups are therefore most worthy of memorialization – often pitting unnecessary lines between Jews, Sinti and Roma, gays, lesbians, disabled and transpeople. This has resulted in fraught debates around whether to include, for example, a plaque to lesbian victims at the memorial site of the Ravensbrück women's concentration camp – with one finally placed at the site in May 2022.[41] The biggest discussions, though, have centred on the so-called 'Homo-Mahnmal' or memorial to homosexual victims of the Holocaust in the central Tiergarten park in Berlin. There, a cuboid cement block invites the viewer in for a closer look at its permanent video installation, which for the first two years featured a continuous loop of a male same-sex kiss.

Contests over this memorial have focused on the prioritization of gay male persecution under Germany's Paragraph 175, and how this has worked to erase the experience of other sex-gender minorities less clearly or straightforwardly persecuted under Nazi law, particularly lesbians. After considerable discussion, a compromise was reached whereby the film changes every two years, showing multiple kisses between people of varying age, gender and colour, with the latest film also drawing out links to the queer and trans past through historical documents from Berlin's Schwules Museum.[42] Debates about how to appropriately remember Nazi LGBTIQ persecution have also crossed national lines, with the pink triangle insignia once applied to homosexual camp inmates taken up in the late twentieth century as a symbol of gay rights more broadly, especially in the context of AIDS activism. Such translations of symbols from one context to another have worked, argues Erik Jensen, to 'foster[] alternate memories' and communities of LGBTIQ shared persecution – even where these are at several removes, both in time and space, from the experiences of the Nazi era.[43]

Disability campaigners have also played a strong role in initiatives to memorialize other victims of the Nazis' genocidal and eugenic policies. A short walk towards the Philharmonie from both the Homo-Mahnmal and the massive, abstract, cemetery-like structure of the Memorial to the Murdered Jews of Europe, covering 19,000 square meters in central Berlin, one finds the smaller 'T4-Denkmal'. This memorial remembers the victims of National Socialist killings euphemistically carried out under the banner of 'euthanasia', and which particularly targeted disabled children and adults.[44] Beyond memory politics, too, German-based disability activists have made gains in achieving recognition of issues around disability and sexuality. They have undertaken vocal sexual health and local government campaigns against discrimination, and fought for rights to intimate relationships, sexual expression and parenthood – rights that have historically been too often downplayed or blatantly dismissed.[45]

Some of these disability rights discourses continue to intersect in complex ways with other branches of sexual activism, such as abortion rights. In 1995, the law that was reached as a compromise between East and West German practices had made abortion due to foetal disability illegal, but doctors could support termination where this was seen to harm the mother's physical or emotional well-being. As Herzog notes, 'this was an understandable postfascist stance, although still an agonizingly problematic one' that ignored the lack of adequate social support for disabled members of society. In 2009, a further law change meant that pregnant women informed of a foetal disability and subsequently seeking late-term abortions were required to undertake a three-day reflection and counselling period – a change promoted by some as an advance for disability rights, and celebrated by the Vatican, even as it had the effect of increasing the anxiety of women and couples seeking termination.[46] In these and many other ways, Germany's traumatic twentieth-century history continues to influence cultural and political discussions around sexuality and reproduction into the present.

* * *

There is much more one could say about the role of sexuality in contemporary Germany – from the rise of online dating apps and cybersex to 'third-wave', 'fourth-wave' and 'post' feminism; from shifting sexual geographies in the face of transnational currents of web-based commerce and consumerism to the emergence of newer identity categories such as non-binary that both build on and diverge from a centuries-old history of creating labels for sexual and gender identity. But such developments no longer strictly fall under the banner of 'history', even as they are unthinkable without the developments examined in this book.

Sexuality in Modern German History has shown how ideas of 'normal' and 'abnormal' sexuality have waxed and waned over time, often open to new definitions and contestations, but at other times the focus of violent policing and naturalization: processes that have always excluded the rights and sexual expressions of some groups at the expense of others. We have seen, for one thing, how the institutions of marriage and the family have prevailed over many centuries as cornerstones of social organization, even as these frameworks have undergone fundamental shifts: from the possibility of divorce opening up with the Protestant Reformation, through to nineteenth-century ideals of bourgeois marital domesticity shoring up larger nationalist and imperialist projects, Weimar-era dreams of gender-equitable 'companionate marriages', Nazi Party appropriations of intimate relationships and family structures to suit its racial hygiene and expansionist goals, the widening acceptance of serial marriages, divorces and patchwork families in the postwar East and West, and 'marriage for all' in the most recent past. What constitutes a 'normal' marriage or a 'normal' family has changed considerably across time and place.

We have also seen how ideas around 'abnormal' sexualities have shifted over time, from being grounds for legal persecution and state violence, to objects of scientific and medical curiosity and diagnosis, to focal points for new political and social movements. Being labelled or labelling oneself according to historically shifting categories of 'deviance' could, we have seen, sometimes be a productive and positive move. For some, such labels have offered a way of forging new spaces in German public life. For others, they have been a way of moving beyond the purview of state censors and authorities to express minority sexual desires and practices. This book has argued, furthermore, that it is impossible to think about how sex has shaped and been shaped by German history without also thinking about gender every step of the way, and how both of these categories intersect, often in complex or unpredictable ways, with ideas of race and ethnicity, class, ability and religion. Rather than arguing for a clear path towards liberation, *Sexuality in Modern German History* has shown that across the centuries that constitute the modern era, and indeed several centuries before that, sexuality has been a consistent focal point for contests, anxieties and negotiations about how people should live their lives. It is impossible to tell the history of sexuality in modern Germany without thinking about how intimate desires and practices clashed and aligned with much more public debates in fields such as politics, religion, the law, medicine and culture. Equally, none of those fields often associated with 'history proper' are truly thinkable without the history of sex.

NOTES

Introduction

Unless otherwise noted, all translations from texts published in German are my own.

1 Ahmed, 'Gender Critical'. On these debates between certain radical 'feminists', sometimes dubbed TERFs (trans-exclusionary radical feminists) and feminist, queer and trans scholars in the German context, see Hark and Villa, *Anti-Genderismus*.

2 Hull, *Sexuality*, 6.

3 In particular, see Foucault, *History*; Giddens, *Modernity*; Giddens, *Transformation*; Taylor, *Sources*. For a survey of Foucault's impact on the field, see Cocks, 'Approaches'.

4 Evans, *Life*, 3.

5 Eley, Jenkins, and Matysik, 'Introduction', 4. More broadly, see essay collections: Eley, Jenkins, and Matysik, *German Modernities*; Ankum, *Women in the Metropolis*.

6 Eley, 'German Modernities', 72.

7 For a summary of debates, see Eley, 63.

8 Eley, Jenkins, and Matysik, 'Introduction', 3.

9 Evans, *Life*, 4.

10 Herzog, 'Hubris and Hypocrisy', 20. See also several important surveys of the historiography of sexuality in the German context: Dickinson and Wetzell, 'Historiography'; Evans, 'Why Queer German History?'; Spector, Puff, and Herzog, *After 'The History of Sexuality'*.

11 As cited in MacGregor, *Germany*, 1.

12 Here I follow the excellent summary in Leng, *Sexual Politics*, 5n5. On the processes leading to unification and nationhood, see Breuilly, *Nineteenth-Century Germany*; Clark, *Iron Kingdom*; Evans, *Rereading*; Fulbrook, *Concise History*; MacGregor, *Germany*.

13 Blackbourn, 'Europeanizing'.

14 See, in particular, Cryle and Stephens, *Normality*; Ernst, *Histories*.

15 On the broad historical shift from 'sovereign' power, centred on spectacular and public exhibitions of state authority such as executions, to modern ideas of 'biopower' and 'biopolitics', focused on regulating and disciplining nominally free, democratic populations, see Foucault, *History*, 1: The Will to Knowledge, 125–45; Cocks, 'Approaches', 42.

16 Roper, *Oedipus*, 8.

17 Foucault, *History*. Scholars following Foucault's 'genealogical' approach to writing history seek to understand the evolution of categories and ideas that give meaning to our lives in the present, viewing this as always responsive to particular historical circumstances rather than as inevitable, rational outcomes. For an introduction to this approach, see Gutting and Oksala, 'Michel Foucault'. On approaching the 'normal' in a genealogical mode see Cryle and Stephens, *Normality*, 10.

18 Wiesner-Hanks, *Gender in History*, 196.

19 Roper, *Oedipus*, 3. Roper and other feminist early modernists such as Natalie Zemon Davis have powerfully countered influential theories of modern subjectivity by Charles Taylor, Jakob Burkhardt and others, arguing that we must also acknowledge the embodied subjectivity of individuals well before this period: Roper, 1–34; Davis, 'Boundaries.' Cf. Taylor, *Sources*; Burkhardt, *Civilisation*. For an overview see Cocks, 'Approaches,' 38–41.

20 Jennifer Evans' work offers a strong model of adopting 'subjectivity' over identity for the history of sexuality in German contexts: Evans, 'Seeing Subjectivity.'

21 Exemplary of such research are the essays collected in: Spector, Puff, and Herzog, *After 'The History of Sexuality'.*

22 On the links between broader sociopolitical movements and shifting historiographical practices see, for example, Jewell, *Women*, 15. In the German context see especially Herzog, *Sex after Fascism*.

23 See, for example, Clark, *Desire*; Herzog, *Sexuality in Europe*; Houlbrook and Cocks, *History of Sexuality*; Wiesner-Hanks, *Gender in History*.

24 Wiesner-Hanks, *Gender in History*, 84.

25 On shifting norms of marriage, see especially introduction and afterword to Lindemann and Halperin, *Mixed Matches*.

26 Scott, 'Gender.'

27 Wiesner, *Gender, Church*, 33–4.

28 Wiesner-Hanks, *Gender in History*, 195.

29 For an overview of the historiography surrounding prostitution in the German context see the introduction to Harris, *Selling Sex*. On terminology see Haak, 'Who Are We Talking About.'

30 For an excellent overview of the development of 'queer' history see Evans, 'Why Queer German History?'

31 Wiesner-Hanks, *Gender in History*, 197.

32 Doan, *Disturbing Practices*, 11; Halperin, *History*, 104.

33 For further discussion see Evans, 'Why Queer German History?,' 379–83.

34 This antinormative capacity of 'queer' has been widely discussed, and at times contested. See, for example, Warner, *The Trouble with Normal*; Wiegman and Wilson, 'Introduction.'

35 Bauer et al., 'Visual Histories,' 2.

36 Doan, *Disturbing Practices*, 13.

37 Sedgwick, *Tendencies*, 197. This has, however, started to change in recent decades, as scholars highlight the need to critically interrogate the history of

heterosexuality, rather than take it as given. See Adams, *Trouble*; Blank, *Straight*; Canaday, *Straight State*; Davis and Mitchell, *Heterosexual Histories*; Gilman and Katz, *Anti-Semitism*.

38 Evans, *Queer Art*, chapter 1.

39 Tobin, *Peripheral Desires*. See also Beachy, 'The German Invention'; Sutton, 'A Tale of Origins.'

40 Puff, *Sodomy*, 7.

41 Karras, *Sexuality*, 30.

42 Doan, *Disturbing Practices*, 72. On the value of such 'ancestral', 'recuperative' and 'backward'-looking approaches see also Love, *Feeling Backward*.

43 On these lists, see Tobin, *Peripheral Desires*, 126–7.

44 For recent analyses of this film see Malakaj, 'Richard Oswald'; Linge, 'Sexology.'

45 Doan, *Disturbing Practices*, 97ff.

46 See, for example, Chiang, *Transtopia*; Evans, *Queer Art*; Love, *Feeling Backward*; Sears, *Arresting Dress*.

47 Martínez, 'Archives,' 174.

48 'Queer' is often also used in cultural criticism to name a broader set of challenges to dominant state or social institutions and processes, highlighting how these have 'not only produced and recognized but also normalized and sustained identity' in ways that often go beyond sexuality. See Eng, Halberstam, and Esbeban Muñoz, 'What's Queer,' 1.

49 Scholars discussing these terms in ways particularly relevant to my approach include Dame, 'Tracing Terminology'; Evans, 'Why Queer German History?'; Stryker, *Transgender History*; Whisnant, *Queer Identities*, 11–12.

Chapter 1

1 Cited in Lindemann, 'Gender Tales,' 138.

2 Cited in Lindemann, 141.

3 Cited in Lindemann, 139.

4 Cited in Lindemann, 144.

5 Lindemann, 131–51, at 131.

6 Lindemann, 134.

7 Tacium, '"Warm Brothers."'

8 For surveys of gender and sexuality in the medieval and early modern periods, see Brundage, *Law, Sex*; Bullough and Brundage, *Handbook*; Jewell, *Women*; Karras, *Sexuality*; Wiesner-Hanks, *Gender in History*; Rublack, *Gender*; Salisbury, *Medieval*. For studies reappraising the history and historiography of medieval sexuality see Dinshaw, *Getting Medieval*; Fradenburg and Freccero, *Premodern*; Freccero, *Queer*; Gowing, Hunter, and Rubin, *Love*; Lochrie, McCracken, and Schultz, *Constructing*; Lochrie, *Heterosyncrasies*.

9 Rublack, *Gender*, 1.

10 Rublack, 'Meanings', 1.

11 Zantop, *Colonial Fantasies*.

12 Hull, *Sexuality*, 2.

13 Luebke, 'Transgressive', 3.

14 Boswell, *Marriage*, 163–5 at 165, 178; Wiesner-Hanks, *Gender in History*, 36–7.

15 Boswell, *Marriage*, 169–70; Karras, *Sexuality*, 81–5; Karras, 'History of Marriage'.

16 Wiesner-Hanks, *Gender in History*, 174.

17 See Brundage, *Law, Sex*, 154ff., with entertaining table overview of proscriptions at p. 162; Karras, *Sexuality*, 97, 111–12.

18 Karras, *Sexuality*, 100.

19 Karras, 150–1.

20 Karras, 100.

21 Karras, 99.

22 Cited in Karras, 89. See also Green, *Trotula*.

23 Karras, *Sexuality*, 89.

24 Karras, 170–1.

25 Karras, 3.

26 Karras, 82.

27 Wiesner-Hanks, *Gender in History*, 38.

28 Karras, *Sexuality*, 99.

29 Boswell, *Marriage*, 171–2, 176.

30 Classen, 'Love, Sex', 63.

31 This tale is recounted in Classen, 63–4.

32 Jarzebowski, 'Meaning', 168. On changing medieval understandings of love see also Reddy, *Making*.

33 On Luther, see e.g. Roper, *Martin Luther*.

34 Roper, *Oedipus*, 79–80, cited at 80.

35 Breul, 'Celibacy'; Luebke, 'Transgressive'. For a detailed study of Reformation-era marriage see Harrington, *Reordering*. On Protestant challenges to Catholic understandings of the relationship between the physical body and the divine, including new perspectives on clerical marriage, see Roper, *Oedipus*, 79–80, 172–4.

36 Sreenivasan, *Peasants*, 204–5.

37 Green, *Women*, 34.

38 Boswell, *Marriage*, 173; Jewell, *Women*, 29.

39 WA32.377,37–378,3; LW21.94, cited in Strohl, 'Luther', n.p. (online version). Strohl, 'Luther on Marriage, Sexuality, and the Family'.

40 Luebke, 'Transgressive', 3–4; Whitford, 'Luther's Pastoral', 14–30.

41 Jewell, *Women*, 42.

42 In particular, see Ozment, *When Fathers*.

43 The craft guilds, first established in the twelfth and thirteenth centuries, oversaw the production and sale of goods under the leadership of master craftsmen, who regulated the quality of materials and work as well as processes of production and sale. Each master craftsman was, in turn, the head of a household – often, they were required to be married – and led his own shop within the household, with several apprentices. Wives, daughters and servants of guild masters worked in guild shops, but without the formal training or influence on the running of the guild. Wiesner-Hanks, *Early Modern Europe*, 43–5. On this economic model and the gender relations it formalized, see also Roper, *Holy*; Jewell, *Women*, 130–1.

44 Lindemann, 'Gender Tales,' 141.

45 Boswell, *Marriage*.

46 Karras, *Sexuality*, 205.

47 Freist, Dagmar, 'One Body'; Luebke, 'Transgressive,' 6.

48 Jewell, *Women*, 126–7; Roper, *Oedipus*, 232.

49 Jarzebowski, 'Meaning,' 166–7. On marriages between former nuns and monks, which opponents viewed as compounding bigamy with (spiritual) incest, see Plummer, 'Married Nuns.' On sibling incest see Bramberger, *Verboten*.

50 Lindemann, 'Aufklärung,' 187–8. On shifting definitions of incest, kinship and 'blood relations' see Braun, 'Die "Blutschande"'; Braun, *Blutsbande*. For a close examination of the Carolina law code's impact on regulating sexual crimes – adopted under Holy Roman Emperor Charles V as a guide for reform rather than a replacement for existing territorial or city laws – see Hull, *Sexuality*, 61–6.

51 Lindemann, 'Aufklärung,' 188. Lindemann cites Art. 'Blutschande,' in Zedler, *Grosses vollständiges Universal Lexicon* (1731), 247–57.

52 Lindemann, 186–8.

53 Luebke, 'Transgressive,' 9. See also Sabean, Teuscher, and Mathieu, *Kinship*.

54 Luebke, 'Transgressive,' 10.

55 Robertson, *Enlightenment*, 1–2 at 1. See also Levitin, 'The Islamic Enlightenment,' 22.

56 Scholars have noted the significance of the Enlightenment for Foucault's chronology of sexuality, although as early modern scholars emphasize, 'the ambivalent effects of sexual regulation about which Foucault wrote so persuasively can be dated well back before the eighteenth century.' Roper, *Oedipus*, 9.

57 The phrase 'social disciplining' (*Sozialdisziplinierung*) was popularized by Gerhard Oestreich to describe the coercive impact of the state during this era, and formed part of what has been described as the larger 'civilizing process' of the early modern era described by scholars such as Norbert Elias. For critical discussion see Hull, *Sexuality*, 53–6.

58 Hull, 55–6. See also Hsia, *Social Discipline*; Roper, *Holy*; Wunder, *He Is the Sun*.

59 Hull, *Sexuality*, 1–4.

60 Hull, 410–11.

61 Gray, *Productive Men*, 180.

62 Hull, *Sexuality*, 411.

63 As Herzog points out, writings by male members of these movements leave a more 'confusing' picture about gender equality, often underlining women's difference from men even as they called for greater female emancipation. Herzog, 'Religious Dissent,' 82.

64 For an open access version of this play: https://www.gutenberg.org/ebooks/9325

65 Inge Stephan, 'Schreibende Frauen der Romantik,' in Beutin et al., *Deutsche Literaturgeschichte*, 212–14. On Levin see also Hahn, 'Rahel Levin Varnhagen (1771–1833).'

66 Cited in Beutin et al., *Deutsche Literaturgeschichte*, 212–14.

67 Beutin et al., 212–14.

68 Hausen, 'Ehepaare,' 92.

69 Justus Möser in Hausen, 94.

70 Blackbourn, 'German Bourgeoisie,' 11. For competing historical narratives about the nineteenth-century German bourgeoisie, which was fragmented into groups including the upper or 'grand' bourgeoisie, the industrial middle classes, and the *Bildungsbürgertum* of university-educated professionals and civil servants, see also other essays in this volume: Blackbourn and Evans, *German Bourgeoisie*.

71 Mosse, *Nationalism and Sexuality*, 18.

72 Richard Evans in Blackbourn and Evans, *German Bourgeoisie*, 128; Hausen, 'Ehepaare,' 95–6; Mosse, *Nationalism and Sexuality*, 17–18. On gender relations in the German bourgeoisie more broadly see Frevert, *Bürgerinnen*; Frevert, *Women*; Hull, *Sexuality*.

73 Hausen, 'Ehepaare,' 95.

74 Blackbourn, 'German Bourgeoisie,' 11.

75 Wiesner-Hanks, *Gender in History*, 46. For a long-view history of birth control methods see Jütte, *Contraception*.

76 For an overview, see Evans, *The Feminist Movement*.

77 Flüchter, 'Transethnic.'

78 Wiesner-Hanks, *Gender in History*, 46. Influential studies of gender and sexuality in colonialist frameworks include McClintock, *Imperial*; Stoler, *Race and the Education*; Stoler, *Carnal*. In the German context, see especially Friedrichsmeyer, Lennox, and Zantop, *Imperialist*; Zantop, *Colonial Fantasies*.

79 This phrase was coined by Stephen Marcus, and plays a prominent role in Foucault's 'genealogy' of modern sexuality: Foucault, *History*, 1: The Will to Knowledge, 1–14; Marcus, *Other Victorians*.

80 On broad shifts in attitudes towards unmarried women see Wiesner, *Gender, Church*, 18–19; Wiesner, 138–9; Rublack, *Gender*.

81 Roper, *Holy*, 231, 257–8. For a detailed study of a 'lesbian' nun in seventeenth-century Italy see Brown, *Immodest*.

82 Image from Philipp Melancthon, Doct. Martinus Luther, *Deuttung der zwo grewlichen Figuren Bapstesels zu Rom un Munchkalbs zu Freyberg in Meyssen funden, Wittenberg*, 1523.

83 Rublack, 'Meanings,' 5.

84 Roper, *Holy*.

85 Roper, *Oedipus*, 43.

86 See Douglas, *Purity*, 120–2; Hull, *Sexuality*, 1–2.

87 Roper, *Oedipus*, 43.

88 Cited in Roper, *Holy*, 230.

89 Roper, 230; Wiesner, *Gender, Church*, 102.

90 Sreenivasan, *Peasants*, 59–60. This is an example of a 'microhistory' approach: in-depth studies of a small community or set of individuals to enable better understanding of the relationships between social expectations and individual experiences than studies with a broader scope. For other examples in the early modern German context see Rublack, *Gender*; Roper, *Oedipus*; Sreenivasan, *Peasants*; Ulbrich, *Shulamith and Margarete*; Wunder, *He Is the Sun*.

91 Wiesner, *Gender, Church*, 102, 109.

92 Hull, *Sexuality*, 258.

93 Hull, 258.

94 Approximately 20 per cent of accused witches in some areas were men, though historians have focused primarily on women: Rublack, 'Meanings,' 10.

95 The literature on witchcraft is vast, but for an excellent study situating the sixteenth-century witchcraft trials within the history of sexuality, gender and religion see Roper, *Oedipus*. For shorter discussions of the gendering of witchcraft persecutions and assumptions about female sexuality and honour, see Jewell, *Women*, 123–4; Wiesner, *Gender, Church*, 138–9; Fuchs, 'Transgressive.'

96 Rublack, *Gender*, 3.

97 Roper, *Oedipus*, 201–3 and passim.

98 The history of the emotions is a rapidly growing field; for an overview see Matt and Stearns, *Doing Emotions*; Gammerl, Nielsen, and Pernau, *Encounters*. Among historians of modern Germany, Ute Frevert's work has been particularly influential: Frevert, *Emotions*.

99 See, in particular, Roper, *Oedipus*, 198–248; Roper, 'Evil Imaginings.'

100 Roper, *Oedipus*, 218, see also 228. For another recent example of studying witchcraft from the perspective of the emotions, see Kounine, *Imagining*.

101 Roper, 'Evil Imaginings,' 103–10.

102 Cunningham, *Children*, 61. For histories of childhood and child sexuality, including competing definitions of these categories, see Ariès, *Centuries*; Classen, *Childhood*; Fishman, 'History.'

103 Tissot, *Treatise*, 192–3 (online version). For an analysis of Tissot's text in the context of other conditions viewed as 'monstrous' or linked to physical and mental deformity see Davidson, *Emergence*, 116–18.

104 Roper, 'Evil Imaginings,' 128–9n88; Braun, *Krankheit*; Hull, *Sexuality*. On the longer history of masturbation see Laqueur, *Solitary Sex*; Singy, 'The History of Masturbation: An Essay Review.'

105 Foucault, *History*, 1: The Will to Knowledge, 121.

106 For critical discussion see, for example, Doan, *Disturbing Practices*; Arondekar et al., 'Queering Archives.'

107 Puff, *Sodomy*, 2; Boswell, *Marriage*, 262. For a close study of competing ninth-century monastic views on sodomy, including whether it represented an individual fault or a broader threat to community and monastic purity, see Diem, 'Teaching Sodomy.'

108 See Roper, *Oedipus*, 25; Roper, *Holy*, 255.

109 Puff challenges what he sees as a 'problematic consensus' among some early modern scholars regarding sodomy's instability as a category, even as he acknowledges that this term meant different things to different people at different times: Puff, *Sodomy*, 1–10, cited at 3 and 8; Puff, 'Localizing,' 177–8, 195. See also Lindemann, 'Gender Tales,' 140–1. For a dissenting view, see Goldberg, *Sodometries*, 18.

110 Puff, *Sodomy*, 2–3.

111 Roper, *Holy*, 255–6.

112 Cited in Clark, *Desire*, 114. See also Ragan, 'Enlightenment.'

113 Foucault, *History*, 1: The Will to Knowledge, 43.

114 Sedgwick, *Epistemology*, 36. Others agree: 'Overall, the occasional cohabitation of research on male and female homosexuality under the roof of a history of sexuality has been an uneasy one': Puff, *Sodomy*, 6.

115 Bennett, '"Lesbian-Like"'; Brown, *Immodest*; Traub, *Renaissance*. In Britain, for example, Doan argues that a popular discourse of 'lesbianism' did not emerge until the court trials of *Well of Loneliness* author Radclyffe Hall in the late 1920s: Doan, *Fashioning Sapphism*.

116 Brown, *Immodest*, 17.

117 Traub, *Renaissance*.

118 Doan, 'Topsy-Turvydom'; Bennett, '"Lesbian-Like."'

119 Puff, *Sodomy*, 32–3. See also Lindemann, 'Gender Tales,' 142–3; Crompton, 'Myth'; Eriksson, 'Lesbian Execution.'

120 On taking a 'topsy turvy' approach to histories of gender and sexuality see Doan, 'Topsy-Turvydom.'

121 Lindemann, 'Gender Tales,' 141. On cross-dressing on the early modern German stage see Colvin, *Rhetorical Feminine*; Krimmer, *In the Company*. For an influential analysis of the carnivalesque tradition, see Bakhtin, *Rabelais*.

122 On premodern histories of 'passing' and women dressed as men, see Bullough and Bullough, *Cross Dressing*; Dekker and Van de Pol, *Frauen in Männerkleidern*; Hotchkiss, *Clothes Make the Man*; Lehnert, *Wenn Frauen*; Lindemann, 'Gender Tales'; Wheelwright, *Amazons*.

123 Lindemann, 'Gender Tales,' 144–5. On intersex and 'hermaphrodite' histories see Dreger, *Hermaphrodites*; Mak, *Doubting Sex*.

124 Laqueur, *Making Sex*.

125 Lindemann, 'Gender Tales,' 143–6, cited at 143–4. See also Wiesner, 'Discourses,' 156–7; Roper, *Oedipus*, 12. For issues with Laqueur's one-sex model see Park, 'Cadden, Laqueur'; Simons, *Sex of Men*, 16.

126 Letter from Johann Wolfgang von Goethe to Duke Karl August, 29 December 1787. Cited in Tobin, *Warm Brothers*, 96–7.

127 Cited in Tobin, 96–7.

128 Roper, *Oedipus*, 45.

129 Tobin, *Warm Brothers*. On male and female friendship in German history and literature see Kraß, *Ein Herz*; Mauser and Becker-Cantarino, *Frauenfreundschaft*.

Scholars of English literature have also written extensively on eroticized male friendship from the Renaissance onwards; see e.g. Haggerty, 'Male Love'; Sedgwick, *Between Men*; Tosh, *Male Friendship*.

130 Smith, 'Same-Sex Male Love,' 405.

131 Cited in Smith, 410.

132 Smith-Rosenberg, 'Female World,' 8.

133 Inge Stephan, 'Subjektivität und Gesellschaftskritik in der Lyrik,' in Beutin et al., *Deutsche Literaturgeschichte*; Baldwin, 'Karsch as Sappho.'

134 Mosse, *Nationalism and Sexuality*. On Mosse's contributions to the history of sexuality in modern Germany and Europe, see Payne, Sorkin, and Tortorice, *What History*.

Chapter 2

1 Stöcker, *Bund*, 16.

2 Stöcker, 'Zur Reform.' On Stöcker, the League and the 'new ethics' see Dickinson, *Sex, Freedom*, 44–5, 191–5; Dickinson, 'Reflections'; Frevert, *Women*, 130–1; Leng, 'Culture, Difference, and Sexual Progress'; Leng, *Sexual Politics*, 52–3; Matysik, *Reforming*, 55–91; Smith, *Berlin Coquette*, 85–92; Wickert, Hamburger, and Lienau, 'Helene Stöcker.'

3 Leng, *Sexual Politics*, 5n5.

4 Leng, *Sexual Politics*, 5n5; Frevert, 'Europeanizing.'

5 See, for example, Beachy, 'The German Invention.'

6 On using 'subjectivity' in relation to early modern history, see Roper, *Oedipus*.

7 See, for example, Oosterhuis, 'Sexual Modernity.'

8 On Hössli see Tobin, *Peripheral Desires*, 27–52, cited here at 40; Leck, *Vita Sexualis*, 105–12. On the term 'sodomy' see chapter 1.

9 Kaan' work has recently been reissued in a critical edition: Kahan, *Heinrich Kaan's 'Psychopathia Sexualis.'* On Kaan's role in helping to shape a 'modern' sexual science see Sigusch, 'Heinrich Kaan'; Sigusch, *Geschichte*, 166–74.

10 Westphal, 'Die conträre Sexualempfindung'; Foucault, *History*, 1: The Will to Knowledge, 43. See discussion of Westphal's contribution in Spector, *Violent Sensations*, 87–8.

11 Krafft-Ebing, *Psychopathia Sexualis* (10th English Ed.). On this work see Oosterhuis, *Stepchildren*.

12 Freud, *Three Essays*.

13 On this and other early journals see Sigusch, *Geschichte*, 81–120.

14 Spector, *Violent Sensations*, 94.

15 Beachy, 'The German Invention,' 810. The following discussion of Kertbeny and Ulrichs is based on Beachy, *Gay Berlin*, 3–25; Tobin, *Peripheral Desires*, 86–92; Whisnant, *Queer Identities*, 20–2; Spector, *Violent Sensations*, 89–99.

16 Kertbeny, 'Paragraph 143,' 51. As cited in Whisnant, *Queer Identities*, 20.

17 Ulrichs, *'Man-Manly' Love*.

18 Ulrichs, 306. On Ulrichs's philosophical, political and legal arguments see Leck, *Vita Sexualis*; Spector, *Violent Sensations*, 89–94.

19 On this recent reception see Spector, *Violent Sensations*, 90. On Ulrichs's place in trans history see Marhoefer, *Racism*, 31–2.

20 Spector, *Violent Sensations*, 89–91.

21 See Sorkin, *Transformation*, 20.

22 Blackbourn, *Long Nineteenth Century*, 216–17; Tobin, *Peripheral Desires*, 230, 233, also 83–110. See also Leck, *Vita Sexualis*, 33–68.

23 Spector, *Violent Sensations*, 89–91, citing Ulrichs at 89.

24 Tobin, *Peripheral Desires*, 111–33.

25 Tobin, *Peripheral Desires*, 92.

26 On the emergence of a German gay rights movement see Beachy, 'The German Invention'; Steakley, *Homosexual Emancipation*; Whisnant, *Queer Identities*, 14–40.

27 Cocks, 'Approaches', 42.

28 Spector, *Violent Sensations*, 80–9, cited at 81; Whisnant, *Queer Identities*, 23. On psychiatric and forensic approaches to male homosexuality see Mildenberger, *Psychiater*; Mildenberger, 'Kraepelin and the "Urnings."'

29 Krafft-Ebing's study was published in multiple editions and translations, for example Krafft-Ebing, *Psychopathia Sexualis (10th English Ed.)*. For details see Oosterhuis, *Stepchildren*.

30 On these connections see Lang, Damousi, and Lewis, *A History of the Case Study*; Schaffner, *Modernism*; Tobin, *Peripheral Desires*.

31 Mr X, cited in Lang, Damousi, and Lewis, *History*, 25.

32 Waters, 'Sexology.'

33 Bloch, *Beiträge*, 222–6; see also Bloch, *Sexualleben*, 551–2, 591–7 (and 539–611 on homosexuality in general). On congenital versus acquired theories of (homo)sexuality see Kahan, *Minor Perverts*.

34 For a brief survey of Hirschfeld's theories and politics see Whisnant, *Queer Identities*, 27–33. For detailed analyses, see Dose, *Magnus Hirschfeld*, 68–78; Herzer, *Magnus Hirschfeld*; Mancini, *Magnus Hirschfeld*; Marhoefer, *Racism*.

35 Weininger, *Sex*, 163. Critics have often emphasized Weininger's antisemitic and misogynist conjoining of ideas, while noting that he was himself Jewish. They also underline the importance of situating his thought in the wider intellectual currents of fin-de-siècle Viennese modernity: Spector, *Violent Sensations*, 171–201. See also Harrowitz and Hyams, *Jews & Gender*; Robertson, 'Historicizing Weininger'; Sengoopta, *Otto Weininger*.

36 Hirschfeld, *Homosexuality*, 506, 525.

37 On these transhistorical connections see the conclusions to Marhoefer, *Sex*; Tobin, *Peripheral Desires*.

38 Bauer, *Hirschfeld Archives*, 90.

39 For a recent translation see Hirschfeld, *Berlin's Third Sex*, cited at 15.

40 Beachy, *Gay Berlin*, 70–84; Ostwald, *Männliche Prostitution*.

41 Hirschfeld, *Die Transvestiten (1910)*; Ellis, *Eonism (1919)*; Karsch-Haack, 'Junggesellin und Junggeselle (Die Transmutistin).'

42 On these certificates and the complex intertwined history of homosexual and trans diagnoses in early sexology, see Herrn, *Schnittmuster*, 139–42 and passim; Hill, 'Sexuality and Gender'; Mak, 'Passing Women'; Prosser, 'Transsexuals'; Sutton, 'From Sexual Inversion.'

43 See, Klöppel, *XX0XY ungelöst*; Mak, *Doubting Sex*; Mak, 'Conflicting Heterosexualities.'

44 For example, Birken, *Consuming Desire*; Weeks, *Sex, Politics and Society*. While such studies tended to cite Foucault's *History*, recent studies have emphasized that Foucault saw such doctor-patient relationships as having simultaneously emancipatory and repressive potential. See Dickinson and Wetzell, 'Historiography,' 298–9; Spector, Puff, and Herzog, *After 'The History of Sexuality.'*

45 See Oosterhuis, *Stepchildren*; Müller, *Homosexuelle Autobiographien*.

46 Freud, *Three Essays*.

47 Bloch, *Sexualleben*, 88ff., 478ff.; Frevert, *Women*, 132–3. See also Cryle and Moore, *Frigidity*, 191–221; Gay, *Bourgeois Experience*.

48 Frevert, *Women*, 132–3; see also Timm and Sanborn, *Gender, Sex*, 106.

49 Freud, 'Fragment,' 50.

50 Dean and Lane, *Homosexuality-Psychoanalysis*; Herzog, *Cold War Freud*.

51 Freud published his first case of a female 'invert' in 1920: Freud, 'Psychogenesis.'

52 Sadger, 'Fragment der Psychoanalyse,' 359.

53 Freud, 'Letter to Anonymous.'

54 On competing sexological and psychoanalytic approaches see Lang and Sutton, 'Queer Cases'; Sutton, *Sex*, 60–90.

55 On the antisemitism pervading German medicine during this period see Gilman, 'Sigmund Freud'; Gilman, *Freud*; Weindling, 'Bourgeois Values.'

56 See, in particular, Leng, *Sexual Politics*; Leng, 'Historicising'; Marhoefer, *Racism*. On the connections between feminism and eugenic thinking during this period see Allen, 'German Radical Feminism'; Dickinson, 'Reflections.'

57 Evans, 'Why Queer German History?,' 378.

58 See Bauer, *Hirschfeld Archives*; Leng, 'Historicising'; Leng, 'Magnus Hirschfeld's Meanings'; Marhoefer, *Racism*.

59 Müller, *Homosexuelle Autobiographien*, 55–110; Tobin, *Peripheral Desires*.

60 Frevert, *Women*, 122.

61 Duc, *Sind es Frauen?*, 5, 54. Duc was a pseudonym for Minna Wettstein-Adelt; for scholarly analyses of this work see Breger, 'Feminine Masculinities'; Martin, 'Extraordinary Homosexuals.'

62 Body, *Memoirs of a Man's Maiden Years*. These are my translations of excerpts included in Ina Linge's study of this text: Linge, 'Gender and Agency,' 393–4.

63 See Homann, *Tagebuch*; Beachy, *Gay Berlin*, 171.

64 Scholars have frequently distinguished two distinct models for thinking of homosexuality at this period, sometimes framed as 'Jewish/sexological' versus 'Greek/cultural'. While this distinction has its limits – proponents of the 'Greek' mode also engaged with scientific theories, and not all sexologists were Jewish – it does provide a useful framework through which to categorize publications on male homosexuality in the Imperial and into the Weimar era. For detailed discussion see Tobin, *Peripheral Desires*. See also Bruns, 'Politics of Masculinity'; Keilson-Lauritz, *Geschichte der eigenen*; Oosterhuis, 'Homosexual Emancipation'; Trask, 'Remaking Men.'

65 On this publication see Tobin, *Peripheral Desires*, 53–82; the journal's title is discussed at 57.

66 Mosse, *Nationalism and Sexuality*, 23–4; Tobin, *Peripheral Desires*, 57–9.

67 On the pre- and post-First World War body culture movements in Germany see Hau, *Cult of Health*; Möhring, *Marmorleiber*; Toepfer, *Empire*. On nudist culture see Grisko, *Freikörperkultur*, 43–140.

68 Mosse, *Nationalism and Sexuality*, 60; Tobin, *Peripheral Desires*, 184.

69 Hochstadt, 'Population,' 333–5.

70 Frevert, *Women*, 107–47; Berghahn, *Imperial Germany*; Wehler, *German Empire*.

71 On the 'new alliances' between groups including sexologists, and the women's, homosexual and youth movements see, for example, Whisnant, *Queer Identities*, 42–79.

72 Foucault, *History*, 1: The Will to Knowledge, 17.

73 Blackbourn and Evans, *German Bourgeoisie*, 11.

74 Mosse, *Nationalism and Sexuality*, 2.

75 Frevert, *Women*, 109. On marriage practices across different classes, and the increasing influence of the middle classes in general, see Berghahn, *Imperial Germany*, 55, 57; Blackbourn and Evans, *German Bourgeoisie*, 98, 115–33; Eley, *Society, Culture, and the State*, 123–5; Frevert, *Bürgerinnen*, 12–15.

76 Blackbourn, 'German Bourgeoisie,' 11.

77 On these broader shifts see, for example, Cocks, 'Approaches,' 39; Coontz, *Marriage*.

78 Holek, as cited in Jensen, 'Bawdy Bodies,' 546–8, also 538, 543.

79 Schulte, 'Peasants and Farmers' Maids,' 158–73.

80 Jones, *Gender*, 81–9.

81 See, in particular, Dickinson, *Sex, Freedom*; Dickinson, 'Men's Christian Morality'; Fout, 'Sexual Politics.'

82 Stark, 'Pornography.'

83 Cited in Fout, 'Sexual Politics,' 277.

84 Dickinson, 'Men's Christian Morality,' 59–60.

85 Dickinson, 'Policing Sex,' 205. For a detailed study of the morality movements see Dickinson, *Sex, Freedom*, 13–136.

86 Cited in Dickinson, *Sex, Freedom*, 88, see also 2. On Wilhelmine censorship history see Stark, *Banned*. On Pappritz see Smith, *Berlin Coquette*, 65ff., 77ff.

87 Frevert, *Women*, 111; König, 'Geburtenkontrolle,' 143; Usborne, 'Social Body,' 142–6; Woycke, *Birth Control*. On infant mortality and attempts to control working class women through public hygiene see Frevert, 'Civilizing Tendency.'

88 Frevert, *Women*, 109–15, and 131–5. On Jewish 'Social feminism' see Kaplan, *Jewish Feminist*. On the 'Jewish question' in the fin-de-siècle women's movement: Omran, *Frauenbewegung und 'Judenfrage.'*

89 Frevert, *Women*, 113.

90 Allen, 'Gender,' 225.

91 On Stöcker, the League and the 'new ethics' see Dickinson, *Sex, Freedom*, 44–5, 191–5; Dickinson, 'Reflections'; Leng, 'Culture, Difference, and Sexual Progress'; Leng, *Sexual Politics*, 52–3; Matysik, *Reforming*, 55–91; Wickert, Hamburger, and Lienau, 'Helene Stöcker.'

92 Leng, *Sexual Politics*.

93 Reagin, *German Women's Movement*, 1–6; Frevert, *Women*, 107–30. On the German women's movement see also Allen, *Feminism*; Dickinson, *Sex, Freedom*; Evans, *The Feminist Movement*; Frevert, *Bürgerinnen*; Greven-Aschoff, *Die bürgerliche Frauenbewegung*; Matysik, *Reforming*.

94 See Reagin, *German Women's Movement*, 2–3, 5–6.

95 On Schirmacher see Lybeck, *Desiring Emancipation*, 44–8.

96 Eley, *Society, Culture, and the State*, 68.

97 Dickinson, *Sex, Freedom*, 305.

98 Zetkin cited in Drewitz, *German Women's Movement*, 65.

99 Abrams, 'Companionship,' 104; Braun, *Selected Writings*, 125.

100 On German socialist feminism see Frevert, *Women*, 138–47; Gaido and Frencia, 'Clara Zetkin'; Lopes and Roth, *Men's Feminism*; Thönnessen, *Emancipation*.

101 Jarausch, 'Students'; Stark, 'Pornography,' 202; Timm and Sanborn, *Gender, Sex*, 106.

102 This statistic is cited in Roos, *Weimar*, 17. There is now a considerable literature on Wilhelmine-era prostitution; see in particular Abrams, 'Prostitutes'; Evans, 'Prostitution, State and Society'; Harris, *Selling Sex*; Roos, *Weimar*, 14–20, 31–2 (and for a list of further sources, 234n2); Schulte, *Sperrbezirke*; Smith, *Berlin Coquette*.

103 Roos, *Weimar*, 14–35; Frevert, *Women*, 135.

104 Timm and Sanborn, *Gender, Sex*, 108–9.

105 On Böhme's text in the context of prostitution reform politics see Smith, *Berlin Coquette*, 69, 92–103.

106 Walkowitz, *City*, 46. See also Rowe, *Representing Berlin*.

107 On these links see, for example, Mosse, *Nationalism and Sexuality*.

108 See Allen, 'German Radical Feminism'; Bauer, '"Race," Normativity'; Doan, 'Marie Stopes,' 596–7; Evans, *The Feminist Movement*; Graham, 'Science'; Leng, 'Historicising'; Marhoefer, 'Race, Empire.' On eugenicist politics in Germany more broadly see Weikart, *Darwin to Hitler*; Weindling, *Health, Race*.

109 Nordau, *Degeneration [Entartung, 1892]*. Cited in Mosse, *Nationalism and Sexuality*, 35. On degeneration theories in late nineteenth-century science, medicine and the arts see Chamberlin and Gilman, *Degeneration*; Pick, *Faces of Degeneration*; Weindling, 'Bourgeois Values,' 80–90.

110 Leng, *Sexual Politics*, 14. See also Leng, 'Historicising.'

111 Hull, 'Kaiser Wilhelm', 198–9. The following summary is based, except where otherwise noted, on Beachy, *Gay Berlin*, 120–39.

112 Cited in Beachy, *Gay Berlin*, 126.

113 On the history of the duel see Frevert, *Men of Honour*.

114 Domeier, *Eulenburg-Skandal*, 10; on the comparison with Dreyfus see pp. 11, 15, 301–61. For a shorter account see Domeier, 'Homosexual Scare'.

115 Hirschfeld in Beachy, *Gay Berlin*, 128. Hirschfeld had apparently hoped to use the trial to continue his advocacy of homosexual emancipation, although his assessment of Moltke's 'unconscious' homosexuality without examining him in person ultimately had a damaging impact on his career. See Domeier, *Eulenburg-Skandal*, 166; Dose, *Magnus Hirschfeld*, 44–5.

116 Beachy, *Gay Berlin*, 123; Domeier, *Eulenburg-Skandal*, 184–6. For a broader account of homophobia and same-sex relations in German government circles see Nieden, 'Homophobie'.

117 See also Deborah Lucas's English translation of the full verse in: Domeier, *Eulenburg*, 127 (German version p. 308).

118 Beachy, *Gay Berlin*, 139.

119 Online archive of full journal: http://www.jugend-wochenschrift.de. For a detailed discussion of these cartoons see Steakley, 'Iconography'.

120 On the 'German scandal' label; the shifting meanings of 'friendship', and the homophobic threat linked to increased visibility – which he also argues helped to encourage heterosexual promiscuity and detabooize the double standard – see Domeier, *Eulenburg-Skandal*, 9, 158–204.

121 Domeier, 'Homosexual Scare', 758.

122 Domeier, *Eulenburg-Skandal*, 13–14, 24, 31–79.

123 Beachy, *Gay Berlin*, 70–5. For an entertaining fictionalized account of fin-de-siècle scandals beginning with Krupp and ending with Nazi SA leader Ernst Röhm see Duberman, *Jew Queers*.

124 Williams, 'Ecstasies'.

125 Cited in Matysik, 'In the Name', 43–4, see also 27–8, 30.

126 Matysik, 33, 44 passim; Lybeck, *Desiring Emancipation*, 108–15.

127 Cited in Leng, *Sexual Politics*, 135. On feminist ideas around female homosexuality see also Dickinson, *Sex, Freedom*, 152–76; Leidinger, 'Anna Rüling'; Matysik, *Reforming*, 152–74.

128 Cited in Leng, *Sexual Politics*, 141.

129 Matysik, 'In the Name', 47.

130 Lybeck, *Desiring Emancipation*, 103.

131 Lybeck, 104.

132 Lybeck, 103–8.

133 Spector, *Violent Sensations*, 1–3. For an example of the 'marginalization' thesis see Evans, *German Underworld*.

134 While backed by powerful manufacturers and businesspeople in the Colonial Association such as Siemens and Krupp, the German colonies ultimately had relatively little economic significance and attracted only few settlers, with most emigrants choosing the United States at this period. For an account of German missionaries from a history of sexuality perspective see Curtis-Wendlandt, 'Missionary Wives.'

135 Tobin, *Peripheral Desires*, 134.

136 Zantop, *Colonial Fantasies*. See also Friedrichsmeyer, Lennox, and Zantop, *Imperialist*; McClintock, *Imperial*; Stoler, *Carnal*.

137 Juergen Zimmerer in Wildenthal et al., 'Forum,' 261.

138 For essays problematizing the changing face of citizenship in Wilhelmine modernity see Eley, Jenkins, and Matysik, *German Modernities*. On gender and citizenship see Canning, 'Of Meaning.'

139 Wildenthal, *German Women*, 74, 79, 82.

140 Wildenthal et al., 'Forum,' 263.

141 On Rechenberg, see Schmidt, 'Colonial Intimacy.' On the colonies as a supposed space of sexual license that extended to same-sex relations see Aldrich, *Colonialism*; Tobin, *Peripheral Desires*, 134–61; Walther, 'Racializing,' 11; Woollacott, *Gender*, 149–50.

142 Walther, 'Racializing,' 12.

143 Wildenthal, *German Women*, 79, 105–7.

144 As a result, concepts such as 'mixed marriage' or 'half-caste' (for the offspring of such marriages) were little more than 'legal mumbo-jumbo': Tobin, *Peripheral Desires*, 134–5.

145 Wildenthal, *German Women*, 86–7.

146 Cited in Fitzpatrick, 'Samoan Women's Revolt,' 211. This article also traces significant opposition to the practice by the 1910s.

147 Wildenthal, *German Women*, 109, 121–2. See also Tobin, *Peripheral Desires*, 142–3.

148 Wildenthal, *German Women*, 103.

149 Lawyer Wilhelm Külz, in Wildenthal, 103.

150 Campt, *Other Germans*, 48–9.

151 Schaper, 'Sex Drives,' 244.

152 Wildenthal, 62–9; 131–71. Cauer is cited here at 135; on her growing cynicism around women's involvement in the colonial project see 137. Not all feminists were in favour of sending women to the colonies; Gertrud Bülow von Dennewitz sharply critiqued the practice of sending male colonists 'suitable female breeding material from the Reich': 134.

153 See also Wildenthal et al., 'Forum,' 161–4; Stoler, *Carnal*.

154 Reagin, *German Women's Movement*, 155–8 at 158.

155 For a detailed analysis of this dynamic see Marhoefer, 'Race, Empire.'

156 Tobin, *Peripheral Desires*, 137, 232.

157 Tobin, 161; Walther, 'Racializing.'

158 Tobin, *Peripheral Desires*, 134–61 at 149–51.

159 Fürth, 'Sexuelle Kriegsfragen,' 133. See also Spengler, *The Decline of the West*; Dickinson, '"A Dark, Impenetrable Wall."'

160 Daniel, *War from Within*, 130–1; Todd, 'Soldier's Wife', 257.

161 Jünger, *In Stahlgewittern*.

162 Killen, *Berlin Electropolis*, 129–30. See also Crouthamel, 'Male Sexuality'; Kaufmann, 'Science'; Lerner, *Hysterical Men*; Sutton, *Sex*, 91–117.

163 On biopolitics see, for example, Cocks, 'Approaches', 42.

164 Usborne, *Politics*, xii.

165 On the social hygiene films see Gertiser, *Falsche Scham*; Killen, 'What Is an Enlightenment Film?'

166 Roos, *Weimar*, 31–5.

167 This untitled source appeared in the journal *Sexual-Probleme* from 1914, cited in Todd, 'Soldier's Wife', 262, see also 265, 269–72.

168 On changing gender roles and sexuality in wartime see Crouthamel, *Intimate History*; Hagemann and Schüler-Springform, *Home/Front*; Kundrus, *Kriegerfrauen*; Todd, *Sexual Treason*.

169 Crouthamel, *Intimate History*, 3–8. On the fusing of feminine and masculine characteristics in notions of 'comradeship' see Crouthamel, '"Comradeship"'; Kühne, *Comradeship*; Kühne, 'Kriegskameradschaft'. On links between soldierly masculinity and citizenship see Crouthamel, 'Hypermasculine'; Frevert, *Die kasernierte Nation*; Frevert, 'Soldaten'; Hagemann and Schüler-Springform, *Home/Front*, 43–86, 233–54; Mosse, *Nationalism and Sexuality*, 114–32.

170 For discussion see Jürgens-Kirchhoff, 'Erotisierung', 97–8.

171 Herrn, *Schnittmuster*, 93.

172 Burchard, 'Sexuelle Fragen', 376.

173 Hirschfeld, *Sexuelle Zwischenstufen*, 2, 145–66; Bauer, *Hirschfeld Archives*, 33–4. On the responses of homosexual rights groups including the WhK to the experience of war and militarisation both during and after the actual conflict see Crouthamel, '"Comradeship."'

174 See, for example, 'Aus der Kriegszeit.'

175 Crouthamel, *Intimate History*, 111.

176 Wolters, 'Transvestiten im Weltkriege.' See also Crouthamel, 'Cross-Dressing'; Herrn, *Schnittmuster*, 76–7, 93–100; Sutton, *Sex*, 106–16.

177 Crouthamel, 'Male Sexuality', 61–2 and passim.

Chapter 3

1 Cited in Friedrich, *Before*, 128.

2 Hans Ostwald, *Berlin und die Berlinerin*, 1911, as cited in Rowe, *Representing Berlin*, 1.

3 For critical explorations of these tropes see Hung, Weiss-Sussex, and Wilkes, *Beyond Glitter*; Kniesche and Brockmann, *Dancing on the Volcano*; Marhoefer, *Sex*, 194–201; Rowe, *Representing Berlin*.

4 Isherwood, *Christopher*, 2.

5   Weitz, *Weimar Germany*, 3. For critical engagements with the 'crisis' narrative of Weimar, see Graf and Föllmer, 'Culture of "Crisis"'; Peukert, *Weimar Republic*.

6   On youth culture, see Peukert, *Weimar Republic*, 89–95; Vendrell, *Seduction of Youth*. On sex reform see Grossmann, *Reforming Sex*; Marhoefer, *Sex*; Usborne, *Politics*. On the 'life reform' and body culture movements see Hau, *Cult of Health*; Möhring, *Marmorleiber*; Toepfer, *Empire*; Wedemeyer, 'Body-Building'; Wedemeyer-Kolwe, *'Der neue Mensch.'*

7   For an overview and links to relevant source material, see pages on the Weimar Republic by the German foreign broadcaster Deutsche Welle (https://www.dw.com/en/weimar-1919-birth-of-germanys-first-democracy/a-47143440) and the German Historical Museum (https://www.dhm.de/en/ausstellungen/permanent-exhibition/epochs/1918-1933.html). Key scholarly surveys of this period include Peukert, *Weimar Republic*; Weitz, *Weimar Germany*.

8   For recent accounts of the opening and work of the Institute see Bauer, *Hirschfeld Archives*, 78–91; Marhoefer, *Sex*, 3–7, Herrn, *Der Liebe und dem Leid*. For a chronology of the building see the archived online exhibition of the Magnus Hirschfeld Society and website of the *Haus der Kulturen der Welt*: https://magnus-hirschfeld.de/institut/gebaeude/chronologie-der-institutsgebaeude/ and https://hkw.de/en/hkw/geschichte/ort_geschichte/magnus_hirschfeld.php.

9   Grossmann, *Reforming Sex*, 6.

10 Koonz, *Mothers*, 47.

11 On demographic shifts, women's work and citizenship, see: Boak, *Women*, 200–7; Bridenthal and Koonz, 'Beyond Kinder, Küche, Kirche'; Canning, 'Claiming Citizenship'; Canning, 'Women and the Politics'; Frevert, *Women*, 151–68; Peukert, *Weimar Republic*, 95–101; Rouette, 'Mothers and Citizens.' On demobilization see introduction to Bridenthal, Grossmann, and Kaplan, *When Biology*.

12 Usborne, *Politics*, 86.

13 Canning, 'Claiming Citizenship,' 116 and passim.

14 Hirschfeld estimated between 90–100 gay bars in the city by 1923; other sources support this estimate: Beachy, *Gay Berlin*, 196–7; Bollé, *Eldorado*, 63; Whisnant, *Queer Identities*, 62.

15 On inflation: Peukert, *Weimar Republic*, 61–6. On changing class structures: Canning, 'Order of Terms'; Frevert, *Women*, 107ff.; Peukert, *Weimar Republic*, 147–64; Weitz, *Weimar Germany*, 129–68.

16 Roos, *Weimar*, 8.

17 Grossmann, 'Girlkultur,' 64.

18 Hung, 'Modernized Gretchen,' 52. Hung offers a useful survey of current historiographical debates around this figure; see also Ankum, *Women in the Metropolis*; Boak, *Women*, 254–91; Smith, *Berlin Coquette*; Sutton, *Masculine Woman*.

19 On postwar 'moral panics' see Usborne, *Politics*, 69–81. On Soviet social policy and its influence on Weimar sex reform, see also 92–4; Beachy, *Gay Berlin*, 183; Melching, 'Left-Wing Intellectuals,' 76–7.

20 Timm, *Politics of Fertility*, 35.

21 On the 'stab in the back' mythology: Leng, *Sexual Politics*, 264. On Jewish involvement in the German military: Frevert, *Die kasernierte Nation*, 95–103.

22 On the New Woman and fears of degeneration: Grossmann, *Reforming Sex*, 6; Leng, *Sexual Politics*, 268, 270. On homophobic and antisemitic connotations: Frame, 'Gretchen, Girl, Garçonne?'; Wallach, *Passing Illusions*, 27–95.

23 Wallach, *Passing Illusions*, 23.

24 Usborne, *Politics*, 88–92.

25 Usborne, 88. On the evolution of this movement into the Weimar era, see Evans, *The Feminist Movement*.

26 Smith, *Berlin Coquette*, 9, 18, passim.

27 Timm, *Politics of Fertility*, 49. Hans Ostwald discussed the links between the Great Inflation, prostitution and crime in his *Moral History of the Inflation*; on this and other examples see Abrams, 'Prostitutes'; Evans, 'Prostitution.'

28 Roos, *Weimar*, 30.

29 Crouthamel, 'Male Sexuality', 70.

30 Theweleit, *Male Fantasies*. For a critical contextualization of this work see Kühne, *Männergeschichte*, 16–19, passim.

31 Kühne, 'Kriegskameradschaft', 178. See also Crouthamel, *Intimate History*.

32 Kühne, *Comradeship*, 6.

33 On shifting ideas of masculinity, see Crouthamel, 'Hypermasculine'; Mosse, *Nationalism and Sexuality*; Trask, 'Remaking Men.' On the dandy see Garelick, *Rising Star*.

34 Such postwar discussions of the state of heterosexuality tended to forget, as scholars point out, the degree to which sexual relations had been contested before the war as well: Leng, *Sexual Politics*, 269; Dickinson, '"A Dark, Impenetrable Wall."'

35 Cited in Williams, *Turning to Nature*, 43.

36 Williams, 47–8. On the popularity of eugenics rhetoric among Weimar-era reformers see Grossmann, *Reforming Sex*; Marhoefer, *Sex*; Marhoefer, *Racism*.

37 Grisko, *Freikörperkultur*; Ross, *Naked Germany*.

38 Cited in Williams, *Turning to Nature*, 41.

39 See discussion in Möhring, *Marmorleiber*, 120–8, see 134–68.

40 Cited in Möhring, 140.

41 See de Ras, *Body, Femininity*; Oosterhuis, *Homosexuality and Male Bonding*; Peukert, *Weimar Republic*; Vendrell, *Seduction of Youth*; Williams, 'Ecstasies.'

42 Williams, *Turning to Nature*, 108–11.

43 On the *Schund und Schmutz* laws: Petersen, 'Harmful Publications'; Springman, 'Poisoned Hearts'; Stieg, '1926 German Law'; Usborne, *Politics*, 76–81.

44 On social hygiene films: Gertiser, *Falsche Scham*; Hagener, *Geschlecht in Fesseln*; Smith, 'Richard Oswald.'

45 On cinema censorship: Lenman, 'Control of the Visual'; Steakley, 'Cinema.' For a broader account of gender and sexuality in Weimar cinema see McCormick, *Gender*.

46 de Ras, *Body, Femininity*, 45. On these connections, particularly at a time when many young people were growing up without fathers, see also Usborne, *Politics*, 76, 86.

47 Williams, *Turning to Nature*, 117–19, 128–9. See also Oosterhuis, *Homosexuality and Male Bonding*, 241–65.

48 Eley, 'German Modernities,' 64. For further discussion of these themes and tensions between rural and urban visions of German identity see, for example, Applegate, *Nation*; Hau, *Cult of Health*; Jenkins, *Provincial*.

49 See de Ras, *Body, Femininity*, 49–50; Vendrell, 'Adolescence,' 396–7, 413–18. On how 'respectability' was used to rein in male and female sexuality see Lybeck, *Desiring Emancipation*; Mosse, *Nationalism and Sexuality*.

50 de Ras, *Body, Femininity*, 40–3, 49–50.

51 Bühler, *Seelenleben*, 167. As translated by de Ras, *Body, Femininity*, 50.

52 Vendrell, 'Adolescence,' 402, 412, 417, passim. See also Vendrell, *Seduction of Youth*.

53 On the friendship societies see Beachy, *Gay Berlin*; Ramsay, 'Rites'; Sternweiler, 'Die Freundschaftsbünde'; Whisnant, *Queer Identities*, 108–9.

54 Crouthamel, '"Comradeship,"' 112.

55 On Radszuweit: Marhoefer, *Sex*, 47–51; Whisnant, *Queer Identities*, 109–11.

56 Ramsay, 'Rites,' 87. On these different branches of the movement see also Tobin, *Peripheral Desires*; Keilson-Lauritz, 'Benedict Friedlaender und die Anfänge.'

57 Lybeck, *Desiring Emancipation*, 151–2. On the gendered codings of queer styles in this era see Schader, *Virile*; Lehnert, *Wenn Frauen*; Sutton, *Masculine Woman*, 90–125.

58 Harvey, 'Culture and Society,' 280–1.

59 On the role of *Anders als die Andern* in Weimar censorship history: Steakley, 'Cinema'; Steakley, *Anders*.

60 On the impact of censorship on queer publishing see Marhoefer, *Sex*, 20–51 and 71–9; Whisnant, *Queer Identities*, 112–21.

61 On these magazines see Whisnant, *Queer Identities*, 112; Beachy, *Gay Berlin*, 164, 189, 192; full list at 276. See also Bollé, *Eldorado*; Lybeck, *Desiring Emancipation*, 151–88; Marhoefer, 'Lesbian Sexuality'; Micheler, *Selbstbilder und Fremdbilder*; Schader, *Virile*.

62 Kollmann, 'Die Liebes-Maske.' On the transvestite magazines, see Herrn, *Schnittmuster*, 142–57; Herrn, *Das 3. Geschlecht*; Marhoefer, *Sex*, 55–64; Sutton, 'Politics.'

63 Scene chronicler Ruth Roellig's contemporary collection, with a preface by Hirschfeld, *Berlins lesbische Frauen* (1928), is reprinted with a critical introduction as Meyer, *Lila Nächte*, 55. On the diversity of Weimar queer nightlife see Bollé, *Eldorado*; Whisnant, *Queer Identities*, 80–106; Gordon, *Voluptuous Panic*.

64 The original sheet music is included in the German Historical Museum press materials for the 2019 exhibition 'Weimar: The Essence and Value of Democracy' https://www.dhm.de/fileadmin/medien/relaunch/presse/pressebilder/Weimar/ Pressebildliste_Weimar_deutsch.pdf. See also: Lareau, 'Lavender Songs'; Jelavich, *Berlin Cabaret*, 103, 193.

65 From the classifieds sections in *Die Freundin*, 3 (1927), No. 7 and 3 (1927), No. 17. The gendering of the German nouns for 'transvestite' suggests this advertisement was posted by someone assigned male at birth who identified as female (Transvestit), seeking intimate companionship with either a ciswoman or 'Transvestitin' – someone assigned female at birth who identified as male.

66 On the codes and significance of the personal ad sections for Weimar queer cultures see Plötz, *Einsame Freundinnen*, 47–53 (here at 48); Schader, *Virile*, 127; Beachy, *Gay Berlin*, 191–2.

67 On middle-class respectability in the LGBTIQ organizations see: Lybeck, *Desiring Emancipation*, 151–88; Marhoefer, *Sex*; Sutton, 'Politics'.

68 On 'rationalism' or 'rationalization' as a mode for interpreting Weimar sex reform see Grossmann, 'The New Woman'; Peukert, *Weimar Republic*, 101–4; Usborne, *Politics*, 98; Timm, *Politics of Fertility*, 51.

69 Eley, 'German Modernities', 65.

70 Cited in Grossmann, *Reforming Sex*, 14.

71 Berghahn, *Modern Germany*, 44. Usborne notes that although 'there was never any conclusive evidence' that sexually transmitted diseases had increased due to the war, 'the image of a "polluted" nation persisted among all political parties': Usborne, *Politics*, 83. See also Grossmann, *Reforming Sex*, 15; Peukert, *Weimar Republic*, 102.

72 Usborne, *Politics*, 1–3, 10–11; Grossmann, Reforming Sex, 99.

73 Usborne, *Politics*, 10–11.

74 Grossmann, *Reforming Sex*, 14–15, cited at 15.

75 Timm, *Politics of Fertility*, 54, see also 35–40. On how these concerns created coalitions that challenged traditional Left-Right divides see also Usborne, *Politics*, xv–xvi, 71 and passim.

76 Usborne, *Politics*, 32; Grossmann, *Reforming Sex*, 15. See also König, 'Geburtenkontrolle'.

77 Boak, *Women*, 205.

78 van de Velde, *Die vollkommene Ehe*; Stopes, *Married Love*.

79 Jagose, *Orgasmology*, 74; Doan, 'Marie Stopes'; Leng, *Sexual Politics*, 270. On other manuals popular in Germany see Usborne, *Politics*, 95.

80 Grossmann, *Reforming Sex*, 28.

81 Lola Landau, 'Kameradschaftsehe', in *Die Tat* 20:11 (February, 1929), 831–5, as translated and reprinted in Kaes, Jay, and Dimendberg, *Weimar Republic Sourcebook*, 702–3, at 703.

82 Hermand and Trommler, *Kultur der Weimarer Republik*, 80–9; Boak, *Women*, 206.

83 Usborne, *Politics*, 3.

84 Grossmann, *Reforming Sex*, 6; Usborne, *Politics*, 93.

85 On how female doctors in particular navigated maternal and eugenic values see Kravetz, *Women Doctors*.

86 Usborne, *Politics*, 142; Dickinson, *Sex, Freedom*, 112.

87 Boak, *Women*, 206.

88 On these centres in the context of the larger Weimar sex reform movement see Grossmann, *Reforming Sex*, 14–77 and 10 on their number and locations; 99 on birth rate in rural areas.

89 Grossmann, 10.

90 For a summary of these debates see Boak, *Women*, 206–7. See also Usborne, 'Rhetoric', 72; Weindling, *Health, Race*, 424–6; Usborne, *Politics*, 142–8. On the sexual counselling centres see especially Grossmann, *Reforming Sex*; Kravetz, *Women Doctors*, 21–54; Soden, *Sexualberatungsstellen*; Timm, *Politics of Fertility*, 54–8 and 80–117.

91 On the Weimar welfare state see Canning, 'Order of Terms'; Crew, *Germans on Welfare*; Hong, *Welfare, Modernity*; Mason, 'Women in Germany'; Usborne, *Politics*, 35–6.

92 See Peukert, *Weimar Republic*, 102; Weindling, *Health, Race*.

93 Grossmann, *Reforming Sex*, vii. See also Timm, *Politics of Fertility*, 82, 85. For accounts of Weimar sexual history that place more emphasis on continuities with the Nazi era, see Harris, *Selling Sex*; Weindling, *Health, Race*.

94 Usborne, *Politics*, 6–7.

95 Usborne, 11.

96 Grossmann, *Reforming Sex*, 15.

97 Dr Max Hodann, 'Methode der Aufklärung über Geburtenregelung,' in Haire, *W.L.S.R. Proceedings of the Third Congress [London]*, 193–4.

98 Timm, *Politics of Fertility*, 36.

99 Aly and Sontheimer, *Fromms*, 28.

100 Usborne, *Politics*, 26–7.

101 On the Weimar-era abortion debates see Usborne, 156–201 (also: 13 on Hope-Bridges; 191–2 on Weimar women doctors); Grossmann, *Reforming Sex*; Grossmann, 'Abortion'; Usborne, *Cultures of Abortion*. On women doctors see Kravetz, *Women Doctors*.

102 Kienle, cited in Usborne, *Politics*, 196.

103 'Frau Dr. Kienle-Stuttgart im Hungerstreik,' 1.

104 Wolf, *Cyankali*, 38.

105 Usborne, *Cultures of Abortion*, 58. See also Grossmann, *Reforming Sex*, 86.

106 Usborne, *Politics*, xvi, 71–2. See also Usborne, 'Christian Churches.'

107 Usborne, *Politics*, 73.

108 Cited in Usborne, 96. On the diverse Catholic positions on eugenics in the Weimar and Nazi periods see: Dietrich, 'Catholic Eugenics.'

109 Timm, *Politics of Fertility*, 50; Hong, *Welfare, Modernity*.

110 Wallach, *Passing Illusions*, 68; Kaplan, *Jewish Feminist*.

111 Roos, 'Nationalism, Racism,' 53, 67–8. See also Boonstra, 'Women's Honour'; Roos, 'Women's Rights'; Wigger, 'Black Shame.'

112 Cited in Roos, 'Nationalism, Racism,' 57.

113 Timm, *Politics of Fertility*, 47; Campt, *Other Germans*, 36–7.

114 Roos, 'Nationalism, Racism,' 69, 71.

115 Campt, *Other Germans*, 55–6, cited at 56. On German racialized stereotypes of African soldiers: Kettlitz, *Afrikanische Soldaten*. On colonial-era sexualities and masculinities, see chapter 2 and Lennox, 'Race, Gender'; Maß, *Weiße Helden*; Wildenthal, *German Women*, 186ff.

116 Report in *Hamburger Nachrichten*, 30 July 1921, cited in Campt, *Other Germans*, 55.

117 Campt, 58–9.

118 On the long history of racialized 'othering' of Jewish physiologies see Gilman, *The Jew's Body*.

119 Bauer, *Hirschfeld Archives*, 7.

120 Roos, *Weimar*, 2. On police regulation of prostitution see also Dickinson, 'Policing Sex'; Freund-Widder, *Frauen unter Kontrolle*; Harris, *Selling Sex*.

121 Cited in Roos, *Weimar*, 1.

122 Roos, 2–3.

123 Smith, *Berlin Coquette*, 21.

124 Marhoefer, *Sex*, 207.

125 Marhoefer, 202.

126 Marhoefer, 197. Smith's study of prostitution and the New Woman also complicates these stereotypes of decadence: Smith, *Berlin Coquette*.

127 Marhoefer, *Sex*, 112–45.

128 Beachy, *Gay Berlin*, 200. Beachy emphasizes the difficulties in characterizing male prostitution in terms of a straightforward commercial transaction, noting that commercialized sex has often been a feature of same-sex erotic subcultures in ways that blur lines of material dependency, remuneration, companionship and love: Beachy, 187–219 at 188–9. See also Lücke, *Männlichkeit in Unordnung*.

129 Beachy, *Gay Berlin*, 201–14, 218.

130 Beachy, 220–1, Kahl cited at 221.

131 Cited in Marhoefer, *Sex*, 122.

132 Marhoefer, 112–21.

133 Beachy, 'The German Invention,' 221.

134 Marhoefer, *Sex*, 119.

135 Marhoefer, 129.

136 Beachy, *Gay Berlin*, 239.

137 Marhoefer, *Sex*, 129–36.

138 These numbers are from an early report on the Institute published in Hirschfeld's *Jahrbuch*: 'Bericht.' For surveys of the Institute and its activities, see Beachy, *Gay Berlin*, 160–3; Dose, *Magnus Hirschfeld*, 51–7; Herrn, 'Vom Traum zum Trauma.' For a comprehensive new history see Herrn, *Der Liebe und dem Leid*.

139 On the Institute's involvement in trans medicine see also Beachy, *Gay Berlin*, 163; Pfäfflin, 'Sex Reassignment.'

140 Grossmann, *Reforming Sex*, 16–17, 28.

141 Isherwood, *Christopher and his Kind*, as cited in Bauer, *Hirschfeld Archives*, 83.

142 On these meetings see Dose, 'World League'; Crozier, 'Becoming a Sexologist.'

143 Beachy, *Gay Berlin*, 162, 182.

144 Hirschfeld, 'Ärztliche Eheberatung.' See also Timm, *Politics of Fertility*, 83.

145 Grossmann, *Reforming Sex*, 16.

146 Usborne, *Politics*, 4–6. On Haeckel and monism see Dickinson, 'Reflections,' 206–22; Weindling, *Health, Race*.

147 Peukert, *Weimar Republic*, 102.

148 On competing models of the 'normal' and 'deviant' see Cryle and Stephens, *Normality*, 261–93.

149 For Steinach's own retrospective account see Steinach and Loebel, *Sex and Life*. For historical accounts of this research: Sengoopta, 'Dr Steinach'; Stoff, *Ewige Jugend*; Walch, *Triebe, Reize und Signale*. On hormone research as a treatment for homosexuality see Sengoopta, 'Glandular Politics'; Sutton, *Sex*, 133–44; Trask, 'Remaking Men'.

150 On the Steinach film: Herrn and Brinckmann, 'Rejuvenation'; Makela, 'Rejuvenation'.

151 On early sex confirmation surgeries undertaken in Germany during these years see Bakker et al., *Others of My Kind*; Beachy, *Gay Berlin*, 176–9; Herrn, *Schnittmuster*; Meyerowitz, *How Sex Changed*, 18–21.

152 Fuechtner, *Berlin Psychoanalytic*, 9.

153 Leng, *Sexual Politics*, 279–80.

154 Deutsch, 'Homosexualität', 225.

155 Horney, 'Gehemmte Weiblichkeit', 72–3.

156 Sutton, *Sex*, 145–72. On scientific theories of frigidity see Cryle and Moore, *Frigidity*. On the contributions of women analysts see Ludwig-Körner, *Wiederentdeckt*; Thompson, 'Early Women'.

157 Cited in Leng, *Sexual Politics*, 195; on Lazarsfeld see also 290–306.

158 Leng, 265.

159 For a recent analysis of such trends see Geissler, 'Critiquing European Ethnography'.

160 Freud, *Totem and Taboo*.

161 See Bauer, *Hirschfeld Archives*, 13–36, 102–23; Fisher and Funke, 'British Sexual Science'; Fisher and Funke, '"Let Us Leave … "'; Fuechtner, Haynes, and Jones, *Towards a Global History*; Funke, 'Navigating'; Fuechtner, 'Indians, Jews'; Herrn and Taylor, 'Magnus Hirschfeld's Interpretation'; Marhoefer, *Racism*.

162 Moreck, *Führer*, 68. On this work see Smith, 'Challenging Baedeker'.

163 Isherwood, *Goodbye to Berlin*, 295.

164 Isherwood, 295–6.

165 On Isherwood as Weimar Berlin's 'most famous sex tourist' and sex tourism, inflation and prostitution more broadly, see Beachy, *Gay Berlin*, 188, 192–209.

166 Marhoefer, *Sex*, 194.

167 Marhoefer, 107, 176–81, 188.

168 In particular, Marhoefer points to the work of Julia Roos, Eric Weitz, Richard McCormick and Richard Evans.

169 'Guest Post: Was There a Backlash against Weimar's Sexual Politics?' (16 November 2015) https://weimarstudies.wordpress.com/2015/11/16/guest-post-was-there-a-backlash-against-weimars-sexual-politics/.

170 Roos, *Weimar*, 8. 'Guest Post: Julia Roos' Response to Laurie Marhoefer' (24 November 2015) See also https://weimarstudies.wordpress.com/2015/11/24/guest-post-julia-roos-response-to-laurie-marhoefer/ See also Roos, 'Backlash'.

171 'Guest Post: Edward Dickinson on Weimar's Sexual Politics and the "Backlash Thesis"' (12 May 2016) https://weimarstudies.wordpress.com/2016/05/12/guest-post-edward-dickinson-on-weimars-sexual-politics-and-the-backlash-thesis/.

Chapter 4

1   Eyewitness report, destruction of Hirschfeld's Institute, 6 May 1933, reprinted in Grau and Schoppmann, *Hidden Holocaust?*, 31–2. Emphasis in original.

2   On the sex reform movement during this period: Grossmann, *Reforming Sex*, 136–65, especially 145–7.

3   Heineman, 'Sexuality and Nazism', 2002, 22.

4   Timm, 'Sex with a Purpose', 223.

5   The use of quotation marks denotes distance from deeply problematic Nazi categorizations; for critical discussion – although she opts against this strategy – see Szobar, 'Telling Sexual Stories', 243n2.

6   Herzog, 'Hubris and Hypocrisy', 6.

7   Evans, 'Why Queer German History?', 377.

8   Herzog, 'Hubris and Hypocrisy', 3–4. Herzog notes that even the widely respected George Mosse subscribed to this view of Nazism as 'profoundly repressive' (5), and that this tendency extends to much German-language scholarship. Cf. Mosse, *Nationalism and Sexuality*; Mosse, *Image of Man*. The essays by Heineman, Timm, and Herzog cited above form part of a pivotal 2002 special issue of the *Journal of the History of Sexuality* on 'Sexuality and German Fascism', edited by Herzog (volume 11, issues 1/2), republished in book form in 2005. Subsequent citations are to this edited collection: Herzog, *Sex after Fascism*.

9   Concerns about writing about sexual violence and rape under Nazism in ways that avoid titillation and recognize the subjectivities of victims are central to a recent special issue of *German History* (March 2021). See Hájková, 'Sexuality, Holocaust'. See also the special issue 'Transgressive Sex, Love, and Violence in World War II Germany and Britain', *Journal of the History of Sexuality* 26:3 (2017), with introduction by Annette Timm, and Hájková and Mailänder, 'Forum: Holocaust'. For a survey of other recent literature on this topic see Dickinson and Wetzell, 'Historiography', 297–8.

10 On ideas of the *Volkskörper* and how this constructed Jewish bodies, in particular, as both foreign and parasitic, see Neumann, 'Phenomenology'.

11 Swett, Ross, and d'Almeida, *Pleasure and Power*, 1–13, at 1. The authors note that such positions involve taking seriously Michel Foucault's insistence on pleasure and power as mutually reinforcing 'spirals' in the history of sexuality.

12 Harvey et al., *Private Life*, 4.

13 Harvey et al., 5.

14 Patrick Farges, in Hájková and Mailänder, 'Forum: Holocaust', 97.

15 For discussion of the birth rate during these decades see Grossmann, *Reforming Sex*, 4; Mouton, *Nurturing*, 108; Noakes and Pridham, *Nazism*, 2: State, Economy and Society 1933–1939, 256.

16 Herzog, *Sex after Fascism*, 10.

17 Nazi race theorist Hans Endres in 1941, cited in Herzog, 'Hubris and Hypocrisy', 9. See also Stibbe, *Women*, 50.

18 Reters, *Liebe, Ehe*, 153. On Nazi sexual ideology see also Stibbe, *Women*, 50; Heineman, 'Sexuality and Nazism', 2005, 50; Maiwald and Mischler, *Sexualität*.

19 Heineman, 'Sexuality and Nazism,' 2005, 32.

20 Cited in Pine, *Nazi Family Policy*, 8.

21 Pine, 9; Stephenson, *Women in Nazi Germany*, 67.

22 See Weindling, *Health, Race*, 291.

23 Pine, *Nazi Family Policy*, 9.

24 For rich imagery reflecting these gendered and racialized Nazi ideal types, although with little analysis of how these were also challenged by everyday Germans, see Pini, *Leibeskult und Liebeskitsch*, 44–5, 109–11, and passim.

25 Haarer, *Die deutsche Mutter*, 5.

26 Cited in Pine, *Nazi Family Policy*, 9. On mother/soldier comparisons see also Mouton, *Nurturing*, 120.

27 Szobar, 'Telling Sexual Stories,' 151. For an important early analysis of the complex imagery of women under Nazism see Rupp, 'Mother of the Volk.' For a survey of recent scholarship see Saldern, 'Innovative Trends.'

28 Campt, *Other Germans*, 65. Feminist historians have been particularly influential in drawing out these connections between Nazi race and gender ideology and its interactions with other social categories such as class or religion. See, for example, Bock, *Zwangssterilisation*; Bridenthal, Grossmann, and Kaplan, *When Biology*; Heineman, *What Difference*; Kaplan, *Between Dignity*; Koonz, *Mothers*; Stephenson, *Women in Nazi Society*. For a survey see Grossmann, 'Feminist Debates.'

29 Sutton, *Masculine Woman*, 86.

30 Gordon, 'Fascism,' 164–7. See also Marschik, 'Eroticism.'

31 Guenther, *Nazi Chic?*; Bertschik, *Mode*, 274–311.

32 Crouthamel, 'Homosexuality and Comradeship.'

33 Gordon, 'Fascism,' 166.

34 Only one organization, the the *Bund für Leibeszucht* (League of Body Culture) managed to resist the official prohibition on nudist movements, and while some historians have declared this a triumph of non-violent resistance, others take a more sober approach: 'Not resistance, but *Gleichschaltung* and assimilation was the strategy of the leadership of organized nudist culture under National Socialism': Linse, 'Freikörperkultur,' 239–41 at 240. For a long-view analysis of shifts in body culture under fascism see Mosse, *Nationalism and Sexuality*.

35 Williams, *Turning to Nature*, 52, on 'strength through joy' see also 100.

36 Linse, 'Freikörperkultur,' 239, 240, 247. On the continuities of the German naturist movement into the Third Reich despite morality-based critiques see also Jefferies, 'German Naturism.'

37 Herzog, 'Hubris and Hypocrisy,' 12–13.

38 Cited in Stephenson, *Women in Nazi Germany*, 163–4.

39 Koonz, *Mothers*, 399; Pine, *Nazi Family Policy*, 51–3; Stibbe, *Women*, 116; Stephenson, *Women in Nazi Germany*, 163–4.

40 Szobar, 'Telling Sexual Stories,' 152. On the Hitler Youth as a space of homoerotic exploration as well as Nazi propaganda, and its problematic legacy in postwar gay representation, see Fleishman, '"Naturgeil."'

41 On marriage policy under the Nazis see Czarnowski, *Das kontrollierte Paar*; Heineman, *What Difference*, 17–74; Klinksiek, *Die Frau im NS-Staat*, 72–81, 87–8; Koonz, *Mothers*; Mouton, *Nurturing*; Reters, *Liebe, Ehe*; Pine, *Nazi Family Policy*; Stephenson, *Women in Nazi Germany*, 27–36; Stephenson, *Women in Nazi Society*, 37–56.

42 Ludwig Nockher, 'Vorschläge zur Gestaltung des deutschen Ehescheidungsrechts', cited in Noakes and Pridham, *Nazism*, 2: State, Economy and Society 1933–1939, 260. See also Klinksiek, *Die Frau im NS-Staat*, 69.

43 Hitler, *Mein Kampf*, 366 in Pine, *Nazi Family Policy*, 15.

44 Noakes and Pridham, *Nazism*, 2: State, Economy and Society 1933–1939, 265; Klinksiek, *Die Frau im NS-Staat*, 15. On the balancing of quality and quantity see also Pine, *Nazi Family Policy*, 11.

45 Cited in Noakes and Pridham, *Nazism*, 2: State, Economy and Society 1933–1939, 260–1.

46 Haarer, *Die deutsche Mutter*, 23.

47 Pine, *Nazi Family Policy*, 16; Mouton, *Nurturing*, 57.

48 Mouton, *Nurturing*, 51.

49 See Heineman, *What Difference*, 24–5; Mouton, *Nurturing*, 51–3.

50 Pine, *Nazi Family Policy*, 16–17.

51 Mouton, *Nurturing*, 54–5.

52 Cited in Mouton, 49–50.

53 Haarer, *Die deutsche Mutter*, 8.

54 Mouton, *Nurturing*, 49. On the closing down of birth control centres and the *Gleichschaltung* of the Weimar sex reform movement see Grossmann, *Reforming Sex*, 136–65; Koonz, *Mothers*, 187; Noakes and Pridham, *Nazism*, 2: State, Economy and Society 1933–1939, 256.

55 Eley, 'German Modernities', 63.

56 Grossmann, *Reforming Sex*, 151–2; Timm, 'Sex with a Purpose', 231.

57 Mouton, *Nurturing*, 151.

58 Pine, *Nazi Family Policy*, 19. On contradictions in the regime's stance see Timm, 'Sex with a Purpose.'

59 Mouton, *Nurturing*, 57, 60. On resistance to the scheme see Heineman, *What Difference*, 24–5; Stibbe, *Women*, 54.

60 On the marriage loan scheme and links to unemployment policy see Mouton, *Nurturing*, 56–61; Noakes and Pridham, *Nazism*, 2: State, Economy and Society 1933–1939, 257–8, 269; Pine, *Nazi Family Policy*, 17.

61 Stephenson, *Women in Nazi Society*, 47.

62 Noakes and Pridham, *Nazism*, 2: State, Economy and Society 1933–1939, 257–8; Koonz, *Mothers*, 185.

63 Stibbe, *Women*, 50.

64 Koonz, *Mothers*, 186.

65 While Bock describes National Socialism as promoting 'a modern cult of fatherhood', Mouton observes that the party focused mostly on men as breadwinners, excluding fathers from much pronatalist propaganda: Bock, 'Antinatalism'; Mouton, *Nurturing*, 124.

66 Koonz, *Mothers*, 108–86; Mouton, *Nurturing*, 116–27; Stephenson, *Women in Nazi Germany*, 31; Stephenson, *Women in Nazi Society*, 49–50.

67 Reproduced in Mouton, *Nurturing*, 116–17. For rich visual materials on the 'cult of mothers' in National Socialism see Schmidt and Dietz, *Frauen unterm Hakenkreuz*, 50–77.

68 Timm, 'Ambivalent Outsider,' 193.

69 Stephenson, *Women in Nazi Germany*, 30; Koonz, *Mothers*, 108. See also Stephenson, *Nazi Organization*, 164–5.

70 See Noakes and Pridham, *Nazism*, 2: State, Economy and Society 1933–1939, 258, 265–6.

71 Haarer, *Die deutsche Mutter*, 5.

72 Koonz, *Mothers*, 187.

73 Stephenson, *Women in Nazi Germany*, 30.

74 Stephenson, 41.

75 Heineman, *What Difference*, 31–2. See also Joshi, 'Maternalism, Race,' 833–40; Stephenson, *Women in Nazi Germany*, 41–2.

76 Cited in Clay and Leapman, *Master Race*, 71.

77 Cited in Heineman, *What Difference*, 31.

78 Cited in Stephenson, *Women in Nazi Society*, 64. See also Stephenson, *Women in Nazi Germany*, 150–1; Koonz, *Mothers*, 398–9; Stibbe, *Women*, 156.

79 Stephenson, *Women in Nazi Society*, 65.

80 Koonz, *Mothers*, 197.

81 Allen, 'Feminism and Eugenics,' 493.

82 This field of research took off in earnest in the 1970s and 1980s thanks to work by scholars such as Claudia Koonz, Jill Stephenson and Gisela Bock. Koonz has argued, for example, that 'Nazi policy rested on the right of the nation to force women to bear children': Koonz, *Mothers*, 197. For Bock, 'compulsory motherhood' and 'prohibition of motherhood' (such as through forced sterilization) formed two sides of the same coin: Bock, 'Racism and Sexism,' 409–10. Scholars have found that it was especially this anti-natalist flipside that differentiated Nazi natalist policy from the celebration of motherhood in other places such as England or France: Mouton, *Nurturing*, 116. See also Bridenthal, Grossmann and Kaplan, *When Biology*; Stephenson, *Women in Nazi Society*; Bock, *Zwangssterilisation*.

83 Stephenson, *Women in Nazi Germany*, 30. See also Stibbe, *Women*, 50.

84 Cited in Bock, *Zwangssterilisation*, 166.

85 Bock, 166. See also discussion in Stephenson, *Women in Nazi Germany*, 30.

86 Bock, *Zwangssterilisation*, 167–8. See also discussion in Stibbe, *Women*, 53–4.

87 Stephenson, *Women in Nazi Germany*, 32; Stibbe, *Women*, 53.

88 On 'mixed' marriages and families see Kaplan, *Between Dignity*, 83–7; Mouton, *Nurturing*, 67–70; Pine, *Nazi Family Policy*, 16; Stoltzfus, 'Limits of Policy'; Stoltzfus, *Resistance*; Szobar, 'Telling Sexual Stories.'

89 Kaplan, *Between Dignity*, 77.

90 Mouton, *Nurturing*, 54.

91 Campt, *Other Germans*, 67.

92 Szobar, 'Telling Sexual Stories,' 131.

93 Mouton, *Nurturing*, 79; Szobar, 'Telling Sexual Stories,' 136.

94 Kaplan, *Between Dignity*, 79.

95 Stibbe, *Women*, 45.

96 Mouton, *Nurturing*, 88.

97 Kaplan, *Between Dignity*, 93. See also Stibbe, *Women*, 70.

98 Cited in Mouton, *Nurturing*, 70.

99 Stoltzfus, *Resistance*.

100 Stoltzfus, 'Limits of Policy,' 117–44 at 117–18. On the diverse motives behind denunciations – 'from base, selfish, personal, to lofty and "idealistic"' see also Gellately, *Gestapo and German Society*, 158.

101 On Nazi divorce law see Noakes and Pridham, *Nazism*, 2: State, Economy and Society 1933–1939, 273–6; Pine, *Nazi Family Policy*, 18–19.

102 Stephenson, *Women in Nazi Society*, 42–3.

103 Noakes and Pridham, *Nazism*, 2: State, Economy and Society 1933–1939, 274. See also Pine, *Nazi Family Policy*, 18; Mouton, *Nurturing*, 93.

104 Becker, 'Zur Funktion.' See also Herzog, 'Hubris and Hypocrisy,' 6–7n9.

105 Stephenson, *Women in Nazi Society*, 42; Mouton, *Nurturing*, 92.

106 Noakes and Pridham, *Nazism*, 2: State, Economy and Society 1933–1939, 273–4.

107 Stephenson, *Women in Nazi Society*, 44; Pine, *Nazi Family Policy*, 18–19.

108 Stephenson, *Women in Nazi Society*, 42–3.

109 For details, see Mouton, *Nurturing*, 90–1.

110 Mouton, 87–9.

111 For these links see in particular, Bock, 'Antinatalism.' See also Mouton, *Nurturing*, 107ff.

112 Heineman, *What Difference*, 24–5; Mouton, *Nurturing*, 61.

113 Amendment to Paragraph 218, cited in Grossmann, *Reforming Sex*, 152. See also Pine, *Nazi Family Policy*, 19–20.

114 Grossmann, *Reforming Sex*, 152; Koonz, *Mothers*, 186–7; Noakes and Pridham, *Nazism*, 2: State, Economy and Society 1933–1939, 256; Stibbe, *Women*, 54, 157.

115 Haarer, *Die deutsche Mutter*, 29.

116 Dickinson, 'Policing Sex,' 232.

117 Pine, *Nazi Family Policy*, 20.

118 Micheler, 'Homophobic Propaganda,' 96.

119 Aly, 'Medicine,' 54–5. For a detailed study of these links see David, Fleischhacker, and Hohn, 'Abortion and Eugenics,' 85–101.

120 Aly, 'Medicine,' 55. See also Evans, *Rereading*, 145–8; Weindling, *Health, Race*, 541–51.

121 Mouton, *Nurturing*, 143; Bock, *Zwangssterilisation*, 386–7, 398. On Catholic women's opposition to abortion see also Koonz, *Mothers*, 267. On Catholic attitudes towards eugenics more broadly see Dietrich, 'Catholic Eugenics.'

122 Proctor, *Racial Hygiene*, 122–3.

123 Haarer, *Die deutsche Mutter*, 27–31, at 28.

124 Mouton, *Nurturing*, 139.

125 Koonz, *Mothers*, 189.

126 Bock, *Zwangssterilisation*, 372. See also Bock, 'Racism and Sexism'; Bock, 'Antinatalism.'

127 See excerpt from the legislation RGB1. I (1933) in Noakes, 'Nazism and Eugenics,' 263.

128 See analysis in Mouton, *Nurturing*, 140–8; Noakes and Pridham, *Nazism*, 2: State, Economy and Society 1933–1939, 261–4; Noakes, 'Nazism and Eugenics'; Pine, *Nazi Family Policy*, 14, 117–24.

129 Cited in Mouton, *Nurturing*, 144–5.

130 Pine, *Nazi Family Policy*, 14, 117–21.

131 Weindling, *Health, Race*, 451–2; Noakes and Pridham, *Nazism*, 2: State, Economy and Society 1933–1939, 263; Noakes, 'Nazism and Eugenics.'

132 Campt, *Other Germans*, 63–80. See also Pommerin, *Sterilisierung*.

133 Grossmann, *Reforming Sex*, vi–vii. On the links between the Weimar welfare state, modern science and Nazi eugenics see also Heineman, 'Sexuality and Nazism,' 2005, 50; Peukert, 'Genesis.'

134 Pine, *Nazi Family Policy*, 124. See also Weingart, 'Rationalization.'

135 Bock, *Zwangssterilisation*, 240; Campt, *Other Germans*, 69; Weindling, *Health, Race*, 533. For comparisons of early twentieth-century German and US euthanasia and eugenic policies see Fischer, 'Maltreatment'; Marhoefer, *Racism*. For a survey of pre-1945 German and international eugenics discourses: Tanner, 'Eugenics before 1945.'

136 Haarer, *Die deutsche Mutter*, 30–1.

137 Bock, *Zwangssterilisation*, 273. See also Bock, 'Racism and Sexism.'

138 Bock, *Zwangssterilisation*, 371.

139 On the Concordat Catholic opposition to Nazi eugenic measures see especially Koonz, *Mothers*, 267, 273, 283. See also Mouton, *Nurturing*, 142.

140 Koonz, *Mothers*, 356, 399.

141 Hitler, *Mein Kampf*, 280.

142 Stephenson, *Women in Nazi Germany*, 45; Stephenson, *Women in Nazi Society*, 68; Stibbe, *Women*, 157.

143 Stibbe, 157; Pine, *Nazi Family Policy*, 122.

144 See Heineman, *What Difference*, 28; Roos, 'Backlash,' 67–9; Stephenson, *Women in Nazi Germany*, 41, 45.

145 Timm, 'Sex with a Purpose,' 224. See also Heineman, 'Sexuality and Nazism,' 2005, 50.

146 Timm, 'Sex with a Purpose,' 224–5.

147 On the swift shutdown of queer culture: Bollé, *Eldorado*; Grau and Schoppmann, *Hidden Holocaust?*; Jellonek, *Homosexuelle*; Whisnant, *Queer Identities*; Sternweiler and Hannesen, *Goodbye to Berlin?*; Stümke, 'Persecution.' Historians emphasize that this proceeded at a different pace in different parts of the country, with Prussia quick to ban gay magazines, organizations, and pubs, while in Hamburg gay pubs remained open until mid 1936. See Micheler, 'Homophobic Propaganda,' 95–6. For essays examining homosexual persecution in various regions (the Palatinate, Würzburg, Düsseldorf, Würzburg and Hamburg as well as Berlin): Zinn, *Homosexuelle in Deutschland*.

148 *Die Freundin* vol. 9, no. 10, 8 March 1933, n.p.; and vol. 5, no. 1, 2 July 1929 (cover).

149 For an overview, see Caplan, 'Administration,' 171–2. Key early works include Grau, *Homosexualität*; Jellonnek, *Homosexuelle unter dem Hakenkreuz*; Müller and Sternweiler, *Homosexuelle Männer*; Schoppmann, *Nationalsozialistische Sexualpolitik*.

150 On this historiography see for example Crouthamel, 'Homosexuality and Comradeship,' 420–1.

151 Giles, 'Institutionalization,' 233. For an overview of scholarship on Nazi homophobia and its inconsistencies see Huneke, 'Duplicity,' 33.

152 For accounts of these events see Hancock, 'Ernst Röhm,' 1998; Hancock, *Ernst Röhm*, 2008; Hancock, 'Purge'; Marhoefer, *Sex*, 146–73; Nieden, 'Aufstieg und Fall'; Whisnant, *Queer Identities*, 212–16; Wackerfuss, *Stormtrooper Families*, 296–318.

153 Wackerfuss, 298–305.

154 Goebbels, cited in Wackerfuss, 302.

155 'Befehl des Obersten SA-Führers,' *Hamburger Tageblatt*, 1 July 1934, cited in Wackerfuss, 302.

156 'Der Führer der Nation gibt seinem Volke Rechenschaft,' *Hamburger Tageblatt*, 13 July 1934, cited in Wackerfuss, 304.

157 Huneke, 'Duplicity,' 33; Oosterhuis, 'Medicine,' 198ff.; Wackerfuss, *Stormtrooper Families*, 305.

158 See Micheler, 'Homophobic Propaganda'; Oosterhuis, 'Medicine.'

159 Giles, 'Denial,' 256–90 especially 256–7.

160 Halberstam, *Queer Art*, 147–72, at 149, 153.

161 Halberstam, 153; see also Herzog, *Sex after Fascism*, 12; Herzog, 'Hubris and Hypocrisy'; Sontag, 'Fascinating Fascism.' See also the special issue 'The Aesthetics of Fascism' published by the *Journal of Contemporary History* in 1996, and Pursell, 'Queer Eyes.' For a critical review of this historiography see Marhoefer, *Sex*, 155.

162 This summary is based on Marhoefer, *Sex*, 146–73. See also Nieden, 'Aufstieg und Fall'; Giles, 'Denial,' 256–7.

163 Whisnant, *Queer Identities*, 215–18 at 215; Giles, 'Legislating Homophobia'; Grau and Schoppmann, *Hidden Holocaust?*; Huneke, 'Duplicity,' 32–4; Micheler, 'Homophobic Propaganda.'

164 Dickinson, 'Policing Sex,' 232.

165 Whisnant, *Queer Identities*, 215–16. See also Grau and Schoppmann, *Hidden Holocaust?*; Giles, 'Institutionalization'; Jellonnek, *Homosexuelle unter dem*

Hakenkreuz; Jensen, 'Pink Triangle'; Micheler, *Selbstbilder und Fremdbilder*; Zinn, *Homosexuelle in Deutschland*.

166 See, in particular, Grau and Schoppmann, *Hidden Holocaust?*, 6–7, 249–53, 282–91; Giles, 'Most Unkindest'; Giles, 'Denial', 259; Herzog, 'European Sexualities', 9 (online); Sparing and Krischel, 'Kastration'.

167 Beck and Heibert, *Underground Life*, 134. This was first published in German as Beck, *Erinnerungen*.

168 Schoppmann, *Days of Masquerade*, 98–113.

169 See introductory essays by Grau and Schoppmann in Grau and Schoppmann, *Hidden Holocaust?*, 2–15. For a careful teasing out of 'tolerance' and 'toleration' in the context of Nazi homophobia, see Huneke, 'Duplicity', 51–2.

170 Grau and Schoppmann, *Hidden Holocaust?*, 7, 9; Stephenson, *Women in Nazi Germany*, 43; Stibbe, *Women*, 53.

171 See Huneke, 'Heterogeneous Persecution', 297. On this club see also Dobler, *Von anderen Ufern*, 182–90; Schoppmann, *Nationalsozialistische Sexualpolitik*, 168.

172 See Schoppmann, 'The Position of Lesbian Women' in Grau and Schoppmann, *Hidden Holocaust?*, 9–14 at 12.

173 Kundrus, 'Frauen', 496. See also Stephenson, *Women in Nazi Germany*, 43–4; Heineman, *What Difference*, 28–9.

174 Stephenson, *Women in Nazi Germany*, 44; Herzog, 'Hubris and Hypocrisy', 15. For surveys of recent scholarship on queer female experience under Nazism see Huneke, 'Duplicity', 31–5; Huneke, 'Heterogeneous Persecution'. Anna Hájková has compiled an online biography covering lesbian and transfeminine histories under Nazism, in conjunction with the 2017 conference 'Holocaust, Sexuality, Stigma: Taking Stock': https://sexualityandholocaust.com/blog/bibliography/.

175 Schoppmann, *Nationalsozialistische Sexualpolitik*, 165–6. On the interwoven experiences of Hahm and other queer women in the years during and following National Socialism see Lybeck, *Desiring Emancipation*, 187; Marhoefer, *Sex*, 200.

176 See Schoppmann, 'The Position of Lesbian Women', in Grau and Schoppmann, *Hidden Holocaust?*, 9–15. For different experiences with categorization as 'asocials' or 'political' prisoners see the oral histories in Schoppmann, *Days of Masquerade*. For a broader analysis of gender in concentration camps see Caplan, 'Gender'.

177 See, in particular, Hájková, 'Sexuality, Holocaust'; Hájková and Mailänder, 'Forum: Holocaust'; Marhoefer, 'Lesbianism, Transvestitism'.

178 Huneke, 'Heterogeneous Persecution', 1–5 and 37 (on 'heterogeneous persecution'); Boxhammer and Leidinger, 'Sexismus'. In a similar vein, see Huneke's close study of the files of eight women investigated by the Gestapo in Huneke, 'Duplicity'.

179 Marhoefer, 'Lesbianism, Transvestitism', 1164–95 at 1173.

180 Marhoefer, 1173.

181 Marhoefer, 1194.

182 See also Vendrell's examination of the case of German-Jewish lesbian Martha Mosse for the way it unpacks intersections of gender, sexuality and collaboration accusations in early postwar West Germany: Vendrell, 'Case'.

183 Evans and Mailänder, 'Cross-Dressing,' 59.

184 Caplan, 'Administration,' 172.

185 Herrn, 'Transvestitismus in der NS-Zeit.'

186 Caplan, 'Administration,' 177. For more information on trans experiences under Nazism – and the relative dearth of research on this topic until very recently – see Herrn, 'Transvestitismus in der NS-Zeit'; Herrn, 'Über den Forschungsstand.'

187 Klöppel, 'Intersex.'

188 Hájková points out that such video testimonies are often oriented towards final scenes in which the witness is surrounded by loving children and grandchildren – archival patterns that can be affirming of family and the future for some, but can also make queer victims further invisible. Hájková, 'Holocaust,' 86–110, esp 90–4. See also Hájková, 'Sexuality, Holocaust'; Hájková, 'Queere Geschichte.'; Hájkova, *Menschen*. Other scholars point to the limitations imposed on witness accounts by survivors' own anxieties around queerness: Ramsden, 'Queer Fear,' 402–3.

189 Beck, *Erinnerungen*, 134.

190 Campt, *Other Germans*, 147.

191 Mouton, *Nurturing*, 64.

192 Heineman, *What Difference*, 46. See also Stibbe, *Women*, 154–5.

193 Mouton, *Nurturing*, 63.

194 Heineman, *What Difference*, 47–8.

195 Heineman, 48. On postmortem marriages see also Kundrus, *Kriegerfrauen*, 391–3; Mouton, *Nurturing*, 65–6; Stibbe, *Women*, 156.

196 Mouton, *Nurturing*, 66; Pine, *Nazi Family Policy*, 97; Stephenson, *Women in Nazi Germany*, 48.

197 Stephenson, *Women in Nazi Germany*, 47.

198 Kundrus, 'Forbidden Company,' 201; Stephenson, *Women in Nazi Germany*, 47.

199 Translated by and cited in Stibbe, *Women*, 155. For the German original quote in the context of a discussion of women's agency in National Socialism, see Heinsohn, *Zwischen Karriere*.

200 Cited in Kundrus, 'Forbidden Company,' 201–2.

201 Stephenson, *Women in Nazi Germany*, 47–8; Stibbe, *Women*, 157–8.

202 Kundrus, 'Forbidden Company,' 204.

203 Heineman, *What Difference*, 56. See also Stibbe, *Women*, 158.

204 Usborne, 'Female Sexual Desire,' 469. On these voluntary relationships and associated illegitimate births see also Joshi, 'Maternalism, Race,' 840–4.

205 Usborne, 'Female Sexual Desire,' 454–7 at 457.

206 Stibbe, *Women*, 155.

207 Kundrus, 'Forbidden Company,' 204. See also Beck, 'Vergewaltigung'; Seifert, 'Der weibliche Körper.' Mühlhäuser productively questions whether it is correct to view rape as an explicit 'strategy' of the Nazis, despite its pervasiveness: Mühlhäuser, 'Reframing Sexual Violence,' 366.

208 See, in particular, Beck, 'Rape'; Mühlhäuser, *Sex and the Nazi Soldier*; Timm, 'Sex with a Purpose.'

209 Mailänder, 'Making Sense,' 489, 493–4, 519.

210 Mühlhäuser, *Sex and the Nazi Soldier*. See also Mühlhäuser, 'Understanding Sexual Violence.'

211 Seifert, 'Der weibliche Körper,' 17–18; Sander and Johr, *BeFreier*, 62.

212 These statistics are from Beck, 'Vergewaltigung'; Grossmann, 'Question'; Tröger, 'Between Rape'; Stibbe, *Women*, 165–9.

213 Cited in Grossmann, 'Sex and Sexual Violence,' 139. First published in the 1950s, this diary received widespread attention when it was republished in the 2000s, before being made into a feature film: Anonymous, *A Woman in Berlin*.

214 On these legacies see especially Grossmann, 'Sex and Sexual Violence'; Grossmann, 'Question'; Heineman, 'Hour of the Woman'; Sander and Johr, *BeFreier*.

215 Beck, 'Vergewaltigung'; Glowacka, 'Sexual Violence.'

216 For rich reflections on these directions in recent research see Evans, 'Why Queer German History?'; Hájková and Mailänder, 'Forum: Holocaust'; Hájková, 'Sexuality, Holocaust.'

217 Hájková, 'Sexual Barter,' 503. See also Gusarov, 'Sexual Barter.'

218 Such work has helped to nuance analyses of relationships not overtly focused on sexuality, such as between working-class female SS guards and inmates. See Mailänder, *Female SS Guards*; Przyrembel, 'Transfixed.'

219 On the ongoing legacies of Nazi eugenics and euthanasia policies, see especially Herzog, *Unlearning Eugenics*.

220 Evans, 'Why Queer German History?,' 378.

Chapter 5

1 Kolano, '" … ein romantisches Ideal" (interview Kurt Starke).' Cited in Herzog, 'Sexual Evolution,' 83.

2 Herzog, 'Sexual Evolution,' 74; McLellan, *Love*, 25.

3 Ghodsee, *Why Women*.

4 Cited in Herzog, *Sex after Fascism*, 142.

5 Heineman, *Before Porn*.

6 Schwarzer, *Der 'kleine Unterschied,'* 10. See also Imke Schmincke, 'Sexualität als "Angelpunkt der Frauenfrage"?,' in Bänziger et al., *Sexuelle Revolution?*, 199–222 at 199.

7 Evans, *Life*, 7.

8 On this moment from a history of sexuality perspective see Evans, *Life*. For an overview of postwar German politics and society see Fulbrook, 'Ossis and Wessis'; Fulbrook, *Concise History*, 205–49.

9 Evans, 'Bahnhof Boys.'

10 Important examples of this approach include Bänziger et al., *Sexuelle Revolution?*; Evans, *Life*; Heineman, *What Difference*; Herzog, *Sex after Fascism*; Timm, *Politics of Fertility*. On 'entanglement' see Evans. Recent queer histories particularly highlight the advantages of viewing histories of law reform, policing, emancipation and memory politics, and queer culture through a pan-German lens; see Evans, *Queer Art*; Huneke, *States*; Rottmann, *Queer Lives*, and Chapter 6. Claudia Roesch's new study of the Pill situates itself slightly differently, as 'transnational' history: Roesch, *Wunschkinder*.

11 Poiger, *Jazz, Rock, and Rebels*, 225.

12 Cited in Heineman, *What Difference*, 108.

13 Herzog, *Sex after Fascism*, 64.

14 W. Byford-Jones, cited in Evans, *Life*, 7.

15 Arendt, cited in Grossmann, 'Trauma, Memory', 215.

16 Evans, *Life*, 27.

17 Evans, 28.

18 Evans, 39.

19 Timm, *Politics of Fertility*, 214–15.

20 Steinbacher, *Wie der Sex*, 87–8.

21 McLellan, *Love*. On the uses of this term see also Evans, *Life*, 78; Timm, *Politics of Fertility*, 214.

22 Evans, *Queer Art*, chapter 1.

23 Evans, *Life*, 67.

24 Evans, *Life*, 123–4. See also Evans, 'Bahnhof Boys'; Whisnant, *Male Homosexuality*, 12.

25 Evans, *Life*, 126–7, at 126.

26 Evans, 127. See also Evans, 'Bahnhof Boys.'

27 For 'reconstruction' arguments see in particular Moeller, 'Reconstructing'; Neumaier, *Familie*, 285.

28 Fulbrook, *History of Germany*, 234, 245–6.

29 Moeller, 'Reconstructing,' 111.

30 Moeller, 112–13.

31 Timm, *Politics of Fertility*. See also Moeller, 'Reconstructing.'

32 This is the title of chapter 3 in Herzog, *Sex after Fascism*, 101.

33 Neumaier, *Familie*, 285.

34 See discussion in Neumaier, *Familie*, 285–6.

35 Heineman, *What Difference*, 109–10 at 110.

36 Baumert, *Deutsche Familien nach dem Kriege*, 1954, cited in Neumaier, *Familie*, 287.

37 Neumaier, *Familie*, 287.

38 See, in particular, Heineman, 109–10, 137–75; Herzog, *Sex after Fascism*, 101–40; Meyer and Schulze, 'Frauen'; Moeller, *Protecting*.

39 Fulbrook, 'Ossis and Wessis,' 425.

40 Steinbacher, *Wie der Sex*, 182–3.

41 On the development of the new *Schund und Schmutz* laws see Steinbacher, 50ff; Timm, *Politics of Fertility*, 297.

42 Herzog, *Sex after Fascism*, 101ff.

43 Cited in Herzog, 102.

44 Poiger, *Jazz, Rock, and Rebels*, 218–23.

45 On the West German postwar morality movement see Steinbacher, *Wie der Sex*, 21–133; Herzog, *Sex after Fascism*, 101–40.

46 Herzog, *Sex after Fascism*, 194, see also 103. For a brief summary of these arguments see Herzog, 'Sexual Evolution,' 73.

47 Herzog, *Sex after Fascism*, 103–4.

48 Herzog, 104; Steinbacher, *Wie der Sex*, 86–7. For this psychoanalytic argument on privatization and Holocaust guilt see also Becker, 'Zur Funktion,' 142–3.

49 Steinbacher, *Wie der Sex*, 14–15.

50 See, in particular, Evans, *Queer Art*; Evans, *Life*; Evans, 'Bahnhof Boys.' See also Bauer and Cook, *Queer 1950s*.

51 Evans, *Life*, 71.

52 McLellan, *Love*, 2–3.

53 Fulbrook, 'Ossis and Wessis,' 425.

54 Harsch, *Revenge*, 133.

55 Harsch, 133.

56 Harsch, 133.

57 Betts, *Within Walls*, 90.

58 Harsch, 'Society, the State,' 57. See also Harsch, *Revenge*, 198; Fenemore, *Sex, Thugs*, 19.

59 Cited in Betts, *Within Walls*, 90. On shifting GDR family politics see also Chapter 7 of Timm, *Politics of Fertility*.

60 Cited in Betts, *Within Walls*, 90.

61 Cited in McLellan, *Love*, 1.

62 Cited in McLellan, 98, 113. For these broader trends, see Chapters 2–4 of McLellan, *Love*.

63 Neumaier, *Familie*, 291.

64 Cited in Betts, *Within Walls*, 100.

65 Moeller, *Protecting*, 71.

66 Neumaier, *Familie*, 293.

67 Herzog, 'Sexual Evolution,' 72.

68 Fulbrook, cited in Fenemore, *Sex, Thugs*, 20.

69 Cited in McLellan, *Love*, 74.

70 On the limits of the official rhetoric of socialist gender equality and sexual progressivism see McLellan, 69–82; Harsch, *Revenge*; Fenemore, *Sex, Thugs*, 19–36; Herzog, 'Sexual Evolution.'

71 McLellan, *Love*, 72–82.

72 Fulbrook, *People's State*, 166; Herzog, 'Sexual Evolution,' 72.

73 Müller, *Männerprotokolle*, 235. Cited in Fenemore, *Sex, Thugs*, 20.

74 Herzog, 'Sexual Evolution,' 91.

75 For examples of more nuanced recent work, see Kościańska, *Gender*; Kurimay, *Queer Budapest*; Lišková, *Sexual Liberation*.

76 Evans, *Life*, 11.

77 Herzog, *Sex after Fascism*, 188.

78 Betts, *Within Walls*, 90–1.

79 Harsch, *Revenge*, 134.

80 Betts, *Within Walls*, 90. On implications of the Law for fertility rights: Timm, *Politics of Fertility*, 249.

81 Moeller, 'Reconstructing,' 112–13.

82 Moeller, 114–15. See also Moeller, *Protecting*, 109ff.

83 Heineman, *What Difference*, 156; Timm, *Politics of Fertility*, 230–5.

84 Moeller, 'Reconstructing,' 114–22.

85 Heineman, *What Difference*, 156–7.

86 Heineman, 157–8.

87 Herzog, *Sex after Fascism*, 118.

88 Herzog, 119–20.

89 Herzog, 'Sexual Evolution,' 72.

90 Heineman, *What Difference*, 155.

91 Herzog, 'Sexual Evolution,' 72. On Catholic approaches to contraception see also Silies, 'Wider die natürliche Ordnung.'

92 Cited in Herzog, *Sex after Fascism*, 118–19, emphasis in original.

93 Neumaier, *Familie*, 289–90.

94 Heineman, *What Difference,* 122–3.

95 Cited in Heineman, 123.

96 Heineman, 131.

97 Heineman, 154.

98 Herzog, *Sex after Fascism*, 118.

99 Frevert, *Women*, 285.

100 Frevert, 286.

101 Fulbrook, 'Ossis and Wessis,' 415–16, 421.

102 McLellan, *Love*, 59.

103 McLellan, 42, 65.

104 McLellan, 42.

105 Volker V., twenty-five years old, graphic designer, interview in McLellan, *Love in the Time of Communism*, 89–90.

106 Schröter, *Ehe*, 29.

107 On the *Babyjahr* and the development of other pronatalist policies between the 1950s and 1970s see McLellan, *Love*, 65.

108 Heineman, *What Difference*, 176. On the combination of institutional structures and rhetoric that 'made women's work for wages not only possible but also much less guilt inducing', see also Herzog, 'Sexual Evolution,' 71, 84.

109 Heineman, *What Difference*, 177.

110 McLellan, *Love*, 56.

111 See, in particular, McLellan, chapter 3.

112 McLellan, 79; Betts, *Within Walls*, 98.

113 Cited in McLellan, *Love*, 41. Socialist sex advice texts often referenced the problems for young couples caused by living with parents: Herzog, 'Sexual Evolution,' 79.

114 Cited in Bronnen and Henny, *Liebe, Ehe*, 32–3.

115 In Bronnen and Henny, 32–3.

116 Betts, *Within Walls*, 88–115.

117 Schröter, *Ehe*, 58.

118 Betts, *Within Walls*, 95, 99, 103. On connections between GDR and older divorce patterns see Mouton, *Nurturing*, 71. On marriage counselling centres see Timm, *Politics of Fertility*, 280–90.

119 Betts, *Within Walls*, 111.

120 Betts, 95–7, at 97.

121 Betts, 101.

122 In Betts, 102.

123 Frau A., cited in Freeland, 'Domestic Abuse,' 253.

124 Freeland, 254.

125 Betts, *Within Walls*, 104–7 at 107. On the many women now in positions of workplace authority see Herzog, 'Sexual Evolution,' 85.

126 Betts, *Within Walls*, 100–1.

127 Betts, 107–9, citing Gaus at 109. On changing understandings of the GDR family and attitudes to divorce see also Harsch, *Revenge*; Mertens, *Wider*.

128 Betts, *Within Walls*, 112–13.

129 Cited in Schröter, *Ehe*, 59.

130 Anita Grandke, *Junge Leute in der Ehe*, 24–5, cited in Schröter, *Ehe*, 30.

131 Cited in Schröter, 32.

132 Schröter, 32–3.

133 Betts, *Within Walls*, 115.

134 McLellan, *Love*, 80.

135 In McLellan, 81.

136 McLellan, 82.

137 McLellan, 82.

138 McLellan, 98–100. On the West German 'sex wave' (*Sexwelle*) see Steinbacher, *Wie der Sex*, 295–324. Some historians use this term synonymously with 'sexual revolution', see Whisnant, *Male Homosexuality*, 10, 167–8.

139 Steinbacher, *Wie der Sex*, 166–7.

140 On the Kinsey Reports in Europe see Herzog, 'Reception'.

141 Steinbacher, *Wie der Sex*, 156–7, 161.

142 Cited in Steinbacher, 161.

143 Cited in Steinbacher, 191–2.

144 Herzog, 'Sexual Evolution', 72.

145 Sager, '"Zeig mal!,"' 63.

146 Sager, 63.

147 Sager, 73.

148 Whisnant, *Male Homosexuality*, 187–8.

149 Whisnant, 167.

150 On Uhse see especially Heineman, *Before Porn*, Steinbacher, *Wie der Sex*, 239-67. More broadly, see Eder, 'Die lange Geschichte'.

151 Herzog, *Sex after Fascism*, 141–5. On the 1970s 'sex films' see Miersch, *Schulmädchen-Report*.

152 Eder, 'Das Sexuelle beschreiben', 97. On postwar erotica and sex education literature see also Eder, 'Die lange Geschichte', 27–34.

153 'Müdes Lächeln', *Der Spiegel* 50 (1969): 82–101, cited in Eitler, 'Die "Porno-Welle,"' 87.

154 Eitler, 91–2.

155 Eitler, 93–4. On *Fanny Hill*, see also Eder, 'Die lange Geschichte', 38.

156 Eitler, 'Die "Porno-Welle,"' 89. On the growing erasure of representations of child sexuality between the 1970s and today see Angelides, 'Feminism, Child Sexual Abuse'. On intergenerational eroticism in postwar German queer contexts see Evans, 'Seeing Subjectivity'; Evans, 'Bahnhof Boys'.

157 Eitler, 'Die "Porno-Welle,"' 94–5. See also Hebditsch and Anning, *Porn Gold*; Lautmann and Schetsche, *Begehren*.

158 McLellan, *Love*, 86.

159 Herzog, 'Sexual Evolution', 82.

160 McLellan, *Love*, 89–90.

161 Cited in Harsch, *Revenge*, 134.

162 Cited in Herzog, 'Sexual Evolution', 74.

163 Cited in Herzog, 'Sexual Evolution', 88.

164 Cited in Herzog, *Sex after Fascism*, 211. See also Fenemore, *Sex, Thugs*, 32–3.

165 On Schnabl see Betts, *Within Walls*, 103; Herzog, *Sex after Fascism*, 212–13; McLellan, *Love*, 84–5.

166 Schnabl, *Mann und Frau*. This text is reproduced in Bronnen and Henny, *Liebe, Ehe*, 74.

167 Schnabl, 'Dämpft die Pille'.

168 McLellan, *Love*, 84.

169 Herzog, 'Sexual Evolution,' 87.

170 Herzog, 74–8. Alongside the marriage manual *Das neue Ehebuch*, Rudolf Neubert was the author of works including the 1968 sex education guide *Wie sag ich es meinem Kinde? Ratschläge für Eltern* (How do I tell my child? Advice for parents). See also Herzog, 'Sexual Evolution,' 74.

171 McLellan, *Love*, 89–90.

172 McLellan, *Love*, 32–3 at 33. See also Fenemore, 'Growing Pains'; Herzog, 'Sexual Evolution,' 86–7.

173 Allendorf and Hirsch, 'Auf dem Lehrplan,' 6.

174 Fenemore, *Sex, Thugs*, 102.

175 McLellan, *Love*, 32, 37.

176 Poiger, *Jazz, Rock, and Rebels*, 81; Fenemore, *Sex, Thugs*, 102.

177 See Herzog, 209–22; McLellan, *Love*, 24–37, 84–92.

178 Herzog, 'Sexual Evolution,' 85.

179 McLellan, *Love*, 100.

180 McLellan, 99.

181 Frackman, 'Homemade Pornography.'

Chapter 6

1   von Mahlsdorf, *Ich bin meine eigene Frau*, 105.

2   von Mahlsdorf, 105. For recent scholarship on Mahlsdorf, homing in on anglophone reception of her life story, see Baer, 'Translation'; Giersdorf, 'Representations.'

3   von Mahlsdorf, *Ich bin meine eigene Frau*, 175.

4   Herzog, 'Syncopated Sex,' 1295.

5   On the origins and progress of the student protest movement across several European contexts see Mercer, *Student Revolt*.

6   Eder, 'Die lange Geschichte,' 25–59, especially 25–6; Eder, 'Long History.'

7   Herzog, 'Sexual Evolution,' 71. See also Herzog, *Sex after Fascism*. For other critical accounts of 'sexual revolution' in Germany and Europe see Eder, 'Long History'; Bänziger et al., *Sexuelle Revolution?*

8   Poiger, *Jazz, Rock, and Rebels*, 3, on the 1950s youth riots and fashions see 71–105. On East German rebel and youth cultures see Fenemore, *Sex, Thugs*.

9   Poiger, *Jazz, Rock, and Rebels*, 77.

10   Poiger, 80.

11   Poiger, 72.

12   Poiger, 84–5.

13   Cited in Fenemore, *Sex, Thugs*, 23, see also 213–16 on 'deviant maschismo'. Fenemore cites this interview by Jürgen Lemke in Lemke, *Gay Voices*. He also points to the gendered tension between the feminizing 'preening' associated with perfect *Halbstarken* haircuts and the maintenance of masculine machismo: 139.

14 Poiger, *Jazz, Rock, and Rebels*, 35.

15 Fenemore, *Sex, Thugs*, 22–4 (citing Armin Schmolling at 24).

16 Steinbacher, *Wie der Sex*, 88–9.

17 Heineman, *What Difference*, 76–7 see also 95–102; Höhn, *GIs and Fräuleins*.

18 Poiger, *Jazz, Rock, and Rebels*, 36.

19 Poiger, 35–6. On links between fraternization, VD fears, and Black GIs, see also Timm, *Politics of Fertility*, 219–21.

20 Steinbacher, *Wie der Sex*, 102; Timm, *Politics of Fertility*, 294ff.

21 McLellan, *Love*, 89.

22 McLellan, 99.

23 McLellan, 101.

24 Fenemore, *Sex, Thugs*, 35–6.

25 McLellan, *Love*, 98–105, citing Wolf at 104.

26 Betts, *Within Walls*, 110. See also McLellan, 'State Socialist Bodies'; McLellan, *Love*, 144–204.

27 McLellan, 145.

28 McLellan, 145.

29 Fenemore, *Sex, Thugs*, 29, 34.

30 Herzog, 'Sexual Evolution,' 83.

31 McLellan cites historians Judith Kruse and Uli Linke: Kruse, 'Nische,' 111; Linke, *German Bodies*, 72.

32 McLellan, *Love*, 171–2.

33 Whisnant, *Male Homosexuality*, 167, 198.

34 This summary draws closely on Poiger, *Jazz, Rock, and Rebels*, 218–23. See also Timm, *Politics of Fertility*, 308–17; Herzog, *Sex after Fascism*, 141–8; Bänziger et al., *Sexuelle Revolution?* For a rich collection of articles, videos and other sources on the 1968 movement see the BPB 'Dossier: 68er-Bewegung' at https://www.bpb.de/geschichte/deutsche-geschichte/68er-bewegung/.

35 Poiger, *Jazz, Rock, and Rebels*, 218–19. On the Prague spring see also 'Prag 1968' in https://www.bpb.de/geschichte/zeitgeschichte/prag-1968/.

36 McLellan, *Love*, 12; Betts, *Within Walls*, 12.

37 See discussion of this film in the context of shifting gender roles in McLellan, *Love*, 69–70.

38 Poiger, *Jazz, Rock, and Rebels*, 220. See also McCormick, *Politics*.

39 McLellan, *Love*, 43, 94–6. This quote from the GDR's chief public prosecutor is reproduced at p. 94.

40 Bronnen and Henny, *Liebe, Ehe*, 15.

41 Volker Petzold, in McLellan, *Love*, 95.

42 McLellan, 38–40; Herzog, 'Sexual Evolution,' 79.

43 Herzog, 170.

44 Cited in Freeland, 'Women's Bodies,' 131.

45 Freeland, 132.

46 Usborne, *Politics*, xiii.

47 Cited in Poiger, *Jazz, Rock, and Rebels*, 221.

48 Frevert, *Women*, 287–303; Freeland, 'Women's Bodies.'

49 Freeland, 132.

50 Cited in Schmincke, 'Sexualität,' 199.

51 Afken, 'From Sisters' Skin.'

52 Freeland, 'Women's Bodies,' 133.

53 Herzog, *Sexuality in Europe*, 171.

54 Freeland, 'Women's Bodies,' 134.

55 Carter, 'Alice.'

56 Steinbacher, *Wie der Sex*, 334. In recent decades, *Bravo*'s Dr. Sommer has moved online: https://www.bravo.de/dr-sommer.

57 Wander, *Guten Morgen*, see also McLellan, Love, 23.

58 Wander, *Guten Morgen*, 13. On Wander's collection and other examples of oral history, interviews or *Protokolle* from this era, see Betts, *Within Walls*, 110; McLellan, Love, 23–4.

59 Herzog, 'Sexual Evolution,' 84.

60 Based on such factors, Fenemore diagnoses a much more 'seismic' shift in GDR attitudes to sexuality around 1968 than Herzog, see esp. Fenemore, *Sex, Thugs*, 33.

61 Cited in Herzog, 'Sexual Evolution,' 90.

62 Herzog, 87.

63 Cited in Herzog, *Sex after Fascism*, 147.

64 Cited in Eder, 'Die lange Geschichte,' 34; Staupe and Vieth, *Die Pille*, 13, 209.

65 Herzog, *Sex after Fascism*, 147.

66 Eder, 'Die lange Geschichte,' 35–6. On the history of the Pill in West Germany see also Roesch, *Wunschkinder*, 138–68; Staupe and Vieth, *Die Pille*.

67 See Roesch, *Wunschkinder*, 7, 153. On the history of the Pill in East Germany see also Leo and König, *Die 'Wunschkindpille'*; Roesch, 'Pro Familia,' 298; Staupe and Vieth, *Die Pille*.

68 McLellan, *Love*, 61. See also Staupe and Vieth, *Die Pille*; Eder, 'Die lange Geschichte,' 34.

69 Wander, *Guten Morgen*, 28.

70 McLellan, *Love*, 61–2, interviewee cited at 61.

71 Harsch, 'Society, the State,' 56; Grossmann, 'Question'; Poutrus, 'Massenvergewaltigungen,' 188–98.

72 Harsch, 'Society, the State,' 57.

73 Harsch, 58–60.

74 Cited in McLellan, *Love*, 63–4.

75 Cited in Harsch, 'Society, the State,' 68.

76 McLellan, *Love*, 57–9.

77 Harsch, 'Society, the State,' 53–4.

78 McLellan, *Love*, 57–8.

79 Harsch, 'Society, the State,' 53–4.

80 Freeland, 'Women's Bodies,' 132; Frevert, *Women*, 287–303, especially 294–5; Steinbacher, *Wie der Sex*, 241.

81 Freeland, 'Women's Bodies,' 132.

82 Frevert, *Women*, 294–5. On 1970s West German abortion reform see also Roesch, *Wunschkinder*, 206–44.

83 Cited in Roesch, 'Pro Familia,' 297. Emphasis in original. On feminist versus Catholic positions on abortion see Heinemann, '"Enttäuschung unvermeidlich?"'. Roesch's article offers a detailed survey of literature on West German abortion debates, including the positions of the two leading Christian denominations.

84 Roesch, 'Pro Familia,' 298–9. See also Roesch, *Wunschkinder*, 81–107.

85 Roesch, 'Pro Familia,' 298.

86 Herzog, *Sexuality in Europe*, 115.

87 Herzog, *Unlearning Eugenics*, 30.

88 Roesch, 'Pro Familia,' 309. On intersections between eugenic thinking, sterilization and family planning for poor and minority groups in West Germany see also Roesch, *Wunschkinder*, 108–37.

89 On the prominence of trans activists in these riots see Stryker, *Transgender History*, 82–6.

90 Evans, *Life*, 123–4.

91 Evans, 126.

92 See, in particular, Griffiths, *Ambivalence*; Huneke, *States*; Whisnant, *Male Homosexuality*.

93 Evans, 'Decriminalization,' 577.

94 On these historical links, see Sieg, 'Deviance.' See also Stümke, *Homosexuelle*, 97–9.

95 Whisnant, *Male Homosexuality*, 12; Evans, *Life*; McLellan, *Love*, 114–43.

96 Cited in McLellan, *Love*, 139.

97 Bühner, 'Rise,' 150. See also the forthcoming Rottmann, *Queer Lives*.

98 Eder, 'Die lange Geschichte,' 36.

99 Whisnant, *Male Homosexuality*, 1–12 and passim.

100 A. Ohm, 'Homosexualität als Neurose,' *Der Weg zur Seele*, 1953, cited in Herzog, *Sexuality in Europe*, 121.

101 Whisnant, *Male Homosexuality*.

102 Dannecker, 'Wunsch,' 37. As cited in Eder, 'Die lange Geschichte,' 36. Dannecker was also co-author of an influential 1970s study of 'ordinary' West German male homosexuality: Dannecker and Reiche, *Der gewöhnliche Homosexuelle*. On the

normalizing tendency of much 1940s–1960s gay activism see Gammerl, 'Männliche Homosexualitäten,' 229–33.

103 Whisnant, *Male Homosexuality*, 66–7, Werres cited at 67. On this magazine and the homophile and art scenes that surrounded it, see Stefan Haupt's 2014 Swiss docudrama *The Circle (Der Kreis)*, and Steinle, *Der Kreis*.

104 Whisnant, *Male Homosexuality*, 64–111 on the broader FRG homophile movement.

105 Cited in Gammerl, 'Männliche Homosexualitäten,' 229.

106 Whisnant, *Male Homosexuality*, 72. On Giese and postwar West German sexual science see also Sigusch, *Geschichte*, 391–414.

107 Eder, 'Die lange Geschichte,' 37. See also Plötz, 'Lesbierinnen.'

108 Evans, *Life*.

109 Whisnant, *Male Homosexuality*, 10. On gender-nonconforming styles and cultures during these decades see Evans, *Queer Art*.

110 Evans, *Life*, 179–80, Mahlsdorf cited at 180.

111 Evans revisits her assessment of this bar's significance from the perspective of queer kinship in Evans, *Queer Art*.

112 Timm and Sanborn, *Gender, Sex*, 244.

113 Könne, 'Schwule und Lesben'; McLellan, *Love*, 117. For a detailed analysis of the pre-1968 legal situation see Grau, 'Return.'

114 Dickinson, 'Policing Sex,' 240.

115 Whisnant, *Male Homosexuality*, 203.

116 Whisnant, 3, 13, 166–203. On these religious arguments see also Herzog, *Sex after Fascism*, 73.

117 Whisnant, *Male Homosexuality*, 177.

118 Cited in Herzog, 'Sexual Evolution,' 76–7, at 76. See also Evans, 'Decriminalization.'

119 Davison, 'Cold War Pavlov.' On GDR sexology see also the chapter by Günter Grau in Sigusch, *Geschichte*, 487–509.

120 Fenemore, *Sex, Thugs*, 33.

121 McLellan, *Love*, 115–17 at 116. See also Grau, 'Ein Leben.'

122 Cited in Whisnant, *Male Homosexuality*, 170.

123 This is the subtitle of a recent collection on German 1970s queer history: Afken and Wolf, *Sexual Culture*.

124 Sieg, 'Deviance,' 97–9.

125 Frackman, 'Homemade Pornography.'

126 Cited and discussed in Whisnant, *Male Homosexuality*, 205.

127 Whisnant, 206. Influential studies of postwar German gay liberation, many of which focus on particular cities, include Dobler, *Von anderen Ufern*; Griffiths, 'Sex, Shame'; Griffiths, *Ambivalence*; Mildenberger, *Die Münchner Schwulenbewegung*; Rosenkranz, Bollmann, and Lorenz, *Homosexuellen-Verfolgung in Hamburg 1919–1969*; Steakley, *Homosexual Emancipation*;

Sternweiler and Hannesen, *Goodbye to Berlin?*; Stümke, *Homosexuelle*. New studies foregrounding connections between gay movements in West and East, and links to longer legacies of National Socialism include Evans, *Queer Art*; Huneke, *States*; and Newsome, *Pink Triangle*.

128 On West German lesbian activism in the 1970s see especially Dennert, Leidinger, and Rauchut, 'Lesben.'

129 For further discussion of this approach see Evans, *Queer Art*.

130 Gammerl, 'Männliche Homosexualitäten,' 224.

131 Florvil, *Mobilizing*. For one of the central texts of this Black feminist movement, see Oguntoye, *Farbe*.

132 In particular, see Gammerl, 'Männliche Homosexualitäten.'

133 Interviewed by and cited in Gammerl, 232.

134 Griffiths, 'Der Tuntenstreit.'

135 Gammerl, 'Männliche Homosexualitäten,' 232. As Evans shows, attitudes to male sex workers had been ambivalent since the early postwar years; see Evans, 'Bahnhof Boys.' On tensions surrounding the leather and fetish scenes see Griffiths, 'Sex, Shame'; Whisnant, 'Styles.'

136 Griffiths, *Ambivalence*, 30.

137 McLellan, *Love*, 120. See also McLellan, 'Glad to Be Gay.'

138 Stapel's interview is from Starke, *Schwuler Osten*, 100. See also von Mahlsdorf, *Ich bin meine eigene Frau*, 173.

139 Fenemore, *Sex, Thugs*, 214. On gay life in the GDR more broadly see Setz, *Homosexualität*.

140 McLellan, *Love*, 48–50, 'Stefan' cited at 49.

141 Frackman, 'Homemade Pornography.' See also McLellan, 'Glad to Be Gay.'

142 Frackman, 'Homemade Pornography,' 97.

143 Rottmann, 'Bubis,' 226. See also Rottmann's forthcoming monograph for a broader exploration of pan-German queer cultures in the decades following the war: Rottmann, *Queer Lives*.

144 von Mahlsdorf, *Ich bin meine eigene Frau*, 175.

145 McLellan, *Love*, 121.

146 McLellan, 121–2. See also McLellan, 'Glad to Be Gay'; Huneke, *States*.

147 McLellan, *Love*, 123–4; Gabriele S. cited at 124.

148 Bühner, 'Rise,' 150.

149 McLellan, *Love*, 127–8.

150 Bühner, 'Rise,' 152.

151 Bühner, 152–5 and passim.

152 Bühner, 'Rise.' See also Könne, 'Schwule und Lesben.'

153 Sieg, 'Deviance,' 101–2; McLellan, *Love*, 122–9; Bühner, 'Rise,' 156. The efforts of GDR lesbians to create recognition of historical persecutions at Ravensbrück have been traced in detail by GDR sociologists and activists Ursula Sillge and Samirah Kenawi,

and examined in recent scholarship, for example, Bryant, 'Queering'; Evans, *Queer Art*, chapter 4; Kenawi, *Frauengruppen*; Sillge, *Un-Sichtbare Frauen*.

154 Augstein, *Transsexuellengesetz*.

155 McLellan, *Love*, 131–2.

156 See Chapter 3 of Evans, *Queer Art*.

157 On these transatlantic links and networks forged between medical and non-medical individuals and groups, see Timm, 'Trans Circles.'

158 See Klöppel, *XX0XY ungelöst*. See also the following helpful review and summary of Klöppel's expansive study: Stoff, 'Rezensionen. Ulrike Klöppel,' 62–4. On the failure of Money's experiments in relation to the David Reimer 'John/Joan' case, see Butler, *Undoing Gender*, 57–74.

159 Timm and Sanborn, *Gender, Sex*, 248; see also Herzog, *Sexuality in Europe*, 177.

160 McLellan, *Love*, 141; Timm and Sanborn, *Gender, Sex*, 245.

161 Beljan, 'Unlust.'

162 Beljan, 327.

163 See activist Ulrich Würdemann's memoirs of and documentary on the German ACT UP movement in the early 1990s: Würdemann, *Schweigen*.

164 Timm and Sanborn, *Gender, Sex*, 245.

165 Hark, *Koalitionen*, 27–8.

166 Herzog, *Sexuality in Europe*, 183.

Conclusion

1 Osmond, 'End of the GDR,' 463.

2 Dennis, 'Coming Out,' 55. On the film's depiction of the ambivalence of LGBTIQ politics under state socialism see also Frackman, 'East German.' The film can be rented from the DEFA film library at the University of Massachusetts: https://ecommerce. umass.edu/defa/film/3538.

3 Sieg, 'Deviance,' 102–4. Lemke's work was also translated into English; see Lemke, *Gay Voices*; Gutsche, *Ich ahnungsloser*.

4 Sieg, 'Deviance,' 105.

5 Sieg, 'Revolution,' 39.

6 Sieg, 39.

7 On the ways in which this transition was represented in the media see also Sharp, 'Sexual Unification.'

8 Herzog, 'Sexual Evolution,' 88.

9 Cited in McLellan, *Love*, 205–6.

10 McLellan, 145, 171.

11 McLellan, 145.

12 Herzog, citing a conversation with Kurt Starke, in Herzog, 'Sexual Evolution,' 89.

13 Herzog, 89–90.

14 Herzog, 90.

15 Lewis, *Eine schwierige Ehe*.

16 Herzog, 'Sexual Evolution', 88.

17 Herzog, 88. For a detailed analysis of these legal reforms and debates see Maleck-Lewy, 'Between Self-Determination'.

18 For an article and podcast reflecting on these legal changes via a series of interviews, see Fiebig, 'Drei Jahre'.

19 For a detailed English-language account of this ruling see the Court's press release: Bundesverfassungsgericht/Federal Constitutional Court, 'Requirements for the Legal Recognition'.

20 'Der wichtigste Satz'; Neukirch, 'Westerwelle'.

21 Reuters, 'Two Transgender Women'.

22 For these critiques in the German context, see especially Marhoefer, *Racism*; Evans, *Queer Art*. For a broader critique of 'homonormativity' and its distinctly nationalist framing, see Puar, *Terrorist*.

23 'Judith Butler drückt die Spaßbremse'; Kögel et al., 'Heftige Diskussionen'.

24 For discussion of these issues see Hark and Villa, *Anti-Genderismus*.

25 See especially Bauer, *Hirschfeld Archives*; Evans, 'Harmless Kisses'; Evans, *Queer Art*; Marhoefer, *Racism*; Leng, 'Historicising'; Marhoefer, 'Race, Empire'.

26 Marhoefer, 92–3. See also Marhoefer, *Racism*.

27 El-Tayeb, 'Queer Muslims'; Haritaworn, *Queer Lovers*.

28 Herzog, *Sexuality in Europe*, 203.

29 A striking example of this is the collection l'Amour laLove, *Beissreflexe*. For a critical survey see Rehberg, 'Gender-Stasi'.

30 Herzog, *Sexuality in Europe*, 198–9.

31 Anderson and Benbow, 'Christoph Meiners' History'.

32 Herzog, *Sexuality in Europe*, 199.

33 Benbow, *Marriage*.

34 For an English-language explanation of these laws, see https://www.bmi.bund.de/SharedDocs/faqs/EN/topics/migration/staatsang/Erwerb_der_deutschen_Staatsangehoerigkeit_durch_Geburt_en.html.

35 Herzog, *Sexuality in Europe*, 200–1.

36 For a feminist analysis of events, see Garraio, 'Cologne'.

37 Hark and Villa, *Unterscheiden*, 9.

38 Herzog, *Sexuality in Europe*, 200–1.

39 On this, see in particular Evans, *Queer Art*.

40 Testament to the ongoing influence of homophobia in shaping public perceptions of this period and its victims are the controversies surrounding research on queer Holocaust experience. For discussion of these issues see: Hájková, 'Holocaust', 110; Grothe, 'Lesbische Beziehungen'.

41 See Hájková and Bosold, *Tagesspiegel* 20 November 2017 ('Ich wollte nicht sterben … '); Bryant, 'Queering.' On the 2022 placing of the 'Gedenkkugel' see video report: Demnitz, 'Lesbische Geschichte wird sichtbar.' https://www.tagesspiegel.de/gesellschaft/queerspiegel/gedenkkugel-in-ravensbrueck-lesbische-geschichte-wird-sichtbar/28308604.html.

42 On debates around these memorials see Huneke, 'Duplicity,' 30–1; Endlich, 'Das Berliner Homosexuellen-Denkmal'; Evans, 'Harmless Kisses'; Oettler, 'The Berlin Memorial'; Tomberger, 'Das Berliner Homosexuellen-Denkmal.'

43 Jensen, 'Pink Triangle,' 320. See also Newsome, *Pink Triangle Legacies.*

44 Pearce, 'Remembering.' For the online memorial site to T4 victims, see https://www.gedenkort-t4.eu/de.

45 Herzog, *Sexuality in Europe*, 198.

46 Herzog, 212–13.

BIBLIOGRAPHY

Abrams, Lynn. 'Companionship and Conflict: The Negotiation of Marriage Relations in the Nineteenth Century.' In *Gender Relations in German History: Power, Agency and Experience from the Sixteenth to the Twentieth Century*, edited by Lynn Abrams, and Elizabeth Harvey, 101–20. London: UCL Press, 1996.

Abrams, Lynn. 'Prostitutes in Imperial Germany, 1870–1918: Working Girls or Social Outcasts?' In *The German Underworld: Deviants and Outcasts in German History*, edited by Richard Evans, 189–209. London and New York: Routledge, 1991.

Adams, Mary Louise. *The Trouble with Normal: Postwar Youth and the Making of Heterosexuality*. Toronto: University of Toronto Press, 1997.

Afken, Janin. 'From Sisters' Skin to Womb Ego: Temporality, Solidarity and Corporeality in Verena Stefan's "Shedding" (1975).' In *Sexual Culture in Germany in the 1970s: A Golden Age for Queers?*, edited by Janin Afken, and Benedikt Wolf, 119–38. Cham: Springer Nature, 2019.

Afken, Janin, and Benedikt Wolf, eds. *Sexual Culture in Germany in the 1970s*. Cham: Springer Nature, 2019.

Ahmed, Sara. 'Gender Critical = Gender Conservative.' *Feministkilljoys* (blog), 31 October 2021. https://feministkilljoys.com/2021/10/31/gender-critical-gender-conservative/.

Aldrich, Robert. *Colonialism and Homosexuality*. London: Routledge, 2003.

Allen, Ann Taylor. 'Feminism and Eugenics in Germany and Britain, 1900–1940: A Comparative Perspective.' *German Studies Review* 23, no. 3 (2000): 477–505.

Allen, Ann Taylor. *Feminism and Motherhood in Germany, 1800–1914*. New Brunswick: Rutgers University Press, 1991.

Allen, Ann Taylor. 'German Radical Feminism and Eugenics, 1900–1908.' *German Studies Review* 11, no. 1 (1988): 31–56.

Allen, Ann Taylor. 'Gender.' In *The Ashgate Research Companion to Imperial Germany*, edited by Matthew Jeffries, 225–44. London: Routledge, 2015.

Allendorf, Marlis, and Ingeburg Hirsch. 'Auf dem Lehrplan steht die Liebe.' *Für Dich*, no. 12, March 1972.

Aly, Götz. 'Medicine against the Useless.' In *Cleansing the Fatherland: Nazi Medicine and Racial Hygiene*, edited by Götz Aly, Peter Chroust, and Christian Pross, translated by Belinda Cooper, 22–98. Baltimore and London: Johns Hopkins University Press, 1994.

Aly, Götz, and Michael Sontheimer. *Fromms. Wie der jüdische Kondomfabrikant Julius F. unter die deutschen Räuber fiel*. Frankfurt am Main: S. Fischer, 2007.

Anderson, Lara, and Heather Benbow. 'Christoph Meiners' History of the Female
    Sex (1788–1800): The Orientalisation of Spain and German Nationalism.'
    History of European Ideas 35, no. 4 (2009): 433–40.
Angelides, Steven. 'Feminism, Child Sexual Abuse, and the Erasure of Child
    Sexuality.' *GLQ: A Journal of Lesbian and Gay Studies* 10, no. 2 (2004):
    141–77.
Ankum, Katharina von, ed. *Women in the Metropolis. Gender and Modernity in
    Weimar Culture.* Berkeley: University of California Press, 1997.
Anonymous. *A Woman in Berlin.* London: Virago, 2011.
Applegate, Celia. *A Nation of Provincials: The German Idea of Heimat.* Berkeley:
    University of California Press, 1990.
Ariès, Philippe. *Centuries of Childhood; A Social History of Family Life.* Translated
    by Robert Baldick. New York: Knopf, 1962.
Arondekar, Anjali, Ann Cvetkovich, Christina B. Hanhardt, Regina Kunzel, Tavia
    Nyong'o, Juana Maria Rodríguez, and Susan Stryker. 'Queering Archives: A
    Roundtable Discussion.' Edited by Daniel Marshall, Kevin P. Murphy, and Zeb
    Tortorici. *Radical History Review* 2015, no. 122 (May 2015): 211–31.
Augstein, Maria Sabine. *Transsexuellengesetz.* Baden-Baden: Nomos, 2012.
'Aus der Kriegszeit.' *Vierteljahresberichte des Wissenschaftlich-humanitären
    Komitees während der Kriegszeit. Herausgegeben statt des Jahrbuch für sexuelle
    Zwischenstufen mit besonderer Berücksichtigung der Homosexualität* 17, no. 4
    (1917): 155, 158.
Baer, Brian James. 'Translation, Transition, Transgender: Framing the Life of
    Charlotte von Mahlsdorf.' *TSQ: Transgender Studies Quarterly* 3, no. 3–4
    (2016): 506–23.
Bakhtin, Mikhail. *Rabelais and His World.* Translated by Helene Iswolsky.
    Bloomington: Indiana University Press, 1984.
Bakker, Alex, Rainer Herrn, Michael Thomas Taylor, and Annette F. Timm, eds.
    Others of My Kind: Transatlantic Transgender Histories, Calgary: University of
    Calgary Press, 2020.
Baldwin, Claire. 'Anna Louisa Karsch as Sappho.' *Women in German Yearbook* 20
    (2004): 62–97.
Bänziger, Peter-Paul, Magdalena Beljan, Franz X. Eder, and Pascal Eitler, eds.
    *Sexuelle Revolution? Zur Geschichte der Sexualität im deutschsprachigen Raum
    seit den 1960er Jahren.* Bielefeld: Transcript, 2015.
Bauer, Heike. '"Race," Normativity and the History of Sexuality: The Case
    of Magnus Hirschfeld's Racism and Early Twentieth-Century Sexology.'
    Psychology and Sexuality 1, no. 3 (2010): 239–49.
Bauer, Heike. *The Hirschfeld Archives: Violence, Death, and Modern Queer
    Culture.* Philadelphia: Temple University Press, 2017.
Bauer, Heike, and Matt Cook, eds. *Queer 1950s: Rethinking Sexuality in the
    Postwar Years.* New York: Palgrave Macmillan, 2012.
Bauer, Heike, Melina Pappademos, Katie Sutton, and Jennifer Tucker. 'Visual
    Histories of Sex: Collecting, Curating, Archiving.' *Radical History Review*, no.
    142 (2022): 1–18.
Beachy, Robert. *Gay Berlin: Birthplace of a Modern Identity.* New York: Knopf,
    2014.
Beachy, Robert. 'The German Invention of Homosexuality.' *The Journal of Modern
    History* 82, no. 4 (2010): 801–38.

Beck, Birgit. 'Rape: The Military Trials of Sexual Crimes Committed by Soldiers in the Wehrmacht, 1939–1944.' In *Home/Front: The Military, War and Gender in Twentieth-Century Germany*, edited by Karen Hagemann, and Stefanie Schüler-Springorum, 255–73. Oxford and New York: Berg, 2002.

Beck, Birgit. 'Vergewaltigung von Frauen als Kriegsstrategie im Zweiten Weltkrieg.' In *Gewalt im Krieg: Ausübung, Erfahrung und Verweigerung von Gewalt in Kriegen des 20. Jahrhunderts*, edited by Andreas Gestrich, 34–51. Münster: Lit, 1996.

Beck, Gad. *Und Gad ging zu David: Die Erinnerungen des Gad Beck 1923 bis 1945*. Edited by Frank Heibert. Berlin: Edition diá, 1995.

Beck, Gad, and Frank Heibert. *An Underground Life: Memoirs of a Gay Jew in Nazi Berlin*. Translated by Allison Brown. Madison: University of Wisconsin Press, 1999.

Becker, Sophinette. 'Zur Funktion der Sexualität im Nationalsozialismus.' *Zeitschrift für Sexualforschung* 14, no. 2 (2001): 130–45.

Beljan, Magdalena. '"Unlust bei der Lust"? Aids, HIV & Sexualität in der BRD.' In *Sexuelle Revolution?*, edited by Peter-Paul Bänziger et al., 323–45. Bielefeld: Transcript, 2015.

Benbow, Heather. *Marriage in Turkish German Popular Culture: States of Matrimony in the New Millennium*. Lanham: Lexington, 2015.

Bennett, Judith M. '"Lesbian-Like" and the Social History of Lesbianisms.' *Journal of the History of Sexuality* 9, no. 1–2 (January 2000): 1–24.

Berghahn, Volker R. *Imperial Germany, 1871–1914: Economy, Society, Culture, and Politics*. Providence, Oxford: Berghahn, 1994.

Berghahn, Volker R. *Modern Germany: Society, Economy, and Politics in the Twentieth Century*. 2nd ed. Cambridge: Cambridge University Press, 1987.

'Bericht über das erste Tätigkeitsjahr (1. Juli 1919 bis 30. Juni 1920) des Instituts für Sexualwissenschaft.' *Jahrbuch für sexuelle Zwischenstufen* 20 (1920): 54–74.

Bertschik, Julia. *Mode und Moderne: Kleidung als Spiegel des Zeitgeistes in der deutschsprachigen Literatur (1770–1945)*. Cologne: Böhlau, 2005.

Betts, Paul. *Within Walls: Private Life in the German Democratic Republic*. Oxford: Oxford University Press, 2010.

Beutin et al., Wolfgang. *Deutsche Literaturgeschichte von den Anfängen bis zur Gegenwart*. 8th ed. Stuttgart, Weimar: Metzler, 2013.

Birken, Lawrence. *Consuming Desire: Sexual Science and the Emergence of a Culture of Abundance, 1871–1914*. Ithaca: Cornell University Press, 1988.

Blackbourn, David. 'Europeanizing German History: Comment on the Eighteenth Annual Lecture of the GHI, November 18, 2004.' *GHI Bulletin* 36 (Spring 2005): 25–32.

Blackbourn, David. *History of Germany 1780–1918: The Long Nineteenth Century*. 2nd ed. Malden, MA: Blackwell, 2003.

Blackbourn, David. 'The German Bourgeoisie: An Introduction.' In *The German Bourgeoisie: Essays on the Social History of the German Middle Class from the Late Eighteenth to the Early Twentieth Century*, edited by David Blackbourn, and Richard J. Evans, 1–45. London: Routledge, 1991.

Blackbourn, David, and Richard J. Evans, eds. *The German Bourgeoisie: Essays on the Social History of the German Middle Class from the Late Eighteenth to the Early Twentieth Century*. London: Routledge, 1991.

Blank, Hanne. *Straight: The Surprisingly Short History of Heterosexuality*. Boston: Beacon Press, 2012.

Bloch, Iwan. *Beiträge zur Aetiologie der Psychopathia sexualis. Mit einer Vorrede von Albert Eulenburg*. Dresden: Dohrn, 1902.

Bloch, Iwan. *Das Sexualleben unserer Zeit in seinen Beziehungen zur modernen Kultur*. Berlin: Marcus, 1907.

Boak, Helen. *Women in the Weimar Republic*. Manchester: Manchester University Press, 2013.

Bock, Gisela. 'Antinatalism, Maternity, and Paternity in National Socialist Racism.' In *Nazism and German Society, 1933–1945*, edited by David F. Crew, 110–40. London and New York: Routledge, 1994.

Bock, Gisela. 'Racism and Sexism in Nazi Germany. Motherhood, Compulsory Sterilization, and the State.' *Signs* 8, no. 3 (1983): 400–21.

Bock, Gisela. *Zwangssterilisation im Nationalsozialismus. Studien zur Rassenpolitik und Geschlechterpolitik*. Münster: MV-Wissenschaft, 2010.

Body, N. O. *Memoirs of a Man's Maiden Years*. Translated by Deborah Simon. Philadelphia: University of Pennsylvania Press, 2005.

Bollé, Michael, ed. *Eldorado: Homosexuelle Frauen und Männer in Berlin 1850-1950. Geschichte, Alltag und Kultur*. Berlin: Rosa Winkel, 1984.

Boonstra, John. 'Women's Honour and the Black Shame: "Coloured Frenchmen" and Respectable Comportment in the Post-World War I Occupied Rhineland.' *German History* 33, no. 4 (2015): 546–69.

Boswell, John. *The Marriage of Likeness: Same-Sex Unions in Pre-Modern Europe*. London: HarperCollins, 1995.

Boxhammer, Ingeborg, and Christiane Leidinger. 'Sexismus, Heteronormativität und (staatliche) Öffentlichkeit im Nationalsozialismus. Eine queer-feministische Perspektive auf die Verfolgung von Lesben und/oder Trans* im (straf-) rechtlichen Kontexten.' In *Homosexuelle im Nationalsozialismus*, edited by Michael Schwartz, 93–100. München: De Gruyter, 2014.

Bramberger, Andrea. *Verboten Lieben: Bruder-Schwester-Inzest*. Pfaffenweiler: Centaurus, 1998.

Braun, Christina von. *Blutsbande. Verwandtschaft als Kulturgeschichte*. Berlin: Aufbau, 2018.

Braun, Christina von. 'Die "Blutschande." Wandlungen eines Begriffs: Vom Inzesttabu zu den Rassegesetzen.' In *Die schamlose Schönheit des Vergangenen. Zum Verhältnis von Geschlecht und Geschichte*, edited by Christina von Braun, 81–111. Frankfurt am Main: Neue Kritik, 1989.

Braun, Karl. *Die Krankheit Onania. Körperangst und die Anfänge moderner Sexualität im 18. Jahrhundert*. Frankfurt: Campus, 1996.

Braun, Lily. *Selected Writings on Feminism and Socialism*. Bloomington: Indiana University Press, 1987.

Breger, Claudia. 'Feminine Masculinities: Scientific and Literary Representations of "Female Inversion" at the Turn of the Twentieth Century.' *Journal of the History of Sexuality* 14, no. 1/2 (January 2005): 76–106.

Breuilly, John, ed. *Nineteenth-Century Germany: Politics, Culture, and Society 1780–1918*. London: Arnold, 2001.

Breul, Wolfgang. 'Celibacy – Marriage – Unmarriage: The Controversy over Celibacy and Clerical Marriage in the Early Reformation.' In *Mixed Matches: Trangressive Unions in Germany from the Reformation to the Enlightenment*, edited by David M. Luebke, and Mary Lindemann, 31–44. New York: Berghahn, 2014.

Bridenthal, Renate, and Claudia Koonz. 'Beyond Kinder, Küche, Kirche: Weimar Women in Politics and Work.' In *When Biology Became Destiny: Women in Weimar and Nazi Germany*, edited by Renate Bridenthal, Atina Grossmann, and Marion Kaplan, 33–65. New York: Monthly Review Press, 1984.

Bridenthal, Renate, Atina Grossmann, and Marion Kaplan, eds. *When Biology Became Destiny: Women in Weimar and Nazi Germany*. New York: Monthly Review Press, 1984.

Bronnen, Barbara, and Franz Henny, eds. *Liebe, Ehe, Sexualität in der DDR*. München: R. Piper, 1975.

Brown, Judith. *Immodest Acts: The Life of a Lesbian Nun in Renaissance Italy*. New York: Oxford University Press, 1986.

Brundage, James A. *Law, Sex, and Christian Society in Medieval Europe*. Chicago: University of Chicago Press, 1987.

Bruns, Claudia. 'The Politics of Masculinity in the (Homo-)Sexual Discourse (1880–1920).' *German History* 23, no. 2 (2005): 306–20.

Bryant, Dara. 'Queering the Antifascist State: Ravensbrück as a Site of Lesbian Resistance.' *Edinburgh German Yearbook* 3. Contested Legacies: Constructions of Cultural Heritage in the GDR (2009): 76–89.

Bühler, Charlotte. *Das Seelenleben des Jugendlichen. Versuch einer Analyse und Theorie der psychischen Pubertät*. Jena: Fischer, 1929.

Bühner, Maria. 'The Rise of a New Consciousness: Lesbian Activism in East Germany in the 1980s.' In *The Politics of Authenticity. Countercultures and Radical Movements across the Iron Curtain, 1968–1989*, edited by Joachim C. Häberlen, Mark Keck-Szajbel, and Kate Mahoney, 151–73. New York and Oxford: Berghahn, 2019.

Bullough, Vern L., and James A. Brundage, eds. *Handbook of Medieval Sexuality*. New York: Garland, 1996.

Bullough, Vern L., and Bonnie Bullough. *Cross Dressing, Sex, and Gender*. Philadelphia: University of Pennsylvania Press, 1993.

Bundesverfassungsgericht/Federal Constitutional Court. 'The Requirements for the Legal Recognition of a Transsexual's Felt Gender Set by § 8 (1)Nos. 3 and 4 of the Transsexuals Act Are Unconstitutional,' 28 January 2011. https://www.bundesverfassungsgericht.de/SharedDocs/Pressemitteilungen/EN/2011/bvg11-007.html.

Burchard, E. 'Sexuelle Fragen zur Kriegszeit.' *Zeitschrift für Sexualwissenschaft* 1, no. 10 (1915): 373–80.

Burkhardt, Jacob. *The Civilization of the Renaissance in Italy*. Translated by S.G.C. Middlemore. Oxford and London: Kegan Paul, 1945.

Butler, Judith. *Undoing Gender*. London: Routledge, 2004.

Campt, Tina. *Other Germans: Black Germans and the Politics of Race, Gender, and Memory in the Third Reich*. Ann Arbor: University of Michigan Press, 2004.

Canaday, Margot. *Straight State: Sexuality and Citizenship in Twentieth-Century America*. Princeton: Princeton University Press, 2009.

Canning, Kathleen. 'Claiming Citizenship: Suffrage and Subjectivity in Germany after the First World War.' In *Gender History in Practice: Historical Perspectives on Bodies, Class & Citizenship*, 212–37. Ithaca: Cornell University Press, 2006.

Canning, Kathleen. 'Of Meaning and Methods: The Concepts of Class and Citizenship in German History.' In *Gender History in Practice: Historical Perspectives on Bodies, Class & Citizenship*, 193–211. Ithaca: Cornell University Press, 2006.

Canning, Kathleen. 'The Order of Terms: Class, Citizenship, and the Welfare State in German Gender History.' In *Gendering Modern German History: Rewriting Historiography*, edited by Karen Hagemann, and Jean H. Quataert, 128–46. New York: Berghahn, 2007.

Canning, Kathleen. 'Women and the Politics of Gender.' In *Weimar Germany*, edited by Anthony McElligott, 146–74. Oxford: Oxford University Press, 2009.

Caplan, Jane. 'Gender and the Concentration Camps.' In *Concentration Camps in Nazi Germany: The New Histories*, edited by Jane Caplan, and Nikolaus Wachsmann, 82–126. London and New York: Routledge, 2010.

Caplan, Jane. 'The Administration of Gender Identity in Nazi Germany.' *History Workshop Journal* 72, no. 1 (2011): 171–80.

Carter, Erica. 'Alice in Consumer Wonderland: West German Case Studies in Gender and Consumer Culture.' In *Gender and Generation*, edited by Angela McRobbie, and Mica Nava, 185–214. London and Basingstoke: Palgrave Macmillan, 1984.

Chamberlin, J. Edward, and Sander L. Gilman. *Degeneration: The Dark Side of Progress*. New York: Columbia University Press, 1985.

Chiang, Howard. *Transtopia in the Sinophone Pacific*. New York: Columbia University Press, 2021.

Clark, Anna. *Desire: A History of European Sexuality*. New York and London: Routledge, 2008.

Clark, Christopher. *Iron Kingdom: The Rise and Downfall of Prussia, 1600–1947*. Cambridge, MA: Belknap, 2006.

Classen, Albrecht, ed. *Childhood in the Middle Ages and the Renaissance. The Results of a Paradigm Shift in the History of Mentality*. Berlin, New York: De Gruyter, 2005.

Classen, Albrecht, ed. 'Love, Sex, and Marriage in Late Medieval German Verse Narratives, Lyric Poetry, and Prose Literature.' *Orbis Litterarum* 49 (1994): 63–83.

Clay, Catrine, and Michael Leapman. *Master Race. The Lebensborn Experiment in Nazi Germany*. London: Hodder & Stoughton, 1995.

Cocks, Harry G. 'Approaches to the History of Sexuality since 1750.' In *The Routledge History of Sex and the Body: 1500 to the Present*, edited by Sarah Toulalan, and Kate Fisher, 38–54. London and New York: Routledge, 2013.

Colvin, Sarah. *The Rhetorical Feminine: Gender and the Orient on the German Stage, 1647–1742*. Oxford: Clarendon Press, 1999.

Coontz, Stephanie. *Marriage, A History: How Love Conquered Marriage*. New York: Penguin, 2006.

Crew, David F. *Germans on Welfare: From Weimar to Hitler*. New York: Oxford University Press, 1998.

Crompton, Louis. 'The Myth of Lesbian Impunity: Capital Laws from 1270 to 1791.' *Journal of Homosexuality* 6, no. 1–2 (1981): 11–25.

Crouthamel, Jason. *An Intimate History of the Front: Masculinity, Sexuality, and German Soldiers in the First World War*. New York: Palgrave Macmillan, 2014.

Crouthamel, Jason. '"Comradeship" and "Friendship": Masculinity and Militarisation in Germany's Homosexual Emancipation Movement after the First World War.' *Gender & History* 23, no. 1 (2011): 111–29.

Crouthamel, Jason. 'Cross-Dressing for the Fatherland: Sexual Humor, Masculinity and German Soldiers in the First World War.' *First World War Studies* 2, no. 2 (2011): 195–215.

Crouthamel, Jason. 'Homosexuality and Comradeship: Destabilizing the Hegemonic Masculine Ideal in Nazi Germany.' *Central European History* 51 (2018): 419–39.

Crouthamel, Jason. 'Hypermasculine Warriors versus Effeminate Men: Masculinity and Sexuality in Print Media by German Veterans of the Great War.' In *Not Straight from Germany: Sexual Publics and Sexual Citizenship since Magnus Hirschfeld*, edited by Michael Thomas Taylor, Annette F. Timm, and Rainer Herrn, 283–305. Ann Arbor: University of Michigan Press, 2017.

Crouthamel, Jason. 'Male Sexuality and Psychological Trauma: Soldiers and Sexual Disorder in World War I and Weimar Germany.' *Journal of the History of Sexuality* 17, no. 1 (2008): 60–84.

Crozier, Ivan. 'Becoming a Sexologist: Norman Haire, the 1929 London World League for Sexual Reform Congress, and Organizing Medical Knowledge about Sex in Interwar England.' *History of Science* 39 (2001): 299–329.

Cryle, Peter, and Alison Moore. *Frigidity: An Intellectual History*. Basingstoke: Palgrave Macmillan, 2011.

Cryle, Peter, and Elizabeth Stephens. *Normality: A Critical Genealogy*. Chicago: Chicago University Press, 2017.

Cunningham, Hugh. *Children and Childhood in Western Society since 1500*. New York: Longman, 1995.

Curtis-Wendlandt, Lisa. 'Missionary Wives and the Sexual Narratives of German Lutheran Missions among Australian Aborigines.' *Journal of the History of Sexuality* 20, no. 3 (2011): 498–519.

Czarnowski, Gabriele. *Das kontrollierte Paar. Ehe- und Sexualpolitik im Nationalsozialismus*. Weinheim: Dt. Studien-Verl., 1991.

Dame, Avery. 'Tracing Terminology: Researching Early Uses of "Cisgender."' *AHA Today (Blog of the American Historical Association)*, 22 May 2017. https://www.historians.org/publications-and-directories/perspectives-on-history/may-2017/tracing-terminology-researching-early-uses-of-cisgender.

Daniel, Ute. *The War from Within: German Working-Class Women in the First World War*. Oxford and New York: Berg, 1997.

Dannecker, Martin. 'Der unstillbare Wunsch nach Anerkennung. Homosexuellenpolitik in den fünfziger und sechziger Jahren.' In *Was heißt hier schwul? Politik und Identitäten im Wandel*, edited by Detlef Grumbach, 27–44. Hamburg: Männerschwarm, 1997.

Dannecker, Martin, and Reimut Reiche. *Der gewöhnliche Homosexuelle. Eine soziologische Untersuchung über männliche Homosexualität in der Bundesrepublik*. Frankfurt am Main: Fischer, 1974.

David, Henry P., Jochen Fleischhacker, and Charlotte Hohn. 'Abortion and Eugenics in Nazi Germany.' *Population and Development Review* 14, no. 1 (1988): 81–112.

Davidson, Arnold I. *The Emergence of Sexuality: Historical Epistemology and the Formation of Concepts*. Cambridge, MA: Harvard University Press, 2001.

Davis, Natalie Zemon. 'Boundaries and the Sense of Self in Sixteenth-Century France.' In *Reconstructing Individualism. Autonomy, Individuality, and the Self in Western Thought*, edited by Thomas C. Heller, Morton Sosna, and David E. Wellbery, 53–63. Stanford, CA: Stanford University Press, 1986.

Davis, Rebecca L., and Michele Mitchell, eds. *Heterosexual Histories*. New York: New York University Press, 2021.

Davison, Kate. 'Cold War Pavlov: Homosexual Aversion Therapy in the 1960s.' *History of the Human Sciences* 34, no. 1 (2021): 89–119.

Dean, Tim, and Christopher Lane, eds. *Homosexuality-Psychoanalysis*. Chicago: Chicago University Press, 2001.

Dekker, Rudolf, and Lotte Van de Pol. *Frauen in Männerkleidern. Weibliche Transvestiten und ihre Geschichte*. Berlin: Verlag Klaus Wagenbach, 1989.

Demnitz, Jana. 'Lesbische Geschichte wird sichtbar.' *Tagesspiegel*, 5 May 2022. https://www.tagesspiegel.de/gesellschaft/queerspiegel/gedenkkugel-in-ravensbrueck-lesbische-geschichte-wird-sichtbar/28308604.html.

Dennert, G., C. Leidinger, and F. Rauchut. 'Lesben in Wut. Lesbenbewegung in der BRD der 70er Jahre.' In *In Bewegung bleiben. 100 Jahre Politik, Kultur und Geschichte von Lesben*, edited by G. Dennert, C. Leidinger, and F. Rauchut, 31–61. Berlin: Querverlag, 2007.

Dennis, David Brandon. 'Coming Out into Socialism: Heiner Carow's Third Way.' In *A Companion to German Cinema*, edited by Terri Ginsberg, and Andrea Mensch, 55–81. Chichester: Wiley-Blackwell, 2012.

'Der wichtigste Satz seines Lebens,' *Frankfurter Allgemeine Zeitung*, 10 June 2021. https://www.faz.net/aktuell/gesellschaft/menschen/klaus-wowereit-20-jahre-coming-out-ich-bin-schwul-und-das-ist-auch-gut-so-17381986.html.

Deutsch, Helene. 'Über die weibliche Homosexualität.' *Internationale Zeitschrift für Psychoanalyse* 18 (1932): 219–41.

Dickinson, Edward Ross. '"A Dark, Impenetrable Wall of Complete Incomprehension": The Impossibility of Heterosexual Love in Imperial Germany.' *Central European History* 40 (2007): 467–97.

Dickinson, Edward Ross. 'Policing Sex in Germany, 1882-1982: A Preliminary Statistical Analysis.' *Journal of the History of Sexuality* 16, no. 2 (2007): 204–50.

Dickinson, Edward Ross. 'Reflections on Feminism and Monism in the Kaiserreich, 1900-1913.' *Central European History* 34, no. 2 (2001): 191–230.

Dickinson, Edward Ross. *Sex, Freedom and Power in Imperial Germany, 1880–1914*. Cambridge: Cambridge University Press, 2014.

Dickinson, Edward Ross. 'The Men's Christian Morality Movement in Germany, 1880–1914: Some Reflections on Politics, Sex, and Sexual Politics.' *Journal of Modern History* 75, no. 1 (2003): 59–110.

Dickinson, Edward Ross, and Richard F. Wetzell. 'The Historiography of Sexuality in Modern Germany.' *German History* 23, no. 3 (2005): 291–305.

Diem, Albrecht. 'Teaching Sodomy in a Carolingian Monastery: A Study of Walahfrid Strabo's and Heito's "Visio Wettini."' *German History* 34, no. 3 (2016): 385–401.

Dietrich, Donald J. 'Catholic Eugenics in Germany, 1920–1945: Hermann Muckermann, S.J. and Joseph Mayer.' *Journal of Church and State* 34, no. 3 (1992): 575–600.

Dinshaw, Carolyn. *Getting Medieval: Sexualities and Communities, Pre- and Postmodern*. Durham: Duke University Press, 1999.

Doan, Laura. *Disturbing Practices: History, Sexuality, and Women's Experience of Modern War*. Chicago: Chicago University Press, 2013.

Doan, Laura. *Fashioning Sapphism: The Origins of a Modern English Lesbian Culture*. New York: Columbia University Press, 2001.

Doan, Laura. 'Marie Stopes's Wonderful Rhythm Charts: Normalizing the Natural.' *Journal of the History of Ideas* 78, no. 4 (2017): 595–620.

Doan, Laura. 'Topsy-Turvydom. Gender Inversion, Sapphism, and the Great War.' *GLQ: A Journal of Lesbian and Gay Studies* 12, no. 4 (2006): 517–42.

Dobler, Jens. *The Eulenburg Affair: A Cultural History of Politics in the German Empire*. Translated by Deborah Lucas Schneider. Rochester, NY: Camden House, 2015.

Dobler, Jens. 'The Homosexual Scare and the Masculinization of German Politics before World War I.' *Central European History* 47, no. 4 (2014): 737–59.

Dobler, Jens. *Von anderen Ufern: Geschichte der Berliner Lesben und Schwulen in Kreuzberg und Friedrichshain*. Berlin: Gmünder, 2003.

Domeier, Norman. *Der Eulenburg-Skandal: Eine politische Kulturgeschichte des Kaiserreichs*. Frankfurt: Campus, 2010.

Dose, Ralf. *Magnus Hirschfeld: The Origins of the Gay Liberation Movement*. Translated by Edward H. Willis. New York: Monthly Review Press, 2014.

Dose, Ralf. 'The World League for Sexual Reform: Some Possible Approaches.' *Journal of the History of Sexuality* 12, no. 1 (2003): 1–15.

Douglas, Mary. *Purity and Danger: An Analysis of Concepts of Pollution and Taboo*. New York: Routledge, 2005.

Dreger, Alice Domurat. *Hermaphrodites and the Medical Invention of Sex*. Cambridge, MA: Harvard University Press, 1998.

Drewitz, Ingeborg, ed. *The German Women's Movement: The Social Role of Women in the 19th Century and the Emancipation Movement in Germany*. Bonn: Hohwacht, 1983.

Duberman, Martin. *Jews Queers Germans: A Novel/History*. New York, Oakland, London: Seven Stories, 2017.

Duc, Aimée (Minna Wettstein-Adelt). *Sind es Frauen? Roman über das dritte Geschlecht*. Berlin: Eckstein, 1901.

Eder, Franz X. 'Das Sexuelle beschreiben, zeigen und aufführen. Mediale Strategien im deutschsprachigen Sexualdiskurs von 1945 bis Anfang der siebziger Jahre.' In *Fragen Sie Dr. Sex! Ratgeberkommunikation und die mediale Konstruktion des Sexuellen*, edited by Peter-Paul Bänziger, Stefanie Duttweiler, Philipp Sarasin, and Annika Wellmann, 94–122. Frankfurt am Main: Suhrkamp, 2020.

Eder, Franz X. 'Die lange Geschichte der "Sexuellen Revolution" in Westdeutschland (1950er bis 1980er Jahre).' In *Sexuelle Revolution?*, edited by Peter-Paul Bänziger et al., 25–59. Bielefeld: Transcript, 2015.

Eder, Franz X. 'The Long History of the "Sexual Revolution" in West Germany.' In *Sexual Revolutions*, edited by Gert Hekma, and Alain Giami, 99–120. London: Palgrave Macmillan, 2014.

Eitler, Pascal. 'Die "Porno-Welle". Sexualität, Seduktivität und die Kulturgeschichte der Bundesrepublik.' In *Sexuelle Revolution?*, edited by Peter-Paul Bänziger, et al., 87–111. Bielefeld: Transcript, 2015.

Eley, Geoff. *Society, Culture, and the State in Germany, 1870–1930*. Ann Arbor: University of Michigan Press, 1996.

Eley, Geoff. 'What Was German Modernity and When?' In *German Modernities from Wilhelm to Weimar: A Contest of Futures*, edited by Geoff Eley, Jennifer L. Jenkins, and Tracie Matysik, 59–82. London and New York: Bloomsbury, 2016.

Eley, Geoff, Jennifer L. Jenkins, and Tracie Matysik, eds. *German Modernities from Wilhelm to Weimar: A Contest of Futures*. London: Bloomsbury Academic, 2016.

Eley, Geoff, Jennifer L. Jenkins, and Tracie Matysik, eds. 'Introduction: German Modernities and the Contest of Futures.' In *German Modernities from Wilhelm to Weimar: A Contest of Futures*, edited by Geoff Eley, Jennifer L. Jenkins, and Tracie Matysik, 1–27. London and New York: Bloomsbury, 2016.

Ellis, Havelock. *Eonism and Other Supplementary Studies*. Vol. 7. 7 vols. Studies in the Psychology of Sex. Philadelphia: F.A. Davis, 1919.

El-Tayeb, Fatima. '"Gays Who Cannot Properly Be Gay": Queer Muslims in the Neo-Liberal European City.' In *Queer Cities Queer Cultures*, edited by Matt Cook, and Jennifer V. Evans, 263–81. London: Bloomsbury, 2014.

Endlich, Stefanie. 'Das Berliner Homosexuellen-Denkmal.' In *Homophobie und Devianz: Weibliche und männliche Homosexualität im Nationalsozialismus*, edited by Insa Eschebach, 167–86. Berlin: Metropol, 2012.

Eng, David L., Judith Halberstam, and José Esbeban Muñoz. 'Introduction: What's Queer about Queer Studies Now?' *Social Text* 23, no. 3–4 (2005): 1–17.

Eriksson, Brigitte. 'A Lesbian Execution in Germany, 1721: The Trial Records.' *Journal of Homosexuality* 6, no. 1/2 (1981): 27–40.

Ernst, Waltraud, ed. *Histories of the Normal and the Abnormal*. Social and Cultural Histories of Norms and Normativity. London: Routledge, 2006.

Evans, Jennifer V. 'Decriminalization, Seduction, and "Unnatural Desire" in East Germany.' *Feminist Studies* 36, no. 3 (2010): 553–77.

Evans, Jennifer V. 'Harmless Kisses and Infinite Loops: Making Space for Queer Place in Twenty-First Century Berlin.' In *Queer Cities Queer Cultures*, edited by Matt Cook, and Jennifer V. Evans, 75–94. London: Bloomsbury, 2014.

Evans, Jennifer V. 'Introduction: Why Queer German History?' *German History* 34, no. 3 (2016): 371–84.

Evans, Jennifer V. *The Queer Art of History: Queer Kinship after Fascism* (Forthcoming). Durham: Duke University Press, 2023.

Evans, Jennifer V. 'Bahnhof Boys: Policing Male Prostitution in Post-Nazi Berlin.' *Journal of the History of Sexuality* 23, no. 3 (2005): 355–70.

Evans, Jennifer V. *Life among the Ruins: Cityscape and Sexuality in Cold War Berlin*. London: Palgrave Macmillan, 2011.

Evans, Jennifer V. 'Seeing Subjectivity: Erotic Photography and the Optics of Desire' *American Historical Review* 118, no. 2 (2013): 430–62.

Evans, Jennifer V., and Elissa Mailänder. 'Cross-Dressing, Male Intimacy and the Violence of Transgression in Third Reich Photography.' *German History* 39, no. 1 (2021): 54–77.

Evans, Richard J. *The Feminist Movement in Germany, 1894–1933*. London: Sage, 1976.

Evans, Richard J. 'Prostitution, State and Society in Imperial Germany.' *Past and Present* 70, no. 1 (1976): 106–29.

Evans, Richard J. *Rereading German History: From Unification to Reunification,
1800-1996*. London and New York: Routledge, 1997.

Evans, Richard J. *The German Underworld: Deviants and Outcasts in German
History*. London: Routledge, 1988.

Fenemore, Mark. *Sex, Thugs and Rock'n'Roll: Teenage Rebels in Cold War East
Germany*. New York: Berghahn, 2007.

Fenemore, Mark. 'The Growing Pains of Sex Education in the German Democratic
Republic.' In *Shaping Sexual Knowledge: A Cultural History of Sexuality in
Twentieth-Century Europe*, edited by Lutz Sauerteig, and Roger Davidson,
71–90. London: Routledge, 2009.

Fiebig, Peggy. 'Drei Jahre Ehe für alle: Viel erreicht – noch viel zu tun.'
Deutschlandfunk, 30 June 2020. https://www.deutschlandfunk.de/drei-jahre-
ehe-fuer-alle-viel-erreicht-noch-viel-zu-tun.724.de.html?dram:article_id=479611.

Fischer, Bernard A. 'Maltreatment of People with Serious Mental Illness in the Early
20th Century.' *The Journal of Nervous and Mental Disease* 200, no. 12 (2012):
1096–100.

Fisher, Kate, and Jana Funke. 'British Sexual Science beyond the Medical: Cross-
Disciplinary, Cross-Historical, and Cross-Cultural Translations.' In *Sexology
and Translation: Cultural and Scientific Encounters across the Modern
World*, edited by Heike Bauer, 95–114. Philadelphia: Temple University Press,
2015.

Fisher, Kate, and Jana Funke. '"Let Us Leave the Hospital; Let Us Go on a Journey
around the World": British and German Sexual Science and the Global Search
for Sexual Variation.' In *A Global History of Sexual Science, 1880–1960*,
edited by Veronika Fuechtner, Douglas E. Haynes, and Ryan M. Jones, 51–69.
Oakland: University of California Press, 2018.

Fishman, Sterling. 'The History of Childhood Sexuality.' *Journal of Contemporary
History* 17, no. 2 (1982): 269–83.

Fitzpatrick, Matthew P. 'The Samoan Women's Revolt: Race, Intermarriage and
Imperial Hierarchy in German Samoa.' *German History* 35, no. 2 (2017):
206–28.

Fleishman, Ian. '"Naturgeil": Homo-Eco-Erotic Utopianism in Hitler Youth Film
Propaganda and "Boy Scout" Porn.' *Colloquia Germanica* 53, no. 2–3 (2022):
269–87.

Florvil, Tiffany. *Mobilizing Black Germany: Afro-German Women and the Making
of a Transnational Movement*. Urbana: University of Illinois Press, 2020.

Flüchter, Antje. 'Transethnic Unions in Early Modern German Travel Literature.'
In *Mixed Matches: Trangressive Unions in Germany from the Reformation to
the Enlightenment*, edited by David M. Luebke, and Mary Lindemann, 150–65.
New York: Berghahn, 2014.

Foucault, Michel. *The History of Sexuality*. Vol. 1: The Will to Knowledge. 3 vols.
London: Penguin, 1998.

Fout, John C. 'Sexual Politics in Wilhelmine Germany: The Male Gender Crisis,
Moral Purity, and Homophobia.' In *Forbidden History: The State, Society, and
the Regulation of Sexuality in Modern Europe*, edited by John C. Fout, 259–92.
Chicago and London: University of Chicago Press, 1992.

Frackman, Kyle. 'Homemade Pornography and the Proliferation of Queer Pleasure
in East Germany.' *Radical History Review*, no. 142 (2022): 93–109.

Frackman, Kyle. 'The East German Film *Coming Out* (1989) as Melancholic Reflection and Hopeful Projection.' *German Life and Letters* 71, no. 4 (2018): 452–572.

Fradenburg, Louise, and Carla Freccero, eds. *Premodern Sexualities*. New York: Routledge, 1996.

Frame, Lynne. 'Gretchen, Girl, Garçonne? Weimar Science and Popular Culture in Search of the Ideal New Woman.' In *Women in the Metropolis*, edited by Katharina von Ankum, 12–40. Berkeley: University of California Press, 1997.

'Frau Dr. Kienle-Stuttgart im Hungerstreik,' *Die Rote Fahne*, 24 March 1931.

Freccero, Carla. *Queer/Early/Modern*. Durham: Duke University Press, 2006.

Freeland, Jane. 'Domestic Abuse and Women's Lives: East and West Policies during the 1960s and 1970s.' In *Gendering Post-1945 German History: Entanglements*, edited by Karen Hagemann, Donna Harsch, and Friederike Brühöfener, 253–73. New York and Oxford: Berghahn, 2018.

Freeland, Jane. 'Women's Bodies and Feminist Subjectivities in West Germany.' In *The Politics of Authenticity. Countercultures and Radical Movements across the Iron Curtain, 1968–1989*, edited by Joachim C. Häberlen, Mark Keck-Szabel, and Kate Mahoney, 131–50. New York and Oxford: Berghahn, 2019.

Freist, Dagmar. 'One Body, Two Confessions: Mixed Marriages in Germany.' In *Gender in Early Modern German History*, edited by Ulinka Rublack, 275–304. Cambridge: Cambridge University Press, 2002.

Freud, Sigmund. 'Fragment of an Analysis of a Case of Hysteria (1905 [1901]).' In *The Standard Edition of the Complete Psychological Works of Sigmund Freud*, 7: 1901–1905: A Case of Hysteria, Three Essays on Sexuality and Other Works. Translated by James Strachey, 1–122. London: Hogarth, 1953.

Freud, Sigmund. 'Letter from Sigmund Freud to Anonymous, April 9, 1935.' In *Letters from Sigmund Freud, 1873–1939*, edited by Ernst L. Freud, 423–4. London: Hogarth, 1961.

Freud, Sigmund. 'The Psychogenesis of a Case of Homosexuality in a Woman.' In *Sexuality and the Psychology of Love*, edited by Philip Rieff, 133–59. New York: Collier, 1963.

Freud, Sigmund. *Three Essays on the Theory of Sexuality*. Translated by James Strachey. London: Imago, 1949.

Freud, Sigmund. *Totem and Taboo: Some Points of Agreement between the Mental Lives of Savages and Neurotics*. Translated by James Strachey. London: Routledge and Paul, 1950.

Freund-Widder, Michaela. *Frauen unter Kontrolle: Prostitution und ihre staatliche Bekämpfung in Hamburg vom Ende des Kaiserreichs bis zu den Anfängen der Bundesrepublik*. LIT Verlag: Münster, 2003.

Frevert, Ute, ed. *Bürgerinnen und Bürger: Geschlechterverhältnisse im 19. Jahrhundert*. Göttingen: Vandenhoeck & Ruprecht, 1988.

Frevert, Ute. *Die kasernierte Nation. Militärdienst und Zivilgesellschaft in Deutschland*. München: C. H. Beck, 2001.

Frevert, Ute. *Emotions in History-Lost and Found*. Budapest: Central European University Press, 2011.

Frevert, Ute. 'Europeanizing Germany's Twentieth Century.' *History and Memory* 17, no. 1-2 (2005): 87–116.

Frevert, Ute. *Men of Honour: A Social and Cultural History of the Duel*. Translated by Anthony Williams. Cambridge: Polity, 1995.

Frevert, Ute. 'Soldaten, Staatsbürger: Überlegungen zur historischen Konstruktion von Männlichkeit.' In *Männergeschichte-Geschlechtergeschichte: Männlichkeit im Wandel der Moderne*, edited by Thomas Kühne, 69–88. Frankfurt and New York: Campus Verlag, 1996.

Frevert, Ute. 'The Civilizing Tendency of Hygiene: Working-Class Women under Medical Control in Imperial Germany.' In *Geman Women in the Nineteenth Century: A Social History*, edited by John C. Fout, 320–44. New York and London: Holmes & Meier, 1984.

Frevert, Ute. *Women in German History: From Bourgeois Emancipation to Sexual Liberation*. Oxford: Berg, 1989.

Friedrich, Otto. *Before the Deluge. A Portrait of Berlin in the 1920s*. New York: Harper and Row, 1972.

Friedrichsmeyer, Sara, Sara Lennox, and Susanne Zantop, eds. *Imperialist Imagination: German Colonialism and Its Legacy*. Ann Arbor: University of Michigan Press, 1998.

Fuchs, Ralf-Peter. 'Transgressive Unions and Concepts of Honor in Early Modern Defamation Lawsuits.' In *Mixed Matches: Trangressive Unions in Germany from the Reformation to the Enlightenment*, edited by David M. Luebke, and Mary Lindemann, 63–79. New York: Berghahn, 2014.

Fuechtner, Veronika. *Berlin Psychoanalytic: Psychoanalysis and Culture in Weimar Republic Germany and Beyond*. Berkeley: University of California Press, 2011.

Fuechtner, Veronika. 'Indians, Jews, and Sex: Magnus Hirschfeld and Indian Sexology.' In *Imagining Germany, Imagining Asia*, edited by Veronika Fuechtner, and Mary Rhiel, 111–30. Rochester, NY: Camden House, 2013.

Fuechtner, Veronika, Douglas E. Haynes, and Ryan M. Jones, eds. *Towards a Global History of Sexual Science, 1880–1950*. Oakland: University of California Press, 2017.

Fulbrook, Mary. *A Concise History of Germany*. Cambridge: Cambridge University Press, 2004.

Fulbrook, Mary. *A History of Germany 1918–2008: The Divided Nation*. 3rd ed. Chichester: Wiley-Blackwell, 2009.

Fulbrook, Mary. 'Ossis and Wessis: The Creation of Two German Societies.' In *German History since 1800*, edited by Mary Fulbrook, 411–31. London: Hodder Arnold, 1997.

Fulbrook, Mary. *The People's State: East German Society from Hitler to Honecker*. New Haven: Yale University Press, 2005.

Funke, Jana. 'Navigating the Past: Sexuality, Race, and the Uses of the Primitive in Magnus Hirschfeld's "The World Journey of a Sexologist".' In *Sex, Knowledge, and Receptions of the Past*, edited by Kate Fisher, and Rebecca Langlands, 111–34. Oxford: Oxford University Press, 2015.

Fürth, Henriette. 'Sexuelle Kriegsfragen.' *Zeitschrift für Sexualwissenschaft* 2 (1915/16): 133–7.

Gaido, Daniel, and Cintia Frencia. '"A Clean Break": Clara Zetkin, the Socialist Women's Movement, and Feminism.' *International Critical Thought* 8 (2018): 277–303.

Gammerl, Benno. 'Ist frei sein normal? Männliche Homosexualitäten seit den 1960er Jahren zwischen Emanzipation und Normalisierung.' In *Sexuelle*

Revolution?, edited by Peter-Paul Bänziger et al., 223–43. Bielefeld: Transcript, 2015.

Gammerl, Benno, Philipp Nielsen, and Margrit Pernau, eds. *Encounters with Emotions: Negotiating Cultural Differences since Early Modernity*. New York: Berghahn, 2019.

Garelick, Rhonda K. *Rising Star: Dandyism, Gender, and Performance in the Fin de Siècle*. Princeton: Princeton University Press, 1998.

Garraio, Júlia. 'Cologne and the (Un)Making of Transnational Approaches to Sexual Violence.' *European Journal of Women's Studies* 28, no. 2 (2021): 129–44.

Gay, Peter. *The Bourgeois Experience: Victoria to Freud*. New York: Oxford University Press, 1984.

Geissler, Christopher. '"Eine Allerweltliebe": Critiquing European Ethnography from within the German Homosexual Emancipation Movement.' *German Studies Review* 42, no. 2 (2019): 239–58.

Gellately, Robert. *The Gestapo and German Society: Enforcing Racial Policy, 1933–1945*. Oxford and New York: Oxford University Press, 1990.

Gertiser, Anita. *Falsche Scham: Strategien der Überzeugung in Aufklärungsfilmen zur Bekämpfung der Geschlechtskrankheiten (1918–1935)*. Göttingen: V&R Unipress, 2015.

Ghodsee, Kristen R. *Why Women Have Better Sex under Socialism: And Other Arguments for Economic Independence*. New York: Nation, 2018.

Giddens, Anthony. *Modernity and Self-Identity: Self and Society in the Late Modern Age*. Cambridge: Polity Press, 1991.

Giddens, Anthony. *The Transformation of Intimacy: Sexuality, Love and Eroticism in Modern Societies*. Cambridge: Polity Press, 1992.

Giersdorf, Jens. 'Why Does Charlotte von Mahlsdorf Curtsy? Representations of National Queerness in a Transvestite Hero.' *GLQ: A Journal of Lesbian and Gay Studies* 12, no. 2 (2006): 171–96.

Giles, Geoffrey J. 'The Institutionalization of Homosexual Panic in the Third Reich.' In *Social Outsiders in Nazi Germany*, edited by Robert Gellately, and Nathan Stolzfus, 233–55. Princeton: Princeton University Press, 2001.

Giles, Geoffrey J. 'Legislating Homophobia in the Third Reich: The Radicalization of Prosecution against Homosexuality by the Legal Profession.' *German History* 23, no. 3 (2005): 339–54.

Giles, Geoffrey J. 'The Denial of Homosexuality: Same-Sex Incidents in Himmler's SS and Police.' In *Sexuality and German Fascism*, edited by Dagmar Herzog, 256–90. New York: Berghahn, 2005.

Giles, Geoffrey J. '"The Most Unkindest Cut of All": Castration, Homosexuality and Nazi Justice.' *Journal of Contemporary History* 27, no. 1 (1992): 41–61.

Gilman, Sander L. *Freud, Race, and Gender*. Princeton: Princeton University Press, 1993.

Gilman, Sander L. 'Sigmund Freud and the Sexologists: A Second Reading.' In *Sexual Knowledge, Sexual Science: The History of Attitudes to Sexuality*, edited by Roy Porter, and Mikuláš Teich, 323–49. Cambridge: Cambridge University Press, 1994.

Gilman, Sander L. *The Jew's Body*. New York: Routledge, 1991.

Gilman, Sander L., and Steven T. Katz. *Anti-Semitism in Times of Crisis*. New York: New York University Press, 1991.

Glowacka, Dorota. 'Sexual Violence against Men and Boys during the Holocaust: A Genealogy of (Not-So-Silent) Silence.' *German History* 39, no. 1 (2021): 78–99.

Goldberg, Jonathan. *Sodometries: Renaissance Texts, Modern Sexualities*. Stanford: Stanford University Press, 1992.

Gordon, Mel. *Voluptuous Panic: The Erotic World of Weimar Berlin*. London; Venice, CA: Feral House, 2001.

Gordon, Terri J. 'Fascism and the Female Form: Performance Art in the Third Reich.' In *Sexuality and Germany Fascism*, edited by Dagmar Herzog, 164–200. New York: Berghahn, 2005.

Gowing, Laura, Michael Hunter, and Miri Rubin, eds. *Love, Friendship and Faith in Europe, 1300–1800*. Basingstoke, New York: Palgrave Macmillan, 2005.

Graf, Rüdiger, and Moritz Föllmer. 'The Culture of "Crisis" in the Weimar Republic.' *Thesis Eleven* 111, no. 1 (2012): 36–47.

Graham, Loren R. 'Science and Values: The Eugenics Movement in Germany and Russia in the 1920s.' *American Historical Review* 82, no. 5 (1977): 1133–64.

Grau, Günter. 'Ein Leben im Kampf gegen den Paragraphen 175. Zum Wirken des Dresdener Arztes Rudolf Klimmer 1905–1977.' In *100 Jahre Schwulenbewegung*, edited by Manfred Herzer, 47–64. Berlin: Rosa Winkel, 1998.

Grau, Günter. *Homosexualität in der NS-Zeit. Dokumente einer Diskriminierung und Verfolgung*. Frankfurt am Main: Fischer, 1993.

Grau, Günter. 'Return of the Past: The Policy of the SED and the Laws against Homosexuality in Eastern Germany between 1946 and 1968.' *Journal of Homosexuality* 37, no. 4 (1999): 1–21.

Grau, Günter, and Claudia Schoppmann, eds. *Hidden Holocaust? Gay and Lesbian Persecution in Germany 1933–1945*. Translated by Patrick Camiller. London: Cassell, 1995.

Gray, Marion W. *Productive Men, Reproductive Women: The Agrarian Household and the Emergence of Separate Spheres during the German Enlightenment*. New York: Berghahn, 2000.

Green, Dennis H. *Women and Marriage in German Medieval Romance*. Cambridge: Cambridge University Press, 2009.

Green, Monica H. *The Trotula: A Medieval Compendium of Women's Medicine*. Philadelphia: University of Pennsylvania Press, 2001.

Greven-Aschoff, Barbara. *Die bürgerliche Frauenbewegung in Deutschland, 1894–1933*. Göttingen: Vandenhoeck & Ruprecht, 1981.

Griffiths, Craig. 'Konkurrierende Pfade der Emanzipation: Der Tuntenstreit (1973–1975) und die Frage des "respektablen Auftretens".' In *Rosa Radikale: Die Schwulenbewegung der 1970er Jahre*, edited by Andreas Pretzel, and Volker Weiß, 143–59. Hamburg: Männerschwarm, 2012.

Griffiths, Craig. 'Sex, Shame and West German Gay Liberation.' *German History* 34, no. 3 (2016): 445–67.

Griffiths, Craig. *The Ambivalence of Gay Liberation: Male Homosexual Politics in 1970s West Germany*. Oxford: Oxford University Press, 2021.

Grisko, Michael, ed. *Freikörperkultur und Lebenswelt. Studien zur Vor- und Frühgeschichte der Freikörperkultur in Deutschland*. Kassel: Kassel University Press, 1999.

Grossmann, Atina. 'A Question of Silence: The Rape of German Women by Occupation Soldiers.' *October* 72, Berlin 1945: War and Rape 'Liberators Take Liberties' (1995): 42–63.

Grossmann, Atina. 'Abortion and Economic Crisis: The 1931 Campaign against §218 in Germany.' *New German Critique* 14 (1978): 119–37.

Grossmann, Atina. 'Feminist Debates about Women and National Socialism.' *Gender & History* 3 (1991): 350–8.

Grossmann, Atina. 'Girlkultur or Thoroughly Rationalized Female: A New Woman in Weimar Germany?' In *Women in Culture and Politics: A Century of Change*, edited by Judith Friedlander, Blanche Wiesen Cook, Alice Kessler-Harris, and Carroll Smith-Rosenberg, 62–80. Bloomington: Indiana University Press, 1986.

Grossmann, Atina. *Reforming Sex: The German Movement for Birth Control and Abortion Reform, 1920–1950*. New York: Oxford University Press, 1995.

Grossmann, Atina. 'The "Big Rape": Sex and Sexual Violence, War, and Occupation in Post-World War II Memory and Imagination.' In *Sexual Violence in Conflict Zones: From the Ancient World to the Era of Human Rights*, edited by Elizabeth D. Heineman, 137–51. Philadelphia: University of Pennsylvania Press, 2011.

Grossmann, Atina. 'The New Woman and the Rationalization of Sexuality in Weimar Germany.' In *Powers of Desire: The Politics of Sexuality*, edited by Ann Snitow, Christine Stansell, and Sharon Thompson, 153–71. New York: Monthly Review Press, 1983.

Grossmann, Atina. 'Trauma, Memory, and Motherhood: Germans and Jewish Displaced Persons in Post-Nazi Germany, 1945–1949.' *Archiv Für Sozialgeschichte* 38 (1998): 215–39.

Grothe, Soveig. 'Lesbische Beziehungen im KZ – zu intim für die Forschung?' *Spiegel*, 17 December 2020. https://www.spiegel.de/geschichte/lesbische-beziehungen-im-kz-zu-intim-fuer-die-forschung-a-74df1056-ec60-44f9-a2b4-5697493d7a3f.

Guenther, Irene. *Nazi Chic? Fashioning Women in the Third Reich*. Oxford: Berg, 2004.

Gusarov, Katya. 'Sexual Barter and Jewish Women's Efforts to Save Their Lives: Accounts from the Righteous among the Nations Archives.' *German History* 39, no. 1 (2021): 100–11.

Gutsche, Kerstin. *Ich ahnungsloser Engel: Lesbenprotokolle*. Berlin: Reiher, 1990.

Gutting, Gary, and Johanna Oksala. 'Michel Foucault.' In *Stanford Encyclopedia of Philosophy*, edited by Edward N. Zalta, Summer 2021. https://plato.stanford.edu/archives/sum2021/entries/foucault/.

Haak, Debra M. 'Who Are We Talking about When We Talk about Prostitution and Sex Work?' *The Conversation*, 15 January 2018. https://theconversation.com/who-are-we-talking-about-when-we-talk-about-prostitution-and-sex-work-88123.

Haarer, Johanna. *Die deutsche Mutter und ihr erstes Kind*. München and Berlin: Lehmanns, 1943.

Hagemann, Karen, and Stefanie Schüler-Springform, eds. *Home/Front: The Military, War and Gender in Twentieth-Century Germany*. Oxford: Berg, 2002.

Hagener, Malte, ed. *Geschlecht in Fesseln: Sexualität zwischen Aufklärung und Ausbeutung im Weimarer Kino 1918–1933*. München: Ed. Text und Kritik, 2000.

Haggerty, George E. 'Male Love and Friendship in the Eighteenth Century.' In *Love, Sex, Intimacy, and Friendship between Men, 1550–1800*, edited by Katherine O'Donnell and Michael O'Rourke, 70–81. Basingstoke: Palgrave Macmillan, 2003.

Hahn, Barbara. 'Rahel Levin Varnhagen (1771–1833).' In *The Shalvi/Hyman Encyclopedia of Jewish Women*. The Jewish Women's Archive, 23 June 2021. https://jwa.org/encyclopedia/article/varnhagen-rahel-levin#pid-17099.

Haire, Norman, ed. *W.L.S.R. World League for Sexual Reform. Proceedings of the Third Congress (London)*. London: Kegan Paul, 1930.

Hájková, Anna. 'Den Holocaust queer erzählen.' *Jahrbuch Sexualitäten* edited by Janin Afken et al., 86–110. Göttingen: Wallstein, 2018.

Hájková, Anna. 'Introduction: Sexuality, Holocaust, Stigma.' *German History* 39, no. 1 (2021): 1–14.

Hájková, Anna. *Menschen ohne Geschichte sind Staub: Homophobie und Holocaust*. Hirschfeld-Lectures no. 14. Göttingen: Wallstein, 2021.

Hájková, Anna. 'Queere Geschichte und der Holocaust.' *Aus Politik und Zeitgeschichte* 38–9 (14 September 2018). http://www.bpb.de/apuz/275892/queere-geschichte-und-der-holocaust.

Hájková, Anna. 'Sexual Barter in Times of Genocide: Negotiating the Sexual Economy of the Theresienstadt Ghetto.' *Signs* 38, no. 3 (2013): 503–33.

Hájková, Anna, and Elissa Mailänder, eds. 'Forum: Holocaust and the History of Gender and Sexuality.' *German History* 36, no. 1 (2017): 78–100.

Halberstam, Jack (Judith). *The Queer Art of Failure*. Durham: Duke University Press, 2011.

Halperin, David M. *How to Do the History of Homosexuality*. Chicago: University of Chicago Press, 2002.

Hancock, Eleanor. *Ernst Röhm: Hitler's SA Chief of Staff*. New York: Palgrave Macmillan, 2008.

Hancock, Eleanor. '"Only the Real, the True, the Masculine Held Its Value": Ernst Röhm, Masculinity, and Male Homosexuality.' *Journal of the History of Sexuality* 8, no. 4 (1998): 616–41.

Hancock, Eleanor. 'The Purge of the SA Reconsidered: "An Old Putschist Trick"?' *Central European History* 44, no. 4 (2011): 669–83.

Haritaworn, Jin. *Queer Lovers and Hateful Others: Regenerating Violent Times and Places*. London: Pluto, 2015.

Hark, Sabine. *Koalition des Überlebens: Queere Bündnispolitiken im 21. Jahrhundert*. Hirschfeld-Lectures 11. Göttingen: Wallstein, 2017.

Hark, Sabine, and Paula-Irene Villa, eds. *Anti-Genderismus: Sexualität und Geschlecht als Schauplätze aktueller politischer Auseinandersetzungen*. Bielefeld: transcript, 2015.

Hark, Sabine, and Paula-Irene Villa, eds. *Unterscheiden und herrschen: Ein Essay zu den ambivalenten Verflechtungen von Rassismus, Sexismus und Feminismus in der Gegenwart*. Bielefeld: transcript, 2017.

Harrington, Joel F. *Reordering Marriage and Society in Reformation Germany*. Cambridge: Cambridge University Press, 1995.

Harris, Victoria. *Selling Sex in the Reich: Prostitutions in German Society, 1914-1945*. Oxford: Oxford University Press, 2010.

Harrowitz, Nancy A., and Barbara Hyams, eds. *Jews & Gender: Responses to Otto Weininger*. Philadelphia: Temple University Press, 1995.

Harsch, Donna. *Revenge of the Domestic: Women, the Family, and Communism in the German Democratic Republic*. Princeton: Princeton University Press, 2007.

Harsch, Donna. 'Society, the State, and Abortion in East Germany, 1950–1972.' *The American Historical Review* 102, no. 1 (1997): 53–84.

Harvey, Elizabeth. 'Culture and Society in Weimar Germany: The Impact of Modernism and Mass Culture.' In *German History since 1800*, edited by Mary Fulbrook, 279–97. London: Arnold, 1997.

Hau, Michael. *The Cult of Health and Beauty in Germany: A Social History, 1890–1930*. Chicago: University of Chicago Press, 2003.

Hausen, Karin. '"… eine Ulme für das schwanke Efeu". Ehepaare im deutschen Bildungsbürgertum.' In *Bürgerinnen und Bürger*, edited by Ute Frevert, 85–117. Göttingen: Vandenhoeck & Ruprecht, 1988.

Hebditsch, David, and Nick Anning. *Porn Gold. Die Geschäfte mit der Pornografie*. München: J&V, 1989.

Heineman, Elizabeth D. *Before Porn Was Legal: The Erotica Empire of Beate Uhse*. Chicago: University of Chicago Press, 2011.

Heineman, Elizabeth. 'The Hour of the Woman: Memories of Germany's "Crisis Years" and West German National Identity.' *American Historical Review* 101, no. 2 (1996): 354–95.

Heineman, Elizabeth D. 'Sexuality and Nazism: The Doubly Unspeakable?' *Journal of the History of Sexuality* 11, no. 1/2 (2002): 22–66.

Heineman, Elizabeth D. 'Sexuality and Nazism: The Doubly Unspeakable?' In *Sexuality and German Fascism*, edited by Dagmar Herzog, 22–66. New York: Berghahn, 2005.

Heineman, Elizabeth D. *What Difference Does a Husband Make? Women and Marital Status in Nazi and Postwar Germany*. Berkeley: University of California Press, 1999.

Heinemann, Isabel. '"Enttäuschung unvermeidlich?" Die Debatten über Ehescheidung, Abtreibung und das Dispositiv der Kernfamilie in der BRD.' In *Enttäuschung im 20. Jahrhundert: Erfahrung und Deutung von politischem Engagement in der Bundesrepublik Deutschland während der 1970er und 1980er Jahre*, edited by Bernhard Gotto, and Anna Ulrich, 55–86. Berlin: De Gruyter Oldenbourg, 2018.

Heinsohn, Kirsten, ed. *Zwischen Karriere und Verfolgung: Handlungsräume von Frauen im nationalsozialistischen Deutschland*. Frankfurt am Main: Campus, 1997.

Hermand, Jost, and Frank Trommler. *Die Kultur der Weimarer Republik*. Frankfurt am Main: Fischer, 1988.

Herrn, Rainer. *Das 3. Geschlecht. Reprint der 1930–1932 erschienenen Zeitschrift für Transvestiten*. Hamburg: Männerschwarm, 2016.

Herrn, Rainer. *Der Liebe und dem Leid: Das Institut für Sexualwissenschaft 1919–1933*. Berlin: Suhrkamp, 2022.

Herrn, Rainer. 'In der heutigen Staatsführung kann es nicht angehen, daß sich Männer in Frauenkleidung frei auf der Straße bewegen. Über den Forschungsstand zum Trans*vestitismus in der NS-Zeit.' In *Homosexuelle im Nationalsozialismus. Neue Forschungsperspektiven zu*

Lebenssituationen von lesbischen, schwulen, bi-, trans*- und intersexuellen Menschen 1933 bis 1945, edited by Michael Schwartz, 101–6. München: De Gruyter, 2014.

Herrn, Rainer. *Schnittmuster des Geschlechts: Transvestitismus und Transsexualität in der frühen Sexualwissenschaft*. Beiträge zur Sexualforschung 85. Gießen: Psychosozial-Verlag, 2005.

Herrn, Rainer. 'Transvestitismus in der NS-Zeit: Ein Forschungsdesiderat.' *Zeitschrift für Sexualforschung* 26, no. 4 (2013): 330–71.

Herrn, Rainer. 'Vom Traum zum Trauma. Das Institut für Sexualwissenschaft.' In *Der Sexualreformer Magnus Hirschfeld: Ein Leben im Spannungsfeld von Wissenschaft, Politik und Gesellschaft*, edited by Elke-Vera Kotowski, and Julius H. Schoeps, 173–200. Berlin-Brandenburg: be.bra wissenschaft, 2004.

Herrn, Rainer, and Christine N. Brinckmann. 'Of Rats and Men: Rejuvenation and the Steinach Film.' In *Not Straight from Germany: Sexual Publics and Sexual Citizenship since Magnus Hirschfeld*, edited by Michael Thomas Taylor, Annette F. Timm, and Rainer Herrn, 212–34. Ann Arbor: University of Michigan Press, 2017.

Herrn, Rainer, and Michael Thomas Taylor. 'Magnus Hirschfeld's Interpretation of the Japanese Onnagata as Transvestites.' *Journal of the History of Sexuality* 27, no. 1 (2018): 63–100.

Herzer, Manfred. *Magnus Hirschfeld: Leben und Werk eines jüdischen, schwulen und sozialistischen Sexologen*. 2nd, revised ed. Hamburg: MännerschwarmSkript, 2001.

Herzog, Dagmar. *Cold War Freud: Psychoanalysis in an Age of Catastrophes*. Cambridge: Cambridge University Press, 2017.

Herzog, Dagmar. 'European Sexualities in the Age of Total War.' In *The Oxford Handbook of European History, 1914–1945*, edited by Nicholas Doumanis, 1–16 (online version). Oxford, New York: Oxford University Press, 2016.

Herzog, Dagmar. 'Hubris and Hypocrisy, Incitement and Disavowal: Sexuality and German Fascism.' In *Sexuality and German Fascism*, edited by Dagmar Herzog, 3–21. New York: Berghahn, 2005.

Herzog, Dagmar. 'Religious Dissent and the Roots of German Feminism.' In *Gender Relations in German History*, edited by Lynn Abrams, and Elizabeth Harvey, 81–100. London: UCL Press, 1996.

Herzog, Dagmar. *Sex after Fascism: Memory and Morality in Twentieth-Century Germany*. Princeton: Princeton University Press, 2005.

Herzog, Dagmar. *Sexuality and German Fascism*. New York: Berghahn, 2005.

Herzog, Dagmar. *Sexuality in Europe: A Twentieth-Century History*. Cambridge: Cambridge University Press, 2011.

Herzog, Dagmar. 'Syncopated Sex: Transforming European Sexual Cultures.' *American Historical Review* 114 (2009): 1287–308.

Herzog, Dagmar. 'The East German Sexual Evolution.' In *Socialist Modern: East German Everyday Culture and Politics*, edited by Katherine Pence, and Paul Betts, 71–95. Ann Arbor: University of Michigan Press, 2008.

Herzog, Dagmar. 'The Reception of the Kinsey Reports in Europe.' *Sexuality & Culture* 10, no. 1 (2006): 39–48.

Herzog, Dagmar. *Unlearning Eugenics: Sexuality, Reproduction, and Disability in Post-Nazi Europe*. Madison: University of Wisconsin Press, 2018.

Hill, Darryl. 'Sexuality and Gender in Hirschfeld's *Die Transvestiten*: A Case of the "Elusive Evidence of the Ordinary."' *Journal of the History of Sexuality* 14, no. 3 (2005): 316–32.

Hirschfeld, Magnus. 'Ärztliche Eheberatung.' *Die Ehe* 1, no. 1 (1926): 3–6.

Hirschfeld, Magnus. *Berlins Drittes Geschlecht [1904]*. Edited by Manfred Herzer. Berlin: Rosa Winkel, 1991.

Hirschfeld, Magnus. *Berlin's Third Sex*. Translated by James J. Conway. Berlin: Rixdorf, 2017.

Hirschfeld, Magnus. *Die Transvestiten. Eine Untersuchung über den erotischen Verkleidungstrieb*. Berlin: Med. Verlag Alfred Pulvermacher, 1910.

Hirschfeld, Magnus. *Sexuelle Zwischenstufen: Das männliche Weib und der weibliche Mann*. 2nd ed. Vol. 2. 3 vols. Sexualpathologie: Ein Lehrbuch für Ärzte und Studierende. Bonn: A. Marcus & E. Webers, 1922.

Hirschfeld, Magnus. *The Homosexuality of Men and Women*. Translated by Michael A. Lombardi-Nash. Amherst, NY: Prometheus Books, 2000.

Hitler, Adolf. *Mein Kampf*. München: Franz Eher, 1942.

Hochstadt, Steve. 'Population: Demography and Mobility.' In *The Ashgate Research Companion to Imperial Germany*, edited by Matthew Jeffries, 333–44. London: Routledge, 2015.

Höhn, Maria. *GIs and Fräuleins: The German-American Encounter in 1950s West Germany*. Chapel Hill: University of North Carolina Press, 2002.

Homann, Walter, ed. *Tagebuch einer männlichen Braut*. Berlin: Dreyer, 1907.

Hong, Young-Sun. *Welfare, Modernity, and the Weimar State, 1919–1933*. Princeton: Princeton University Press, 1998.

Horney, Karen. 'Gehemmte Weiblichkeit. Psychoanalytischer Beitrag zum Problem der Frigidität.' *Zeitschrift für Sexualwissenschaft* 13, no. 2 (1926): 67–77.

Hotchkiss, Valerie R. *Clothes Make the Man: Female Cross Dressing in Medieval Europe*. New York: Garland, 1996.

Houlbrook, Matt, and Harry Cocks, eds. *Palgrave Advances in the Modern History of Sexuality*. Basingstoke: Palgrave Macmillan, 2006.

Hsia, R. Po-Chia. *Social Discipline in the Reformation: Central Europe, 1550–1750*. London: Routledge, 1989.

Hull, Isabel V. 'Kaiser Wilhelm and the "Liebenberg Circle."' In *Kaiser Wilhelm II, New Interpretations: The Corfu Papers*, edited by John Röhl and Nicolaus Sombart, 193–220. Cambridge: Cambridge University Press, 1982.

Hull, Isabel V. *Sexuality, State and Civil Society in Germany, 1700–1815*. Ithaca: Cornell University Press, 1996.

Huneke, Samuel Clowes. 'Heterogeneous Persecution: Lesbianism and the Nazi State.' *Central European History* 54, no. 2 (2021): 297–325.

Huneke, Samuel Clowes. *States of Liberation: Gay Men between Dictatorship and Democracy in Cold War Germany*. Toronto: University of Toronto Press, 2022.

Huneke, Samuel Clowes. 'The Duplicity of Tolerance: Lesbian Experiences in Nazi Berlin.' *Journal of Contemporary History* 54, no. 1 (2019): 30–59.

Hung, Jochen. 'The Modernized Gretchen: Transformations of the "New Woman" in the Late Weimar Republic.' *German History* 33, no. 1 (2015): 52–79.

Hung, Jochen, Godela Weiss-Sussex, and Geoff Wilkes, eds. *Beyond Glitter and Doom: The Contingency of the Weimar Republic*. London: IMLR, 2012.

Isherwood, Christopher. *Christopher and His Kind*. New York: Farrar, Straus and Giroux, 1976.

Isherwood, Christopher. *Goodbye to Berlin*. London: Hogarth, 1939.

Jagose, Annamarie. *Orgasmology*. Durham: Duke University Press, 2012.

Jarausch, Konrad H. 'Students, Sex and Politics in Imperial Germany.' *Journal of Contemporary History* 17 (1982): 285–303.

Jarzebowski, Claudia. 'The Meaning of Love: Emotion and Kinship in Sixteenth-Century Incest Discourses.' In *Mixed Matches: Transgressive Unions in Germany from the Reformation to the Enlightenment*, edited by David M. Luebke, and Mary Lindemann, 166–83. New York: Berghahn, 2014.

Jefferies, Matthew. '"For a Genuine and Noble Nakedness"? German Naturism in the Third Reich.' *German History* 24, no. 1 (2006): 62–84.

Jelavich, Peter. *Berlin Cabaret*. Cambridge, MA: Harvard University Press, 1993.

Jellonnek, Burkhard. *Homosexuelle unter dem Hakenkreuz: Die Verfolgung von Homosexuellen im Dritten Reich*. Paderborn: Schöningh, 1990.

Jenkins, Jennifer L. *Provincial Modernity: Local Culture and Liberal Politics in Fin-de-Siècle Hamburg*. Ithaca: Cornell University Press, 2003.

Jensen, Birgit A. 'Bawdy Bodies or Moral Agency? The Struggle for Identity in Working-Class Autobiographies of Imperial Germany.' *Biography* 28, no. 4 (2005): 534–57.

Jensen, Erik N. 'The Pink Triangle and Political Consciousness: Gays, Lesbians, and the Memory of Nazi Persecution.' *Journal of the History of Sexuality* 11, no. 1/2 (2002): 319–49.

Jewell, Helen M. *Women in Late Medieval and Reformation Europe 1200–1550*. Basingstoke: Palgrave Macmillan, 2007.

Jones, Elizabeth. *Gender and Rural Modernity: Farm Women and the Politics of Labor in Germany, 1871–1933*. Farnham: Ashgate, 2009.

Joshi, Vandana. 'Maternalism, Race, Class and Citizenship: Aspects of Illegitimate Motherhood in Nazi Germany.' *Journal of Contemporary History* 46, no. 4 (2011): 832–53.

'Judith Butler drückt die Spaßbremse.' *taz*, 20 June 2010, https://taz.de/Eklat-beim-Berliner-CSD/!5140677/.

Jünger, Ernst. *In Stahlgewittern: Historisch-kritische Ausgabe*. Edited by Helmuth Kiesel. Stuttgart: Klett-Cotta, 2013.

Jürgens-Kirchhoff, Annegret. '"Sterbelust und Opferdrang." Die Erotisierung des Krieges.' In *Gewalt im Krieg. Ausübung, Erfahrung und Verweigerung von Gewalt in Kriegen des 20. Jahrhunderts*, edited by Andreas Gestrich, 75–98. Münster: Lit, 1996.

Jütte, Robert. *Contraception: A History*. Cambridge: Polity, 2008.

Kaes, Anton, Martin Jay, and Edward Dimendberg. *The Weimar Republic Sourcebook*. Berkeley: University of California Press, 1994.

Kahan, Benjamin, ed. *Heinrich Kaan's 'Psychopathia Sexualis' (1844)*. Translated by Melissa Haynes. Ithaca: Cornell University Press, 2016.

Kahan, Benjamin. *The Book of Minor Perverts: Sexology, Etiology, and the Emergences of Sexuality*. Chicago: University of Chicago Press, 2019.

Kaplan, Marion A. *Between Dignity and Despair: Jewish Life in Nazi Germany*. New York, Oxford: Oxford University Press, 1999.

Kaplan, Marion A. *The Jewish Feminist Movement in Germany: The Campaign of the Jüdischer Frauenbund 1904–1938*. Westport, CT: Greenwood, 1979.

Karras, Ruth Mazo. *Sexuality in Medieval Europe: Doing Unto Others.* 3rd ed. London, New York: Routledge, 2017.

Karras, Ruth Mazo. 'The History of Marriage and the Myth of Friedelehe.' *Early Medieval Europe* 14, no. 2 (2006): 119–51.

Karsch-Haack, Ferdinand. 'Junggesellin und Junggeselle (Die Transmutistin).' *Garçonne* 4 (1931): 1–4.

Kaufmann, Doris. 'Science as Cultural Practice: Psychiatry in the First World War and Weimar Germany.' *Journal of Contemporary History* 34, no. 1 (1999): 125–44.

Keilson-Lauritz, Marita. 'Benedict Friedlaender und die Anfänge der Sexualwissenschaft.' *Zeitschrift für Sexualforschung* 18, no. 4 (2005): 311–31.

Keilson-Lauritz, Marita. *Die Geschichte der eigenen Geschichte: Literatur und Literaturkritik in den Anfängen der Schwulenbewegung.* Berlin: Rosa Winkel, 1997.

Kenawi, Samirah. *Frauengruppen in der DDR.* Berlin: GrauZone, 1995.

Kertbeny, Karoly Maria. 'Paragraph 143 and the Prussian Penal Code.' In *Sodomites and Urnings: Homosexual Representations in Classic German Journals*, edited and translated by Michael A. Lombardi-Nash, 46–78. New York: Harrington Park, 2006.

Kettlitz, Eberhardt. *Afrikanische Soldaten aus deutscher Sicht seit 1871: Stereotype, Vorurteile, Feindbilder und Rassismus.* Frankfurt am Main: Peter Lang, 2006.

Killen, Andreas. *Berlin Electropolis. Shock, Nerves, and German Modernity.* Berkeley: University of California Press, 2005.

Killen, Andreas. 'What Is an Enlightenment Film? Cinema and the Rhetoric of Social Hygiene in Interwar Germany.' *Social Science History* 39, no. 1 (2015): 107–27.

Klinksiek, Dorothee. *Die Frau im NS-Staat.* Stuttgart: Dt. Verl.Anst., 1982.

Klöppel, Ulrike. 'Intersex im Nationalsozialismus.' In *Homosexuelle im Nationalsozialismus*, edited by Michael Schwartz, 107–14. München: De Gruyter, 2014.

Klöppel, Ulrike. *XX0XY ungelöst: Hermaphroditismus, Sex und Gender in der deutschen Medizin. Eine historische Studie zur Intersexualität.* Bielefeld: Transcript, 2010.

Kniesche, Thomas W., and Stephen Brockmann. *Dancing on the Volcano: Essays on the Culture of the Weimar Republic.* Columbia, SC: Camden House, 1994.

Kögel, Annette, Jörn Hasselmann and Ferda Ataman. 'Heftige Diskussionen nach Kritik an CSD.' *Der Tagesspiegel*, 20 June 2010. https://www.tagesspiegel. de/berlin/stadtleben/butler-auftritt-heftige-diskussionen-nach-kritik-an-csd/1864540.html.

Kolano, Uta. '"… ein romantisches Ideal" (interview with Kurt Starke).' In Uta Kolano, *Nackter Osten*, 83–86. Frankfurt/Oder: Frankfurter Oder Editionen, 1995.

Kollmann, Gertrud. 'Die Liebes-Maske.' *Die Welt der Transvestiten/Die Freundin*, 18 May 1932, n.p.

König, Malte. 'Geburtenkontrolle. Abtreibung und Empfängnisverhütung in Frankreich und Detuschland, 1870–1940.' *Francia. Forschungen zur westeuropäischen Geschichte* 38 (2011): 127–48.

Könne, Christian. 'Schwule und Lesben in der DDR und der Umgang des SED-Staates mit Homosexualität.' *BpB: Bundeszentrale für politische Bildung*, 28 February 2018. https://www.bpb.de/geschichte/zeitgeschichte/deutschlandarchiv/265466/schwule-und-lesben-in-der-ddr.

Koonz, Claudia. *Mothers in the Fatherland: Women, The Family, and Nazi Politics.* New York: St. Martin's Press, 1987.

Kościańska, Agnieszka. *Gender, Pleasure, and Violence: The Construction of Expert Knowledge of Sexuality in Poland.* Bloomington: Indiana University Press, 2021.

Kounine, Laura. *Imagining the Witch: Emotions, Gender, and Selfhood in Early Modern Germany.* Oxford: Oxford University Press, 2018.

Krafft-Ebing, R. von. *Psychopathia Sexualis with Especial Reference to Antipathic Sexual Instinct: A Medico-Forensic Study.* English translation of 10th German ed. London: Rebman, 1899.

Kraß, Andreas. *Ein Herz und eine Seele: Geschichte der Männerfreundschaft.* Frankfurt am Main: Fischer, 2016.

Kravetz, Melissa. *Women Doctors in Weimar and Nazi Germany: Maternalism, Eugenics, and Professional Identity.* Toronto: University of Toronto Press, 2019.

Krimmer, Elisabeth. *In the Company of Men: Cross-Dressed Women around 1800.* Detroit: Wayne State University Press, 2004.

Kruse, Judith. 'Nische im Sozialismus.' In *Endlich Urlaub! Begleitbuch zur Ausstellung im Haus der Geschichte der Bundesrepublik Deutschland, Bonn, 6. Juni bis 13. Oktober 1996*, edited by Hans Walter Hütter, 106–11. Cologne: DuMont Reiseverlag, 1996.

Kühne, Thomas. '"… aus diesem Krieg werden nicht nur harte Männer heimkehren": Kriegskameradschaft und Männlichkeit im 20. Jahrhundert.' In *Männergeschichte – Geschlechtergeschichte: Männlichkeit im Wandel der Moderne*, edited by Thomas Kühne, 174–92. Frankfurt and New York: Campus, 1996.

Kühne, Thomas, ed. *Männergeschichte – Geschlechtergeschichte. Männlichkeit im Wandel der Moderne.* Frankfurt and New York: Campus, 1996.

Kühne, Thomas. *The Rise and Fall of Comradeship: Hitler's Soldiers, Male Bonding and Mass Violence in the Twentieth Century.* Cambridge: Cambridge University Press, 2017.

Kundrus, Birthe. 'Forbidden Company: Romantic Relationships between Germans and Foreigners, 1939 to 1945.' In *Sexuality and German Fascism*, edited by Dagmar Herzog, 201–22. New York: Berghahn, 2005.

Kundrus, Birthe. 'Frauen und Nationalsozialismus. Überlegungen zum Stand der Forschung.' *Archiv für Sozialgeschichte* 36 (1996): 481–99.

Kundrus, Birthe. *Kriegerfrauen. Familienpolitik und Geschlechterverhältnisse im Ersten und Zweiten Weltkrieg.* Hamburg: Hans Christians Verlag, 1995.

Kurimay, Anita. *Queer Budapest, 1873–1961.* Chicago: University of Chicago Press, 2020.

LaLove, Patsy l'Amour, ed. *Beissreflexe: Kritik an queerem Aktivismus, autoritären Sehnsüchten, Sprechverboten.* Berlin: Querverlag, 2017.

Lang, Birgit, Joy Damousi, and Alison Lewis. *A History of the Case Study: Sexology, Psychoanalysis, Literature.* Manchester: Manchester University Press, 2017.

Lang, Birgit, and Katie Sutton. 'The Queer Cases of Psychoanalysis: Rethinking the Scientific Study of Homosexuality, 1890s–1920s.' *German History* 34, no. 3 (2016): 419–44.

Laqueur, Thomas. *Solitary Sex: A Cultural History of Masturbation*. New York: Zone, 2003.

Laqueur, Thomas Walter. *Making Sex: Body and Gender from the Greeks to Freud*. Cambridge, MA: Harvard University Press, 1990.

Lareau, Alan. 'Lavender Songs: Undermining Gender in Weimar Cabaret and Beyond.' *Popular Music and Society* 281 (2005): 15–33.

Lautmann, Rüdiger, and Michael Schetsche. *Das pornographische Begehren*. Frankfurt am Main: Campus, 1990.

Leck, Ralph M. *Vita Sexualis: Karl Ulrichs and the Origins of Sexual Science*. Urbana: University of Illinois Press, 2016.

Lehnert, Gertrud. *Wenn Frauen Männerkleider tragen: Geschlecht und Maskerade in Literatur und Geschichte*. München: dtv, 1997.

Leidinger, Christiane. '"Anna Rüling": A Problematic Foremother of Lesbian Herstory.' *Journal of the History of Sexuality* 13, no. 4 (2004): 477–99.

Lemke, Jürgen. *Gay Voices from East Germany. Interviews by Jürgen Lemke*. Edited by John Borneman. Bloomington: Indiana University Press, 1991.

Leng, Kirsten. 'Culture, Difference, and Sexual Progress in Turn-of-the-Century Europe: Cultural Othering and the German League for the Protection of Mothers and Sexual Reform, 1905–1914.' *Journal of the History of Sexuality* 25, no. 1 (2016): 62–82.

Leng, Kirsten. 'Historicising "Compulsory Able-Bodiedness": The History of Sexology Meets Queer Disability Studies.' *Gender & History* 31, no. 2 (2019): 319–33.

Leng, Kirsten. 'Magnus Hirschfeld's Meanings: Analysing Biography and the Politics of Representation.' *German History* 35, no. 1 (2017): 96–116.

Leng, Kirsten. *Sexual Politics and Feminist Science: Women Sexologists in Germany, 1900–1933*. Ithaca: Cornell University Press, 2017.

Lenman, Robin. 'Control of the Visual Image in Imperial Germany.' In *Zensur und Kultur/Censorship and Culture*, edited by John A. McCarthy and Werner von der Ohe, 111–22. Tübingen: Max Niemeyer Verlag, 1995.

Lennox, Sara. 'Race, Gender, and Sexuality in German Southwest Africa: Hans Grimms "Südafrikanische Novellen."' In *Germany's Colonial Pasts*, edited by Eric Ames, Marcia Klotz, and Lora Wildenthal, 63–75. Lincoln and London: University of Nebraska Press, 2005.

Leo, Annette, and Christian König. *Die 'Wunschkindpille': Weibliche Erfahrung und staatliche Geburtenpolitik in der DDR*. Göttingen: Wallstein, 2015.

Lerner, Paul Frederick. *Hysterical Men: War, Psychiatry, and the Politics of Trauma in Germany, 1890–1930*. Ithaca: Cornell University Press, 2003.

Levitin, Dmitri. 'Misrepresentations. The Islamic Enlightenment.' *London Review of Books* 40, no. 22, 22 November 2018. https://www.lrb.co.uk/the-paper/v40/n22/dmitri-levitin/misrepresentations.

Lewis, Alison. *Eine schwierige Ehe. Liebe, Geschlecht und die Geschichte der deutschen Wiedervereinigung im Spiegel der Literatur*. Freiburg: Rombach, 2009.

Lindemann, Mary. 'Aufklärung, Literature, and Fatherly Love: An Eighteenth-Century Case of Incest.' In *Mixed Matches: Trangressive Unions in Germany from the Reformation to the Enlightenment*, edited by David M. Luebke, and Mary Lindemann, 184–203. New York: Berghahn, 2014.

Lindemann, Mary. 'Gender Tales: The Multiple Identities of Maiden Heinrich, Hamburg 1700.' In *Gender in Early Modern German History*, edited by Ulinka Rublack, 131–51. Cambridge: Cambridge University Press, 2002.

Linge, Ina. 'Gender and Agency between "Sexualwissenschaft" and Autobiography: The Case of N.O. Body's "Aus eines Mannes Mädchenjahren".' *German Life and Letters* 68 (2015): 387–405.

Linge, Ina. 'Sexology, Popular Science and Queer History in "Anders Als Die Andern" ("Different from the Others").' *Gender & History* 30, no. 3 (2018): 596–610.

Linke, Uli. *German Bodies: Race and Representation after Hitler*. New York: Routledge, 1999.

Linse, Ulrich. 'Sonnenmenschen unter der Swastika. Die FKK-Bewegung im Dritten Reich.' In *Freikörperkultur und Lebenswelt: Studien zur Vor- und Frühgeschichte der Freikörperkultur in Deutschland*, edited by Michael Grisko, 239–96. Kassel: Kassel University Press, 1999.

Lišková, Katerina. *Sexual Liberation, Socialist Style: Communist Czechoslovakia and the Science of Desire, 1945–1989*. Cambridge: Cambridge University Press, 2018.

Lochrie, Karma. *Heterosyncrasies: Female Sexuality When Normal Wasn't*. Minneapolis: University of Minnesota Press, 2005.

Lochrie, Karma, Peggy McCracken, and James A. Schultz, eds. *Constructing Medieval Sexuality*. Minneapolis: University of Minnesota Press, 1997.

Lopes, Anne, and Gary Roth. *Men's Feminism: August Bebel and the German Socialist Movement*. Amherst, NY: Humanity, 2000.

Love, Heather. *Feeling Backward: Loss and the Politics of Queer History*. Cambridge, MA: Harvard University Press, 2007.

Lücke, Martin. *Männlichkeit in Unordnung. Homosexualität und männliche Prostitution in Kaiserreich und Weimarer Republik*. Frankfurt: Campus, 2008.

Ludwig-Körner, Christiane. *Wiederentdeckt-Psychoanalytikerinnen in Berlin*. Gießen: Psychosozial-Verlag, 1999.

Luebke, David M. 'Introduction: Transgressive Unions.' In *Mixed Matches: Trangressive Unions in Germany from the Reformation to the Enlightenment*, edited by David M. Luebke, and Mary Lindemann, 1–13. New York: Berghahn, 2014.

Luebke, David M. and Mary Lindemann, eds. *Mixed Matches: Trangressive Unions in Germany from the Reformation to the Enlightenment*. New York: Berghahn, 2014.

Lybeck, Marti M. *Desiring Emancipation: New Women and Homosexuality in Germany, 1890–1933*. Albany: State University of New York Press, 2014.

MacGregor, Neil. *Germany: Memories of a Nation*. London: Penguin, 2016.

Mahlsdorf, Charlotte von. *Ich bin meine eigene Frau. Ein Leben*. München: dtv, 1995.

Mailänder, Elissa. *Female SS Guards and Workaday Violence: The Majdanek Concentration Camp, 1942–1944*. Translated by Patricia Szobar. East Lansing: Michigan State University Press, 2015.

Mailänder, Elissa. 'Making Sense of a Rape Photograph: Sexual Violence as Social Performance on the Eastern Front, 1939–1944.' *Journal of the History of Sexuality* 26, no. 3 (2017): 489–520.

Maiwald, Stefan, and Gerd Mischler. *Sexualität unter dem Hakenkreuz. Manipulation und Vernichtung der Intimsphäre im NS-Staat.* Hamburg and Vienna: Europa, 1999.

Mak, Geertje. 'Conflicting Heterosexualities: Hermaphroditism and the Emergence of Surgery around 1900.' *Journal of the History of Sexuality* 24, no. 3 (2015): 402–27.

Mak, Geertje. *Doubting Sex: Inscriptions, Bodies and Selves in Nineteenth-Century Hermaphrodite Case Histories.* Manchester: Manchester University Press, 2012.

Mak, Geertje. '"Passing Women" im Sprechzimmer von Magnus Hirschfeld. Warum der Begriff "Transvestit" nicht für Frauen in Männerkleidern eingeführt wurde (transl. Mirjam Hausmann).' *Österreichische Zeitschrift für Geschichtswissenschaften* 9, no. 3 (1998): 384–99.

Makela, Maria. 'Rejuvenation and Regen(d)eration: "Der Steinachfilm," Sex Glands, and Weimar-Era Visual and Literary Culture.' *German Studies Review* 38, no. 1 (2015): 35–62.

Malakaj, Ervin. 'Richard Oswald, Magnus Hirschfeld, and the Possible Impossibility of Hygienic Melodrama.' *Studies in European Cinema* 14, no. 3 (2017): 216–30.

Maleck-Lewy, Eva. 'Between Self-Determination and State Supervision: Women and the Abortion Law in Post-Unification Germany.' *Social Politics: International Studies in Gender, State & Society* 2, no. 1 (1995): 62–75.

Mancini, Elena. *Magnus Hirschfeld and the Quest for Sexual Freedom.* New York: Palgrave Macmillan, 2010.

Marcus, Stephen. *The Other Victorians: A Study of Sexuality and Pornography in Mid-Nineteenth-Century England.* London: Weidenfeld & Nicolson, 1966.

Marhoefer, Laurie. 'Lesbianism, Transvestitism, and the Nazi State: A Microhistory of a Gestapo Investigation, 1939–1943.' *American Historical Review* 121, no. 4 (2016): 1167–95.

Marhoefer, Laurie. *Racism and the Making of Gay Rights: A Sexologist, His Student, and the Empire of Queer Love.* Toronto: University of Toronto Press, 2022.

Marhoefer, Laurie. *Sex and the Weimar Republic: German Homosexual Emancipation and the Rise of the Nazis.* Toronto: University of Toronto Press, 2015.

Marhoefer, Laurie. '"The Book Was a Revelation, I Recognized Myself in It": Lesbian Sexuality, Censorship, and the Queer Press in Weimar-Era Germany.' *Journal of Women's History* 27, no. 2 (2015): 62–86.

Marhoefer, Laurie. 'Was the Homosexual Made White? Race, Empire and Analogy in Gay and Trans Thought in Twentieth-Century Germany.' *Gender & History* 31, no. 1 (2019): 91–114.

Marschik, Matthias. 'A Fascinating Spectacle of Inconsistencies: Eroticism in the Nazi Era.' *European Journal of Cultural Studies* 6, no. 1 (2003): 95–116.

Martin, Biddy. 'Extraordinary Homosexuals and the Fear of Being Ordinary.' *Differences* 6, no. 2–3 (1994): 100–25.

Martínez, María Elena. 'Archives, Bodies, and Imagination: The Case of Juana Aguilar and Queer Approaches to History, Sexuality, and Politics.' *Radical History Review*, no. 120 (2014): 159–82.

Mason, Tim. 'Women in Germany, 1925–1940: Family, Welfare and Work. Part I.' *History Workshop* 1 (1976): 74–113.

Maß, Sandra. *Weiße Helden, Schwarze Krieger: Zur Geschichte kolonialer Männlichkeit in Deutschland, 1918–1964*. Cologne: Böhlau, 2006.

Matt, Susan J., and Peter N. Stearns, eds. *Doing Emotions History*. Urbana: University of Illinois Press, 2014.

Matysik, Tracie. 'In the Name of the Law: The "Female Homosexual" and the Criminal Code in Fin de Siècle Germany.' *Journal of the History of Sexuality* 13, no. 1 (2004): 26–48.

Matysik, Tracie. *Reforming the Moral Subject: Ethics and Sexuality in Central Europe, 1890–1930*. Ithaca: Cornell University Press, 2008.

Mauser, Wolfram, and Barbara Becker-Cantarino, eds. *Frauenfreundschaft-Männerfreundschaft. Literarische Diskurse im 18. Jahrhundert*. Tübingen: Niemeyer, 1991.

McClintock, Anne. *Imperial Leather: Race, Gender, and Sexuality in the Colonial Contest*. New York: Routledge, 1995.

McCormick, Richard W. *Gender and Sexuality in Weimar Modernity: Film, Literature, and 'New Objectivity.'* New York: Palgrave, 2001.

McCormick, Richard W. *Politics of the Self: Feminism and the Postmodern in West German Literature and Film*. Princeton: Princeton University Press, 1991.

McLellan, Josie. 'Glad to Be Gay behind the Wall: Gay and Lesbian Activism in 1970s East Germany.' *History Workshop Journal*, 74, no. 1 (2012): 105–30.

McLellan, Josie. *Love in the Time of Communism: Intimacy and Sexuality in the GDR*. Cambridge: Cambridge University Press, 2011.

McLellan, Josie. 'State Socialist Bodies: East German Nudism from Ban to Boom.' *Journal of Modern History* 79 (March 2007): 48–79.

Melching, Willem. '"A New Morality": Left-Wing Intellectuals on Sexuality in Weimar Germany.' *Journal of Contemporary History* 25, no. 1 (1990): 69–85.

Mercer, Ben. *Student Revolt in 1968: France, Italy and West Germany*. Cambridge: Cambridge University Press, 2019.

Mertens, Lothar. *Wider die sozialistische Familiennorm: Ehescheidungen in der DDR, 1950–1989*. Opladen und Wiesbaden: VS Verlag für Sozialwissenschaften, 1998.

Meyer, Adele, ed. *Lila Nächte: Die Damenklubs im Berlin der zwanziger Jahre*. Berlin: Edition Lit.Europe, 1994.

Meyer, Sibylle, and Eva Schulze. 'Frauen in der Modernisierungsfalle – Wandel von Ehe, Familie und Partnerschaft in der Bundesrepublik Deutschland.' In *Frauen in Deutschland, 1945–1992*, edited by Gisela Helwig, and Hildegard Maria Nickel, 166–89. Berlin: Akademie Verlag, 1993.

Meyerowitz, Joanne. *How Sex Changed: A History of Transsexuality in the United States*. Cambridge, MA: Harvard University Press, 2002.

Micheler, Stefan. 'Homophobic Propaganda and the Denunciation of Same-Sex-Desiring Men under National Socialism.' In *Sexuality and German Fascism*, edited by Dagmar Herzog, 95–130. New York: Berghahn, 2005.

Micheler, Stefan. *Selbstbilder und Fremdbilder der 'Anderen.' Männer begehrende Männer in der Weimarer Republik und der NS-Zeit*. Konstanz: UVK-Verl.-Ges., 2005.

Miersch, Annette. *Schulmädchen-Report. Der deutsche Sexfilm der 70er Jahre*. Berlin: Bertz + Fischer, 2003.

Mildenberger, Florian. *Die Münchner Schwulenbewegung 1969 bis 1996: Eine Fallstudie über die zweite deutsche Schwulenbewegung.* Bochum: D. Winkler, 1999.

Mildenberger, Florian. '*In Richtung der Homosexualität verdorben.*' *Psychiater, Kriminalpsychologen und Gerichtsmediziner über männliche Homosexualität. 1850–1970.* Hamburg: MännerschwarmSkript, 2002.

Mildenberger, Florian. 'Kraepelin and the "Urnings": Male Psychiatry in Psychiatric Discourse.' *History of Psychiatry* 71, no. 3 (2007): 321–35.

Moeller, Robert. *Protecting Motherhood: Women and the Family in the Politics of Postwar West Germany.* Berkeley: University of California Press, 1993.

Moeller, Robert G. 'Reconstructing the Family in Reconstruction Germany: Women and Social Policy in the Federal Republic, 1949–1955.' In *West Germany under Construction: Politics, Society, and Culture in the Adenauer Era*, edited by Robert G. Moeller, 109–33. Ann Arbor: University of Michigan Press, 1997.

Möhring, Maren. *Marmorleiber: Körperbildung in der deutschen Nacktkultur (1890–1930).* Köln: Böhlau, 2004.

Moreck, Curt. *Ein Führer durch das 'lasterhafte' Berlin: Das deutsche Babylon 1931.* Berlin: Bebra, 2018.

Mosse, George L. *Nationalism and Sexuality: Respectability and Abnormal Sexuality in Modern Europe.* New York: H. Fertig, 1985.

Mosse, George L. *The Image of Man: The Creation of Modern Masculinity.* New York: Oxford University Press, 1996.

Mouton, Michelle. *From Nurturing the Nation to Purifying the Volk: Weimar and Nazi Family Policy, 1918–1945.* Cambridge: Cambridge University Press, 2007.

Mühlhäuser, Regina. 'Reframing Sexual Violence as a Weapon and Strategy of War: The Case of the German Wehrmacht during the War and Genocide in the Soviet Union, 1941–1944.' *Journal of the History of Sexuality* 26, no. 3 (2017): 366–401.

Mühlhäuser, Regina. *Sex and the Nazi Soldier: Violent, Commercial and Consensual Contacts during the War in the Soviet Union, 1941–1945.* Translated by Jessica Spengler. Edinburgh: Edinburgh University Press, 2020.

Mühlhäuser, Regina. 'Understanding Sexual Violence during the Holocaust: A Reconsideration of Research and Sources.' *German History* 39, no. 1 (2021): 15–36.

Müller, Christine. *Männerprotokolle.* Berlin: Buchverlag Der Morgen, 1985.

Müller, Joachim, and Andreas Sternweiler, eds. *Homosexuelle Männer im KZ Sachsenhausen.* Berlin: Rosa Winkel, 2000.

Müller, Klaus. *Aber in meinem Herzen sprach eine Stimme so laut: Homosexuelle Autobiographien und medizinische Pathographien im neunzehnten Jahrhundert.* Berlin: Verlag rosa Winkel, 1991.

Neukirch, Ralf. 'Westerwelle nimmt Mronz auch künftig mit an Bord.' *Der Spiegel*, 9 March 2010. https://www.spiegel.de/politik/deutschland/auslandsreisen-westerwelle-nimmt-mronz-auch-kuenftig-mit-an-bord-a-682660.html.

Neumaier, Christopher. *Familie im 20. Jahrhundert. Konflikte um Ideale, Politiken und Praktiken.* Berlin and Boston: De Gruyter, 2019.

Neumann, Boaz. 'The Phenomenology of the German People's Body (Volkskörper) and the Extermination of the Jewish Body.' *New German Critique* 36, no. 1 (2009): 149–81.

Newsome, W. Jake. *Pink Triangle Legacies: Coming Out in the Shadow of the Holocaust.* Ithaca: Cornell University Press, 2022.

Nieden, Susanne zur. 'Aufstieg und Fall des virilen Männerhelden: Der Skandal um Ernst Röhm und seine Ermordung.' In *Homosexualität und Staatsräson*, edited by Susanne zur Nieden, 147–88. Frankfurt: Campus, 2005.

Nieden, Susanne zur. 'Homophobie und Staatsräson.' In *Homosexualität und Staatsräson. Männlichkeit, Homophobie und Politik in Deutschland 1900-1945*, edited by Susanne zur Nieden, 17–51. Frankfurt and New York: Campus, 2005.

Noakes, Jeremy, and Geoffrey Pridham, eds. *Nazism 1919–1945. A Documentary Reader.* Vol. 2: State, Economy and Society 1933–1939. 4 vols. Liverpool: Liverpool University Press, 2000.

Noakes, Jeremy. 'Nazism and Eugenics: The Background to the Nazi Sterilization Law of 14 July 1933.' In *Ideas into Politics: Aspects of European History, 1880-1950*, edited by R. J. Bullen, H. Pogge von Strandmann, and A. B. Polonsky, 75–95. Totowa, NJ: Barnes and Noble, 1984.

Nordau, Max. *Degeneration [Entartung, 1892].* New York: Howard Fertig, 1968.

Oettler, Anika. 'The Berlin Memorial to the Homosexuals Persecuted under the National Socialist Regime: Ambivalent Responses to Homosexual Visibility.' *Memory Studies* 14, no. 2 (2021): 333–47.

Oguntoye, Katharina. *Farbe bekennen: afro-deutsche Frauen auf den Spuren ihrer Geschichte.* Frankfurt am Main: Fischer, 1992.

Omran, Susanne. *Frauenbewegung und 'Judenfrage': Diskurse um Rasse und Geschlecht nach 1900.* Frankfurt: Campus, 2000.

Oosterhuis, Harry. 'Homosexual Emancipation in Germany before 1933: Two Traditions.' In *Homosexuality and Male Bonding in Pre-Nazi Germany: The Youth Movement, the Gay Movement, and Male Bonding before Hitler's Rise*, edited by Harry Oosterhuis, 1–34. New York: Haworth, 1991.

Oosterhuis, Harry, ed. *Homosexuality and Male Bonding in Pre-Nazi Germany: The Youth Movement, the Gay Movement, and Male Bonding before Hitler's Rise.* New York: Haworth, 1991.

Oosterhuis, Harry. 'Medicine, Male Bonding and Homosexuality in Nazi Germany.' *Journal of Contemporary History* 32, no. 2 (1997): 187–205.

Oosterhuis, Harry. 'Sexual Modernity in the Works of Richard von Krafft-Ebing and Albert Moll.' *Medical History* 56, no. 2 (2012): 133–55.

Oosterhuis, Harry. *Stepchildren of Nature: Krafft-Ebing, Psychiatry, and the Making of Sexual Identity.* Chicago: University of Chicago Press, 2000.

Osmond, Jonathon. 'The End of the GDR: Revolution and Voluntary Annexation.' In *German History since 1800*, edited by Mary Fulbrook, 454–72. London: Arnold, 1997.

Ostwald, Hans. *Männliche Prostitution im kaiserlichen Berlin.* Leipzig: Fiedler, 1907.

Ozment, Steven. *When Fathers Ruled: Family Life in Reformation Europe.* Cambridge, MA: Harvard University Press, 1985.

Park, Katharine. 'Cadden, Laqueur, and the "One-Sex Body."' *Medieval Feminist Forum* 46, no. 1 (2010): 96–100.

Payne, Stanley G., David J. Sorkin, and John S. Tortorice, eds. *What History Tells. George L. Mosse and the Culture of Modern Europe.* Madison: University of Wisconsin Press, 2004.

Pearce, Caroline. 'Remembering the "Unwanted" Victims: Initiatives to Memorialize the National Socialist Euthanasia Program in Germany.' *Holocaust Studies* 25, no. 1–2 (2019): 118–40.

Petersen, Klaus. 'The Harmful Publications (Young Persons) Act of 1926. Literary Censorship and the Politics of Morality in the Weimar Republic.' *German Studies Review* 15, no. 3 (1992): 505–23.

Peukert, Detlev. *The Weimar Republic: The Crisis of Classical Modernity*. Translated by Richard Deveson. London: Penguin, 1991.

Peukert, Detlev J. K. 'The Genesis of the "Final Solution" from the Spirit of Science.' In *Reevaluating the Third Reich*, edited by Thomas Childers, and Jane Caplan, 234–52. London, New York: Holmes and Meier, 1993.

Pfäfflin, Friedemann. 'Sex Reassignment, Harry Benjamin, and Some European Roots.' *International Journal of Transgenderism* 1, no. 2 (5 July 2012).

Pick, Daniel. *Faces of Degeneration: A European Disorder, c. 1848–1918*. Cambridge: Cambridge University Press, 1989.

Pine, Lisa. *Nazi Family Policy, 1933–1945*. Oxford: Berg, 1997.

Pini, Udo. *Leibeskult und Liebeskitsch: Erotik im Dritten Reich*. München: Klinkhardt und Biermann, 1992.

Plötz, Kirsten. '"Echte" Frauenleben? "Lesbierinnen" im Spiegel öffentlicher Äußerungen in den Anfängen der Bundesrepublik.' In *Homosexualitäten in der Bundesrepublik Deutschland 1949 bis 1972 (=Invertito. Jahrbuch für die Geschichte der Homosexualitäten 1)*, edited by Fachverband Homosexualität und Geschichte, 47–69. Hamburg: Männerschwarm, 1999.

Plötz, Kirsten. *Einsame Freundinnen. Lesbisches Leben während der zwanziger Jahre in der Provinz*. Hamburg: MännerschwarmSkript-Verl., 1999.

Plummer, Marjorie Elizabeth. '"Nothing More Than Common Whores and Knaves": Married Nuns and Monks in the Early German Reformation.' In *Mixed Matches: Trangressive Unions in Germany from the Reformation to the Enlightenment*, edited by David M. Luebke, and Mary Lindemann, 45–62. New York: Berghahn, 2014.

Poiger, Uta G. *Jazz, Rock, and Rebels: Cold War Politics and American Culture in a Divided Germany*. Berkeley: University of California Press, 2000.

Pommerin, Reiner. *Sterilisierung der Rheinlandbastarde: Das Schicksal einer farbigen deutschen Minderheit, 1918–1937*. Düsseldorf: Droste, 1979.

Poutrus, Kirsten. 'Von den Massenvergewaltigungen zum Mutterschutzgesetz. Abtreibungspolitik und Abtreibungspraxis in Ostdeutschland, 1945-1950.' In *Die Grenzen der Diktatur. Staat und Gesellschaft in der DDR*, edited by Richard Bessel, and Ralph Jessen, 170–98. Göttingen: Vandenhoeck & Ruprecht, 1996.

Proctor, Robert. *Racial Hygiene: Medicine under the Nazis*. Cambridge, MA: Harvard University Press, 1988.

Prosser, Jay. 'Transsexuals and the Transsexologists: Inversion and the Emergence of Transsexual Subjectivity.' In *Sexology in Culture: Labelling Bodies and Desires*, edited by Lucy Bland, and Laura Doan, 116–31. Cambridge: Polity, 1998.

Przyrembel, Alexandra. 'Transfixed by an Image: Ilse Koch, the "Kommandeuse of Buchenwald."' *German History* 19, no. 3 (2001): 369–99.

Puar, Jasbir. *Terrorist Assemblages: Homonationalism in Queer Times*. Durham: Duke University Press, 2007.

Puff, Helmut. 'Localizing Sodomy: The "Priest and Sodomite" in Pre-Reformation Germany and Switzerland.' *Journal of the History of Sexuality* 8, no. 2 (1997): 165–95.

Puff, Helmut. *Sodomy in Reformation Germany and Switzerland, 1400–1600.* Chicago: University of Chicago Press, 2003.

Pursell, Tim. 'Queer Eyes and Wagnerian Guys: Homoeroticism in the Art of the Third Reich.' *Journal of the History of Sexuality* 17, no. 1 (2008): 110–37.

Ragan, Jr., Bryant T. 'The Enlightenment Confronts Homosexuality.' In *Homosexuality in Modern France*, edited by Bryant T. Ragan, Jr., and Jeffrey Merrick, 8–29. Oxford: Oxford University Press, 1996.

Ramsay, Glenn. 'The Rites of Artgenossen: Contesting Homosexual Political Culture in Weimar Germany.' *Journal of the History of Sexuality* 17, no. 1 (2008): 85–109.

Ramsden, Roseanna. '"Something Was Crawling All over Me": Queer Fear in Women's Holocaust Testimonies.' *Holocaust Studies* 26, no. 3 (2020): 401–15.

Ras, Marion E. P. de. *Body, Femininity and Nationalism: Girls in the German Youth Movement 1900–1934.* New York and London: Routledge, 2008.

Reagin, Nancy R. *A German Women's Movement: Class and Gender in Hanover, 1880–1933.* Chapel Hill: University of North Carolina Press, 1995.

Reddy, William M. *The Making of Romantic Love: Longing and Sexuality in Europe, South Asia, and Japan, 900–1200 CE.* Chicago: University of Chicago Press, 2012.

Rehberg, Peter. 'Die queer-feministische Gender-Stasi.' *Die Zeit*, 16 June 2017. https://www.zeit.de/kultur/2017-06/beissreflexe-judith-butler-queer-sexualitaet-gender?utm_referrer=https%3A%2F%2Fwww.google.com.

Reters, Torsten. *Liebe, Ehe und Partnerwahl zur Zeit des Nationalsozialismus: Eine soziologische Semantikanalyse.* Dortmund: Projekt-Verlag, 1997.

Reuters. 'Two Transgender Women Win Seats in German Parliament.' 28 September 2021. https://www.reuters.com/world/europe/two-transgender-women-win-seats-german-parliament-2021-09-27/.

Robertson, John. *The Enlightenment: A Very Short Introduction.* Oxford: Oxford University Press, 2015.

Robertson, Ritchie. 'Historicizing Weininger: The Nineteenth-Century German Image of the Feminized Jew.' In *Modernity, Culture and 'the Jew,'* edited by Bryan Cheyette, and Laura Marcus, 23–39. Cambridge: Polity, 1998.

Roesch, Claudia. 'Pro Familia and the Reform of Abortion Laws in West Germany, 1967–1983.' *Journal of Modern European History* 17, no. 3 (2019): 297–311.

Roesch, Claudia. *Wunschkinder: Eine transnationale Geschichte der Familienplanung in der Bundesrepublik Deutschland.* Göttingen: Vandenhoeck & Ruprecht, 2021.

Roos, Julia. 'Backlash against Prostitutes' Rights: Origins and Dynamics of Nazi Prostitution Policies.' In *Sexuality and German Fascism*, edited by Dagmar Herzog, 67–94. New York: Berghahn, 2005.

Roos, Julia. 'Nationalism, Racism and Propaganda in Early Weimar Germany: Contradictions in the Campaign against the "Black Horror on the Rhine."' *German History* 30, no. 1 (2012): 45–74.

Roos, Julia. *Weimar through the Lens of Gender: Prostitution Reform, Woman's Emancipation, and German Democracy, 1919–33.* Ann Arbor: University of Michigan Press, 2010.

Roos, Julia. 'Women's Rights, Nationalist Anxiety, and the "Moral" Agenda in the Weimar Republic: Revisiting the "Black Horror" Campaign against France's African Occupation Troops.' *Central European History* 42, no. 3 (2009): 473–508.

Roper, Lyndal. '"Evil Imaginings and Fantasies": Child-Witches and the End of the Witch Craze.' In *Gender in Early Modern German History*, edited by Ulinka Rublack, 102–30. Cambridge: Cambridge University Press, 2002.

Roper, Lyndal. *Martin Luther: Renegade and Prophet*. London: The Bodley Head, 2016.

Roper, Lyndal. *Oedipus and the Devil: Witchcraft, Sexuality and Religion in Early Modern Europe*. London: Routledge, 1994.

Roper, Lyndal. *The Holy Household. Women and Morals in Reformation Augsburg*. Oxford: Clarendon Press, 1989.

Rosenkranz, Bernhard, Ulf Bollmann, and Gottfried Lorenz. *Homosexuellen-Verfolgung in Hamburg 1919–1969*. Hamburg: Lambda, 2009.

Ross, Chad. *Naked Germany: Health, Race and the Nation*. Oxford: Berg, 2005.

Rottmann, Andrea. 'Bubis behind Bars: Seeing Queer Histories in Postwar Germany through the Prison.' *Journal of the History of Sexuality* 30, no. 2 (2021): 225–52.

Rottmann, Andrea. *Queer Lives across the Wall: A Different History of Divided Berlin, 1945–1970 (Forthcoming, Working Title)*. Toronto: University of Toronto Press, 2023.

Rouette, Susan. 'Mothers and Citizens: Gender and Social Policy in Germany after the First World War.' *Central European History* 30, no. 1 (1997): 48–66.

Rowe, Dorothy. *Representing Berlin: Sexuality and the City in Imperial and Weimar Germany*. Aldershot: Ashgate, 2003.

Rublack, Ulinka. *Gender in Early Modern German History*. Cambridge: Cambridge University Press, 2002.

Rublack, Ulinka. 'Meanings of Gender in Early Modern History.' In *Gender in Early Modern German History*, 1–20. Cambridge: Cambridge University Press, 2002.

Rupp, Leila J. 'Mother of the Volk: The Image of Women in Nazi Ideology.' *Signs: Journal of Women in Culture and Society* 3, no. 2 (1977): 362–79.

Sabean, David Warren, Simon Teuscher, and Jon Mathieu, eds. *Kinship in Europe: Approaches to Long-Term Developments (1300–1900)*. New York: Berghahn, 2007.

Sadger, Isidor. 'Fragment der Psychoanalyse eines Homosexuellen.' *Jahrbuch für sexuelle Zwischenstufen mit besonderer Berücksichtigung der Homosexualität* 9 (1908): 339–424.

Sager, Christin. '"Zeig mal!" – aber wie viel?! Sexualaufkläungsbücher und ihre Fotografien um 1968.' In *Sexuelle Revolution?*, edited by Peter-Paul Bänziger, et al., 63–86. Bielefeld: Transcript, 2015.

Saldern, Adelheid von. 'Innovative Trends in Women's and Gender Studies of the National Socialist Era.' *German History* 27, no. 1 (2009): 84–112.

Salisbury, Joyce E. *Medieval Sexuality: A Research Guide*. New York: Garland, 1990.

Sander, Helke, and Barbara Johr, eds. *BeFreier und Befreite: Krieg, Vergewaltigungen, Kinder*. München: Antje Kunstmann, 1992.

Schader, Heike. *Virile, Vamps und wilde Veilchen. Sexualität, Begehren und Erotik in den Zeitschriften homosexueller Frauen im Berlin der 1920er Jahre.* Königstein/Taunus: Ulrike Helmer, 2004.

Schaffner, Anna Katharina. *Modernism and Perversion: Sexual Deviance in Sexology and Literature, 1850–1930.* Basingstoke: Palgrave Macmillan, 2011.

Schaper, Ulrike. 'Sex Drives, Bride Prices and Divorces: Legal Policy Concerning Gender Relations in German Cameroon, 1884–1916.' In *Gender History in a Transnational Perspective. Biographies, Networks, Gender Orders*, edited by Oliver Janz and Daniel Schönpflug, 243–69. New York and Oxford: Berghahn, 2014.

Schmidt, Heike I. 'Colonial Intimacy: The Rechenberg Scandal and Homosexuality in German East Africa.' *Journal of the History of Sexuality* 17, no. 1 (2008): 25–59.

Schmidt, Maruta, and Gabi Dietz, eds. *Frauen unterm Hakenkreuz: Eine Dokumentation.* München: dtv, 1985.

Schmincke, Imke. 'Sexualität als "Angelpunkt der Frauenfrage"? Zum Verhältnis von sexueller Revolution und Frauenbewegung.' In *Sexuelle Revolution?*, edited by Peter-Paul Bänziger et al., 199–222. Bielefeld: Transcript, 2015.

Schnabl, Siegfried. 'Dämpft die Pille das Verlangen?' *Für Dich*, no. 6, February 1972.

Schnabl, Siegfried. *Mann und Frau intim.* Berlin: VEB Volk und Gesundheit, 1974.

Schoppmann, Claudia. *Days of Masquerade: Life Stories of Lesbians during the Third Reich.* New York: Columbia University Press, 1996.

Schoppmann, Claudia. *Nationalsozialistische Sexualpolitik und weibliche Homosexualität.* 2nd ed. Pfaffenweiler: Centaurus, 1997.

Schröter, Anja. *Ehe und Scheidung in der DDR.* Erfurt: Landeszentrale für politische Bildung Thüringen, 2019.

Schulte, Regina. 'Peasants and Farmers' Maids: Female Farm Servants in Bavaria at the End of the Nineteenth Century.' In *The German Peasantry: Conflict and Community in Rural Society from the Eighteenth to the Twentieth Centuries*, edited by Richard J. Evans, and W. R. Lee, 158–73. London: Routledge, 2015.

Schulte, Regina. *Sperrbezirke: Tugendhaftigkeit und Prostitution in der bürgerlichen Welt.* Hamburg: Europäische Verlagsanstalt, 1994.

Schwarzer, Alice. *Der 'kleine Unterschied' und seine großen Folgen: Frauen über sich.* Frankfurt am Main: Fischer, 1975.

Scott, Joan W. 'Gender: A Useful Category of Historical Analysis.' *The American Historical Review* 91, no. 5 (1986): 1053–75.

Sears, Clare. *Arresting Dress: Cross-Dressing, Law, and Fascination in Nineteenth-Century San Francisco.* Durham and London: Duke University Press, 2015.

Sedgwick, Eve Kosofsky. *Between Men: English Literature and Male Homosocial Desire.* New York: Columbia University Press, 1985.

Sedgwick, Eve Kosofsky. *Epistemology of the Closet.* Berkeley: University of California Press, 1990.

Sedgwick, Eve Kosofsky. *Tendencies.* Durham: Duke University Press, 1993.

Seifert, Ruth. 'Der weibliche Körper als Symbol und Zeichen. Geschlechtsspezifische Gewalt und die kulturelle Konstruktion des Krieges.' In *Gewalt im Krieg.*

Ausübung, Erfahrung und Verweigerung von Gewalt in Kriegen des 20. Jahrhunderts, edited by Andreas Gestrich, 13–33. Münster: Lit, 1996.

Sengoopta, Chandak. 'Dr Steinach Coming to Make Old Young! Sex Glands, Vasectomy and the Quest for Rejuvenation in the Roaring Twenties.' *Endeavour* 27, no. 3 (2003): 122–6.

Sengoopta, Chandak. 'Glandular Politics: Experimental Biology, Clinical Medicine, and Homosexual Emancipation in Fin-de-Siècle Central Europe.' *Isis* 89 (1998): 445–73.

Sengoopta, Chandak. *Otto Weininger: Sex, Science, and Self in Imperial Vienna*. Chicago: University of Chicago Press, 2000.

Setz, Wolfram, ed. *Homosexualität in der DDR. Materialien und Meinungen*. Hamburg: Männerschwarm, 2006.

Sharp, Ingrid. 'The Sexual Unification of Germany.' *Journal of the History of Sexuality* 13, no. 3 (2004): 348–65.

Sieg, Katrin. 'Deviance and Dissidence: Sexual Subjects of the Cold War.' In *Cruising the Performative: Interventions into the Representation of Ethnicity, Nationality, and Sexuality*, edited by Sue-Ellen Case, Philip Brett, and Susan Leigh Foster, 93–111. Bloomington and Indianapolis: Indiana University Press, 1995.

Sieg, Katrin. 'The Revolution Has Been Televised: Reconfiguring History and Identity in Post-Wall Germany.' *Theatre Journal* 45, no. 1 (1993): 35–47.

Sigusch, Volkmar. *Geschichte der Sexualwissenschaft*. Frankfurt: Campus Verlag, 2008.

Sigusch, Volkmar. 'Heinrich Kaan: der Verfasser der ersten "Psychopathia sexualis": Eine biographische Skizze.' *Zeitschrift für Sexualforschung* 16 (2003): 116–42.

Silies, Eva-Maria. 'Wider die natürliche Ordnung. Die katholische Kirche und die Debatte um Empfängnisverhütung seit den 1960er Jahren.' In *Sexuelle Revolution?*, edited by Peter-Paul Bänziger et al., 153–79. Bielefeld: Transcript, 2015.

Sillge, Ursula. *Un-Sichtbare Frauen. Lesben und ihre Emanzipation in der DDR*. Berlin: Ch. Links, 1991.

Simons, Patricia. *The Sex of Men in Premodern Europe: A Cultural History*. Cambridge: Cambridge University Press, 2011.

Singy, Patrick. 'The History of Masturbation: An Essay Review.' *Journal for the History of Medicine and Allied Sciences* 59, no. 1 (2004): 112–21.

Smith, Camilla. 'Challenging Baedeker through the Art of Sexual Science: An Exploration of Gay and Lesbian Subcultures in Curt Moreck's Guide to "Depraved" Berlin (1931).' *Oxford Art Journal* 36, no. 2 (2013): 231–56.

Smith, Helmut Walser. 'Same-Sex Male Love and Patriotic Sacrifice in Prussia: On the Death of Ewald von Kleist, 1759.' *German History* 34, no. 3 (2016): 402–18.

Smith, Jill Suzanne. *Berlin Coquette: Prostitution and the New German Woman, 1890–1933*. Ithaca: Cornell University Press, 2013.

Smith, Jill Suzanne. 'Richard Oswald and the Social Hygiene Film: Promoting Public Health or Promiscuity?' In *The Many Faces of Weimar Cinema: Rediscovering Germany's Filmic Legacy*, edited by Christian Rogowski, 13–30. Rochester, NY: Camden House, 2010.

Smith-Rosenberg, Carroll. 'The Female World of Love and Ritual: Relations between Women in Nineteenth-Century America.' *Signs* 1, no. 1 (1975): 1–29.

Soden, Kristine von. *Die Sexualberatungsstellen der Weimarer Republik, 1919-1933.* Berlin: Hentrich, 1988.

Sontag, Susan. 'Fascinating Fascism.' *New York Review of Books*, 6 February 1975.

Sorkin, David. *The Transformation of German Jewry, 1780–1840.* Detroit: Wayne State University Press, 1999.

Sparing, Frank, and Matthis Krischel. 'Kastration von homosexuellen Männern im Nationalsozialismus.' In *Justiz und Homosexualität*, edited by Ministerium der Justiz des Landes NRW, and Michael Schwartz, 52–73. Geldern: jva druck + medien, 2019.

Spector, Scott. *Violent Sensations: Sex, Crime & Utopia in Vienna and Berlin, 1860–1914.* Chicago: University of Chicago Press, 2016.

Spector, Scott, Helmut Puff, and Dagmar Herzog, eds. *After 'The History of Sexuality'? German Genealogies with and beyond Foucault.* New York: Berghahn, 2012.

Spengler, Oswald. *The Decline of the West.* Translated by Charles Francis Atkinson. London: Allen & Unwin, 1922.

Springman, Luke. 'Poisoned Hearts, Diseased Minds, and American Pimps: The Language of Censorship in the *Schund und Schmutz* Debates.' *The German Quarterly* 68, no. 4 (1995): 408–29.

Sreenivasan, Govind P. *The Peasants of Ottobeuren, 1487–1726: A Rural Society in Early Modern Europe.* Cambridge: Cambridge University Press, 2004.

Stark, Gary. *Banned in Berlin: Literary Censorship in Imperial Germany, 1871-1918.* New York: Berghahn, 2009.

Stark, Gary. 'Pornography, Society, and the Law in Imperial Germany.' *Central European History* 14, no. 3 (1981): 200–29.

Starke, Kurt. *Schwuler Osten. Homosexuelle Männer in der DDR.* Berlin: Ch. Links, 1994.

Staupe, Gisela, and Lisa Vieth, eds. *Die Pille. Von der Lust und von der Liebe.* Berlin: Rowohlt, 1996.

Steakley, James D. *'Anders als die Andern.' Ein Film und seine Geschichte.* Hamburg: Männerschwarm, 2007.

Steakley, James D. *The Homosexual Emancipation Movement in Germany.* New York: Arno Press, 1975.

Steakley, James D. 'Cinema and Censorship in the Weimar Republic: The Case of Anders als die Andern.' *Film History* 11, no. 2 (1999): 181–203.

Steakley, James D. 'Iconography of a Scandal. Political Cartoons and the Eulenburg Affair.' In *History of Homosexuality in Europe and America*, edited by Wayne R. Dynes, and Stephen Donaldson, 323–85. New York and London: Garland, 1992.

Steinach, Eugen, and Josef Loebel. *Sex and Life: Forty Years of Biological and Medical Experiments.* London: Faber, 1940.

Steinbacher, Sybille. *Wie der Sex nach Deutschland kam: Der Kampf um Sittlichkeit und Anstand in der frühen Bundesrepublik*, München: Siedler, 2011.

Steinle, Karl-Heinz. *Der Kreis: Mitglieder, Künstler, Autoren.* Berlin: Rosa Winkel, 1999.

Stephenson, Jill. *The Nazi Organisation of Women.* London: Helm, 1981.

Stephenson, Jill. *Women in Nazi Germany.* Harlow: Pearson, 2001.

Stephenson, Jill. *Women in Nazi Society.* London: Croom Helm, 1975.

Sternweiler, Andreas. 'Die Freundschaftsbünde – Eine Massenbewegung.' In *Goodbye to Berlin?* edited by Andreas Sternweiler, and Hans Gerhard Hannesen, 95–104. Berlin: Rosa Winkel, 1997.

Sternweiler, Andreas, and Hans Gerhard Hannesen, eds. *Goodbye to Berlin? 100 Jahre Schwulenbewegung*. Berlin: Rosa Winkel, 1997.

Stibbe, Matthew. *Women in the Third Reich*. London: Hodder Education, 2003.

Stieg, Margaret F. 'The 1926 German Law to Protect Youth against Trash and Dirt: Moral Protectionism in a Democracy.' *Central European History* 23, no. 1 (1990): 22–56.

Stöcker, Helene. 'Bund für Mutterschutz.' *Moderne Zeitfragen*, no. 4, edited by Hans Landsberg. Berlin: Pan-Verlag, 1905.

Stöcker, Helene. 'Zur Reform der sexuellen Ethik.' *Mutterschutz* 1, no. 1 (1905): 3–12.

Stoff, Heiko. *Ewige Jugend. Konzepte der Verjüngung vom späten 19. Jahrhundert bis ins Dritte Reich*. Köln: Böhlau, 2004.

Stoff, Heiko. 'Rezensionen. Ulrike Klöppel, XX0XY ungelöst. Hermaphroditismus, Sex und Gender in der deutschen Medizin.' *Berichte zur Wissenschaftsgeschichte* 35 (2012): 62–4.

Stoler, Ann Laura. *Carnal Knowledge and Imperial Power: Race and the Intimate in Colonial Rule*. Berkeley: University of California Press, 2002.

Stoler, Ann Laura. *Race and the Education of Desire: Foucault's 'History of Sexuality' and the Colonial Order of Things*. Durham: Duke University Press, 1995.

Stoltzfus, Nathan. *Resistance of the Heart. Intermarriage and the Rosenstrasse Protest in Nazi Germany*. New Brunswick: Rutgers University Press, 2001.

Stoltzfus, Nathan. 'The Limits of Policy: Social Protection of Intermarried German Jews in Nazi Germany.' In *Social Outsiders in Nazi Germany*, edited by Robert Gellately, and Nathan Stolzfus, 117–44. Princeton: Princeton University Press, 2001.

Stopes, Marie. *Married Love*. Oxford: Oxford University Press, 2008.

Strohl, Jane E. 'Luther on Marriage, Sexuality, and the Family.' In *The Oxford Handbook of Martin Luther's Theology*, edited by Robert Kolb, Irene Dingel, and L'ubomir Batka, Online. Oxford: Oxford University Press, 2014. https://www.oxfordhandbooks.com/view/10.1093/oxfordhb/9780199604708.001.0001/oxfordhb-9780199604708.

Stryker, Susan. *Transgender History*. Berkeley: Seal Press, 2008.

Stümke, Hans-Georg. *Homosexuelle in Deutschland: Eine politische Geschichte*. München: Beck, 1989.

Stryker, Susan. 'The Persecution of Homosexuals in Nazi Germany.' In *Confronting the Nazi Past. New Debates on Modern German History*, edited by Michael Burleigh, 154–66. New York: St Martin's Press, 1996.

Sutton, Katie. 'From Sexual Inversion to Trans*: Transgender History and Historiography.' In *Was ist Homosexualität? Forschungsgeschichte, gesellschaftliche Entwicklungen und Perspektiven*, edited by Florian Mildenberger, Jennifer Evans, Rüdiger Lautmann, and Jakob Pastötter, 181–204. Hamburg: Männerschwarm, 2014.

Sutton, Katie. 'Review Essay: A Tale of Origins: The Emergence of Sexual Citizens in German Modernity.' *Journal of the History of Sexuality* 27, no. 1 (2018): 186–206.

Sutton, Katie. *Sex between Body and Mind: Psychoanalysis and Sexology in the German-Speaking World 1890s–1930s*. Ann Arbor: University of Michigan Press, 2019.

Sutton, Katie. *The Masculine Woman in Weimar Germany*. New York: Berghahn, 2011.

Sutton, Katie. '"We Too Deserve a Place in the Sun": The Politics of Transvestite Identity in Weimar Germany.' *German Studies Review* 35, no. 2 (2012): 335–54.

Swett, Pamela E., Corey Ross, and Fabrice d'Almeida, eds. *Pleasure and Power in Nazi Germany*. Basingstoke: Palgrave Macmillan, 2011.

Szobar, Patricia. 'Telling Sexual Stories in the Nazi Courts of Law: Race Defilement in Germany, 1933 to 1945.' In *Sexuality and German Fascism*, edited by Dagmar Herzog, 131–63. New York: Berghahn, 2005.

Tacium, David. '"Warm Brothers" in 18th-Century Berlin.' *The Gay & Lesbian Review Worldwide* 26, no. 4 (2019): 19–20.

Tanner, Jakob. 'Eugenics before 1945.' *Journal of Modern European History* 10, no. 4 (2012): 458–77.

Taylor, Charles. *Sources of the Self: The Making of the Modern Identity*. Cambridge, MA: Harvard University Press, 1989.

Theweleit, Klaus. *Male Fantasies*. Cambridge: Polity, 1987.

Thompson, Nellie. 'Early Women Psychoanalysts.' *International Review of Psychoanalysis* 14 (1987): 391–408.

Thönnessen, Werner. *The Emancipation of Women: The Rise and Decline of the Women's Movement in German Social Democracy*. London: Pluto, 1973.

Timm, Annette F. '"I Am So Grateful to All You Men of Medicine": Trans Circles of Knowledge and Intimacy.' In *Others of My Kind: Transatlantic Transgender Histories*, edited by Alex Bakker, Rainer Herrn, Michael Thomas Taylor, and Annette F. Timm, 71–132. Calgary: University of Calgary Press, 2020.

Timm, Annette F. 'Sex with a Purpose: Prostitution, Venereal Disease, and Militarized Masculinity in the Third Reich.' In *Sexuality and German Fascism*, edited by Dagmar Herzog, 223–55. New York: Berghahn, 2005.

Timm, Annette F. 'The Ambivalent Outsider: Prostitution, Promiscuity, and VD Control in Nazi Berlin.' In *Social Outsiders in Nazi Germany*, edited by Robert Gellately, and Nathan Stoltzfus, 192–211. Princeton: Princeton University Press, 2001.

Timm, Annette F. *The Politics of Fertility in Twentieth-Century Berlin*. Cambridge: Cambridge University Press, 2010.

Timm, Annette F., and Joshua A. Sanborn. *Gender, Sex and the Shaping of Modern Europe: A History from the French Revolution to the Present Day*. 2nd ed. London and New York: Bloomsbury Academic, 2016.

Tissot, S. A. D. *A Treatise on the Crime of Onan*. Project Gutenberg (2020). London: B. Thomas, n.d. https://www.gutenberg.org/ebooks/61621.

Tobin, Robert. *Warm Brothers: Queer Theory and the Age of Goethe*. Philadelphia: University of Pennsylvania Press, 2000.

Tobin, Robert Deam. *Peripheral Desires: The German Discovery of Sex*. Philadelphia: University of Pennsylvania Press, 2015.

Todd, Lisa M. *Sexual Treason in Germany during the First World War*. London: Palgrave Macmillan, 2017.

Todd, Lisa M. '"The Soldier's Wife Who Ran Away with the Russian": Sexual
    Infidelities in World War I Germany.' *Central European History* 44, no. 2
    (2011): 257–78.
Toepfer, Karl Eric. *Empire of Ecstasy: Nudity and Movement in German Body
    Culture, 1910–1935.* Berkeley: University of California Press, 1997.
Tomberger, Corinna. 'Das Berliner Homosexuellen-Denkmal: Ein Denkmal für
    Schwule *und* Lesben?' In *Homophobie und Devianz: Weibliche und männliche
    Homosexualität im Nationalsozialismus*, edited by Insa Eschebach, 187–207.
    Berlin: Metropol, 2012.
Tosh, Will. *Male Friendship and Testimonies of Love in Shakespeare's England.*
    London: Palgrave Macmillan, 2016.
Trask, April. 'Remaking Men: Masculinity, Homosexuality and Constitutional
    Medicine in Germany, 1914–1933.' *German History* 36, no. 2 (2018):
    181–206.
Traub, Valerie. *The Renaissance of Lesbianism in Early Modern England.*
    Cambridge: Cambridge University Press, 2002.
Tröger, Annemarie. 'Between Rape and Prostitution: Survival Strategies and
    Chances of Emancipation for Berlin Women after World War II.' In *Women in
    Culture and Politics: A Century of Change*, edited by Judith Friedlander, Blanche
    Wiesen Cook, Alice Kessler-Harris, and Carroll Smith-Rosenberg, translated by
    Joan Reutershan, 97–117. Bloomington IN: Indiana University Press, 1986.
Ulbrich, Claudia. *Shulamit and Margarete: Power, Gender, and Religion in a Rural
    Society in Eighteenth-Century Europe.* Boston: Brill, 2004.
Ulrichs, Karl Heinrich. *The Riddle of 'Man-Manly' Love.* Translated by Michael A.
    Lombardi-Nash. 2 vols. New York: Prometheus, 1994.
Usborne, Cornelie. *Cultures of Abortion in Weimar Germany.* New York:
    Berghahn, 2007.
Usborne, Cornelie. 'Female Sexual Desire and Male Honor: German Women's Illicit
    Live Affairs with Prisoners of War during the Second World War.' *Journal of the
    History of Sexuality* 26, no. 3 (2017): 454–88.
Usborne, Cornelie. 'Rhetoric and Resistance: Rationalisation of Reproduction in
    Weimar Germany.' *Social Politics* 4, no. 1 (1997): 65–89.
Usborne, Cornelie. 'Social Body, Racial Body, Woman's Body. Discourses, Policies,
    Practices from Wilhelmine to Nazi Germany, 1912–1945.' *Historical Social
    Research / Historische Sozialforschung* 36, no. 2 (2011): 140–61.
Usborne, Cornelie. 'The Christian Churches and the Regulation of Sexuality in
    Weimar Germany.' In *Disciplines of Faith: Studies in Religion, Politics and
    Patriarchy*, edited by Jim Obelkevich, Lyndal Roper, and Raphael Samuel,
    99–112. London: Routledge, 1987.
Usborne, Cornelie. *The Politics of the Body in Weimar Germany: Women's
    Reproductive Rights and Duties.* Basingstoke: Macmillan, 1992.
Velde, Dr. Th. H. van de. *Die vollkommene Ehe.* 5th ed. Leipzig: Benno Konegen,
    1927.
Vendrell, Javier Samper. 'Adolescence, Psychology, and Homosexuality in the
    Weimar Republic.' *Journal of the History of Sexuality* 27, no. 3 (2018): 395–
    419.
Vendrell, Javier Samper. 'The Case of a German-Jewish Lesbian Woman: Martha
    Mosse and the Danger of Standing Out.' *German Studies Review* 41, no. 2
    (2018): 335–53.

Vendrell, Javier Samper. *The Seduction of Youth: Print Culture and Homosexual Rights in the Weimar Republic*. Toronto: University of Toronto Press, 2020.

Wackerfuss, Andrew. *Stormtrooper Families: Homosexuality and Community in the Early Nazi Movement*. New York: Harrington Park, 2015.

Walch, Sonja. *Triebe, Reize und Signale: Eugen Steinachs Physiologie der Sexualhormone*. Göttingen: Böhlau, 2016.

Walkowitz, Judith R. *City of Dreadful Delight: Narratives of Sexual Danger in Late-Victorian Britain*. Chicago: University of Chicago Press, 1992.

Wallach, Kerry. *Passing Illusions: Jewish Visibility in Weimar Germany*. Ann Arbor: University of Michigan Press, 2017.

Walther, Daniel J. 'Racializing Sex: Same-Sex Relations, German Colonial Authority, and Deutschtum.' *Journal of the History of Sexuality* 17, no. 1 (2008): 11–24.

Wander, Maxie. *Guten Morgen, Du Schöne*. Berlin: Aufbau Verlag, 2003.

Warner, Michael. *The Trouble with Normal: Sex, Politics, and the Ethics of Queer Life*. Cambridge, MA: Harvard University Press, 1999.

Waters, Chris. 'Sexology.' In *Palgrave Advances in the Modern History of Sexuality*, edited by H. G. Cocks, and Matt Houlbrook, 41–63. Basingstoke: Palgrave Macmillan, 2006.

Wedemeyer, Bernd. 'Body-Building or Man in the Making: Aspects of the German Bodybuilding Movement in the Kaiserreich and Weimar Republic.' *International Journal of the History of Sport* 11, no. 3 (1994): 472–84.

Wedemeyer-Kolwe, Bernd. *'Der neue Mensch': Körperkultur im Kaiserreich und in der Weimarer Republik*. Würzburg: Königshausen & Neumann, 2004.

Weeks, Jeffrey. *Sex, Politics and Society: The Regulation of Sexuality since 1800*. London: Longman, 1981.

Wehler, Hans-Ulrich. *The German Empire, 1871–1918*. Leamington Spa: Berg, 1985.

Weikart, Richard. *From Darwin to Hitler: Evolutionary Ethics, Eugenics, and Racism in Germany*. New York: Palgrave Macmillan, 2004.

Weindling, Paul. 'Bourgeois Values, Doctors and the State: The Professionalization of Medicine in Germany 1848–1933.' In *The German Bourgeoisie*, edited by David Blackbourn, and Richard J. Evans, 198–223. London: Routledge, 1991.

Weindling, Paul. *Health, Race, and German Politics between National Unification and Nazism, 1870–1945*. Cambridge: Cambridge University Press, 1989.

Weingart, Peter. 'The Rationalization of Sexual Behavior: The Institutionalization of Eugenic Thought in Germany.' *Journal of the History of Biology* 20, no. 2 (1987): 159–93.

Weininger, Otto. *Sex and Character: An Investigation of Fundamental Principles*. Edited by Daniel Steuer. Translated by Ladislaus Löb. Bloomington and Indianapolis: Indiana University Press, 2005.

Weitz, Eric D. *Weimar Germany: Promise and Tragedy*. Princeton: Princeton University Press, 2007.

Westphal, Carl. 'Die conträre Sexualempfindung.' *Archiv für Psychiatrie und Nervenkrankheiten* 2, no. 1 (1869): 73–108.

Wheelwright, Julie. *Amazons and Military Maids: Women Who Dressed as Men in the Pursuit of Life, Liberty, and Happiness*. London: Pandora, 1989.

Whisnant, Clayton. 'Gay German History: Future Directions?' *Journal of the History of Sexuality* 17, no. 1 (2008): 1–10.

Whisnant, Clayton J. 'Styles of Masculinity in the West German Gay Scene, 1950–1965.' *Central European History* 39, no. 3 (2006): 359–93.

Whisnant, Clayton J. *Male Homosexuality in West Germany: Between Persecution and Freedom*, 1945–69. Basingstoke: Palgrave Macmillan, 2012.

Whisnant, Clayton J. *Queer Identities and Politics in Germany: A History, 1880–1945*. New York: Harrington Park, 2016.

Whitford, David M. '"It Is Not Forbidden That a Man May Have More Than One Wife": Luther's Pastoral Advice on Bigamy and Marriage.' In *Mixed Matches: Trangressive Unions in Germany from the Reformation to the Enlightenment*, edited by David M. Luebke, and Mary Lindemann, 14–30. New York: Berghahn, 2014.

Wickert, Christl, Brigitte Hamburger, and Marie Lienau. 'Helene Stöcker and the Bund für Mutterschutz (The Society for the Protection of Motherhood).' *Women's Studies International Forum* 5, no. 6 (1982): 611–18.

Wiegman, Robyn, and Elizabeth A. Wilson. 'Introduction: Antinormativity's Queer Conventions.' *Differences* 26, no. 1 (2015): 1–25.

Wiesner, Merry E. 'Disembodied Theory? Discourses of Sex in Early Modern Germany.' In *Gender in Early Modern German History*, edited by Ulinka Rublack, 152–73. Cambridge: Cambridge University Press, 2002.

Wiesner, Merry E. *Gender, Church, and State in Early Modern Germany. Essays*. London and New York: Longman, 1998.

Wiesner-Hanks, Merry E. *Early Modern Europe, 1450–1789*. Cambridge: Cambridge University Press, 2013.

Wiesner-Hanks, Merry E. *Gender in History: Global Perspectives*. 2nd ed. Malden, MA: Wiley-Blackwell, 2011.

Wigger, Iris. '"Black Shame" – the Campaign against "Racial Degeneration" and Female Degradation in Interwar Europe.' *Race & Class* 51, no. 3 (2010): 33–46.

Wildenthal, Lora. *German Women for Empire, 1884–1945*. Durham: Duke University Press, 2001.

Wildenthal, Lora, Juergen Zimmerer, Russell A. Berman, Jan Rüger, Bradley Naranch, and Birthe Kundrus. 'Forum: The German Colonial Imagination.' Edited by Maiken Umbach. *German History* 26, no. 2 (2008): 251–71.

Williams, John Alexander. 'Ecstasies of the Young: Sexuality, the Youth Movement, and Moral Panic in Germany on the Eve of the First World War.' *Central European History* 34, no. 2 (2001): 163–89.

Williams, John Alexander. *Turning to Nature in Germany: Hiking, Nudism, and Conservation, 1900-1940*. Stanford, CA: Stanford University Press, 2007.

Wolf, Friedrich. *Cyankali §218 (mit Materialien)*. Edited by Michael Kienzle, and Dirk Mende. Stuttgart: Klett, 2001.

Wolters, Emi. 'Transvestiten im Weltkriege [8-part series, 24 February to 13 April 1932, in "Die Welt der Transvestiten" supplement].' *Die Freundin* 8, no. 8–15 (1932), n.p.

Woollacott, Angela. *Gender and Empire*. Basingstoke: Palgrave Macmillan, 2006.

Woycke, James. *Birth Control in Germany 1871–1933*. London: Routledge, 1988.

Wunder, Heide. *He Is the Sun, She Is the Moon: Women in Early Modern Germany*. Cambridge, MA: Harvard University Press, 1998.

Würdemann, Ulrich. *Schweigen = Tod, Aktion = Leben: ACT UP in Deutschland 1989 bis 1993*. epubli, 2017. https://www.2mecs.de/wp/2017/07/schweigen-tod-aktion-leben-act-up-in-deutschland-1989-bis-1993/

Zantop, Susanne. *Colonial Fantasies: Conquest, Family and Nation in Precolonial Germany, 1770–1870*. Durham: Duke University Press, 1997.

Zinn, Alexander, ed. *Homosexuelle in Deutschland 1933–1969: Beiträge zu Alltag, Stigmatisierung und Verfolgung*. Göttingen: Vandenhoeck & Ruprecht, 2020.

INDEX